Dinah's Daughters

Dinah's Daughters

Gender and Judaism from the Hebrew Bible to Late Antiquity

Helena Zlotnick

PENN

University of Pennsylvania Press

Philadelphia

Copyright © 2002 University of Pennsylvania Press
All rights reserved
Printed in the United States of America on acid-free paper

10 9 8 7 6 5 4 3 2 1

Published by
University of Pennsylvania Press
Philadelphia, Pennsylvania 19104-4011

Library of Congress Cataloging-in-Publication Data
Zlotnick, Helena.
  Dinah's daughters : gender and Judaism from the Hebrew Bible to late antiquity / Helena Zlotnick.
    p. cm.
  Includes bibliographical references and index.
  ISBN 0-8122-3644-0 (cloth : alk. paper) — ISBN 0-8122-1797-7 (paper : alk. paper)
  1. Dinah (Biblical character)   2. Women in the Bible.   3. Women in rabbinical literature.   4. Women in Judaism   I. Title.
BS580.D55 Z56 2001
221.8'3054—dc21   2001037332

To
Peter Brown
Michael Thomas Davis
David Noel Freedman
who trusted me

Contents

List of Abbreviations   ix

Introduction: Setting the Stage   1
  Words of Warning   1
  Sex, Status, and Homecoming: A Jewish Penelope?   4
  Sin, Shame, and Sanctity: The Tale of the Lusty Wife and Rabbi Meir   15
  Contents   25

Part I. Projections of Biblical Spheres of Women

1. From Dinah to Cozbi: Rape, Sex, and Foundational Moments   33
  From Rape to Parental Reticence   35
  Why Not Marry a Shechemite?   42
  Dinah and Matriarchal Betrothals   45
  A Woman of the Wilderness: The Rape of Cozbi   49
  Foundation Murders and Rapes   52

2. Patriarchy and Patriotism: Integrating Sex into Second Temple Society   57
  Birth of a Nation: Marriage and Patriotism in Ezra   58
  Private and Public in Yehud   61
  Sin, Scripture, and Intermarriage   63
  The Fate of Foreign Spouses   66
  The Case of the Defiant Daughter: Jubilees' Dinah   69

3. From Esther to Aseneth: Marriage, Familial Stereotypes, and Domestic Felicity   76
  Marriage Between Gentiles, Model 1: Ahasuerus and Vashti   77

Marriage Between Gentiles, Model 2: Haman and Zeresh 82
The Jewish Family 84
Intermarriage: Ahasuerus and Esther 89
Integrating Brides into the Family: Aseneth and Joseph 92

Part II. Visions of Rabbinic Order

4. Keeping Adultery at Bay: The Wayward Wife in Late Antiquity 105
Theologies and Theories of Sexuality: Roman and Rabbinic Perspectives 105
Suspecting Adultery 110
Preliminaries: Singling Out Adulteresses 113
The Right to Accuse: Constantinian and Rabbinic Innovations 118
The "Other": Lovers and Aftermath 125

5. The Harmony of the Home in Late Antiquity: Jewish, Roman, and Christian Perspectives on Intermarriage 132
Why Not Marry a Goy? 137
Early Christianity and Marital Peripheries 151
Banning Jewish-Christian Marriage: Roman Legal Perspectives 155

Conclusion: To Die like a Woman? To Live like a Woman? Is There a Jewess in Judaism? 161

Notes 173

Bibliography 215

General Index 235

Index of Citations 241

Acknowledgments 247

Abbreviations

Hebrew Bible (in canonical order)

Gen.	Genesis
Exod.	Exodus
Lev.	Leviticus
Num.	Numbers
Deut.	Deuteronomy
Josh.	Joshua
Judg.	Judges
1 Sam.	1 Samuel
2 Sam.	2 Samuel
1 Kgs.	1 Kings
2 Kgs.	2 Kings
Isa.	Isaiah
Jer.	Jeremiah
Ezek.	Ezekiel
Ps.	Psalms
Prov.	Proverbs
Eccl.	Ecclesiastes
Neh.	Nehemiah

New Testament

1 Cor.	1 Corinthians
2 Cor.	2 Corinthians

Rabbinic Sources

BT AZ	Babylonian Talmud, Avodah Zarah
BT BM	Babylonian Talmud, Baba Metzia
BT Ket.	Babylonian Talmud, Ketubbot
BT Kidd.	Babylonian Talmud, Kiddushin
BT Ned.	Babylonian Talmud, Nedarim

BT Nid.	Babylonian Talmud, Nidda
BT San.	Babylonian Talmud, Sanhedrin
BT Shab.	Babylonian Talmud, Shabbat
BT Sot.	Babylonian Talmud, Sotah
BT Yeb.	Babylonian Talmud, Yebamot
M Avot	Mishnah, Avot
M Git.	Mishnah, Gittin
M Ket.	Mishnah, Ketubbot
M Kidd.	Mishnah, Kiddushin
M Meg.	Mishnah, Megillah
M Ned.	Mishnah, Nedarim
M San.	Mishnah, Sanhedrin
M Sot.	Mishnah, Sotah
M Yeb.	Mishnah, Yebamot
PT AZ	Palestinian Talmud, Avodah Zarah
PT Ket.	Palestinian Talmud, Ketubbot
PT Kidd.	Palestinian Talmud, Kiddushin
PT Shab.	Palestinian Talmud, Shabbat
PT Sot.	Palestinian Talmud, Sotah
PT Yeb.	Palestinian Talmud, Yebamot
T Hull.	Tosefta, Hullin
T Ket.	Tosefta, Ketubbot
T Kidd.	Tosefta, Kiddushin
T Yeb.	Tosefta, Yebamot

Roman Legal Sources

CJ	Codex Justinianus
CTh	Codex Theodosianus
D	Digest
Nov.	Justinian Novellae

Introduction

Setting the Stage

Words of Warning

The basic hypothesis of this book is simple enough—to identify who belongs and who does not, who behaves in an acceptable social manner and who transgresses divinely ordained and man-made boundaries, it is necessary to examine the human body in specific contexts. These are, in turn, explored and resolved through situations of intimate sexual contacts. At the heart of the ancient intellectual or rather ideological ventures to define identity through a sexual code of conduct as a key to communal affiliation gender distinctions loom large.[1] So do real and perceived differences between Israelites/Jews on the one hand and non-Israelites/gentiles on the other. To be a Jew involves a complex series of prescriptive and preventive injunctions, do's and don'ts. To be a Jewess primarily means the latter.

In ways that cannot always be traced with great precision, women, and particularly gentile females, have come to symbolize the forbidden. Foreign women are also endowed with a curious freedom of action and choice that does not necessarily reflect realities. Delilah, for example, is one of the most autonomous women in the Bible, appearing without either patronymic or family ties and wealthy enough to command her own price.[2] To be a Jewess implies, by contrast, an adherence to modes of life within perimeters carefully delineated by men through contrasts. A Jewess does not go out to mingle with gentile female friends. If she does, she may meet the fate of Dinah (Gen. 34). She does not freely dispense sexual favors to men outside her own group lest she usher in idolatry and bring calamity, as do the Moabite daughters of the desert (Num. 25), and the wives of Jewish men in the time of Ezra and Nehemiah. A Jewess does not marry a gentile unless, perhaps, he is a king and she is destined to become a queen, like Esther, in order to save her people from extinction. If she defies paternal precepts she condemns herself to a painful death, as the anonymous author of Jubilees asserts in an elaborate reworking of the Dinah affair. And, needless to say, a Jewess does not commit adultery, a command originally issued, it seems, to Israelite males only (Exod. 20:14). If she does, or is merely suspected of it, she must bear the consequences, as does a Jewess who denies her own husband his sexual due (*moredet*).

Such premises may appear obvious. Yet, no modern study has examined the formation and transformation of the ideology of female Jewishness in antiquity.[3] The question addressed in this book is, therefore, what does being and becoming a Jewess entail in antiquity? I should add that "ancient Judaism" in this study embraces a wide textual chronology, from exilic and postexilic canonizations of the Israelite past (i.e., the dawn of the Hebrew Bible as we know it) down to late antiquity and its codifications (i.e., the Mishnah and the two Talmuds, to mention only the canonic compilations). It thus covers periods that are conventionally known as Israelite or biblical, Second Temple or postbiblical, and rabbinic or late antiquity, each now falling under different academic disciplines and departments.[4] No apology, I believe, is needed for selecting from so wide a span. While the makers and shapers of the texts varied, as did the cultural contexts in which they reflected, wrote, revised, and redacted their texts, the symbols and stereotypes here explored experienced long gestations that do not necessarily conform to modern notions of periodization.[5] Between recollection and articulation it is often impossible to date with any precision either the "originals" or the mutations of ideas and ideals. Ancient Jewish authors had little interest in matters pertaining to standard or common chronologies.[6]

The varieties of Judaism(s) in antiquity are clearly reflected in the literary genres on which my book draws.[7] Besides dealing with a sacred text whose precise origins, development, redaction, and canonization have been and are hotly contested,[8] the sources utilized range from anonymous and ill-dated postbiblical "scriptures," including the Apocrypha, Pseudepigrapha, and the Qumran writings, to equally anonymous and ill-dated, if not altogether antihistorical rabbinic writings.[9] Such diversity is well matched by the plethora of modern approaches to these texts.[10] Who, exactly, did these genres represent and who, specifically, adopted their agendas as guidelines or aspired to follow their recommended ways of life is equally difficult to decide.[11]

Recent research into the Jewish communities in the Roman provinces, for example, throws light on startling differences between Roman Palestine, the subject so often discussed in rabbinic works of late antiquity, and Diaspora communities.[12] It would be hazardous, then, to draw conclusions about Jewish life around the Mediterranean from Palestinian compositions in any period throughout antiquity. Even in Palestine itself ideas of the identity of Jews and Judaism appear to vary greatly. Scholars of late ancient synagogal liturgy (*piyyut*) in Eretz Israel have emphasized important differences between popular and rabbinic ideas.[13] In this light it would be futile within the framework of a study of gender and national identity to venture into the abyss of formulating grand theories about the historical and intellectual formation of the canonically aspiring works of ancient Judaism.[14] Suffice it, I hope, to alert readers to the pitfalls involved in the use of ancient Jewish sources, to their problematization, and to the heterogeneity of modern interpretations.

The tales and situations explored here are extraordinarily flexible and free from chronological constraints. They lend themselves to repeated narration in vastly different historical and social contexts because they share a basic timeless conviction of the Israelites/Jews as a locus of holiness.[15] In no case are we made privy to the identity of the "original" narrator or of the redactor(s). And it is precisely because our sources are so careful in stripping irrelevant identities and dates that I have recruited Greek and Roman lore and law not only to provide illuminating comparisons but also to account for alternative readings.

The beginnings of the ideology that crafted a Jewess in antiquity must be sought in the central sacred text of Judaism.[16] Through a series of episodic narratives the Hebrew Bible provides images of women that have become icons of the desirable or of the unacceptable, each contributing to the limits of female identity. The figures of the temptress, the seducer and seduced, the chaste and the female guardian of chastity provide critical modules and stereotypes. In my reading, a Jewess often emerges as the implied antithesis of a gentile woman.[17] To meet a Jewess it is often necessary to penetrate the domicile, in itself an allusive and elusive space; to encounter a non-Jewess one has to venture into the wilderness and the public. When one does meet a Jewess in antiquity the temporal frame nearly invariably relates to marriage. In other words, the surviving sources capture a Jewess mostly when her orbit touches on that of men, be it when she is considered ready or unready for nuptials, when she enters matrimony, or when she transgresses its boundaries. What happens in the women's quarters or among women remains mostly outside the perimeters of ancient Jewish literature. Rarely do speculations, of any kind, comic, satiric, or dramatic, enter its pages.

Since the nature of the evidence is spotty, at best, the treatment of the subject of Jewessness largely depends on an analysis of specific episodes. I do not believe that it is possible, at present, to construct a continuous history of women in ancient Judaism.[18] Besides obvious problems relating to chronology, the Jewess of antiquity, with few exceptions, remains an iconic image, remote and static. There are no biographies (or autobiographies) of Jewish women, real or mythic, nor an archaeology of Jewessness.[19] Women appear in specific contexts when there is need to demonstrate, primarily, what not to do, what to avoid rather than what to follow. In this light, the choice of characters and themes in this study is deliberate, not arbitrary.

One obvious difficulty of the present reconstruction is the gender-biased nature of the evidence.[20] The women so artfully described, praised, or censured hardly ever speak for themselves. Their hypothetical voices need to be derived from evidence that is, in itself, composite and tendentious.[21] To tease subtexts from these texts I have set out to explore defining moments and characters in an act of shaping the facial contours of their Judaism, from the reconstructed annals of patriarchal history to rabbinic reflections on straying wives and on (inter)marriage. To probe hidden human emotions and the subtle intertwining of fate, humanity, and the domicile in the Hebrew Bible, I have often resorted to classical literature (Greek and Roman) which, to my mind at least, provides provocative insights into the terse but suggestive biblical narratives. To investigate rabbinic formulations of the harmony of the home and of infractors of the domicile I used Roman law. The breadth and effectiveness of these comparative endeavors can be measured by the two following tales, the stories of Rachels and the adventures of a blameless sage.

Sex, Status, and Homecoming: A Jewish Penelope?

In the pages of Genesis the love of Jacob for Rachel and her inability to bear sons are two dominant themes of the tale of the fourth matriarch. When she lives, she is consumed by the desire to procreate. When she dies, it is in the act of giving birth, the most common cause of female death in antiquity. Yet, in the Hebrew Bible she is the only mother fated, or reported, to pass away in this manner. The scene of her demise is placed outside the domicile and the choice of the location contrasts sharply with the privacy that ordinarily envelops the dying moments of women in antiquity.[22] Rachel does not die in the marriage chamber, a space that encapsulates the symbolism of women's life by echoing the pattern of marriage and maternity that society prescribes to ensure their inexorable intertwining with the lives of men. Nor does she die in her marital bed, a locus of recollections of the pleasures of marital sex and of the fact that women die because of men and for men. Deprived of the consolation of her bed, her room, and her memories, Rachel dies violently and untimely. In death she is further singled out for the ultimate separation, for she is buried not with her husband or her ancestors but on the road where her grave becomes a monument (Gen. 35:19–20).

Rachel's last moments brim with anomalies. During the last stages of pregnancy she is in exile from the elements that provide women with stability in crucial times. A solitary midwife, appearing ex nihilo, mediates the delivery that the biblical text repeatedly qualifies as "difficult" (Gen. 35:16–17). Above all, Rachel's agonizing and solitary death is, to an extent, self-inflicted, fulfilling two predictions. One is a curse, uttered by Jacob, on the head of a thief of holy objects who turns out to be Rachel herself (Gen. 31:32). The episode involved a theft, breach of hospitality, and the mapping of a domain of secrecy between a husband who unknowingly consigns his own wife to death, and a wife who steals and conceals from her father without telling her husband (Gen. 31). The second prediction is Rachel's, voiced by her when she confronts Jacob with the demand: "Give me sons or else I die" (Gen. 30:1). The words forge an intimate link between motherhood and self-destructiveness and Rachel experiences both. Her transformation from a wife to a mother also brings to an end the Genesis narrative of the cycle of wives-mothers that had begun with Eve.

Rachel's tragedy unravels a threat to the order that patriarchal preferences had established. For her the child comes first. Her paradigm of motherhood highlights the relevance of males to the process of generation and reproduction but also the irrelevance of Yahweh, in spite of the deity's unversality that the narrator/redactor had been at pains to establish. God may open closed wombs but Jacob, according to Rachel, is expected to plant his seed there at her will and behest. She dies, then, not only for breaching the bond between fathers and daughters by stealing from her father and lying to him, but also because she has threatened the divine-male establishment that guarantees the role of Yahweh as the Creator of all.

In her body Rachel combines all the main functions that a woman *qua* women ever fulfills in the Hebrew Bible. She is a daughter, a sister, a wife, and a mother. No other woman in the Hebrew Bible is presented in all these manifestations at once. Rachel, then, is unique, a symbolic figure of all that is feminine. By the end of antiquity, in Lamentations Rabbah,

Rachel becomes the mother par excellence and the only parent with power to redeem the whole of Israel by successfully invoking divine mercy with an autobiographical tale. Between the midrashic image of Rachel in Lamentations Rabbah and Genesis's Rachel a few lines of the prophet Jeremiah chart the way for this remarkable metamorphosis:

Thus says the Lord: A voice is heard in Rā'mah, lamentation and bitter weeping. Rachel is weeping for her children; she refuses to be comforted for her children because they are not. Thus says the Lord: Keep your voice from weeping and your eyes from tears, for your work shall be rewarded, declares the Lord, and they shall come back from the land of the enemy. There is hope for the future, declares the Lord, and your children shall come back to their own country. (Jer. 31:15–17, Oxford translation)

In inner biblical interpretation "Rachel" had been recast as the most effective mourner over the disaster of exile. The prophetic choice is particularly poignant for the most haunting parental dirges in the Hebrew Bible belong to David and not to Rachel. In fact, Yahweh does not speak to Rachel at all in the pages of Genesis. Yet, for Jeremiah, the great prophet of doom, it is Rachel and not the famed and eloquent king, who encapsulates the tragedy and the sorrow of separation. Instead of a "national" figure of a mourning father Rachel emerges as the mother of all mothers and as a metaphor of maternity that brings consolation. Ignoring Rachel's more earthly aspects, not the least her willingness to "hire out" her own husband to her sister for a potent potion (Gen. 30:14–16), Jeremiah's elevation of Rachel to a level of direct intermediary between Israel and Yahweh remains unaccounted for. This is precisely the gap that a late ancient midrashic narrative attempts to bridge by exploring the figure of the biblical Rachel against a context of destruction, exile, and redemption. In this rabbinic incarnation Rachel becomes a spokeswoman for all of Israel not through personal proof of fertility but through evidence of sibling affection.

Said [Moses] to Him: "Sovereign of the Universe, You have written in Your Torah: *whether it be a cow or a ewe, you shall not kill it and its young on one and the same day* (Lev. 22:28). But have You not killed many mothers and sons and remained silent?"

At that moment Rachel leaped in front of the One Above and said: "Lord of the Universe, it is known to you that Jacob your servant loved me very much and toiled for me for seven years in my father's house and that when these seven years were complete my father planned to substitute my sister for me as a wife. I knew his plan and therefore was cast into a dilemma. I informed my husband [of my father's plot] and gave him a sign to distinguish between me and my sister. But later I had a change of heart. I suppressed my desire [for Jacob] and conceived pity for my sister's shame.

In the evening, when my sister was substituted for myself, I disclosed to my sister the signs I had given to my husband so that he would believe her to be me. I even crawled under their bed. When he talked to her she maintained her silence while I answered him lest he recognized her voice. I did her kindness. Nor was I envious of her or exposed her shame. And if I, a mere mortal, dust and ashes, overcame my envy and did not shame my sister, why should You, the merciful King, be jealous of idolatry that has no substance and exile my children to be put to death by the sword and to become a prey to their enemies?"

And immediately the mercy of the Lord was stirred and He said: "For you, Rachel, I will restore Israel to her place." For it was said (Jer. 31:15): *A voice is heard in Rā'mah . . . Rachel is weeping for her children*.[23]

Lamentations Rabbah transforms sisterly jealousy, a hallmark of the biblical narrative, into a supreme sacrifice based on collaboration between sisters. Rachel not only helps Leah to deceive Jacob but she also becomes a vicarious participant in their wedding night. From a woman wholly attentive to the needs of her own body Rachel becomes sensitive to the sentiments of other women in a way rarely depicted in the Hebrew Bible. The tale of Ruth and Naomi provides an exception in its understanding of the nature and mutual needs of women *qua* women and among women. When the widowed Naomi is ready to go back home to "the land of Judah" she is faced with the pain of leaving behind a hospitable land (Moab), the burials of her beloved husband and sons, and two loving relatives with whom she had shared happiness and grief. Ahead of her is an uncertain future at the mercy of relatives she barely knows and in a home territory that she had left long ago. Ruth's beautiful words to her—"where you go, I will go; where you sleep, I will sleep; your people are my people and your God is my god; where you die there I, too, shall be buried" (Ruth 1:16–17)—capture the dilemma of a woman who feels that she no longer has the right to occupy a space in her adoptive land but is still apprehensive of her rightful place in her society of origin. By accompanying her into the unknown, ready to share her vicissitudes, Ruth becomes Naomi's daughter of blood. Her readiness to forgo her citizen's privileges in her native land and to assume the identity of a foreigner in an alien country, just as Naomi had done, recreates the bond between the two women that Ruth's marriage with Naomi's son had initiated but that his death threatened to sever.[24]

Rachel under the bed, like Ruth in "the land of Judah," is willing herself to alienation from what is hers by right. Ostensibly comic and crafty, yet vulnerable and merciful, the midrashic Rachel symbolizes the power inherent, paradoxically, in female weakness as a key to an understanding of the voice of women through biblical exegesis.[25] She is still a "trickster" as she had been in the biblical narrative and she still stage-manages the entire scene. Leah is seen, right on the bed, but she is not heard. Rather, she is a listener, a voiceless and a passive presence in a naked body that goes through the motions. Listening can be a fatal occupation, as Lamentations Rabbah does not note but as Phaedra learns when she becomes an invisible participant in a dialogue that unravels her love for her stepson (see below). Leah's sentiments are not recorded in the midrash.[26] Instead, the midrashic tale focuses on Rachel's display of sisterhood as a key to her humanness and to full membership in the Jewish community. She becomes a true matriarch, indeed *the* matriarch par excellence, not by promoting the inheritance of a favorite son, as Rebecca does in Genesis, nor through the production of heirs or her capacity for mourning, but because she protects the human and moral dignity of her sister. In the process she demonstrates that the fickleness ordinarily associated with women can turn into faithfulness and constancy.

Above all, the midrash provides a unique insight into the kind of solidarity of which women are capable and men rarely record or comprehend. Its insistence on Rachel's sibling empathy as a key to future national redemption reflects an exceptional comprehension of the closeness of the domicile to the divine, and of the ability of women, as women, to reach Above through means that men could not share and via domestic realms in which men remain passive.

By taking apart the biblical components of the figure of Rachel and by reassembling and modifying them to suit the needs of the age, Lamentations Rabbah hints at the intricacies of reconstructing female imagery, of stereotypes and of ideologies of Jewessness in antiquity. Rachel, the bride-turned-mother, demonstrates how a biblical archetype can undergo far-reaching transformations on the basis of a single prophetic allusion. The very malleability of the image of Rachel also accounts for the predominance of problematic rather than of straightforwardly positive female icons in ancient Jewish sources. It seems hardly worth emphasizing that Lamentations Rabbah does not sketch a path that sisters are expected to follow and, at any rate, Leviticus 18:18 prohibits the marriage of two sisters to the same man unless one sister has died first. But the delineation of an ideal Rachel underlines the elusiveness of female imagery in biblical and post-biblical discourses. It also explains, in part, why the determination of gender and identity has relied less on penetrating the domicile and more on erecting boundaries around it.

Rachel's continuing appeal is evident from the association of her name with wives of well-known sages. Such links, based ostensibly on no more than the coincidence of names or of events, often serve as a rationale behind edifying tales regarding women. In one notable example the significance of the name (Rachel = ewe), combined with biblical data regarding Rachel, inspired a rabbinic tale about a famous sage of the early second century C.E., Rabbi Akiva, and his wife, Rachel. Akiva is a historical figure; she is less clearly so. What mattered, however, in the talmudic context in which the story is narrated, was the casting of Akiva's Rachel as a sharer in the multiple images of the biblical matriarch.

Existing in several versions (BT Ned. 50a; Ket. 62b-63a; Avot de Rabbi Nathan A1 and B12), perhaps relating to one archetype, the tales about Akiva and Rachel partake in the theme of an absent husband who disappears for many years and of a wife who remains fiercely loyal to him in spite of enormous difficulties at home.[27] In all the versions the wife invariably belongs to a higher social and economic class than her husband but the initial gap is brought to a final close upon the triumphant return of the husband as a famed "hero." The most elaborate embellishment of the core tale appears in the Babylonian tractate on vows:

The daughter of Kalba Savua (or his granddaughter) became engaged to Rabbi Akiva. Kalba Savua heard and disinherited her. Nevertheless she married Akiva. In the autumn they used to sleep in a barn where he picked straw out of her hair. He said to her: "If it were in my power, I would have given you Jerusalem of Gold." Then Elijah came in the guise of a mortal man and knocking on the gate he said: "Give me some straw for my wife has just given birth to a baby and I have nothing to make her a bed with" Rabbi Akiva told his wife: "Here is a man who does not even have straw."

She said to Akiva: "Go and stay in the house of a sage." He did and studied for a dozen years with Rabbis Eliezer and Joshua. At the end of this period he went back home. As he stood nearby he heard a wicked man telling his wife: "Your father did the right thing [by disinheriting you]. He [Akiva] is not like you [or: not of your mettle]. He left you a widow, bereft of life, all these years." She told him: "If he heeds me, he will stay away for another dozen years." Akiva said [to himself]: "Since she gives me permission I will return [to school]." And so he did. He stayed away from home for another twelve years.

After this period he returned with twenty four thousand pairs of pupils and the whole world came to greet him. So did she. But that wicked man said to her: "Where are you going?" She replied: "The righteous man knows his beast." She went [to meet Akiva] to demonstrate [to the wicked man that she was right?] but his pupils shoved her aside. Akiva said: "Leave her alone. What is mine and yours is hers." Kalba Savua heard and came to inquire about [abolishing] his earlier oath [to disinherit her]. And he was permitted [to annul it]. (BT Ned. 50a)

Plainly put, the tale of Rachel and Akiva recounts how a man and a woman of vastly different backgrounds meet, fall in love, and marry over the objections of her family. It continues to narrate how she lives with her beloved in penury and how she encourages him to overcome his humble beginnings by becoming a Jewish hero, namely a sage. Her (his?) success is then measured not only by the number of pupils that he acquires and by his triumphal return home but also by her staunch loyalty to his cause and finally, and chillingly, by her admission of inferiority.

It is easy to see why the wife in the tale is called Rachel, as in the name of an animal and the biblical matriarch, even though it is unclear whether this indeed was her name or whether the tale has a historical core. Nor does it greatly matter. Like the biblical couple, the bond between the rabbinic one is so strong that it can bridge years of separation. Indeed, the fourteen years of labor that Jacob invests in the acquisition of Rachel in Genesis are expanded in the Talmud to twenty-four, as though to illustrate the temporal meaningless of their relationship. Rachel and Akiva are first separated by class, then by her family's disowning of the couple, and finally by many years of male schooling. The mental state of the biblical Rachel during the years of forced abstention is not explored. But they explain the sense of urgency gleaned from the ultimatum she issues to Jacob to provide her with sons or to see her dying. The rabbinic tale emphasizes the wife's uncompromised devotion to her husband through the absence of children from the relationship and her comments on neighborly gossip.

Akiva's Rachel is thrown into a legal and social limbo from which her innate sense of compassion (like that of Lamentations Rabbah's Rachel), no less than Akiva's actual return, finally extricates her. According to one version of the story, when mocked by a neighbor on account of Akiva's absence, Rachel responds that "a righteous man has regard for the life of his beast" (Prov. 12:10, Oxford). In the context of Proverbs, where this reference appears, "a good wife is the crown of her husband but she who brings shame is like rottenness in his bones" (12:4, Oxford). There is, therefore, an intimate link between the public image of a Jewish man and the private doings of his wife.[28]

Notwithstanding, Rachel's self-imposed isolation may be seen also as a result of her own earlier decision to marry in spite of her father's wishes.

The departure and lengthy absence of her husband may be construed as a punishment for her own departure from her father's house and not only as an expression of his desire to pursue wisdom. If this is the case, however, Akiva's Rachel seemingly fails to fulfill a critical role, namely that of a mediator between father and husband. Here, too, are echoes of the biblical Rachel whose actions hastened an open confrontation between Laban, her father, and Jacob. Yet, Rachel's extraordinary loyalty to Akiva, even by rabbinic standards, redeems her in the end. Or so it appears.

Modern analyses of the tale(s) of Akiva and Rachel have emphasized its links with Palestinian and Babylonian rabbinic debates over the seemingly contradictory demands of married life on the one hand and of total commitment to the Torah on the other.[29] Analyzed within the larger narrative and legal framework of the Talmuds, such scholarly perspectives help to explain the final redactional mind and its concern to record and to account for Palestinian and Babylonian views on the meaning of marital relations. But they fail to penetrate the intent or the underlying theme of the "original" Akiva-Rachel tales that, to my mind at least, endeavored not to sympathize with the "wife"-"widow" of an absent man but rather to illuminate the permanent tension between husbands and wives that a prolonged absence further exacerbates. What the tales imply is that a returning husband may come home not to find rest and peace but rather chaos and perhaps death. Here, the most vivid and expressive parallels belong to a realm not of biblical myth or rabbinic ideology but to the domain of Greek mythology. I am thinking, of course, of Penelope and Odysseus.

To begin with, there are some striking similarities between the basic components of the two tales. Odysseus gains the throne of Ithaca through his marriage with Penelope.[30] In other words, it is her status and position, and not his, that confers royalty on him. In the household of Rachel and Akiva the "nobility" is likewise all hers, as is the background of wealth and of class. Odysseus leaves home, presumably with the compliance, if not the support, of his wife to join a war that promises to turn its combatants from rulers by courtesy of marriage into heroes in their own right. Only in this manner can he finally close the initial gap between himself and Penelope. To become a hero, then, a Greek man in this context must sever, temporarily, his family ties and abandon his household. Through the *Iliad* we can glimpse the activities of Odysseus and his partners during the last year of the war; through the *Odyssey*, we can, exceptionally, also glean the domicile or the sphere of actions and reflections of one woman, Penelope, during the lengthy absence of her husband. The Jewish narrative does not have to illustrate the doings of Akiva in the course of his years of study. Such a description would have been superfluous. Nor does it elaborate the life of the wife left at home since its pattern should have conformed to a host of regulations, not the least the avoidance of adultery. With the exception of two solitary encounters between Rachel and a nosy neighbor, Akiva's wife does not provide any comment on her years of solitude.

Yet, underlying the period of separation is a basic gap that has steadily widened. On his lengthy and tortuous way home Odysseus visits the underworld where, among departed comrades, he meets Agamemnon, the leader of the Trojan expedition. During his absence, Agamemnon's wife, Clytemnestra, ruled their kingdom, took a lover and made him king. She knew only too well how her husband had spent his time at Troy. He had no idea of her activities at home. When he finally returns, a great and renowned victor, Agamemnon expects a triumphal reception. What he gets is, indeed, a purple carpet, a banquet, a hot bath, all leading to more bloodshed, his own this time. Under these circumstances it is hardly surprising that Agamemnon warns Odysseus of the hazards of the return, even when the wife at home is the loyal and loving Penelope.

Nothing is more frightful or shameless than a woman who puts such deeds into her heart and contrives the murder of her wedded husband.... You may be sure that I had planned a homecoming to my children and to my household, but she ... had brought shame on herself and on women yet to be, even on her who does what is right ... [therefore] in your house never be gentle even to your wife. Do not declare to her every thought you have in mind but reveal some and hide others.... Death will not come to you from your wife ... wise Penelope, who is both prudent and understanding ... a newly wed bride when the expedition set sail.... Yet, do not bring your ship to the shore of your native land in the open, but rather in secret, for no longer is there truth in women.[31]

The loyal woman at home, then, can turn into an unexpected threat.[32] Even when she is reputedly steadfast she is still dangerous and unpredictable. Odysseus follows the advice of the dead Agamemnon and returns home in disguise. After many verbal skirmishes with Penelope, who remains suspicious of his identity longer than everyone else, and a successful competition with his rivals, Odysseus regains his place with the added prestige won in war.[33] Yet, even after this "happy end" the words of Agamemnon continue to resound in the concluding narrative:

How good and understanding was flawless Penelope.... How well she kept before her the image of Odysseus, her wedded husband. Therefore, the fame of her excellence shall never perish.... Not in this manner did Clytemnestra devise evil deeds and kill her wedded husband. Hateful shall the song regarding her be among men and evil reputation does she bring to all womankind, even upon her who does rightly.[34]

Neither Penelope nor Rachel reveals her sentiments in full, the former in spite of numerous attributed speeches, the latter because women hardly ever express their feelings in rabbinic tales. But neither narrative even attempts to penetrate the mind of women, nor their "immeasurable mourning," not only because it was largely a closed book to male authors but also because of simple lack of interest.[35] Odysseus attempts to consult his mother about the "will and mind" of his wife; Akiva's Rachel does not appear with a mother at all. She does come, however, with a wealthy and irate father who disinherits her for insubordination.

When addressing their husbands, both women, Penelope and Rachel, issue commands. Penelope does it by virtue of her position, as does Rachel. For both this type of discourse is habitual. It is also the manner of speaking that Akiva acquires after many years of study when he finally assumes a social position equal to the one that Rachel had by birth. The "happy end" of each tale is not, in fact, the return of the husband and conjugal reunification after years of separation. It is rather the leveling of gaps between spouses that brings satisfaction to the husband and possibly, but only possibly, to the wife too.

Odysseus and Akiva return home as heroes, although the lengthy absence of Odysseus undermines a heroic reception. Not even his successful skirmish with the greedy suitors of his wife enables Odysseus to claim the position of a hero. He has to prove to his own wife, the legal ruler of the land, that he, and only he, is her legally wedded husband. In Penelope's domicile, the glory of battle between men had waned into insignificance. Akiva's homecoming is accompanied by a reception accorded to a hero and, above all, by an admission of inferiority on the part of his own wife. Herein lies the essence of his ultimate triumph. For Penelope and Rachel the return of their husbands involves a loss and a gain: Penelope is no longer the sole ruler in her domain, nor is Rachel in hers. With the husbands at home, the women become wives once more.

Marriage for women like Rachel, then, involves a transition from riches to rags, from conjugality to forced celibacy, and from the status of a matron and an object of love and husbandly admiration, to that of a widow, a target of pity and derision. Matrimony guarantees neither security nor stability for the wife under certain circumstances. Nor is there anything specifically Jewish about such a conclusion. In the societies envisioned in the Talmuds, Rachel's position remains ambiguous, just like that of Odysseus's Penelope. Tied to their habitat, either by choice or by force of circumstances, they do not enjoy the physical mobility that so characterizes the life of men in the recorded tales of male heroisms. Yet, women like Rachel and Penelope can exercise a certain freedom of choice: Rachel chooses Akiva over parental objections; Penelope chooses to remain loyal to the memory of Odysseus in spite of being besieged by numerous suitors.

Significantly, neither the Greek nor the Jewish stories about "Rachel" deal with the "ever after" of the respective spousal returns. Telemachos, Penelope's and Odysseus's son, had become irrelevant long before the return of his father.[36] To prevent a Jacob-Rachel confrontation over procreation the talmudic tales of Akiva's return do not feature children at all.[37] Marital beds, however, play a crucial role in the Homeric recognition scene and in the tale of Rachel in Lamentations Rabbah. They are the matrix through which female identity is explored, precisely because this is the most important shared territory of the domicile. Here, again, is a touch of irony—in the *Odyssey* the revelations of the marriage bed convince Penelope of the identity of the stranger claiming to be her husband, and complete her transformation from a "widow" back into a wife. In the midrashic tale, Rachel under the bed is transformed into a sister through vicariously experiencing the meaning of marriage and sex. In the Talmud there is no bed at all but only a makeshift straw heap in a barn that guarantees eventual recognition in spite of the far-reaching changes that had taken place.

Perhaps, however, the most meaningful contribution of the Greek epic to a fuller understanding of the rabbinic text lies in the latter's final twist. Homer places the burden of recognition on Penelope while the Talmud shifts the weight to Akiva. In the former it is the familiar who has to come to terms with the unfamiliar, but in the Jewish version it is the returning "foreigner" who acts as an arbiter of the territory of the domicile that had remained a closed book to him for years.

Embedding Jewish tales, then, in a broader cultural context contributes to an alternative reading of allusive and taciturn texts. And while such associations appear to dispel the uniqueness of rabbinic tales, they nevertheless underline their claims of universality. And they further help to weave invisible threads between tales of different periods, thus demonstrating both continuity and change of mental outlooks and attesting to shifting modules of exegetical modes. When read in a comparative context it is possible to appreciate the originality and the commonality of rabbinic reflections on the ideology of Jewishness, female and male, as the following tales that focus on the twin themes of avowed chastity and shame suggest.

Sin, Shame, and Sanctity:
The Tale of the Lusty Wife and Rabbi Meir

An ill-dated midrash on the Seventh Commandment, "thou shalt not commit adultery" (Exod. 20:14), projects a seemingly conventional triangle in order to illustrate the ills that befall one who transgresses the forbidden.[38] Its protagonists are a virtuous rabbi, a lusty wife, and an indifferent husband. The tale provides wonderful twists on the original biblical ban with which, in effect, it has little to do.[39]

The following was told about Rabbi Meir who used to make a pilgrimage to Jerusalem every major festival. When in Jerusalem he usually stayed in the house of Rabbi Judah the butcher (cook?). Judah's wife was beautiful and modest and most attentive to Rabbi Meir's needs every time he came. When she died Judah married another. He bid her as follows: "If a young sage (= a pupil of the sages) by the name of Rabbi Meir arrives be sure to pay him respect, allow him to enter the house, bring him food and drinks, serve him while he eats and drinks, make his bed and provide him with bed cloths." She replied: "I will do so."

When the festival approached Rabbi Meir made his customary pilgrimage to Jerusalem and went to the house of Rabbi Judah. He told Judah's new wife: "Show me (or bring forth) Judah's wife." She said: ["His wife has died and he has married me."] Thereupon Meir wept and turned away to go. She grabbed him by his garment and said:] "My lord, my husband has bidden me to pay utmost respect to a sage by the name of Rabbi Meir, saying that when he comes here I must bring him food and drinks. [Rest assured that] I will pay you even greater respect than the first wife." But Meir said to her: "I cannot enter the house with the permission of the wife only. I must have the husband's permission to enter his home." He left the house and went to look for Judah. The latter told him: "My first wife has died [and this one is more zealous for your honor than her predecessor]." Meir immediately returned to Judah's house.

Rabbi Judah's new wife was attentive to all his needs. She prepared food and brought it to him, and when he ate she served him. Now, Meir was a good-looking man and she kept gazing at him. She made him drunk till he no longer knew his right hand from his left. She made his bed. He fell upon it in a stupor. The woman took off his clothes and slept with him. He knew nothing of this and slept with her the whole night. In the morning he went to pray (in the house of study? the synagogue?). When he returned, she put food and drinks before him. He ate and drank. As she served him she kept chatting and laughing. Rabbi Meir thought that she was being rather cheeky. He averted his gaze, looking at the ground, reluctant to look at her. She said to him: "Why do you avoid looking at me? You have slept with me throughout the night and were not ashamed then. And now you are shy of me?" He said: "Nonsense, this never happened." She said: "If you do not believe me [I will tell you that] you have such and such mark on your body."

Rabbi Meir then realized that he had slept with her and became rather resentful. Crying, he uttered: "What a pity I lost the Torah that I have studied. What remedy do I have now? What shall I do? I will go to the head of the academy (yeshiva) and tell him of my sin and I will accept his judgment regardless." Returning home he kept wailing and crying, rending his clothes and putting ashes on his hair. All his relatives immediately came out and asked him: "What do you intend to do?" He replied: "I will go to the head of the academy in Babylon and will abide by his judgment." They said to him: "You have sinned inadvertently and not deliberately. The Lord will forgive you. Do not cry out in a loud voice lest your sons are ashamed." But he replied: "If I listen to you the Lord will never forgive my sins, as it is said: *the one who conceals his sin can never succeed*" (Prov. 28:13).

He then headed to the academy in Babylon. Its head said to him: "What do you want?" He replied: "Such and such things happened to me and for this reason I have come to you. Everything you say, whether condemning me to death or to be fed to the beasts I will accept." The head said: "Let me inquire into the matter." The next day he told Rabbi Meir: "We have examined the matter and decided to feed you to the beasts" (i.e., lions). Meir replied: "I accept this judgement of heaven. Let your command be executed." The head called for two strongmen and told them to take Meir to the forest to a place frequented by lions, to bind his legs and arms, and to leave him there. He further ordered them to stay put on a tall tree to observe Meir's fate. "If he is eaten," he said, "bring me his bones so that I can bury them in a solemn ceremony since he had accepted the judgement of heaven." . . . (And so they did but nothing happened for three days.)

On the third night, a lion came, growled and roared around Meir, and put his teeth into him. Wrenching one of Meir's ribs he took, however, only a bite out of it. The next day the witnesses informed the head of this and he said: "Go and bring Meir to me since the lion barely touched his rib." They brought him and the head ordered the doctors to heal him.

When Rabbi Meir returned home a voice came out of heaven declaring: "Rabbi Meir will gain life in the next world." For this reason a man should not touch the wife of another man and not even the fiancée of one lest she pulls him to hell (*gehenom*) where he will burn forever.

At a basic reading, the story features a man who is wholly committed to the pursuit of the Torah, seduced against his will and conscience; a female seducer who is bent on the fulfillment of her bodily needs; and a third party who is the host of the seduced and husband of the seducer. The tale is littered with the echoes of a multitude of similar narratives, from the biblical encounter between Joseph and the wife of his master Potiphar (Gen. 39:12–18), through Homer's Bellerophon, Pindar's Peleus, the Roman foundational myth of the rape of Lucretia, and the myth of Hippolytus and Phaedra.[40] It is this last tale, in its Euripidean guise, that provides, I think, the most insightful parallels with the rabbinic midrash.

Euripides' tragedy presents a young man (Hippolytus) sworn to a life of chastity and celibacy whose unruffled and happy existence is shattered when he learns, through a third party, that his stepmother (Phaedra) is in love with him.[41] His anger upon this revelation knows no bounds; her shame at his rejection and her fear of exposure are so great that she commits suicide. But she also takes vengeance by leaving for Theseus, her husband (and his father) who had been away, a note accusing Hippolytus of raping her. Theseus is shocked, dismayed, and furious at this violation of his marriage bed. He banishes his son from the realm in spite of the latter's protestation of innocence. On his way to the location of exile Hippolytus loses control over his beloved horses. At the sight of a monster rising from the sea they trample him to death. In his dying moment, however, Artemis, the goddess whom he had venerated in life, reveals the truth, effects a reconciliation between father and son, and brings to a closure the cycle of love, revenge, and death that Aphrodite had set in motion even before the play started.

The surviving *Hippolytus* is, in fact, Euripides' second try at dealing with the myth.[42] In the first version Phaedra, like Judah's wife in the midrash, communicates her passion directly to Hippolytus. In the second and much revised play there is no trace of the impudent Phaedra. Instead, like Hippolytus himself, she is a paragon of virtue who courageously attempts to overcome her passion for her stepson. Nor is there a trace of physical sexual encounter in the altered drama. An ever present but unfulfilled carnal desire motivates the words and actions of the characters, just as Meir's fear of the perpetual presence of sin dictates his tenacious quest for absolution. In the *Hippolytus* the mere verbal suggestion, if not the possibility of actual adultery, puts the potential seducer and her object of passion in untenable positions. What makes the *Hippolytus*, as we have it, even more powerful are both the absence of direct confrontation between Phaedra and Hippolytus and the potency of words and insinuations. As she listens, unseen, to Hippolytus's angry retort to the revelation of her love, Phaedra is convinced that she must die. The alternative of living with shame is unacceptable:

. . . I must die. And die dishonored . . .
The anger of Hippolytus is whetted.

> He will tell his father all the story . . .
> To my disparagement. He will tell old Pittheus too
> And will fill all the land with my dishonor.⁴³

What she does not know is that her forbidden sentiments had been planted in her heart by a goddess (Aphrodite) as a prelude to a divine punishment of Hippolytus. She is then in no position to argue, as Penelope had done when defending Helen that:

> A god, in fact, prompted her to do the shameful deed. And she did not realize beforehand the fatal, divinely inspired folly out of which first came suffering also to us.⁴⁴

Forbidden love, then, is not an inborn passion but is invented and disseminated by a power stronger than the control that humans can exercise over their emotions. In the play, Aphrodite, Hippolytus's enemy, although set on punishing his devotion to Artemis (and to celibacy), inspires Phaedra (rather than Hippolytus) with passion. But the recasting of Phaedra as the chaste spouse enabled Euripides to highlight the tragedy of a woman who is ashamed to come to terms with her sexuality and of a man whose avoidance of women provides an illusion of security from sex.

Judah's wife, like Euripides' first Phaedra, is straightforward, conforming to the familiar tradition of the temptress initiating adultery.⁴⁵ Her subsequent fate, like that of Potiphar's wife but unlike Phaedra's, is of no relevance to the subject and the lesson of the story. For all that we know she and Judah lived happily ever after. The midrash is not interested in the ordeal (Num. 5) relating to suspected adultery nor in her redemption. But Phaedra's fate suggests that the mere hint of adultery in the domicile is sufficient to drive a woman to destruction and to ruin the home. In the absence of the husband the social conventions that govern the household become the sole responsibility of the wife. This is why Akiva's "Rachel" nips gossip in the bud by referring to the proverb about the righteous man who knows his own beast.

Within so delicate a balance silence and discretion are crucial.⁴⁶ This is precisely what Phaedra's self-appointed emissary of love (her nurse) realizes and what Hippolytus fails to understand:

> *Hippolytus.* You cannot expect that I hear horror and stay silent.
> *Nurse.* I beg of you, I entreat you by your right hand,

>   Your strong right hand—do not speak of this! . . .
> *Hippolytus.* What is this? Do you maintain that you have done
>   nothing wrong?
> *Nurse.* Yes, but the story, son, is not for everyone.
> *Hippolytus.* Why not? A pleasant tale makes pleasanter telling,
> When there are many listeners.
> *Nurse.* You will not break your oath to me, surely you will not?
> *Hippolytus.* My tongue swore, but my mind was still unpledged.[47]

Choosing death, Phaedra avoids shame and infamy. Her suicide silences the body that could have been accused of adultery but it does not banish her from the stage. Communicating with the living beyond death she turns the tables by implicating Hippolytus in a rape. The charge effectively counters his possible accusation of adultery. What Phaedra fails to take into account is Hippolytus's readiness to abide by the promise of silence that he had reluctantly proffered.

In the midrash Meir's sexual chastity is compromised as is that of Hippolytus. The agent of ruin is a wife of an honored friend who uses wine as her weapon. Meir becomes an unconscious participant in the sexual encounter that she initiates. And although he can choose to forget that night, as Hippolytus can elect to ignore Phaedra's passion and the nurse's entreaty, Meir insists on atoning for what he regards as a sin. His willingness to undergo a purifying ordeal is emphasized by the narrator's insistence on his foggy mind during the sexual act. Emerging out of Judah's bed, Meir is as ignorant of his unconscious if willing participation as both Phaedra and Hippolytus are of the fact that their chastity had been a subject of wager between two goddesses.

Strictly speaking, Phaedra is innocent of adultery, and Hippolytus is not culpable of either adultery or rape. But Phaedra's efforts to repress her love are undermined by her nurse who cannot see her suffering, and Hippolytus's commitment to virginity, of which he is inordinately proud, is threatened by the sudden information that the nurse reveals and then by Phaedra's accusation. In the eyes of his father he is guilty of rape. Meir's relatives consider him innocent since in their eyes what happened was a rape and not adultery. The head of the academy in Babylonia shares Meir's sentiments and decrees that he must bear the consequences of the act itself. Phaedra judges herself and condemns herself to death.[48] Hippolytus, who knows the truth but abides by his oath of silence, has to submit to his father's judgment and to face exile, a sentence tantamount to death. Both

Meir and Hippolytus confront nature in its crudest form through an encounter with beasts, domestic in the case of Hippolytus, and wild in Meir's case. Having created a culture of selfishness by a ruthless devotion to the Torah and to the life of the hunt, Meir survives the lion's attack but Hippolytus is killed by his own horses.[49]

Meir is seduced with food and drink, rather than with words. Awakened, his reaction is as furious as that of Hippolytus. He denies that sex had ever taken place. The compact rabbinic tale has no space for fulminating gender-based rhetoric yet it casts the woman as a person entirely controlled by physical needs that others must fulfill. The male characters, by contrast, are self-absorbed and self-sufficient and their commitments and sexual integrity are compromised by women. As far as Hippolytus is concerned, the mere act of listening to a confession of love is polluting; Meir feels polluted by the invasion of his sexual privacy; and both men seek to purify themselves by running away from all women.

Secure in their knowledge of their self-righteousness, the two, when put to the test, fail to come to grips with the true meaning of male virtue. Hippolytus gleans its depth when he has to deal with an accusation of a sexual transgression that he cannot refute because Phaedra is not there to counter or to countenance it. Meir becomes a hero not because of his manifest and much vaunted devotion to the Torah but because he experiences sufferings and learns to know himself. Hippolytus is made to share Phaedra's fate in order to acquire the knowledge that he had not possessed. In the process he becomes aware that he had not been, after all, the most pious of men as he had often claimed. Meir chooses to pay for a loss of sexual integrity in which he had been an unconscious participant, and by being left to the mercy of heaven he also has a chance of survival.

Underlying the tale of Phaedra and Hippolytus is an acknowledgment of the power of love (*eros*), the source of words and actions that can destroy the domicile.[50] In the tale of Meir the lust of the unnamed wife of Judah threatens the integrity of Meir's body and mind. Hippolytus inveighs against a domestic landscape which, as he claims, forces men to come to terms with the life cycle and emotions of women.

> Why, why, Zeus, did you put a woman into the world,
> In the light of the sun? . . .
> The father who begets her, rears her up,
> Must add a dowry gift to pack her off
> To another's house and thus be rid of the load.

> And he again that takes the cursed creature
> Rejoices and enriches his heart's jewel
> With dear adornment, beauty heaped on vileness . . .
> The husband who has the easiest life is one whose wife
> Is a mere nothingness, a simple fool,
> Uselessly sitting by the fireside.
> I hate a clever woman—God forbid
> That I should ever have a wife at home
> With more than woman's wits! Lust breeds mischief
> In the clever ones . . .
> At home the mistress plots mischief . . .
> bargaining and trafficking
> in the sanctity of a father's marriage bed . . .
> It is my piety that saves you.
> Had you not caught me off my guard and bound
> My lips with an oath, by heaven I would not refrain
> From telling this to my father . . .[51]

But Phaedra depicts a landscape, essentially of the same domicile, in which the lives of women are seriously circumscribed by the nature of women and, above all, by a culture of shame and the necessity to conceal their true feelings:

> At first when love had struck me, I reflected
> How best to bear it. Silence was my first plan.
> Silence and concealment . . .
> Then I believed that I could conquer love,
> Conquer it with discretion and good sense.
> And when that too failed me, I resolved to die . . .
> When I do wrong I could not endure to see
> A circle of condemning witnesses.
> I know what I have done. I know the scandal.
> And all too well I know that I am a woman,
> Object of hate to all. Destruction lights
> Upon the wife who herself plays the tempter
> And strains her loyalty to her husband's bed.[52]

In her reading of essentially the same panorama there is no language that women and men can share. This is why there is also no solution, other than death, to the proposed adultery in the play. Ultimately, but beyond the action on the stage, Hippolytus dies to be reborn as a hero, and Phaedra becomes, finally, a part of him precisely because of her unrequited love.

Meir's rebirth is enacted through a repetition of the divine act of creation itself. The midrash aspires to teach a lesson to anyone, or rather to any male contemplating adultery. But the very survival of Meir may result in a contradictory conclusion. Can men commit adultery, pay for it, and be redeemed? The answer proposed by the midrash is a recreation of the beginning of humanity itself. Its moralizing revolution resows Adam's rib in order to recover a primordial state of innocence without women and without temptations. This is precisely the manly "paradise" that Hippolytus conjures up:

> Why, Zeus, did you put women in the world and
> In the light of the sun? If you were so determined
> To breed the race of man, the source of it
> should not have been women. Men might have dedicated
> in your temples images of gold, silver or weight of bronze,
> and thus have bought the seed of progeny . . .
> So we might have lived in our houses
> Free of the taint of women's presence . . .[53]

In Meir's mind the night with Judah's wife disqualified him as a Torah scholar. But it was his single-minded pursuit of the Torah that generated the circumstances that led to his sin. In the end, the story of Meir has little to do with adultery and much to do with man's perception of his place in society. By excluding the woman from the rest of the tale the rabbinic narrators implied that Meir's punishment atoned for both his and her sin. They made the man responsible for the domicile and for the behavior of its female members. By choosing a member of their own class as an example of the Seventh Commandment the rabbis also reinforced their status as a model elite, echoing Phaedra's conviction that: "when shameful practices are countenanced by the nobility, they will also be approved by the low born."[54]

Underlying the two stories, the Greek and the Jewish, are also issues of knowledge and education. Hippolytus had believed that knowledge is innate and granted only "to those to whom rectitude in everything is inborn."[55] But he learns that chastity and innocence do not offer protection, just as Meir discovers that his passion for the Torah can be easily compromised unless he learns to know himself. In the Judaism of this midrash men can be "raped" but can also survive to prove, metaphorically, that women are altogether superfluous. By recasting the most famous biblical foundation tale not as the beginning of conjugality but rather as the regaining of male primordial virginity, the Judaism of the midrash reverses the order of the creation itself. Eve's successors become the aggressors that must be excised through the removal of the rib by a savage act of a beast.

It is idle to speculate whether the narrator of the tale of the rape of Rabbi Meir was familiar with any classical tale.[56] Nor is it of particular importance. What these two versions, Jewish and Greek, of "adultery" demonstrate is a commitment to cultural and moral standards that are disseminated through the narration of episodes involving invasions of the male body. Jews and Greeks, men and (to a degree) women, are judged by their responsibility vis-à-vis the integrity of their body and its place in an ordained society. When read against the myth of Hippolytus, Meir's tale appears to depict an idyllic rabbinic landscape, like that of Hippolytus's fantasy land, in which there are no women at all, either chaste or lusty, and where men learn to live without women.

By putting the brunt of the guilt on the object rather than on the initiator of adultery the two tales provide precious insights into a web of gender relations in which moral intentions rather than actions are decisive. The assumed guilt of the adulteress in the Jewish tale is not discussed. Readers of the midrash need not have pondered on her subsequent absence from the tale or on her fate since she merely furnishes a point of departure for Meir's search for his moral self and manhood. But there is no doubt that she is cast as a negative stereotype for the kind of behavior that a virtuous Jewess should avoid. She has no moral redemption.

What makes this fanciful rabbinic episode also meaningful within a context of sexual and social identities is its choice of names and approximate chronology. Both the casting of the young sage as Rabbi Meir and the reference to a Jerusalem pilgrimage suggest an attempt to link the chief protagonist with a famed tanna of that name in the second century.[57] What, precisely, were the sources that contributed to the midrashic narrative remains unclear.[58] By a curious coincidence, perhaps, Meir's wife, Beruriah, a person of some standing in her own right, becomes the subject of a similar tale of seduction.[59] Rashi, one of the greatest medieval interpreters of rabbinic law and lore, has a unique and bizarre tale about Beruriah based, some maintain, on a Babylonian talmudic tradition.[60] According to Rashi, Beruriah and Meir disagreed over definitions regarding the nature of women, the latter supporting sages who maintained that women were fickle by nature, the former strenuously objecting to so facile a view.[61] To prove her wrong Meir incited one of his pupils to seduce her. After initial failures the pupil succeeded. Beruriah discovered the plot and strangled herself. Meir left home in disgrace. The terse tale dispenses with details altogether. Hippolytus's story and the midrash about Meir provide valuable clues to its missing parts.

Casting respectable married women as parties in an adultery is hardly novel. But Beruriah and Phaedra are also characterized by fatal ignorance about the real power behind the seduction. Not sex but strife (between goddesses and between sages) are the causes of their eventual disgrace and demise. And neither has the option that the midrash offers straying males. In the Greek play, neither the married couple (Phaedra and Theseus) nor, for that matter, the putative one (Phaedra and Hippolytus) share marital or sexual intimacy in the domicile, the natural environment for such modes of communication. They are never seen in the privacy of their bedroom and the only time men on stage gaze at the body of a woman is when she is lifeless. Beruriah's tale is launched, oddly enough, with an intellectual debate over a philosophical question. The argument betrays uneasiness about the place of women in the learning domain of men. Its conclusion is as inevitable as Phaedra's passion and Meir's seduction. But the Greek tale endeavors to feature the woman as a heroine; the Jewish stories cast women as villains and sinners.

To be a Greek or a Jewish wife, then, somehow entailed situations over which the woman had no control but in which she was embroiled without, ultimately, a way out. Chaste wives, as well as erudite and outspoken ones, meet the same deadly end because stereotypic male visions of the domain of women cannot be reconciled with breached morals, regardless of the innocence or guilt of the women involved. Even the absence of a moralizing tenor vis-à-vis the errant wife of the Meir midrash does not undermine this conclusion for its underlying assumption is that women, married or otherwise, are fickle, precisely the point that Beruriah is trying to refute. In the sophisticated environment of classical Athens where Euripides produced his version(s) of the myth it was possible to heroize Phaedra, not, however, without moralizing about female fickleness. Indeed, Euripides had to change the way he cast Phaedra because his original reading of her character, as a proverbial temptress, elicited much criticism.

Values, such as those gleaned from rabbinic literature, appear to contrast with the apparently nonchalant manner in which patriarchs like Abraham and Isaac used their wives' bodies as a guarantee of their own safety. Even the chaste Esther seemed barely bashful when translated into Ahasuerus's harem. That a revolution of mores had taken place between the return from Babylon under Ezra and Nehemiah in the fifth century B.C.E. and late antiquity (ca. 250–650 C.E.) is evident and has been often noted. This change in the ideology of Jewishness, and especially of Jewessness, may have accelerated with the late ancient shaping of Christian sexual morality.[62] In both contexts a process of redefining membership in the community of creed focused on the body as a locus of a metamorphosis of values in which the figure of biblical women, such as Rachel, actively contributed to the mutation.[63]

Our surviving sources offer limited perspectives of what it meant to be a woman in ancient society, Greek, Roman, or Jewish. Rather they illustrate a variety of circumstances, each requiring different stereotypic responses. What seems clear, however, is that amid a host of female stereotypes there is no single universal "positive" prototype of a Jewess. Instead, we have a series of situational and stereotypic behaviors, some positive, the majority negative, and all ambiguous and open to different interpretations. If becoming a Jew (male) entails an eternal pursuit of 613 positive "musts," becoming a Jewess involves a process of avoidance. A Jewess has to avoid gentiles, adultery, defending her gender, offending her sister, and so on. A perusal of such patterns of abstention or avoidance, as well as the pursuit of the forbidden, resides at the heart of this study.

Contents

The book falls into two distinct parts, one dealing with literary sources and with specific cases or characters, the other with legal sources and legal theories. In terms of "chronology," the first part focuses on the Hebrew Bible with two excursions into the realm of postbiblical extensions. The second part is anchored in Roman law and rabbinics in late antiquity. To justify the apparent temporal gap between the two parts, I can recruit the rabbis who forged a direct, if ahistorical concatenation between themselves and their biblical "ancestors" (Avot 1.1). Between the last recorded "events" in the Hebrew Bible and Hillel and Shamai, the great pre-70 C.E. forerunners of the rabbis, Jewish history had become a blank. Through a process of remembrance and obliteration the men who shaped and canonized the writings of the Israelite/Jewish past removed an intermediary stage, rich in literary creativity but judged poor in the right spirit. The Judaism of antiquity as bequeathed to the Jews of the Middle Ages and of modernity does not include the so-called Jewish-Hellenistic corpus. Neither Philo nor Josephus, nor even the library that the caves of the Judaean desert suddenly revealed barely half a century ago, made their way into the canonized corpus. Between visible poles of destruction and restoration, marked by the history and metahistory of the Temples in Jerusalem, the Judaism(s) that contextualize my study had grown out of the Hebrew Bible and the rabbinic corpora.

The first chapter ("From Dinah to Cozbi: Rape, Sex, and Foundational Moments") focuses on the transition of the body of a woman from adolescence to womanhood. It analyzes the history of an illegal invasion of the female body as reflected in the so-called rape of Dinah (Gen. 34) and it ends with a postscript dealing with a metaphorical rape and the delegitimization of marriage between a noble Israelite and an aristocratic Midianite (Num. 25). The ultimate fate of the matriarch Dinah is intriguing precisely because we know nothing about it. We know, of course, what happens to her unfortunate suitor but we can only guess her own lot. Patriarchy had specific uses for a virgin daughter and sister but a single woman with a compromised hymen was a liability. She had to assume widowhood without ever having been married, turning from a victim into an object of concealment. Yet, a careful reading of the Dinah narrative also shows that women can become potential agents of conversion and of peaceful coexistence rather than, as so often asserted in the Bible, agents of apostasy and destruction.

In the making of both matriarchy and patriarchy the episode of Dinah's "rape" proved as critical as were the rapes of the Sabine women for the foundation of the Roman state, and of Lucretia for the demise of the Roman monarchy and the rise of the Republic. The investigation of sex as a social marker of power and authority in patriarchal Canaan has, indeed, useful and illuminating parallels in the tales of passion and violence that accompany the emergence of the Roman commonwealth and of the Roman constitution. Such a comparative approach further highlights the formation of a distinctly Jewish point of view of history. In Judaism, the turning points of the past are determined through a wholesale rejection of foreign spouses, as an investigation of the foreign women of Persian Yehud (Ezra 9–10) endeavors to show in Chapter 2 ("Patriarchy and Patriotism: Integrating Sex into Second Temple Society"). At Rome, by startling contrast, it is rather the wholesale integration of foreign bodies, especially female, that shapes the course of its history. A new sense of Jewish patriotism entails a redefinition of criteria of affiliation. The men of Yehud/Judaea have to send away their wives and children to sustain their membership in the exilic community. At Rome, the Sabine women, newly married to their Roman abductors, have to reject their fathers and brothers to prove their loyalty to their husbands. The erasure of ethnic boundaries is accomplished in their bodies.

In the painstakingly reconstructed Temple-state of Ezra and of Nehemiah there is room only for faceless and voiceless Jewesses but none for childbearing foreigners who are the legally wedded wives of Jewish men and mothers of half-Jews. Like the Shechemites of patriarchal Canaan, the foreign women of Yehud become objects of rejection and a test of their husband's "patriotism." Controlling women, either by rape or through marriage, becomes a bloodless victory but a triumph nevertheless.

Nor is there room in the ideal Jewish state for a father who authorizes marriage for his daughter with a non-Jewish male or a daughter who dreams of such a step. The Jewish family of the Second Temple, as seen through the book entitled Jubilees, has a pure pedigree based on careful marital strategies. In a sense, Jubilees is a direct heir of the ideology of the nascent "state" of Ezra and hence an appropriate postscript to the second chapter. A Jewish daughter and wife in the landscape drawn by the anonymous author of Jubilees has one model that she must not follow, namely that of Dinah. Defiance does not become a Jewess, especially when it comes to marriage. A disobedient daughter who marries a gentile is to be burned to death. A Jewish wife who defies her husband, a topic of much rabbinic discussion, either by denying him sexual favors or by neglecting her duties (*moredet*), risks losing her dowry and divorce, thus endangering the social status acquired through marriage.

Yet, in fantasy lands women do acquire distinct personalities. But do they become models of Jewessness? The third chapter ("From Esther to Aseneth: Marriage, Familial Stereotypes, and Domestic Felicity") deals with the formation of families and with moments rarely captured, namely the "ever after" nuptial "bliss." In Susa, the capital of the mighty Achaemenid-Persian empire, a mixed couple is conjured up and an intermarriage is engineered by a Jewish patriarch. As Esther enters, the Temple, the Jewish state, and even God disappear. Between the mute foreign women of Ezra-Nehemiah and the vociferous Esther of the scroll lies a vast zone of ambiguity. Is Esther to become a model for an ideal Jewish wife? Is she a prototype of a female Jewish martyr? Hardly. The familial stereotypes that dwell in the scroll of Esther do not inspire emulation. Nor does the independent-minded Vashti or her less recalcitrant Jewish successor.

Neither the biblical Dinah nor the biblical Esther bear children, failing thus to fulfill the prime obligation of a matriarch. Equally poignant is the question whether the ideal relationship between a Jew and a woman is the one that depicts a marriage between a Jewish male and a gentile woman. In the tale known as "Joseph and Aseneth" a pagan woman falls in love with a Jewish man. He, a virtuous believer, rejects her. She, a single-minded woman, is determined to win his heart through a mysterious search for the "Right One." Aseneth might or might not be a prototype of a woman who converts out of love. But is she an ideal Jewess? Can she provide a model of the correct form of affiliation within the community of faith? Although elevated to a position of an arbiter of male and of "national" fate, figures such as Esther, Aseneth, Jubilees' counter-Dinah, and the rebellious wife are perforce evasive or, perhaps, timeless and inapplicable.

Within these traditional perceptions of who is a Jewess, or rather who she ought not to be, the rabbis, guardians of law in late antiquity, developed their social discourse of belonging. They set out to create a community in which a sense of communal identity was shaped in response to real or perceived communal needs. In such a society, the "law" is often predicated on the delineation of the illegal other as the embodiment of negative values and practices. The survival of this society depends on the construction of a "framework of fidelity" and the sanctification of the conjugal act.[64] Already in the Bible, woman's fidelity to her husband is often taken as a symbol of the bond between Israel and its God. Such mutual sanctification ensured and assured the truth of carnal filiation and the legitimization of the genealogical chain.

Infractors of marital harmony, primarily adulterous wives, emerge as transgressors and as violators of the law (Chapter 4: "Keeping Adultery at Bay"). Extensive discussions of suspected adultery took place in Roman Palestine in late antiquity. The debates recorded in the Talmuds (Babylonian and Palestinian) demonstrate how ideology and legal theories combine to define the boundaries of appropriate conduct of Jewish matrons/Roman citizens. Within the vast canvas of Roman legalities, the rabbis carved out a specific niche for their womenfolk. In this part there is a deliberate emphasis on Roman and rabbinic comparative perspectives. Late ancient Judaism did not develop in a vacuum.

Suspected adultery has a long ancestry. The image of a straying wife as a powerful negative icon is all-pervasive in ancient cultures. In the Bible

(Num. 5:10–31), a husband who suspected his wife of adultery had the right to subject her to an ordeal meant to establish her innocence or to prove her guilt. In the course of this public procedure at the heart of the sacred sanctuary, the suspected woman was exposed to the public gaze as priests loosened her hair and bared her breasts. The very exposure was meant to constitute a threat and a punishment. In rabbinic interpretations, elaborated in a space without a central sanctuary, the issue of suspected adultery was moved from the sacred public precincts to the domicile to be dealt with, if possible, at home. If the husband insisted on exposing his wife, he was given an opportunity to reconsider his actions and intentions at every stage of the legal road. By relying on powerful images of the forbidden the rabbis may have hoped to induce women to conform to their ideal boundaries of the wifely domain.

To be a Jewess, then, meant staying within specific marital bonds, resisting extramarital temptations, and marrying within communal boundaries. To produce Jews, namely full-fledged members of the community, a Jewish woman had to abide by the correct paternal wishes and to be allied to a man with the requisite lineage. Intermarriage posed, therefore, a grave problem as rabbinic discussions, the subject of Chapter 5 ("The Harmony of the Home"), show. Such marital alliances violated the prescribed code of female conduct and introduced genealogical confusion. Jewish objections to intermarriage are based on, essentially, ethnic and religious grounds.

Jewish women never marry gentiles, at least in theory. Yet, under the umbrella of Roman law, they could still contract valid matrimony with a non-Jew. Until the late fourth century C.E. marital impediments in Roman law never recognized distinctions of cult and ethnicity. The legal closure of marital boundaries along ethnic and creedal lines in Roman law emerges in late antiquity as a result of communal discourses, Jewish, Roman, and Christian, of inclusion and exclusion. Definitions of marital ineligibility cement the negative stereotypes that had shaped thinking about Jewessness for generations. They are informative as negative directives. They rarely reassure or inspire confidence.

Who is, finally, a Jewess? Perhaps the question ought to be rephrased: What is a Jewess? She is an entity whose strongest outlines are drawn against powerful reliefs of female judges, warriors, prophetesses, and queens that cannot become stereotypes.[65] Even the first four matriarchs, in spite of their continuing rhetorical appeal (Ruth 4:11), present problematic and ambiguous models. A more plausible Jewess is ultimately an ordinary woman who may desire to "go out" and meet eligible gentile men; who may harbor a craving to taste sex outside marriage; and who may dream of marrying a gentile monarch. And precisely because of the ordinariness of such cravings, these prospects are more threatening than the feats of biblical heroines. In Jewish ideology, Jewish women, beginning their life as well-guarded virgins, are to become marketable marital commodities and, eventually, the chaste wives and mothers of more Jews. This common course of life has been, needless to say, prescribed by men who, paradoxically, fail to provide consistently positive ideals and stereotypes for their womenfolk.

PART I

PROJECTIONS OF BIBLICAL SPHERES OF WOMEN

I

From Dinah to Cozbi

Rape, Sex, and Foundational Moments

> We see that women have been the cause of great dissensions and much ruin to states, and have caused great damage to those who govern them. We have seen in the history of Rome that the outrage committed upon Lucretia deprived the Tarquins of their throne. . . . Aristotle mentions as one of the first causes of the ruin of tyrants the outrages committed by them upon the wives and daughters of others, either by violence or by seduction.
>
> —Machiavelli, *Discourses*, Book III, Chapter 26

Love and lust appear in biblical narratives as a fatal combination, at least for the female objects of such emotions. In fact, women are rarely if ever made to experience these sentiments in the Bible. When Amnon, son of David and heir to the throne, conceives an irrepressible passion for his half-sister, Tamar, she begs him to seek permission to marry her (2 Sam. 13). Tamar is fully aware of the hazardous consequences for herself if coerced into sex with her sibling. "To whom shall I carry my disgrace?" (2 Sam. 13:13). Who, indeed, is likely to sympathize with her plight? Rejecting her plea, he rapes her. Love turns to hate and Amnon sends her away to become a useless and unwanted member of her brother's household.[1] Did she love him? No answer is forthcoming. When Shechem, heir to the wealth of the ruler of Hivite land, sees Dinah, his lust can be ostensibly assuaged only through violence (Gen. 34). Lust, however, turns to love. But the suitor of Jacob's daughter is singularly unacceptable. He has to be killed; Dinah becomes a widow without ever having been married.

To sustain membership in the family, the clan, and the community, an unmarried daughter, if the lessons of the two tales are to be applied literally, ought to stay at home and never stir even from her room. Otherwise, a visit to the bedside of a sick brother may result in a rape. An innocent outing to see local female friends may kindle the passion of a local man and lead to a disaster. Dinah's behavior becomes a model of inappropriateness. Marriage outside the group of blood and faith, at least when contemplated along the line proposed by Genesis 34, is threatening to the solidarity of society. But such impressions may be misleading.

Simply put, the story of Dinah and Shechem presents an unlikely chronology which begins with an apparent rape of an unsuspecting woman and continues with a rapist who falls in love with his victim. The tale then proceeds to recount how this man asks his father to negotiate marriage with her family and how her family, represented by two elder brothers, embarks on marital negotiations with covert anger but open glee. It ends by narrating the onslaught which the victim's brothers lead on a group of prospective bridegrooms as the latter are recovering from an operation of circumcision.

Numerous commentators have enlisted various theories to explain this bizarre tale.[2] With hardly an exception they have all operated on the assumption that Genesis 34 reports a crisis generated by a rape, in the conventional, contemporary sense of the term.[3] With this focus in mind, discussions have invariably revolved around the guilt or innocence, the indifference or concerns of the Israelite avengers.[4] But this point of departure provides a false premise and shaky foundations. Analyzed within a larger socioeconomic context, the main hypothesis of this section is that Dinah's tale reflects a clash between two marital strategies, or ideologies, and specifically between arranged marriage and the so-called abduction marriage or bride theft. Only within this specific framework of marital alternatives, does Dinah's tale and its intricate presentation in Genesis 34 become intelligible as does the behavior of its protagonists. Beyond this scope, a further attempt is made to throw light on the mechanisms that turned friendships into feuds in an environment in which the institution of hospitality carried a clearly defined code of conduct.

Genesis 34 has not come down in its original formulation. Its current state reflects a succession of revisions that convey editorial concerns rather than attempts to transmit accurately the original. It seems clear that the narrator who inserted Dinah's story into its present place had an agenda that went far beyond any interest in either "rape" or retaliation.[5] In the present context, then, it is imperative to offer a reading that explores the employment of the symbolism of this story (whether real or fictitious) to engender a discourse about the present. Underlying this query is also the question of the redactor's own comprehension of what, precisely, had taken place long ago in patriarchal Canaan. Given these seemingly disparate strands, a comparative approach provides promising clues and valuable means in any attempt to recover the ancient layers of the tale and to strip it of modern assumptions based on contemporary perceptions of the role that a rape plays.[6] The work done by anthropologists, such as the series of articles that appeared in a 1974 issue of *Anthropological Quarterly* on kidnapping and elopement as alternative systems of marriage, has been particularly useful.[7]

The chapter ends with an exploration of a metaphorical rape of a Midianite princess married to an Israelite aristocrat by a zealous priest (Num. 25). Here the drama takes place at the heart of the wilderness camp and on the verge of the entry to the promised land. Against this critical junction the "rape" of Dinah is reenacted with a curious reversal and a settling of scores. Descendants of Dinah's vindictive brothers turn against each other in a deadly encounter over the correctness of marital alliances for the people of Israel/children of Jacob. As the image of the armed priest is brought to life in the pages of Numbers the text offers a means to reexperience the ritualized moment that provided the focus of belonging and of self-definition.

From Rape to Parental Reticence

In spite of its bloody end, the tale of Dinah is launched on a quiet enough note with Jacob peacefully settling on a plot purchased from Hamor of Shechem (Gen. 33:18–19). The first interaction between the Israelites and the Shechemites is, then, an ordinary commercial transaction conducted and completed, as one would expect, between two patriarchs, Jacob, the elder of the clan, and Hamor, the ruler of the land. The latter, somewhat surprisingly, is designated in Gen. 33:19 not in a ruling or possessive capacity but as "father of Shechem," an appellation carefully chosen to serve as a link between this episode and its sequel that features Jacob's daughter and Hamor's son. Hamor's hospitality and the grant of freedom of worship to the newcomers is further highlighted by reference to Jacob's construction of an altar honoring "the God of Israel" (Gen. 33:20).

In terms of ancient host/guest-friendship relations, familiar, for example, from the poetic compositions of Homer and Hesiod, as well as from patriarchal episodes in Genesis, Hamor and Jacob entered a specific realm of exchange with its own set of regulations.[8] Two critical aspects of this relationship were reciprocity and voluntary association. By entering the territory of Hamor "in peace" (Gen. 33:18), Jacob demonstrated his willingness to respect the law of the land. By alienating his property in favor of a stranger Hamor indicated his readiness to accommodate the needs of his guest-friend. This voluntary selling of land to newcomers outside the settled group further generated a type of patron/client relationship or friendship.[9] Economically advantageous to both sides, this friendship between strangers also entailed mutual obligations as it operated side by side with the duties generated by kin ties and blood.[10] In the Homeric realm the obligations further passed from fathers to sons.

At an unspecified point in time after the Israelites had settled in the land of Shechem, a daughter of Jacob visits friends among "the women of the land" (Gen. 34:1). No further information is forthcoming about Dinah. A tacit assumption is made that she has not been betrothed previously. Had she been, there would have been no room for subsequent negotiations since Israelite law, at least to judge by Deuteronomy 22, admittedly sequentially later, prescribed death for the rapist. Nor should this type of interaction between women of different ethnic and cultic affiliation occasion surprise or disapproval.[11] While the Pentateuch transmits bans on sexual association between Israelites and non-Israelites, there is no prohibition on friendship between women of different cultic affiliation. Moreover, by becoming a guest-friend of Hamor, Jacob effectively initiated a set of friendships between members of the two households.

According to Gen. 34:2 Shechem the Hivite "saw" Dinah, "took" her, "slept" with her and "tormented," or raped her.[12] What, precisely, prompted so violent a reaction remains unclear. Perhaps, as Hermann Gunkel saw, Shechem's behavior reflects an editorial doublet.[13] Perhaps the description was a result of a carefully crafted rhetorical sequence that aimed to cast Shechem as the villain of the piece from its very beginning.[14] At any rate, the outcome was a crowded scene that the author/editor presented in such a way as to create the impression of an impetuous act, with Shechem embarking on seduction as soon as he laid eyes on Dinah. But had she been entirely unknown to him prior to their first and fatal encounter?

Dinah's apparent vulnerability at the moment of her "rape" is puzzling. Perhaps she never suspected that she would become an object of desire. If, however, her sexual integrity had been as critically important as her brothers made it out to be, why was she allowed to "go out" all by herself in the first place?[15] Her family claimed that her rape was a first-rate violation (Gen. 34:7), but of what? Nor did the editor-narrator bother to explain why she had been unaccompanied in a society that clearly placed a high value on the virginity of its daughters. Such an omission is curious if not altogether deliberate. It strikes an ominous note in the midst of an otherwise bucolic scene of guest/host friendship and patronage.

Genesis 34 refrains from providing the precise location where the rape of Dinah occurred. In the case of a rape of a betrothed woman the locality determined her fate and that of her abductor. Deuteronomy 22, where cases of rape are dealt with, does not refer to a location of a rape if the woman in question has not previously been betrothed. In fact, the implication is that the girl's consent or resistance to her rape does not at all matter as long as her rapist is willing to pay her father the bride price and to marry her, and the father is willing to consent to this transaction. The location of a rape, then, determined the degree of collusion, if any, between the "rapist" and the "raped." The omission of so critical an aspect in Dinah's tale intimates that the subject of Genesis 34 is not a rape at all, and certainly not in our contemporary understanding of this term.

Gen. 34:26 implies that Dinah had remained in Shechem's house throughout the negotiations regarding her impending marriage with her abductor.[16] Her absence from home for a significant length of time was, in itself, sufficient to tarnish her reputation and to minimize the opportunities of her male relatives to ally her with an eligible man of their choice.[17] If Dinah's brothers were as furious as Gen. 34:7 made them out to be, why did they not demand the immediate return of their sister as part of the negotiations? Instead, they utilized her location as an instrument of threat to her prospective family: "If you do not comply with our demand of circumcision we shall take our daughter and depart" (Gen. 34:17).[18]

There is, then, no indication whether Dinah had been carried away to be raped outdoors in a field, or whether she was raped in her local friend's house. Nor is it clear if she had been carried into Shechem's house and then raped. Who were her local women friends? Were they female members of Hamor's household? Who were Shechem's accomplices, if any? In the course of the ensuing negotiations between the two households Hamor proposes marriage not only between his son and Dinah but also between other Shechemites and other Israelite women.[19] Such an extension of marital bonds, hardly sensible under ordinary circumstances, hints at a general participation in Shechem's activities.

Perhaps the most revealing aspect of the violence and silence that characterize the initial contacts between Dinah and Shechem is an unreported dialogue represented by a curt reference to Shechem's emotions after the reported rape. In a verbal triad the narrator asserts that Shechem's soul "cleaved" to Dinah's as he fell in love with her and "spoke to her heart" (Gen. 34:3). But what did Shechem tell Dinah? Livy, the Roman historian (59 B.C.E.-17 C.E.), supplies valuable clues to bridge the gap. In his account of the so-called rape of the Sabine women (written, as that of Dinah's, centuries after its presumed date), he made Romulus, the engineer of the wholesale abduction marriage between Roman males and Sabines, address the abducted women at a critical moment when their male relatives were gathering to avenge the wrong done to their dignity, religion, and hospitality:

"Your fathers' pride denied marriage (*conubium*) to us, their neighbors. But you [i.e., their daughters] will have a share in our fortunes, our civic rights, and in that which is dearest to human kind, namely our children. Let wraths subside and let your hearts be won over by those to whom fate handed over your bodies. It often happened that gratitude arose out of injuries. You will find that your [Roman] husbands will treat you better because each of them will strive not only to do his own duty toward you but also to make up for the loss of your parents and country." The men then resorted to blandishments, making passion and love the excuse for their action, the type of entreaty that is especially effective with women. (Livy, 1.9.14–16)[20]

One simple and economical interpretation of the sequence in Genesis 34, then, is that Shechem, having subdued Dinah by force, wanted to win her over with words. Another is that the redactor deliberately inverted the order in which events had taken place, beginning with forced sexual contacts and ending with genuine emotions.

Dinah's response to her abductor's importunate plea is not recorded, but the possibility of her assent to his marriage proposal cannot be dismissed.[21] As a daughter of an unloved wife of Jacob her position at home must have been rather unpleasant. With irritable and righteous full brothers, like Shimon and Levi, Dinah could have hardly been a happy young woman. Between a hostile environment at home with its fair share of sibling violence and a potentially loving spouse, there was not much of a choice for a young woman, but the latter, at least, carried a promise of peace. Dinah's possibly tacit assent, then, casts a wholly different light on the affair. Given the redactor's order of happenings, with its echoes of Livy's reconstruction of the affair of the Sabine women, the question of what, precisely, is at stake in Genesis 34 must be asked.

According to Deuteronomy 22 a rape of an unbetrothed woman is a crime only if the rapist refuses to pay the bride price to the girl's father.[22]

Since Shechem obviously was more than happy to pay, he could have hardly been accused of a rape.[23] Nor is there a reference to any rape in the course of the negotiations that followed it. The reticence can be best explained if Dinah's rape was perceived as a component in a larger and more meaningful context of contemporary marital strategies. Such an assumption is clearly reflected in the following:

> If someone who had not previously made any agreement with a girl's parents should seize her (*rapuerit*) against her will or if he should lead her away (*abduxerit*) with her consent, and hoping to gain immunity through (the favorable) response of one whom our ancestors had prevented from suing and from giving testimony and from all legal matters on account of the vice of frivolity and the fickleness of her gender and judgment, her response would be of no avail to him according to the ancient law and the girl herself would be liable for collusion in the crime. . . . If the virgin is found to have consented (to the abduction), she should be punished with the same severity as her abductor (*raptor*). Nor shall impunity be offered to those abducted against their will for they could have stayed at home until their marriage day and, if the doors had been broken through the audacity of the abductor, they should have sought help of the neighbors by raising a cry and by defending (themselves) with all their efforts. . . . If the abductor had been proven guilty without a shade of a doubt no appeal from him should be heard. . . . We order that partners and helpers of the abductor, without regard to their sex, be subjected to the same penalties.[24]

Although a worthy addition to the Pentateuch, this law is, in fact, a late Roman constitution issued in 326 C.E. by the emperor Constantine. It deals with a phenomenon usually described as abduction marriage or bridal theft. Containing elements familiar to any reader of the Dinah tale the law indicates a continuing discomfort of ancient authorities with a mode of marriage that did not receive parental sanction. Indeed, in a society in which marriage served as a vital instrument of economic, political, and social bonds, the retention of marital decisions in the hands of fathers and/or close kin male relatives was clearly of critical importance. Needless to say, the wishes of a young couple were hardly ever taken into account. In this, young men barely fared better than young women.

Ancient literature and law, as well as modern anthropological research on bride theft or abduction marriage, demonstrate a variety of configurations as a result of an unplanned and unsanctioned transfer of a potential bride from her father's to a strange household. In extreme cases, such as the mythic Helen whose face reputedly launched a thousand ships, the abduction (in this case apparently with the consent of the woman) led to a major war and to the destruction of a major city.[25] More often than not, however, an abduction led to marriage and reconciliation. In practically every case, as the above-quoted Constantinian law shows, the authorities frowned on this type of marriage alternative not because it involved a forcible seizure (the consent of the woman is, in fact, nearly always assumed) and a violation of the body of the woman seized but because these thefts thwarted parental plans.

Abduction marriages created an awkward situation for the fathers of the two parties involved. Shechem's bride theft had placed his father in a somewhat untenable position, precisely the same awkwardness that Jacob experienced when he heard of the affair. By disrupting, through abduction, an established pattern of premarital negotiations, the father of the bridegroom, if wealthy as Hamor had been, was practically bound by any demand that her family might pose. But Shechem compounded the problem by also violating the rules of guest-friendship through the abduction and rape of a woman who was, technically, under his father's protection. The case scenario is not unlike the one that provoked the Trojan War, with Paris, a guest-friend of Agamemnon and his brother Menelaus, abducting (and marrying) the latter's wife. The Achaeans who set out to Troy cared little about the abduction of the beautiful Helen, a "crime" that at any rate her husband should have avenged. What summoned them to a long and arduous overseas expedition was the violation of the basic rule of a society which could not function without respecting the sanctity of guest-friendship between males.

Like Hamor, Jacob had to deal with delicate and embarrassing preconditions. He had been a guest-friend of the father but he was also the father of the woman whose marriageability had been impaired by his host's son. By selling him a piece of his own land Hamor extended a bond of hospitality to the Israelite newcomers. By abducting Dinah, Shechem undermined not only patriarchal strategies of prearranged marriages but, more seriously, he also caused a disruption of the delicate set of male relationships that supported a socioeconomic structure carefully calculated to retain a balance of power between nomads and sedentary populations.[26]

Jacob reveals his helplessness when he decides to await his sons' return. His reticence, then, makes sense not so much as a symbol of his indifference to Dinah's fate,[27] but rather as a token of his inability to reconcile two opposing marital strategies and his own role as Hamor's guest-friend. Dinah's rape, whether real or assumed, constituted an integral segment of an acknowledged marital procedure that the Canaanites evidently practiced, if not approved of. A brief comparison with two other reported cases of rape illustrates this point.²⁸ When Amnon has his half-sister Tamar in his power and asks her to sleep with him she reminds him that rather than raping her he can ask their father, David, for permission to wed her (2 Sam. 13:13b). The story, as has been often observed, bears striking verbal similarities with that of Dinah. But its main resonance resides in the assumed clash between marital strategy that focuses on parental assent and prenuptial negotiations on the one hand and bride theft or abduction marriage on the other. Even the tale of Amnon and Tamar could have ended happily but for Amnon's change of heart from love to hatred (2 Sam. 13:15). The juxtaposition of these two sentiments results in a crisis and eventually leads to the avenging of Tamar by her blood brother through blood. David's absence from the proceedings is as notable as is his presumed assent to a mediated marriage between his two children. Amnon's crime had been not only cheating his half-sister but also deceiving their father who had sent her to his sickbed in good faith.

An even more significant parallel is offered by the equally infamous rape of a woman who is identified solely as a Levite's concubine (Judg. 19).²⁹ A man of the tribe of Levi, stranded in a Benjaminite city for a night on his way home, is finally given shelter by a local man. When the inhabitants demand the host to provide his guest for their entertainment the host offers instead his own daughter and the guest his concubine. The latter is duly produced and the local men proceed to gang-rape her. She reaches her host's home in time to die on its threshold. Her "husband" advertises her murder by cutting her body and dispatching its severed parts to various Israelite settlements. A civil war ensues when the Benjaminites refuse to turn over the residents responsible for the violence. The Israelites further swear not to "intermarry" with the Benjaminites. Although the Levite remains clearly unharmed, the Benjaminites are deemed guilty of a triple violation, namely the very spirit of hospitality, its rules, and man's sole right to the body of his concubine. In other words, the Benjaminites' behavior, compounded by their solidarity with the criminals, undermines the very structures on which the proper functioning of their society depends.³⁰

In all three tales the protagonists reach a sore end. In all three vengeance is wreaked not only on the direct perpetrator of the crime but also on a wide circle of accomplices. In two instances the brothers of the victims organize the revenge.³¹ All three serve to cast into sharp relief a process of fragmentation of the family and, by implication, of society as a whole. The affair of Dinah put an end to any ideology of coexistence in patriarchal

Canaan/the promised land; that of the concubine signified the culmination and the end of a chaotic and lawless period in which "every man did as he wished"; the rape of Tamar demonstrated that even the model royal family carried within itself the seeds of familial and national destruction. But these similarities need not obscure their differences. Shechem was, of course, no Israelite, and certainly not a kinsman of Dinah. His breach of the patriarchal marital code elicited a new debate.

Why Not Marry a Shechemite?

Dinah's abduction upset the process of decision-making regarding the fate of daughters by taking the initiative out of parental hands and by presenting Jacob's family with a fait accompli. Dinah's brothers, irate as the text makes them to be, opt for negotiations, becoming the sole representatives of the family. The ensuing negotiations between the Israelites and the Shechemites illustrate even more clearly the validity of perceiving the process as a clash of two marital ideologies. Pursuant to most cases of abduction marriage the family of the abductor makes the opening overtures in an effort to reconcile the two sides. Hamor asks for the hand of Dinah in marriage on behalf of his son.

In the course of the negotiations, Hamor effectively suggests the extension of the personal hospitality ties between himself and Jacob to the whole peoples. In his speech he uses the verb "to marry" or "to bind oneself by marriage" (Gen. 34:9) to denote the type of the envisaged marital bonds. This verb captures the essence of a legal alliance even more than the more familiar "give and take" of daughters (Gen. 34:9). From a patriarchal point of view, Genesis 34 outlines a type of marital negotiations in which brides are given and taken as part of a financial transaction between elders of clans. From the Canaanite point of view, abduction marriage presents an acceptable if not necessarily endorsable strategy. That the Israelites understood this point rather well is reflected in the very absence of any reference to the rape as such.

By extending the negotiations from two individuals involved in a specific marital strategy to include the whole of the Israelites and the Hivites, Genesis 34 presents intermarriage as an instrument of peace and prosperity, going so far as to suggest that it can pave the way to the creation of "one people" (Gen. 34:16). Hamor's proposal appears generous. He even outlines the economic advantages that would accrue to the Israelites as a result of the wholesale marriage with local men and women. Dinah's brothers, who became the spokespersons of the clan, are tempted, at least ostensibly, to respond favorably. But they raise a single and surprising objection. They are quite willing to marry Dinah off to Shechem but he is uncircumcised. Whether circumcision as a sign of the covenant between Israel and Yahweh had already been an integral part of Israelite cultic requirements or whether the demand is anachronistic remains unclear. The objection could have been planned in order to prompt a rejection of the whole proposal. But the brothers underestimate Shechem's love for their sister. He immediately complies (Gen. 34:19). Hamor, however, needs to discuss the matter with the prospective Shechemite bridegrooms.

Accounts of abduction marriage in contemporary Mediterranean societies, where bride theft has been practiced in spite of legal strictures and possible parental disapproval, show that the abduction often involved a raiding party consisting of friends of the abductor. Roman law explicitly recognized the role of accomplices and called for their execution and the confiscation of their property.[32] Even those who were not directly involved but aided the abductor in some capacity (such as not disclosing the whereabouts of the abducted) were condemned to capital punishment, regardless of whether the abducted woman was willing or not.[33] The complicity of other Shechemites may explain their fate.

Within the setting of Genesis 34 the negotiations between Hamor and Jacob's sons make little sense. Jacob's family represented a tiny clan of nomads who had just settled on a small piece of land purchased from a local potentate. Hamor's family controlled a considerable stretch of land and represented the multifold advantages that a settled society in a pre-urbanized environment could offer. Prior to the encounter between Shechem and Dinah the advantages were all on the side of Hamor's people. Nor did they have a reason to seek marital bonds with Jacob's family. Paradoxically, then, Dinah's abduction created a situation in which the hosts found themselves at the mercy of the guests. Jacob's silence, already alluded to, underscores the fragility of the situation that the abduction marriage created. This unusual set of circumstances, highlighted by the silence of one patriarch, is further emphasized by the absence of another patriarch, Isaac, whose death is reported in Gen. 35:28 and thus falls, at least according to the redactional order of Genesis, after the conclusion of the Shechem affair.[34]

In relating the gist of the negotiations to his people (with his own interpretation), Hamor presents the Israelites as peaceful people (Gen. 34:21a), using thus the same adjective that the narrator employed to characterize the coming of Jacob to Hamor's territory. Hamor then dwells on the economic advantages that the alliance is bound to offer to the Shechemites. Of the terms used in the private negotiations and the public presentation, that of "one people" (Gen. 34:16, 22) deserves attention for it articulates the ideology of abduction marriage. The traditional Israelite way of betrothal was a carefully orchestrated process which cemented existing clannish bonds. Abduction marriages, by contrast, had the potential of amalgamating entire nations. This was indeed the rhetoric that Romulus harnessed in the passage cited above. Such rhetoric also advanced women from the role of passive recipients (victims) and observants to that of active participants in shaping national destinies.

For Hamor, as for Jacob, marriage primarily signifies a transaction in which daughters are transferred from the guardianship of their fathers to that of their husbands (Gen. 34:9, 21). He further interprets the expression "one people" to signify shared assets (34:23). And he faithfully conveys to his people the condition of circumcision for every male. The introduction of this factor into the economic-political negotiations between Dinah's and Hamor's families shows that at stake is not crime against the body of an individual woman but against the very foundations of political balance and the institution of guest-friendship. In other words, it is the covenant itself that Shechem's act violated.

Being in a position of a guest-friend entailed a code of conduct that Hesiod, the Greek poet, articulated with striking simplicity:

Be friendly with the friendly, and visit him who visits you
Give to one who gives, but do not give to one who does not give.
(*Works and Days*, 353–54, trans. A. N. Athanassakis)

At the heart of this type of male bonding were certain assumptions, obligations, and expectations that each side needed to abide by.[35] There were, obviously, also frequent abuses. A recurring Greek complaint was that of betrayal and deceit, precisely the two major elements of the Dinah tale.[36] The Shechemites, administering circumcision to an unspecified number of males, were "rewarded" with the sword.[37] In a context, such as patriarchal Canaan, in which rules of hospitality and specific marital strategies were of paramount importance for the very survival of the clan, Shechem's sexual initiative assumed proportions well beyond its immediate implications for either Dinah or himself.

Dinah and Matriarchal Betrothals

If Dinah's tale hints at alternative (and irreconcilable) marriage cultures it may be useful to clarify patriarchal marital strategies. The book of Genesis provides two accounts of what amounts to legitimate betrothals, each serving as a foil for the perceptions of illegality of Genesis 34.[38] The betrothals of the three matriarchs, Rebecca, Leah, and Rachel, also offer insights into the type of acceptable marriages that Yahweh's young clan was willing to accept at that stage of their formation. Prenuptial agreements, in company with calculated matrimonial choices and decisions, instantly emerge as a prominent feature.

Thus the rationale that dictates the dispatch of a patriarchal representative all the way from Canaan back to Mesopotamia in search of a bride for Isaac points to a basic clannish endogamy (Gen. 24:4). Abraham's articulation of his opposition to exogamy, namely to marriage with local women (Gen. 24:3), reinforces this perception. Although Rebecca's tale subsequently reads more like a romantic novel than a carefully planned set of negotiations between males over the fate of a given daughter it underscores the critical bond that familial ties created in spite of geographical distances.

In order to secure the right wife Abraham sends his slave, laden with golden gifts, to a specific location. When the slave sees Rebecca, outdoors and near the local well, he approaches her without disclosing his identity. Somewhat unaccountably he rewards her with precious gifts in exchange for a glass (or possibly a jar) of water. Neither Rebecca's good looks nor her hospitality escape the eyes of the watchful servant of Abraham. Her brother, similarly anxious to demonstrate his family's hospitality, runs out to meet the guest (as humble as a slave might have been) but finds a moment to comment on Rebecca's newly acquired golden accoutrements.

The dramatic setting of this wonderful scene prompted the editor-narrator to ignore the rules of the economy of biblical narrative and to retell the tale of the encounter between Abraham's slave and Rebecca at some length. The occasion also presented an opportunity to expose patriarchal marital strategies in time for the readers to appreciate the full enormity of Dinah's abduction marriage. Once introduced to Abraham's quest,

Rebecca's male relatives (her father and her brother) consent without further ado to the vicarious proposal of marriage. "Behold Rebecca in front of you, take her and go and she shall be a wife to your master's son as God had spoken" (Gen. 24:51). These are generous words, confirmed by an exchange of more gifts and with a general feast. Even Rebecca is consulted, possibly a perfunctory gesture, about the timing of her departure. Such questioning recalls the view of Roman law on the vitality of mutual consent in any arranged marriage. But the law never questioned the pressure that parents put on their daughters to comply with the parental choice. The consent of a prospective wife, although a legal requirement, was in most cases a mere formality.

Jacob's wooing of Rachel reveals other aspects of patriarchal betrothal strategies. Both Rebecca and Rachel make their debut outdoors as they engage in fetching water. This time, however, the intended couple meets in person. Jacob, although armed with foreknowledge of the boundaries of his marital circle, nonetheless falls in love with his beautiful cousin Rachel (Gen. 29). Rachel proves as hospitable as Rebecca had been, but her father has his own marital agenda in mind. Nor does Jacob conceal his identity as Abraham's slave had done when he met Rebecca. Once apprised of their kinship ties Jacob kisses Rachel (clearly a ritualized gesture) and bursts into tears (29:11).

In spite of the emotional bond between Jacob and Rachel and their blood ties, Rachel's father still exacts a hefty bride price from his nephew. Laban's commercial instincts are at work as is his adherence to a marital tradition that requires the marriage of the oldest daughter first. Jacob's ignorance of this matrimonial code is surprising but he pays dearly for his attempt to breach it. There was clearly no question of resorting to abduction marriage in this case. Jacob might have saved seven years of forced labor but the biblical narrator would not have been able to use Dinah's tale to illustrate the results of a violent clash between coexisting marital strategies.

By the time Dinah reached a marriageable age, then, negotiations over marital arrangements had become an integral component of patriarchal marital strategy as was clannish endogamy. Shechem's deed introduced a new concept of betrothal through abduction marriage. Nor was he a member of the clan. With a double disadvantage, Jacob had to consider carefully his course of action. In the event, the decision was taken out of his hands through the impetuousness of his sons. Dinah's tale symbolizes the shifting of generational perceptions of marital norms as words and actions are transferred from traditional agents (namely fathers) to new agents (namely sons/brothers).

Perhaps the most instructive similarity among the three matriarchal tales is the implication that Israelite daughters fetched a high bride price and that even blood relatives insisted on payment in full. The scarcity of appropriate matrimonial matches in Canaan made these women particularly desirable. In Dinah's case, the abduction, compounded by genuine affection, as well as the economic status of the abductor's family and the breach of hospitality, ensured a high bride price. In all cases marriage was intended to cement existing alliances. What complicated Shechem's position was his cultic affiliation.

Hospitality played a critical role in all three narratives, but in Genesis 24 and 29 the prospective groom or his father's emissary were in a position of a guest-friend, while in Genesis 34 the groom's father was the host-friend and ruler of the land. Rebecca and Laban were fully conscious of their role as the first representatives of their families to meet a "stranger" in need of hospitality. In Dinah's tale the expectations had already been established with the sealing of the land sale to Jacob. In all these tales the code of hospitality forms a critical background component of subsequent arrangements.

Abduction marriage, then, points to the availability of one alternative in a marital culture that emphasized familial consent and betrothal negotiations. It was an option that Shechem adopted either because he had anticipated objections to his suit or, as the editor-narrator wished his readers to believe, because love changed his initial plan to commit solely a sexual act. But like all doomed loves the story of Dinah and Shechem was accompanied by violence and by a breach of a code of conduct predicated on relations formed through guest-friendship.

Accompanied or unaccompanied by a rape, the abduction of women by men for marital purposes is a familiar feature in nation-building myths of the ancient world. The abduction of the Sabine women in Rome of the eighth century B.C.E. provides a striking example and, unlike Dinah's tale, a happy end. The "father of history," Herodotus of Halicarnassus (fifth century B.C.E.), opens his tale of the hostilities between Persia and the Greeks with a series of bygone abductions and rapes that had ultimately led to a mighty clash. This was as good as any explanation to account for deep-seated animosities, even though such explanations had their fair share of ancient critics. Thucydides is worth quoting as he criticized "poets . . .

and prose chroniclers . . . whose authorities cannot be checked, and whose subject matter, owing to the passage of time, is mostly lost in the unreliable streams of mythology."[39] Nor did the severity of ancient (and modern) legislation against the practice of abduction marriage achieve its curtailment. Even the church, making abduction marriage an impediment, proved helpless.[40]

By the time Dinah's tale reached an editorial stage, the institutions of abduction marriage and guest-friendship had been forgotten. In an effort to harmonize events that had resulted from two distinct manners of contracting marriage the redactor created a sequence based on the only item that was fully understood in his time, namely a rape. Yet it proved impossible to suppress the worldview that had informed the words and actions of the protagonists in Genesis 34.

Sadly, the biblical narrator also inflicts on Dinah, implicitly, the most severe handicap that a woman could bear, namely childlessness. She, like Tamar after her rape by Amnon, becomes an object of concealment, the bearer of an ironic fate for a woman whose story begins with going out in public. Condemned to obscurity, Dinah is denied an appropriate suitor. In a culture in which the survival of what is human takes place when women give birth, a childless woman is patently worthless. She cannot be a sharer of the promise made to Eve and Adam at the dawn of humanity and to Abraham, the first "Jew" at the dawn of Jewish history. In the retelling of the affair of Dinah and Shechem the narrator turned a familial and intimate matter into a "national" concern. The frontiers between the private and the public were deliberately blurred in order to convey a series of messages, one of which aimed at delineating the perimeters of female freedom of movement and of choice. In Dinah's case, marriage outside the boundaries of the paternal group presented insoluble problems. Had Dinah married Shechem she would have become the last matriarch, mother of tribal eponyms, the heirs of Abraham, Isaac, and Jacob.

When intimate relations extend to men or women deemed by biblical narrators as "foreigners," and hence as potentially dangerous to genealogical and religious cohesion, drastic solutions are applied to resolve the situation. Shechem has to die. Dinah disappears. But their tale required an additional, if not a symmetrical ending that explores what happens when an Israelite male is attached to a non-Israelite woman. This is why the narrative sequence that begins with the "rape" of Dinah leads to the "rape" of a Midianite. And this is why stories of "miscegenation" are crucial keys in shaping the identity of a Jewess.

A Woman of the Wilderness: The Rape of Cozbi

As it stands, the tale of Cozbi the Midianite and of Zimri, a member of the tribe of Shimon (Num. 25:6–18), appears to have neither rhyme nor reason.[41] A respectable couple, each a member of a highly distinguished clan, are murdered in the privacy of their own bedroom by a zealous priest carrying a deadly weapon. Their murder apparently puts a stop to a general plague generated by an equally bizarre account of sex and apostasy (Num. 25:1–5) that involves an untold number of Israelite males and Moabite women. The couple's killer becomes an arbiter of communal fate.

To decode Numbers 25 it is not only necessary to bear in mind the fate of Dinah but also to use the lens of a Roman foundational myth in which a revolution is constructed around a rape. I am thinking specifically about the rape of Lucretia that figures in Roman historiography as the launching pad of the demise of the monarchy and the rise of the republic. In both tales, the Jewish and the Roman, the ostensible central place of the women masks profound rivalries between men. In either, the violent death of a woman heralds a far-reaching transformation of the relationships between the private and the public. Above all, each illustrates how Jews came to think of themselves as Jews, and Romans as Romans, through a reconceptualization of the foreign other and the extrapolation of female boundaries of acceptable behavior.[42]

In the redacted version of Num. 25:6–18 the identity of the chief actors is only gradually revealed, as though the redactor attempted to create a drama with mounting suspense. First, a "man of the sons of Israel" approaches the tent of the assembly in the company of a "Midianite woman." Then a priest who, unlike his victims, is fully and immediately endowed with a full pedigree, chases the unknown Israelite and pierces him and "the woman" to death. The priest then receives divine approval and blessings. Readers who may have wondered about so great a prize for so bloody an act are finally made privy to the identity of the dead couple. He is Zimri, a blue-blooded member of the tribe of Shimon; she is Cozbi, a scion of a royal house of Midian. Once the two are out of the way, Moses is ordered to chase the Midianites to death (Num. 25:16–18).

More is omitted than said. No reason, for example, is given to account for the presence of the couple near the tent of the assembly, the heart of the sacred, at a highly sensitive moment. None is provided to explain the seemingly irrational anger that the couple provokes in Phineas. No resistance is offered by either Zimri or Cozbi to the wrathful clergyman. The atonement provided by the death of a single couple for the general sin with Moabites remains inexplicable. Indeed, the juxtaposition of the Moabite and the Midianite tales of Numbers 25 seems to have been inspired solely by the locality where both occurred, namely Moabite Shittim, and by the involvement of foreign women in each narrative.

The precise nature of the relationship between Zimri and Cozbi poses a problem. By timing their public appearance to coincide with an upheaval caused by (illicit?) sexual alliances between Israelite males and foreign women in general, the text strongly suggests that besides sex and apostasy the two had little in common. Yet this can hardly be the case. As ultimately divulged in the narrative, both were far from commoners seeking a momentary sexual gratification. They were aristocrats, members of powerful and distinguished clans, she of an even more respectable stock than he. The assumption that their relationship was perfectly legal, a result of careful paternal negotiations, cannot be dismissed.

Intermarriage has a curious and ambiguous history in the Bible.[43] Patriarchal preferences emphasize strict clannish endogamy, at least for designated heirs. Joseph, however, marries an Egyptian and produces through her two more tribal eponyms. Judah ensures his succession through copulating with his Canaanite daughter-in-law. Moses, of course, marries a Midianite. Among the list of the liberated Israelites, the tribe of Shimon numbers "Shaul son of the Canaanite woman" (Exod. 6:15). Notwithstanding such marital alliances, the Pentateuch also transmits strongly worded prohibitions on marriage outside the group of birth and faith (Exod. 34:15-16; Deut. 7:3-4). It also provides a chilly tale of "rape" and revenge that powerfully illustrates the ills of intermarriage, namely Dinah's story (Gen. 34).

Neither Exodus 34 nor Deuteronomy 7, the *loci classici* of the bans on intermarriage, specifically includes Moabites and Midianites in their list of undesirable matches. But the lists, in themselves, may convey little more than a rhetorical flourish. The Deuteronomist castigates Solomon for allowing his foreign wives, most of whom belonging to ethnic affiliations outside the list, to lead his heart astray into the worship of multiple divinities (1 Kings 11).[44] Ezra-Nehemiah insists that foreign wives, regardless of national or ethnic affiliation, ought to be dismissed, along with their children (see Chapter 2).

Since the Pentateuch fails to provide ordinances in case intermarriage does take place, suggesting neither the ruthless elimination of the couple nor the legitimization of their relationship, the place of mixed couples in the Israelite, or Jewish, social fabric remains subject to subjective circumstances. In the case of Zimri and Cozbi, their social and economic status raised a problem regarding the role of Cozbi as a potential matriarch and the inheritance of their issue. Cozbi was not a Canaanite, like Tamar, who could be ignored after delivering two sons (Gen. 38:26). Zimri did not marry within his clan to secure paternal inheritance as the heirs of Zelophehad had been bidden (Num. 36).

Tales involving intimate relations beyond the boundaries of patriarchal structures of genealogy and inheritance are often doomed to disaster. Already in the family of founding fathers the narrative of the episode of Dinah and Shechem set out not only to censure intermarriage but also to ensure the demise of, potentially, a thirteenth Israelite patriarch. Had Dinah and Shechem married, as suggested by his family and ostensibly approved by hers, their children would have had a stake in Jacob's inheritance. These sons would have been, however, patriarchs with only a partial Abrahamic lineage. But Dinah's "going out" (Gen. 34:1) cast her as a "prostitute" (Gen. 34:31), a labeling that rendered her unworthy of becoming a full-fledged member of the clan.

Numbers 25 forms an important complement to Genesis 34. Each features two levels of intimate relations, one between an individual couple (Dinah-Shechem/Cozbi-Zimri), the other between large ethnic groups (Israelite-Shechemite/Israelite-Moabite). Both types of intimacy are termed abominations. The proposed match in Genesis 34 and the existing one in Numbers 25 have also the potential of disrupting patterns of patriarchal inheritance. Like Shechem, Cozbi comes with a full pedigree and with a great deal to offer. Neither she nor Dinah are victims of sexual desire alone. They are, in fact, pawns in a deadly game between men. Both occupy a critical and, therefore, vulnerable position between male rivals. One is cast as the outsider within, the other as the external outsider. Cozbi's presence in the Israelite camp, like Dinah's presence in Shechem's house, serves as a reminder of women's sole power, the ability to generate more patriarchs and, by implication, to perpetuate or disrupt existing patterns of succession.[45]

Even the differences are significant. In Num. 25:1–6 it is the Israelites and not their foreign partners who are singled out as the sinners destined to die. Dinah, unlike Cozbi, is not executed. Her fate is not disclosed but she probably spends the rest of her life in enforced celibacy as a useless object in the house of her brothers (cf. Tamar, 2 Sam. 13:20). In Genesis 34, Dinah's blood brothers, Shimon and Levi, undertake the execution of their prospective brother-in-law. In Numbers 25, the sibling partnership disintegrates over a similar bone of contention.

Shechem dies not because he treated Dinah "as a whore," as her brothers allege, but because his potential incorporation into Jacob's family presents insoluble problems. Cozbi dies because she cannot be integrated into existing patriarchal and tribal order. Her very foreignness is a threat as is her status. Her putative sons would be able to lay claim to a tribal land as well as to Midianite royalty. Her chief attribute as a woman, namely her potential to bear children, is her undoing.

Phineas kills Cozbi by piercing her belly. Her mode of death is clearly symbolic, as has been often observed. But the symbolism must be fully appreciated. By wielding a spear Phineas uses a weapon that resembles a male sexual organ. By selecting her womb as a target he rapes her. To be precise, he impregnates her in a manner calculated not only to inflict death but also to degrade her legal relationship to a level of arbitrary passion. This delegitimization of the tie between Cozbi and Zimri puts the couple in precisely the same position in which the redactor of Genesis 34 places Dinah and Shechem. And since the killer in Numbers 25 is a priest it is also possible to view the killing as an act of sacrifice made on the altar of atonement for the general sin at Baal Peor.[46]

By providing powerful negative icons the stories of Cozbi and Dinah contribute to the shaping of Israelite female identity. The mechanics of their presentation can be further glimpsed through a comparison with foundational tales in other cultures where the reporting is considerably more expansive than the one provided in the Bible. One such is the Roman tale of the rape of Lucretia whose sequence illuminates a similar shift of relationship between the private and the public over a breach of morality.

Foundation Murders and Rapes

In the narrative of the Roman historian Livy, itself crafted centuries after the events it purports to record, a family drama is turned into a revolution (1.57–59).[47] According to Livy, during a lull in a war, a group of bored aristocrats entered a contest over the chastity of their wives. "Each of them extravagantly praised his own [wife] and the rivalry grew hotter and hotter until Collatinus suggested riding to Rome to test their wives in person" (Livy, 1.57).[48] In an alcoholic stupor the men ride off to Rome only to find their wives, seemingly oblivious to the dangers facing their husbands on the battlefield, whiling away their time in banquets with male friends. One exception is Collatinus's wife, Lucretia, who dutifully remains at home, engaged in wifely pursuits. She thus emerges as a winner in a competition of which, ironically, she knows nothing whatsoever.

Unfortunately for all concerned the wager does not come to this happy end. The "victorious" Collatinus invites his "defeated" friends to dinner at his home. During the meal Sextus Tarquinius, heir to the throne of Rome and a relative of Collatinus himself, decides to seduce Lucretia since her chastity evidently inflames his lust. He returns to her home in the absence of her husband. In the middle of the night, still as an honored guest, he invades Lucretia's bedroom and, threatening her with death, he "urged his love, begged her to submit, pleaded, threatened, using every weapon that may conquer a woman's heart" (Livy, 1.58). Lucretia, however, prefers to die than to submit to seduction. Sextus then informs her that if she refuses to be raped he will kill a slave, lay his naked body next to hers, and kill her as though he caught them both in an act of adultery. This time Lucretia yields. After Tarquinius leaves she summons her male relatives, divulges her disgrace and the name of her ravisher, asserts her innocence, and commits suicide in spite of the protestations of her family. Brutus, a relative of the couple and of Sextus, vows revenge as he holds the bloody knife that Lucretia wielded to kill herself.

> Lucretia's body was carried from the house into the public square. Crowds gathered, as crowds will, to gape and wonder—and the sight was unexpected enough, and horrible enough to attract them. Anger at the criminal brutality of the king's son and sympathy with the father's grief stirred every heart. . . . Brutus made a speech painting in vivid colors the brutal and unbridled lust of Sextus Tarquinius, the hideous rape of the innocent Lucretia, and her pitiful death, the bereavement of her father . . . the king's arrogant behavior, the sufferings of the commons. . . . He reminded them of the foul murder of Servius Tullius, of the daughter who drove her carriage over her father's corpse in violation of the most sacred of relationships, a crime that God alone could punish. (1.59)

Lucretia's death apparently engineers a revolution as Brutus steers the populace against the kings. In place of a monarchy the Roman Republic comes into being. The real story is, needless to say, considerably more intricate. The three men, Collatinus, Tarquinius, and Brutus are relatives. The "revolution" that dismisses Tarquinius and ushers in Brutus's "Republic" may be regarded as an extension of family affairs into the public domain. Tarquinius, although a guest in Lucretia's household, acts as though he is the master. The real contest is not so much between him and his female victim as between males over winning a challenge. Lucretia submits since "this kind of rape is by definition a contest of words: hers against his."[49] Her subsequent suicide induces a vow of revenge, the expulsion of the entire royal family, and the rise of the Republic. Ultimately, both the rapist and his victim appear as "pawns in a struggle to legitimize revolution, insurrection, expulsion and murder."[50]

Lucretia commits suicide in the presence of her family, thus vindicating herself through revealing what the prince had done. Silenced through coercion, she chooses to reveal her disgrace to a familial public. But Brutus advertises it further afield and includes the public itself as both listeners and participants in the family tragedy. Ironically, the kind of shame that costs Lucretia her life becomes a cause for a general revolution based ostensibly on revulsion. What the family may have chosen to keep a secret is turned into a public affair because Brutus requires a reason to dislodge the royal family of Rome.

In Numbers 25 the story begins with a public display of passion and idolatry as Israelite males cling passionately to Moabite females. It continues with an intrusion of the private domain as Phineas invades Cozbi and Zimri's space. The drama unfolds by moving from the edge of the camp, where the worship of Baal takes place, to its very heart, the tent of the Tabernacle. Family ambitions, as reflected in the liaison between Zimri and Cozbi, are entangled with public desires and the violation of the sacred bond between Yahweh and Israel. By revealing in public the private crime of Tarquinius, Brutus lays the foundations of the Republic. By exposing Zimri and Cozbi out of thousands of mixed couples, the narrative engineers the shift of power from secular to priestly hands. Whatever judgment Moses was to pass on the erring Israelites, God and Phineas took the initiative out of his hands. By executing Zimri, Phineas also severs the ties that Shimon and Levi, their ancestors, had forged over Dinah's rape and the execution of the Shechemites.

Just as the Roman foundational myth of the rape of Lucretia and the founding of the Republic also conceals the settling of private scores (between Tarquinius and his two relatives, Collatinus, Lucretia's husband, and Brutus), the "rape" of Cozbi brings to conclusion a critical sibling issue, namely the cooperation of Levi and Shimon over the settling of the Dinah affair. In Genesis 34 both brothers appear to espouse the purity of Israelite descent. In Numbers 25 it is Phineas the priest who alone opposes a potential contamination of this scheme by killing a descendant of Shimon. In Genesis 34 Shimon expresses, in private, his opposition to intermarriage while lending support, in public, to the plan of wholesale intermarriage. In Numbers 25 Zimri becomes the literal executor of his ancestor's public opinion by actively engaging in a relationship with a non-Israelite, presumably with the support of his entire clan. The opposition is transferred entirely into priestly hands.

In both the Jewish and the Roman cases, public and private, the individual and the community, are brought together through a public drama meant to engender a sense of communal identity. In this context perhaps the most meaningful comparison between the two foundational rapes is the reconceptualization of both as a sacrifice:

As the others were absorbed in mourning, Brutus snatched the knife from the wound (caused by her suicide) and holding it before him, still dripping with blood, said: By this blood, the most chaste before the royal injustice, I swear and I make you gods my witnesses, to drive out with fire, sword and whatever force I might, Tarquinius Superbus together with his criminal wife and children.[51]

The purity of the victim, human or animal, turns the private transgression of the body of a chaste matron into a national affair. In Numbers 25 it is not even Phineas who makes an oath but Yahweh himself.

Both narratives, the biblical account of the "rape" of Cozbi (and of Dinah), and the Roman (Livian) account of the rape of Lucretia act as catalysts in effecting a change in social and political structures.[52] They illustrate how Jews came to think of themselves as Jews, and Romans as Romans. In either case a family affair is deliberately turned into a "national" cause at the cost of the female protagonist. In both, boundaries between family and the larger social context in which families operate appear blurred. Distinctions are applied not to matters of intimacy and public interest but to patterns of behavior. Zimri commits an unforgivable sin by willingly allying himself with a foreign woman; Lucretia commits one unwittingly, but sin it is nevertheless.

Ultimately each set of foundational myths is more indicative of their creators, or rather redactors, than of the original circumstances that gave rise to them. The tale of Cozbi comes at a moment when the great promise to the patriarchs is at risk of unfulfillment. The plague decimates many people. According to a later census only two males of the generation that had known Egyptian slavery survive. The sudden and complete demise of the older generation engenders problems of succession as seen in the legal case of the daughters of Zelophehad. But such problems are not to be solved through intermarriage.

In Numbers 25 and Genesis 34, as in royal Rome, configurations of gender relations are primarily based on familial calculations. Cozbi, like Dinah, is a "daughter" and a "sister" (Num. 25:18) but of Midianite stock. Zimri is a "son" of a patriarch but, in redactional perspectives, a traitor to the bloody heritage of Genesis 34. Above all, he acts against the interests of the community as interpreted by Phineas and by the priestly redactor of the text. By conjuring up a sacrifice of the couple as an atonement, the textual recreation of the spectacle of killing offers a means for every member of the community to experience as a participant the ritualized moment that more than any other provides the focus of belonging and self-definition.[53] In republican Rome Brutus recreates what it means to be a Roman over the body of Lucretia. In the wilderness, Phineas redefines a sense of belonging as he chases Cozbi to her death.

In the biblical and the Roman context women are assailed without deriving protection from the males whose responsibility it is to defend them. Cozbi is equipped with a powerful clan of origin. Yet, the power of execution that Phineas assumes over her body implies that by marrying into the Israelite community the family of origin relinquishes its authority over its female members. In order to be avenged Lucretia has to die. In the biblical narrative, a strange inversion casts the Midianites as the offending side and the Israelites as the injured one. Cozbi becomes a symbol of strife and a worthy company of Balak and Balaam (Num 25:18).

Tales of erotic violence, then, disguise male rivalries and mask historical procedures. Between Genesis 34 and Numbers 25 it is possible to discern a process of identity formation that elevates and maintains patrilineal and priestly principles at the expense of individual desires and ambitions. In hindsight it is best, perhaps, to regard the rapes of Dinah and Cozbi as two bookends, one signaling the demise of the last matriarch, the other effecting the elimination of a potential matriarch. The priestly redactor of the texts punctuated ancient Israelite history with two tales that feature women, foreign lovers, and violence. Ultimately, such stories also provide negative stereotypes of behavior: a Jew is not to marry outside the group; a Jewess behaves neither like Dinah who leaves the domestic space to encounter a "rapist," nor like Cozbi who enters her domicile to encounter a murderer.

2

Patriarchy and Patriotism

Integrating Sex into Second Temple Society

In the book of Genesis, Jewish women marry relatives; non-Jewish women, when they are married to Jewish patriarchs, receive scant attention. This imbalance is, perhaps, not entirely coincidental. The matriarchs of Genesis hardly set a model of wifely behavior. Sarah forces her husband to send away a favorite sexual partner and ruthlessly advances the interests of her own son. Rebecca tricks Isaac into conferring the rights of primogeniture on their younger son. Leah and Rachel leave their parental home in anger, feeling that they have been cheated of their rightful inheritance. Nor does Jacob's household set an example of blissful domesticity. Leah desperately uses her fertility as a weapon against her barren sister.

Jewish or, rather, Israelite women emerge, at least in the pages of Genesis, as independent agents, either ferociously promoting the interests of their favorite sons or doing their best to win their husband's love. Laudable as such portrayals may have been, neither proved attractive or useful to later interpreters. In a battle over the integrity of Jewish society in the nascent province of Persian Yehud (= Judaea), married women whose marriage is threatened and whose children face disinheritance have no voice. Whatever they feel for their husbands remains immaterial. Nor do they have a mother to fight for their marital or parental rights. When sex becomes an instrument of defining patriotism, as it did in the postexilic period, the subordination of men to the new state is measured by that of wives to husbands.

In the pages of Ezra-Nehemiah foreign wives, and by extension all wives, are scrutinized. No defiance is recorded on the part of the women whose dismissal is demanded by the state. But a theoretical case dealing with a defiant daughter illustrates how the behavior of individual Jewesses bears on the welfare of the community at large. In Jubilees the contours of the Jewish family are drawn either around the relationships between mothers and sons (in biblical recollection) or between fathers and daughters (in contemporary elaboration). Through such pairs the text measures the ability and the viability of the family to survive and to cope in an ideal Jewish society. To judge by Jubilees, readers of the Dinah affair in the Judaean society of the Second Temple appear considerably more puzzled by Jacob's than by Dinah's silence or silenced voice. As Jubilees recreates Genesis 34, it harnesses fathers and daughters to participate in a national program of purification. Any failure to comply entails capital punishment. Neither Jubilees nor Ezra-Nehemiah provides concrete suggestions relating to what wives and daughters should do. Both are obsessed with what women ought not to become.

That daughters ought not to be like Dinah seems understandable in the climate generated by Ezra in Yehud. I begin this chapter with an analysis of a curious episode in the annals of the Second Temple, namely the wholesale rejection of "foreign" women in Yehud. I continue with the remaking of biblical matriarchs, especially Dinah, in Jubilees. Ezra throws into relief the institution of the family, and particularly the function of women within the larger context of the "commonwealth." Jubilees shows how notions of belonging must begin at home, with fathers and daughters. Ezra appears to assert that foreigners in general, and foreign women in particular, constitute a divisive element in society. Jubilees claims that divisiveness is generated when daughters reject social norms of behavior. In either case, the models discussed are models to be shunned.

Birth of a Nation: Marriage and Patriotism in Ezra

In 539 B.C.E., a victorious Cyrus issued an edict that permitted Jews in Persian exile to return to their Judaean home. The vision of the dry bones, so eloquently depicted by Ezekiel, became a reality. Laden with valuables that had belonged to the Temple, those who responded to the call returned to the ancestral land. They found a landscape that had been altered, not the least due to governmental policies of population transplantation. They also realized that the joy of restoration was hardly shared by the other inhabitants of Yehud (Judaea). Jews who had not been deported were in bad economic shape; transplanted settlers who had adopted the Jewish theological worldview were flourishing; Persian central authorities were far away, bent on ensuring law and order at any cost.

It is hardly surprising, perhaps, that the growing pains of the exilic community occupy a major portion in the narrative that bears the name of Ezra, the leader of one exilic group. Issues of identity and boundaries become critical in the efforts of leaders to preserve the special character of the community that had experienced exile and return.[1] At the climax of a succession of astounding events that extend from Cyrus's edict to Ezra (mid-fifth/early fourth century B.C.E.?),[2] a group of Jewish men are pressured to dismiss their foreign wives. In the middle of a battle to survive in a changed environment the hostilities shift from clashes with neighbors to a domestic front. The ideology that Ezra forges emphasizes separation rather than harmony and concord. But cohesiveness is evidently achieved at the cost of marital relations and specifically at the expense of "foreign" wives.

There are no "Jewish" wives in Ezra. To be precise, there are names that can be associated with female Jewish names but these women have neither face nor voice. Nor are the foreign women whose dispatch becomes so critical endowed with words. The women of Yehud, whether deemed Jewish or foreign, remain silent. What is the significance of this silence?[3] Ezra-Nehemiah features three main themes: the "reading" of a sacred text, public spectacles, and the vilification of the foreign other.[4] All three are intimately linked. Scripture and spectacles are often staged in a manner calculated to exclude the nonaffiliated other. Indeed, in the foundational tales that Ezra-Nehemiah unites, foreigners are cast as the inevitable foes of the founders, and spectacles emerge as assertions of authority and legitimacy against the other. But even such a crude dichotomy appears less startling than the emphasis placed on foreign women. With the exception of the Dinah tale (Gen. 34) no other biblical story proposes a wholesale rejection (or integration, for that matter) of foreign spouses out of (or into) the community. None makes so explicit the intimate link between sex and society.

On its own terms it is difficult to understand fully from the Ezra text what transpired in Jerusalem and in the Jewish households of Persian Yehud during the campaign of sexual separation.[5] What can be clearly discerned is an attempt to formulate rites of separation between husbands and wives rather than rituals of sexual unions. This is important, for the Bible does not contain a single description of marital rites. There are no formulas uttered by either the bride or the bridegroom and no officiating authority. Male-female bonding is not a subject of narrative descriptions, nor of legal ordinances.

The prelude to the episode of marital separation includes complaints by a group of unnamed "officials," in public, about another group of "traitorous" men who are married to "foreign women." The situation is presented as a violation of Pentateuchal bans on intermarriage.[6] The marriages are defined as an unholy mixture of the "holy seed" with "the peoples of the land" (Ezra 9:1-2).[7] Although refraining from naming individuals, the categories of offenders are carefully constructed, beginning with a general allusion to the "people of Israel, priests and Levites" and ending with "officials and leaders," in other words, starting from the general and moving to the particular, and from the lower to the upper class. The precise identity of the women to whom they are married remains elusive. They are invoked, collectively, through a deliberately manipulated Pentateuchal list of forbidden marital partners.

The rhetoric of collectivity of Ezra 9:1-2 emphasizes the women's dispensability and, paradoxically, their power.[8] Although anonymous and invisible, their implied presence is dangerous. The text, ostensibly focusing on the Jewish husbands, nevertheless targets these women. Their dispatch is a guarantee of future peace and prosperity. Foreign wives, it may be surmised, dilute the seed of exilic Jewish males, thereby undermining the unique character of the community.[9] In the scheme of Yehud-exilic procreation foreign women have no place. The community can and should survive without them. They are a collective negativity.

How extraordinary this perception is can be measured against the presentation of groups of foreign women in Roman reconstructions of the annals of early Rome.[10] Of the foundational tales commemorated by historians and poets of Rome, that of the rape of the Sabine women enjoyed considerable vogue.[11] Its appeal is reflected in the number of surviving versions that aspire to "record" the events surrounding this wholesale abduction of foreign women by the Romans of Romulus's time. In its longest version, that of Livy (*ab urbe condita*, 1.9-15), the historian highlights the critical significance of these women as a guarantee of Rome's future. Briefly recounted, Livy depicts an acute scarcity of women in newly founded Rome as a motivation behind a Roman drive to seek brides from their neighbors. The latter, both fearful and contemptuous of the upstart Romans as prospective bridegrooms, reject the Roman proposals of marriage. Undaunted, the crafty Romulus devises a stratagem. He stages elaborate games to which he invites the unsuspecting Sabines and other neighbors. When the men are engrossed in the spectacles, the Romans abduct the female spectators. A war ensues. The abducted women, now married to their Roman abductors, become mediators of peace and all live happily ever after.

> This happy and unlooked-for end to a bitter war strengthened the bond between the Sabine women and their parents and husbands. Romulus moreover marked his own special awareness of this deepened feeling by giving the women's names to the thirty wards into which he then divided the population. (Livy, 1.13)

In Livy's pages the foreign women talk with a unified voice in spite of their varied geographical and ethnic affiliations. They are not all Sabine but their very vocality highlights the discord among the male groups. At Rome their presence means survival; for their male relatives it represents an affront of the first order. In Ezra 9–10 the foreign women do not find their own voice. But their implied centrality signifies just as broad and deep a communal crisis. At stake is the perpetuation of the community through procreation as well as the very identity of the new establishment. In either case it is the foreign women-turned-residents that determine the character of the fledgling community. But the receptivity of the Romans to foreigners in general, and to marriage with foreign women in particular, is precisely what makes Rome great in the perspective of memory and recollection.

Private and Public in Yehud

In Judaea, or Persian Yehud, the result of the campaign to get rid of foreign women is hardly a foregone conclusion. While the women do not appear to have advocates, their husbands do not readily bow to pressure. To advance the cause of marital separation and the dispensability of foreign women in the Judaean exilic state, the proponents of exclusion have to mount elaborate spectacles to enlist public opinion to their side. They begin with a public accusation at a sensitive moment in the history of the community, when a new leader and new immigrants have just arrived. Amid euphoric celebrations, the subject of marriage, or rather intermarriage, introduces a jarring note. Yet, in spite of its suddenness, at least in the recorded version of Ezra 9, the problem could have hardly been novel. As surfaces later, some couples have children.

Ezra, the newly appointed leader and the recipient of the criticism concerning intermarriage in the community, reacts, to begin with, like Jacob when he hears of his daughter's abduction and rape. He remains silent. Instead of words, he adopts a series of dramatic gestures, ripping his clothes, tearing his hair out, and sitting in demonstrative desolation. This unusual spectacle of mourning draws attention and "all those who tremble at the words of the Lord regarding the betrayal of the Golah (exile)" (9:4) gather around him. Ezra's demonstrative reaction implies that the men charged with intermarriage are also guilty of impiety. In narrative perspectives, then, a judgment is passed on these men before the matter is discussed or resolved. Their wives are doomed to silence and to rejection.

Abhorrent as the presence of foreign women as wives of Jewish men appears in the eyes of Ezra, the indictment may have also occasioned surprise, if not indignation. Marriage with "foreigners," of whatever affiliation or creed, appears neither rare nor unacceptable. Jewish brides may not have been always readily available or even desirable.[12] A public debate on this score is, however, out of the question, falling outside the redacted scope of the narrative. Its results would have been unpredictable.

On the verge of what must become a momentous decision regarding the shape of marriage in the community of the Second Temple, Ezra turns first to the ultimate source of power, God. Kneeling and spreading his palms he prays publicly, thus appropriating an essentially private act from both the accusing and the accused. His piety strikes a visible contrast with the alleged impiety of the (absent?) men involved in marriage outside the community. By addressing God, rather than the audience, about a matter of public interest, Ezra constitutes himself the sole mediator between the people and Yahweh. He alone is able to engage the power of Yahweh on behalf of the state, and only he can decipher the will of God. Interpreting the divine message appears to have become the monopoly of priests and scribes, rather than of prophets.

Watching Ezra in tears, his audience weeps inconsolably.[13] Their imitation reflects approval. His piety is reassuring but the possibility of failure must also be taken into account. This complex set of relationships between an individual and a community is staged against an eloquent landscape. Ezra dictates his drama within an urban context that had experienced vastly disparate fortunes and whose fate was still hanging in the balance.[14] The monuments of Jerusalem, some real, others conjured, participate in the invocation of the past and the present.[15] They lent mute assent to Ezra's presentation and interpretation of Scriptures and they act as visual testimonies of the antithetical possibilities of resolution and disaster. Against a cityscape of half-raised walls, a testimony of catastrophe and exile, Ezra's disheveled appearance provides a reminder of the shifting fortunes of the community, of its fragility, and of the mutations of the covenant between Israel and Yahweh. Domesticity becomes secondary.

Ezra's words reinforce the message that his appearance and the visual context of his prayer have projected. His listeners are called upon to share his revulsion and to avoid precisely what the "sinners" had done, namely intermarriage. He reminds them of Pentateuchal bans on intermarriage (Exod. 34:15–16; Deut. 7:3–4). But instead of emphasizing the risks of idolatry and apostasy entailed in intimate sexual relations with non-Jews, as the Pentateuch does, Ezra rejects intermarriage for economic reasons. To be precise, he links the well-being of the community with a rejection of intermarriage in terms that echo the arguments employed in the Dinah tale (Gen. 34). Negotiating marriage on behalf of his son Shechem, Hamor promotes wholesale marital alliances between Israelites and Shechemites as means to promote the economic interests of both sides (see Chapter 1). Ezra insists that peace with the locals and the economic advantages of intermarriage are hindrances, rather than guarantees of the covenant between Yahweh and Israel. Ezra's marital ideology strives, then, to undermine the role of women as potential mediators of peace and prosperity. In this, he reflects a remarkable continuity with the spirit of the final redactor of Genesis 34.

Sin, Scripture, and Intermarriage

In Ezra's recapitulation of history, intermarriage becomes the sin par excellence.[16] It is impiety itself.[17] Indeed, it becomes an institutionalized public crime, just like adultery.[18] That such an attitude presented something of a novelty can be maintained on the basis of the recorded biblical annals of ancient Israel. Opposition to intermarriage, in itself, may have already been part of the ideological equipment of the Deuteronomist, but the demand in Ezra's Yehud for a dissolution of marital bonds was unprecedented.[19] Significantly, the very grammar of intermarriage provided a mechanism for social communication.

Paradoxically perhaps, intermarriage becomes a strategy for establishing distinctions within the community itself and for creating an arena where events affecting the lives of its members can be controlled. By elevating the sin of intermarriage to the degree of a national crisis, and by insisting on repentance, Ezra appropriates for himself a prophetic tradition of moral authority. The powers that the Persian monarch has invested in him are now put to the test. They are, however, interpreted not in terms of political and legal arbitration but rather in terms of models of morality.

In the struggle over the precise identity and loyalties of the community, it is precisely this tradition that Ezra endeavors to recapture. Placing intermarriage within a sequence of historical covenants and their violation enables Ezra to present his stand as a traditional approach to the problem. If the new settlement is to survive and succeed, this tradition needs to be reconstructed, reestablished, and reimposed. A correct marriage, therefore, must be defined, for birth becomes a basis of membership. Ezra thus uses his superior moral position to reinforce an agenda of genealogy and to propose a new ideology of what it means to be a Jew.[20]

More recent traditions, established in the course of the brief history of the exilic resettlement itself, and including an inherited animosity vis-à-vis the locals, further assist Ezra to solidify his position. Already in the early years of their return to the land the returnees exclude the "other," first from sharing in the reconstruction of the Temple (Ezra 4:1–5), then from participation in rituals and feasts (Ezra 6:19–22), and finally from the family. Such human exclusion entails a redefinition of space. Thus the public sacred space, the sacred feasts and finally the households become foci of bonding as the boundaries between "us" and "them" are drawn.[21] Viewed from this vantage point, the issue of domestic partners appears a natural conclusion and an inevitable climax as the scale of exclusion leads from public to private and from feasts to families.

Yet, even Ezra's prayer of atonement proves insufficient incentive to dissolve existing marriages. Another speaker appears on the Jerusalem horizon. He is a man named Shechania, a "man in whom God resides," and he is the first to refer to the targeted wives. In his public address the spouses of the Jewish men who had been accused of intermarriage are called "foreign."[22] In the initial complaint, they were designated as "daughters" (*banot*) of local men, a designation that emphasized their nonexilic affiliation. In Ezra's prayer all these locals, daughters and fathers collectively, become impure.[23] In Shechania's speech the emphasis on "foreignness" places these women in a category of transient people standing outside the protective fold of the community.[24] Legally speaking, "foreign" hardly applies to legal spouses of Jewish men, whatever their ethnic or religious affiliation might have been. But the term anticipates their fate.[25] They will become foreign since they will not stay in the community.

Shechania also proposes a concrete solution to the dilemma facing Ezra and the community, namely a new covenant based on the dismissal of these women and their children. He thus exercises pressure on the leader to follow the exegesis he had already applied when reacting to the crisis. The resolution, however, appears to lack scriptural basis.[26] Although the initial complaint skillfully blended Scriptures with actualities by associating Deut. 7:3–4 (a general ban on intermarriage with seven named peoples) with Deut. 23:4–9 (the banning of Moabites and Ammonites from the community in perpetuity), such a mixture does not "logically" require a subsequent legal move of expulsion.[27] Nor does Scripture propose the expulsion of people who had been legally barred from admission. The Pentateuch is preventive rather than prescriptive. It refrains from envisaging the possibility of inclusion.[28]

In spite of Shechania's insistence on the application and execution of everything "according to God's precepts and to the Law" (Ezra 10:3), he fails to produce the latter. There was simply no law that either encouraged or authorized the wholesale dismissal of families of Israelite men. No interpretation of either Deuteronomy 23 or 7, or of Exodus 34 for that matter, could produce a solution of forced separation. The opposite appears to have been the case since later the rabbis found a way to reinforce the integration rather than the exclusion of Moabite women into the community and the Book of Ruth provides a narrative proof of openness to (select) foreign women.

When Ezra, then, presented intermarriage as the great historic transgression, he could but did not propose repudiation. Pentateuchal bans on intermarriage did not provide a solution in case a mixed marriage did take place. Any Jewish man had, of course, a right to terminate his marriage on practically any ground, whatever the "nakedness/indecency of a thing/matter" (Deut. 24:1) might have meant.[29] Yet, neither Ezra nor Shechania appears to have relied on this scriptural reference when they proposed and embarked on the detachment of the foreign wives from their husbands.[30] Had so simple a rule been in effect for spouses of differing religious and ethnic affiliation, Ezra would not have required an elaborate series of spectacles to effect separation. The law of divorce, it may be surmised, applied only to Jewish men married to Jewish women.

To lend authority to the call to send away foreign women and children, Shechania calls for a reenactment of the covenant itself. The idea of enlisting the ancient covenant between Yahweh and Israel to dissolve individual marriages bears no resemblance to any Pentateuchal provision. A further novelty resides in the idea of legally penalizing the seemingly innocent wives rather than their guilty husbands. After all, the initial accusation had been made against the latter. Here, however, the narrative of the rape of Dinah (Gen. 34) could provide ideological ammunition.[31] In patriarchal Canaan a general plan of intermarriage between Israelite women and non-Israelite males was rejected with vehemence and with the slaughter of prospective bridegrooms.

Indeed, the narrative of Dinah and Shechem provides a functional foil for that of Ezra 9–10. Each involves a wholesale rejection of foreign spouses and both do so after the actual bonding had taken place. In Genesis 34, Dinah's brothers allege that her abduction had been an abomination, precisely the term that colors the attitude of the accusers in Ezra 9 to intermarriage. In each case, what is really at stake is the "cleanness" of the divinely defined clan and territory. Thus, neither in patriarchal genealogy nor in a postexilic one is room made for the inclusion of foreign spouses within the boundaries of the covenantal land.

The foreign women of Yehud must leave. They become a bone of contention and a divisive element in the newly formed Jewish society. Instead of mediating between their families of origin and of marriage, as the Sabine women do in Romulean Rome, they have to be removed. Unlike the Sabine women who start as outsiders and end as fully integrated insiders, the foreign women in Yehud begin as insiders only to become unwanted outsiders.[32] If at Rome marriage is the surest method of cementing friendships between men, in Yehud it becomes a test of male patriotism.[33] For the Sabine women patriotism meant devotion to the new household with its values and gods. It arose out of love for their husbands and children. In Ezra-Nehemiah, it is this familial love that the husbands of foreign women must eschew in order to demonstrate their attachment to the community. Equally ironic is the possibility that these husbands manipulated their wives' affection to convince them to abide by the new law of separation. Patriarchy and patriotism assert themselves in both accounts at the expense of foreign women.[34]

The Fate of Foreign Spouses

The call to abide by Yahweh's interpreted will through voluntary separation from "the peoples of the land" and from "the foreign women" (Ezra 10:11) is followed by a public oath and by opposition (Ezra 10:15). In the end, a list of offenders is drawn. As it stands, it seems to be incomplete. This is where the text comes to an end. Its most glaring omission is a recording of the reaction of the women themselves. It is precisely this disregard for the sentiments of the victims that Plutarch, in another version of the Sabine tale, amends with an eloquent reconstruction of the voice of the Sabine women as they address their insulted male relatives on the eve of war with Rome:

When have we done you wrong or harm that we had to suffer in the past, and must still suffer now such cruel evils? We were violently and lawlessly ravished away by those to whom we now belong. But though thus ravished, we were neglected by our brethren and fathers and kinsmen until time had united us by the strongest ties with those whom we had most hated [i.e., their Roman abductors]. Time has made us now fear for those who had treated us with violence and lawlessness when they go to battle and mourn for them when they are slain. You [i.e., their relatives] did not come to avenge us upon our ravishers while we were still maidens, but now you would tear wives from their husbands and mothers from their children, and the help that you now render us is more pitiful than your former neglect. (*Romulus* 19.2–5)[35]

This protest, as eloquent as the silence of the foreign women of Yehud, also alludes to another seemingly missing element in the Jewish narrative, namely the relatives of the women or their families of origin. Their involvement, however, can be surmised. The offers of help that unnamed "foes" make to the exilic settlers may have stemmed from such familial links (Ezra 4:1–2). Nehemiah's proverbial enemies, Sanballat the Samaritan, Tobias the Ammonite, and Geshem the Arab, are related, by marriage, to eminent members of the exilic community. Their failed attempt to negotiate a settlement with Nehemiah may have been due to political as well as to personal concerns.

Above all, repeated references to children of mixed marriage indirectly convey the poignancy of the situation, at least for the women. The concluding phrase of Ezra refers to sons of foreign women by their Jewish husbands.[36] Roman literary recapitulations of the Sabine tale feature children, actualized or implied, as critical components. In Livy's prose account, Romulus, the engineer of the wholesale abduction, suggests to the abducted women that "in marriage they will have a share in all the fortunes of the state, and in children, the fondest desire of the human race."[37] In this formula of Romulean marriage, "children perform the same function in relation to mother and father that the Sabine women perform in relation to husband and blood relations: they are the mutually valuable object that will bring parties together."[38] Their role as catalysts is further reflected in their mothers' call to their own parents to conjure up these children as their grandchildren, and hence as valid reasons for the cessation of Sabine-Roman hostilities.

Children remain a powerful visual illustration of the marriage bond as well as a striking manifestation of the woman's most critical role in shaping and perpetuating society. Ovid's poetic version of the abduction of the Sabine women endows the women with visible and audible children. He also places them, rather effectively, in their mothers' arms at a crucial moment on the battlefield itself. When the two armies, that of Rome, now counting the women's husbands, and that of the Sabines and their allies, numbering the women's relatives, are about to join battle, the children, rather than the women, become mediators of peace.

As though they understood, with ingratiating clamor, the grandchildren were holding out their small arms to their own grandfathers. He who could was calling out to his grandfather, then seen for the first time; and he who was hardly able to had been forced to be able.[39]

The children of mixed marriages in Yehud have, similarly, a variety of roles. Although they are never heard, in Ezra 10:44 they serve as a silent testimony of the length of the marriage between their foreign mothers and Jewish fathers. In the course of the spectacles advocating separation the children are a point of repeated reference. Their implied presence cannot be divorced from that of their mothers. Mixed marriage, as presented in Ezra and Nehemiah, is not merely an affair of the heart between two individuals. Its very existence is a barometer of the community's commitment to its new location and vocation.

Ezra-Nehemiah is essentially a tale of transition between exilic and postexilic identity. The human and physical boundaries of the new homeland are dictated by the associations of the past. Its frontiers are shaped by a map of historical-geographical affiliations. Within this binding cartography Ezra crafts his notions of belonging. In his ideal creation distinctions between public and private, between family and community, are achieved through the imposition of public oaths and rituals. The foreign women and children whose discharge is demanded in Ezra become a symbol of national disunity. In Jubilees, a work that in some sense can be regarded as a coda to the book(s) of Ezra and Nehemiah, the integrity of a Jewish family is preserved through the maintenance of correct relations between fathers and daughters. By extension, Ezra's silent women become Jubilees' defiant daughters, both destined for excision.

The Case of the Defiant Daughter: Jubilees' Dinah

Social constructs of the ideal postexilic family emphasize both male dominance within the household (coupled with obedience to the state) and the importance of correct lineage on both sides. Within this framework a choice of a spouse becomes a critical matter not only for individuals about to enter matrimony and produce children but also for society at large. The point is forcefully illustrated in the apocryphal work known as "Jubilees," whose author(s) forged a new and improved covenant for Israel, at least in their own terms.[40] According to scholarly calculations Jubilees is a product of a transition period, perhaps even of Hasmonaean origin.[41] It reflects the centrality of the tales of Genesis and of Egyptian bondage in the life of the community that it addressed.[42] Its aim is ostensibly to recapture Genesis 1 to Exodus 12 through exegetical paraphrase.[43] But numerous digressions in the course of the retelling of the biblical past provide clues to contemporary attitudes and to the impact of Ezra's marital ideology.[44]

Jubilees' hostile attitude to gentiles in general, and to marriage partners outside the faith in particular, is remarkable and uncompromising. But perhaps its most curious aspect is the freedom which the author takes with the original biblical text to advance different agendas. Within a chronology based on a solar calendar and on the appropriate maintenance of the Sabbath and the festivals (2:25–27; 50:8, 12–13; 6:17–36; 16:20–31; 24:18–19, 40), Jubilees presents biblical events and genealogies as texts recorded in "heavenly tablets" (1:27).[45] It exhibits a tendency to integrate notions of sacred space and sanctified liturgy into the sanctity of the human (Jewish) body. In this, Jubilees emerges as a continuator of Ezra's concept regarding the sexual exclusivity of Jewish identity. Yet, to advance his agenda of marital separation Ezra resorted to a recollection of the history of the covenants between Yahweh and Israel in the desert; Jubilees, by contrast, provides a running commentary on marital tales of Genesis, using the tale of Dinah as a platform for the prevention of intermarriage. If a Jewess, in Ezra, is born, one assumes, in a purely Jewish wedlock, the Jewess of Jubilees is made through rigorous application of the interpreted lessons of the past.

That a series of moral essays on correct deportment and on sexual mores can be based on Genesis is hardly surprising. Genesis has the added advantage of focusing on one household, the founding family of Judaism. And although Jubilees' matriarchs are neither silent nor invisible, they, like the women of Yehud, are ultimately subordinate to overriding patriarchal and patriotic concerns. Communications in Jubilees' household are maintained along two lines, one linking fathers and daughters, the other mothers and sons. To begin with, Abraham provides the following guidelines:

> If any woman among you commits a sexual offense, burn her in fire. They are not to commit sexual offenses [by] following their eyes and their hearts lest they take wives for themselves from among Canaanite women. The descendants of Canaan are destined to be uprooted from the earth. (Jub. 20:4, VanderKam, slightly emended)[46]

To judge by this difficult passage,[47] the correct marriage has no room for love or lust. Such a premise echoes repeated patriarchal insistence on limiting of the marital circle to one's own kin, regardless of one's own inclinations. Yet, Israelites (the subject of "they"), women and men alike (?), can stumble into wrong alliances if they, like Esau, disobey paternal precepts. By adopting the harsh penalty of burning that the Pentateuch reserves for fornicating daughters of priests (Lev. 21:9), Abraham implies that all female Israelites share the same degree of priestly purity. But Jubilees' Abraham does not dwell on the nature of the women's "sexual offenses" nor on the fate of Israelite males who follow Esau's suit. It is, perhaps, oblivion. In other words, males who marry "Canaanites" are bound to participate in the anticipated extinction of their wives' families. They lose membership, memory and identity.

These are curious comments. Abraham's discourse, moreover, is aimed at his grandson, Jacob. The two, at least according to the chronology of Genesis, had never met. In the "original" the warning against marriage with Canaanites is issued to Abraham's slave (Gen. 24:3–4) and Abraham dies before the birth of Jacob (Gen. 25:8–9). Notwithstanding, Jubilees transmits directly from one patriarch to another a crucial message. And it appoints a matriarch, Rebecca, as the chief guardian of Abraham's moral legacy. Her words to Jacob echo faithfully the patriarch's injunctions:

> My son, do not marry any of the Canaanite women like your brother Esau who has married two wives from the descendants of Canaan. . . . Listen to me and do the will of your mother. Do not marry any of the women of this land but [someone] from my father's house (*bēit av*) and from my father's clan (*mīshpakhah*). Marry someone from my father's house so that the One Above will bless you and your sons become righteous and your seed holy. (Jub. 25:1, 3, VanderKam)[48]

The choice of a matriarch, rather than a patriarch, as a preserver of male sexual purity emphasizes the importance of the correct lineage on both sides, maternal and paternal, in an Israelite/Jewish family.[49] Jubilees'

Rebecca is a woman imbued with "a spirit of holiness" (*rŏo'akh ha-kodesh*, 25:14), like a prophet.⁵⁰ Perhaps her prominence in the text reflects the closeness of mothers and sons in Jubilees' conjectured community; perhaps it indicates the role of mothers as matrimonial brokers for their sons. Be that as it may, Jubilees casts Rebecca as a full participant in the promotion of the interests and welfare of the family. She is a representative of endogamy and isolation par excellence. In the middle of Canaan she rejects Canaanite daughters-in-law while insisting on sending her beloved son away from home in search of a bride of her own kin.

Jubilees clearly endorses the marital patterns that the founding fathers had established in patriarchal Canaan. Like Rebecca, the text insists on the significance of marriage within specific perimeters of blood. But it says nothing regarding the eligibility or ineligibility of Canaanite males or the applicability of such strictures to its own time. To illustrate the disastrous results of a departure from patriarchal marital norms Genesis provides the tale of Dinah and Shechem. In Jubilees, a representation or, rather, misrepresentation of the same story provides a platform for the promotion of a specific familial agenda.

> There [i.e., in Salem, near Shechem] Jacob's daughter Dinah was taken by force to the house of Shechem, the son of Hamor the Hivite, the ruler of the land. He lay with her and defiled her. Now she was a small girl, twelve years of age. He begged her father and her brothers that she be given to him as a wife. Jacob and his sons were angry with the Shechemites because they had defiled their sister Dinah. They spoke deceptively with them, acted in a crafty way toward them, and deceived them. Simeon and Levi entered Shechem unexpectedly and effected a punishment on all the Shechemites. They killed every man whom they found in it. They left absolutely no one in it. They killed everyone in a painful way because they had violated their sister Dinah. (Jub. 30:2–4, VanderKam)

One of Jubilees' most blatant violations of the Genesis sequence is the suppression of the Shechemites' readiness to undergo circumcision in compliance with the Israelite demands as a precondition of marrying Israelite women. Jubilees also identifies Dinah as a daughter of Jacob while Gen. 34:1 specifically affiliates her with Leah, her mother. Nor is Dinah's age an issue in the Bible but it spices the latter tale with an imagery of a brutal rape. Through such process of exegesis the ambiguities of the original tale, including the circumstances that militated in favor of Shechem and of his people, are systematically removed. Genesis 34 becomes, in Jubilees, a sordid tale of a premeditated sexual assault and an act repeatedly described as desecration and defilement. Its key phrase, "the defilement of an Israelite virgin" (30:6), recaptures the last defying words of Dinah's brothers (Gen. 34:31): "Will our sister be treated as a whore?"

On the basis of the Dinah tale Jubilees advocates a new and radical agenda of moral behavior for members of its Jewish commonwealth.[51] One unusual feature of this program is its emphasis on intimate links between fathers and daughters. A father who authorizes a marriage of a daughter with a gentile is to be stoned to death; a daughter who marries a gentile in defiance of parental wishes is to be burned to death. The penalties, if they were ever to be applied, are interesting. The father's proposed stoning recalls the fate of blasphemers (Lev. 24:9); the woman's punishment harks back to the penalty prescribed for daughters of priests who had sexual relations prior to their betrothal (Lev. 21:9 = Jub. 30:7). Violators of the Jubilees' ban on intermarriage are deemed guilty of a double crime, prostitution and blasphemy, and are accordingly placed outside the pale of the community. In Jubilees' society there is no room for the non-Jewish other or for Jews who dilute identity.

> Nothing like this, namely the defilement of an Israelite woman, is to be done anymore from now on. For their punishment [i.e., of the Shechemites] had been decreed in heaven. . . .
> If there is a man in Israel who wishes to give his daughter or his sister to any who is from the seed of the gentiles, he is to die. He is to be stoned because he has caused sin and shame in Israel; and the woman is to be burned and uprooted from Israel because she has defiled the reputation of her father's house.
> Let no adultery or defilement be found in Israel throughout all the days of the generations of the earth because Israel is holy to the Lord. Any person who causes defilement is to die by stoning, for thus it has been decreed and written in the heavenly tablets concerning all the seed of Israel: Let anyone who defiles die and let him be stoned. And there is no limit of days for this law, nor is there a remission or forgiveness. The man who allows his daughter to be defiled will be rooted out since he had given of his seed to the Molech and has sinned by defiling it.
> And you, Moses, command the children of Israel and testify to them that they are not to give any of their daughters to the gentiles, nor take in marriage from the daughters of the gentiles because it is despicable before the Lord. Therefore I have written for you in the words of the law everything that the Shechemites had done to Dinah and how the sons of Jacob told them: "We shall not give our daughter to an uncircumcised man because it is a disgrace for us" (Gen. 34:14). And it is a disgrace for the Israelites to give and take gentile women in marriage because it is a defilement and despicable for Israel. Nor will Israel be cleansed from this defilement as long as it has one wife of the daughters of the gentiles or if anyone has given one of his daughters to a man who is of any of the gentiles. For it is a blow upon blow and curse upon curse, and every punishment, blow, and curse will come. (30:5–15, based on Wintermute, VanderKam, and Cahana)

As a tissue of biblical allusions the passage is a splendid example of an imaginative interpretation based on a single biblical story. The killing of the Shechemites becomes an occasion for the establishment of a general rule against intermarriage, thus "anticipating" both Exodus 34 and Deuteronomy 7. The assault on the city of Shechem, an action condemned by Jacob in the original tale, is justified in Jubilees by a heavenly decree. The sexual inviolability of "an Israelite virgin," a concept that remains dormant in the biblical context, emerges as a paradigm of behavior. Fairly and squarely Jubilees shifts the biblical balance as it puts the weight of moral responsibility on the shoulders of the father rather than on those of the brothers. It does, however, elevate Levi to the status of Israel's guardian of chastity. As an avenger of sexual transgressions Levi and his descendants, in particular Phineas, guarantee the special place that priests occupied in Judaism. Somehow between Phineas, the avenger of a single transgression concerning intermarriage (Num. 25), and Levi, the avenger of a single rape (Gen. 34), an elusive process produced a third character, Levi, who in Jubilees emerges as Abraham's chief moral heir.

In its concern to recruit all the available Pentateuchal support regarding marital frontiers and the behavior appropriate to a Jewess, Jubilees turns to the basic Pentateuchal bans on intermarriage. Jub. 30:11 repeats Deut. 7:3–4 without, however, subscribing to its specific banned peoples. In this it provides a perfect complement to the ideology of separation that Ezra and Nehemiah had advocated. And like them, it binds marriage, family, and the common good in an inextricable link that can be snapped through violation of sexual mores (Jub. 30:15). But whether Jubilees reflects a general anti-gentile mood or a specific objection to sexual contacts is difficult to assess. Besides advocating the purity of Jewish descent, Jubilees also attacks those who neglect the circumcision of their sons (15:33), as well as Jews who appear to favor idolatry (20:8). It advocates a strict separation (22:16–18) between Jews and gentiles, characterizing the latter as necromancers and devil worshipers (22:18).

Who are Jubilees' Jews and who are Jubilees' Jewesses? In the eyes of its unnamed author(s) Judaism is a construct of correct celebrations and of pure worshipers (49:5). Women, especially the bodies of virgins ripe for marriage, are a threat for they constitute potential transgressors and vehicles of apostasy. Ezra had targeted Jewish men and their wives; Jubilees aimed its arrows at Jewish daughters and their fathers. Ezra-Nehemiah takes for granted foreign women as divisive; Jubilees regards Jewish women in precisely the same light. Between the two texts the formation of Jewish identity shifted its goalposts from the removal of the former to the confinement of the latter.

The orientation of Jubilees, especially its insistence on external reflections of bodily purity, is echoed in a Hebrew document, Miqṣat Ma'asé ha-Torah (MMT), unique among the texts of the Dead Sea Scrolls, that likewise insists on a solar calendar and on separation.[52] It is a letter addressed to a leader whose identity has been contested and with whom the writer's group shares its rules and its eschatology. Inserted into a list of rules are a few lines that clearly echo the view of Ezra on sexual mores in general and on intermarriage in particular.[53]

The similarities between Jubilees 30 and MMT on this score have been widely recognized although there are various interpretations of MMT's criticism of the mingling of the holy seed of priests and of the people with "whores." Between Ezra's statement and Jubilees' strictures MMT provides a *halakha* (rule) that deals ostensibly with mixed marriage but is probably aimed at marriage with proselytes and their descendants. If this is indeed the case, the caves of the Judaean desert yield an astonishing evidence of the extension of contemporary polemics in which issues of sexual relations, and especially the possibility of acquiring purity through marriage with a Jew, had become central, at least in some circles.

In Ezra's time the controversy over the purity of the returning community had taken place in Jerusalem, itself a focus of holiness. Jubilees transferred the debate, metaphorically, to patriarchal Canaan, a territory sanctified by association with Israelite founding narratives. The writer of MMT addressed his words to an audience beyond the confines of the desert community in an effort to clarify its halakhic stance on issues of purity. All three focus on women as agents of impurity. Regardless, then, of affiliation, the Hebrew/Aramaic texts that deal with intermarriage in the Second Temple appear to link the sanctity of the land and its people with the correct maintenance of the body of individuals and of the family.

In Judaea, as in the rest of the Mediterranean in antiquity, the core of society was the family. The desire to procreate created an emotional bond between its members, as did the sharing of familial religious rites and goals. In the Jewish and Roman narratives here surveyed, the family is pitted, however, against the commonwealth or the general good. Wives are asked to give up what is dearest to them, fathers and husbands. Husbands are expected to fight against their relatives or to demonstrate their loyalty to the community by giving up their wives and children.

In the tale of the first Roman marriages, foreign women and children function in a precisely contrary fashion to their Jewish counterparts, although in both the Roman and the Jewish contexts marriage is represented as an institution subordinate to male purposes, and women as subordinate to men. The Romans, new migrants like the exilic settlers of Yehud, nevertheless cast their founder as a leader who promotes integration through marriage. In collective Jewish memory Ezra becomes an advocate of marital separation. In comparative terms the Roman shift of culture from the local to the universal is exactly a reversed image of the Jewish shift from biblical universalism to an increasingly parochial discourse. In a perfectly ordered Jewish society there is no room for outsiders, either as cobuilders or as feasting or domestic partners. Foreigners, especially foreign women, even proselytes, cannot be fully integrated into the painstakingly reconstructed fabric of society. Nor is there room, apparently, for women who convert out of love.

Beyond the intricate sets of familial relationships in Ezra and in Jubilees lies a history that can no longer be recovered. The affair of the foreign marriages in Ezra is carefully placed so as to create a sensation and to generate a crisis. Lacking in vital details, Ezra's redactor aimed to convey what mattered most in his own environment, namely the reproduction of public spectacles as bonding matters of religious and political associations. In Ezra, as in the Roman tale about the Sabine women, an array of conflicting and overlapping concerns is presented. Ezra, who begins his life in Babylonia, must found a new commonwealth with specific boundaries in a society with constantly shifting frontiers. If Rome grows through the absorption of new citizens, especially women, Ezra's Yehud shrinks through the rejection of foreigners, especially women. If Romans are made, Jews are born.

3

From Esther to Aseneth

Marriage, Familial Stereotypes, and Domestic Felicity

Only rarely do ancient texts allow us to probe the "happily ever after" stage. Divorce documents hint at marital tension but, on the whole, biblical and postbiblical narrators display a remarkable lack of interest in the intricacies of married life.[1] How ancient Judaism perceived the basic conjugal unit in specific Diaspora settings can be glimpsed through two texts that feature postnuptial "bliss" and a series of married couples. The Hebrew text bearing the name of Esther supplies an astonishing wealth of information regarding familial stereotypes and women in a state of matrimony, as does the tale entitled "Joseph and Aseneth." In the former several types of families are explored; the latter features the adventures of a woman whose marriage engenders family feud, abduction, and carnage.

In the endless and fascinating scholarly debates about the tiny scroll of the Masoretic text (MT) of Esther, the presence, as well as the absence, of crucially important elements in Jewish history has been frequently noted.[2] We have, for example, a Jewish protagonist who ostensibly, at least, shared the trauma of exile from Jerusalem to Babylon, and a gentile monarch whose vagaries reflect the vicissitudes of exilic life. There is also a Jewess whose "marriage" with a gentile does not require a conversion of any sort. We do not have, however, God, the one and only God whose presence has been so critical for a history of Israel. There is also an absence that, to my mind at least, has not been sufficiently emphasized, namely the lack of a Jewish family. To be precise, there is no conventional conjugal Jewish unit in Esther and no children born in Jewish wedlock. This omission is all the more striking against the presence of no less than three couples in the brief biblical narrative.

A careful scrutiny of the (Hebrew) text reveals how the story of Esther is crafted as a parable on family ethics and on marriage outside the faith.[3]

The subject of the family in general, and of marriage in particular, also highlights the localized nature of the entire tale of Esther. Most of its episodes take place at or near the royal palace and often within a familial context. This is important: the story, humorous, ironic, and sarcastic, is basically a family narrative, beginning with a marital dispute at the palace and ending with the success of one family, that of Mordechai and Esther, and the failure of another, that of Haman and Zeresh. As such, the scroll provides unique commentary on the functioning of the family unit through a series of relationships which include married couples, (adoptive) father and daughter, and the imperial *familia*, namely the royal household with its slaves, officials, and public and private quarters, all dominated by the figure of the "king of kings."[4]

Amidst these familial configurations it may be asked whether a "normal" model of Jewish life, based on a "normal" family unit, can exist in a Diaspora context. Ezra-Nehemiah demanded the severance of marital ties but stopped short of proposing a model of domestic bliss. In an ill-dated romance featuring Joseph and Aseneth in a reconstructed Egyptian environment the absorption of a gentile wife into a Jewish family entailed considerable disruption. What, then, is a "normal" couple or a conventional family? What are the behavioral ingredients of women in marriage as delineated in these texts?

In a narrative littered with paradoxes, such as Esther, or an imaginative novel favored by an unknown group of readers, such as "Joseph and Aseneth," a search for normalcy appears, perhaps, paradoxical. Yet, there is no full understanding of either tale without an evaluation of their most important ingredient, namely the family and its concomitant issue of marriage. I begin with a presentation of couples in Esther, and continue with an exploration of what happens after a "happy end" when the presence of a bride introduces strife rather than satisfaction. Underlying the quest is also an attempt to comprehend the texts as an interpretative venture of Scripture itself.[5]

Marriage Between Gentiles, Model 1: Ahasuerus and Vashti

Esther's narrative opens with an introduction of a gentile royal couple, Ahasuerus and Vashti. They set a curious model of spousal relationship. Just how striking this model is, is partly reflected in the concomitant absence of a model of a Jewish couple (below). Ahasuerus, the foremost of the four main protagonists in rank and power (Esther 1:1–8), is an ostentatious monarch eager to show off his wealth to all and sundry; Vashti is a woman remarkable for her beauty and, as one learns soon, for independence of mind. As the story unrolls, the audience gazes at the court of the palace (1:6b; cf. 7:7–8) where the most important activities are to take place. There the king entertains his people (all males, it seems) while his queen, Vashti, duplicates her spouse's actions by presiding over an all-female banquet (Esther 1:9).[6] A strict and predicable separation, architectural and human, is maintained between the female and male realms in the palatial landscape. By imitating her spouse's activities Vashti also recognizes their respective roles vis-à-vis the public, male and female alike, as well as her own subordinate social position.

When the king desires, however, to cross the boundaries of gender and space by displaying his wife's beauty to his assembled guests, the queen exhibits a singular and somewhat improbable obstinacy. She refuses to obey the royal summons. Her husband, whose will to show off his queen had been apparently inspired by a state of drunken euphoria (1:10), subsequently reveals his short temper and his inability to deal with his own wife. He turns to his councillors for advice on this score. They deem her action a "national" crime and an affront to all men.[7] In spite of this interpretation, suspicion lingers that what irked her royal husband most was rather her daring to introduce a somber note into a general atmosphere of hilarity. Ahasuerus clearly did not anticipate an objection to his request; Vashti might not have expected the summons. Perhaps she considered it rude to leave her own banquet and guests in the midst of the party. Perhaps she dreaded an exposure to the gaze of an inebriate male public.

Ahasuerus and Vashti never confront each other face to face.[8] Her refusal to attend the banquet is never explained. But who is responsible for a breach of marital and royal etiquette? The king for wishing to show off his wife's beauty in public, or the queen for refusing to obey? No answer is forthcoming in the scroll. But the brief mirroring of gentile marital liaisons at the court is critical. It provides a functional foil for the relations between Ahasuerus and Esther and lays down the rules of domestic relations within the specific orbit of the palace.

On the basis of this episode, then, the marriage of Ahasuerus and Vashti is characterized by spousal strain rather than by marital harmony. It is further cast as a relationship between a ruler and a subject rather than between husband and wife.⁹ In other words, even when a woman attains what may appear as the height of any female fantasy and becomes a queen, all is not well. She gains neither peace nor security. Does the text mock female stereotypic ambitions or is it an attempt to probe the vagaries of queenly life?

Vashti's recalcitrance, ostensibly a matter to be settled in the intimacy of the bedroom, is nonetheless discussed in public, between the king and his legal advisers. These men interpret her action as a gesture of contempt for husbandly authority in general (1:16). They further assert that her behavior, unless punished, is likely to create a dangerous precedent. Other wives, mindful of the example set by the queen, would likewise defy their husband's wishes and men would be held in contempt in their own homes. In other words, the episode is interpreted as an undermining of the basic principle of marital relations, namely a complete and unquestioning obedience of wives to husbands.¹⁰ That the private and public realms are here entangled in a merry web is an obvious implication of the fact that this is no ordinary couple. Yet, the councillors' insinuations concerning Vashti's power over all the women of the kingdom appear far-fetched. They are not sustained anywhere else in the narrative.

Esther's text implies that prior to the encounter between Ahasuerus and Vashti no regulation dealt with wifely disobedience, presumably because kings were expected to control their own household without the aid of legal experts. Underlying the search for legal procedures in this case was the contrast between Vashti's sense of propriety, based on her understanding of queenly stereotypes, and the law of the land that had yet to be written. In the mind of the assembled males marriage was a state institution founded on an unconditional compliance of wives with their husbands' commands and on male authority to command the bodies and even the tongues of their wives.

Perceptions of this sort dictated an exemplary penalty. The king readily concurred with his councillors' advice, banning his own wife from marital intimacy and announcing her demotion. Whether such penalties were to apply to every recalcitrant woman in the realm remains an open question. Perhaps a divorce could have been easily and unilaterally effected in Achaemenid Persia. "Persian" law in Esther, however, echoes Pentateuchal regulations that enabled a man to divorce his wife practically on any ground (Deut. 24:1–2).

The royal decree concerning Vashti's fate also included a rider enjoining all men in the kingdom to be masters in their own households

(Esther 1:22). The means to ensure the execution of this command were not provided—only a general recommendation to adopt the language of the fathers of each establishment (Esther 1:22).[11] This surprising attention to the linguistic aspects of domestic relations had little to do with the specific couple on the stage. But it echoed, somewhat perversely, a controversy that marred Nehemiah's efforts in Persian Yehud to cleanse Jerusalem of its gentile dwellers (Neh. 13:23–29) and to "Judaize" the Judaean landscape (Neh. 13:15–18).

A survey of the conjugal map of the Temple-state community of Yehud ignited Nehemiah's anger as he witnessed Jewish men living with Ammonite, Moabite, and Ashdodite women. Nehemiah's displeasure apparently had been prompted not only by the very existence of mixed marriages but also by their educational repercussion. In the mind of the builders of the exilic community in Yehud, intermarriage signaled major regressions.[12] Its immediate result was the breeding of half-Jews, unaware of their own linguistic and ritual heritage.[13]

Similarities between the language of the scroll and that of Nehemiah 13 are, perhaps, not coincidental. Both texts evince an extraordinary interest in the linguistic implications of marriage and in the position of the patriarch in individual households. Neh. 13:24 uses the expression "the language of each people" in order to illustrate the pedagogical evils of intermarriage. Ahasuerus's decree in Esther 1:22a insists that the decision regarding the language at home must remain with husbands/fathers. Nehemiah's understanding of what it meant to belong to the community appears linked with the issue of its language—"Jews" speak "Judaean" (Neh. 13:23–24). Strangely enough, Ahasuerus's government seems to agree on this score. It is difficult to escape the notion that, in a way, Neh. 13:23–24 was a proof text for both Esther 1:22 and 2:5: Esther 1:22 calls for male domination through the exclusive use of patriarchal language at home; Esther 2:5 identifies Mordechai as a Jew and a patriarch, one example of the general rule just prescribed. Yet, if Neh. 13:23–24 was indeed put to such a use, Esther's redactor undermined its general applicability by translating Esther into a gentile environment where not only her Judaean identity but also her Judaean language had to be stored away.[14]

Who, then, is Vashti? In the MT Esther she has neither kin nor previous history.[15] The author's reticence regarding her background is indicative more of the story's general mood than of historical marital alliances of the Achaemenid (Persian) ruling house. Had she been the king's major spouse and a member of a powerful aristocratic clan her dismissal was hardly likely to have been a trivial matter. But such considerations fall outside the framework of a tale in which the only item needed to advance the plot is a vacancy in the palace. Nor is Vashti's fate disclosed.[16]

Just how important and unusual is the emphasis of the opening chapter of Esther on a gentile couple may be gleaned from the fact that only one other gentile couple features in the entire Bible. Potiphar, the Egyptian master of Joseph and an important man in the pharaonic administration, and his wife, provide curious insights into exilic redactional views of gentile marriage (Gen. 39).[17] She is unnamed but is clearly a woman of both words and actions and a stereotype of the rebuffed seducer (cf. Phaedra, above, Introduction). Potiphar's (potentially) adulterous wife emerges as a contrasting character to the seemingly chaste Vashti. She leaves her allotted female domain, crosses boundaries of gender (by venturing out of the women's quarters), of status (by making advances at a slave), and of appropriate marital behavior (by desiring sex with a man other than her husband). When rejected, she accuses Joseph, the target of her amorous advances, of mocking and raping her (Gen. 39:17). Her husband reacts precisely as Ahasuerus does—both men are enraged. Pharoah's minister is angry at the alleged male seducer, while his Persian successor, ironically, directs his wrath at his virtuous wife (cf. Gen. 39:19 with Esther 1:12). Readers of Genesis are apprised of Joseph's innocence; Esther's readership is left in doubt regarding Vashti's precise crime. The presentation of the gentile Egyptian couple, surely unrepresentative of Egyptian society in the assumed time of Joseph, appears calculated to promote associations with the image of foreign women as seducers, so clearly delineated in patriarchal bans on intermarriage (Exod. 34:16; Deut. 7:4).[18]

Vashti remains a woman whose sexual preferences go unrecorded. She seems stubborn, insubordinate, and disobedient but also courageous and defiant.[19] Her characterization also prompts a question regarding the absence of a motherly figure in a text dominated by women. Vashti, disgraced and demoted, has apparently no one to turn to, either mother or father. Nor is Esther endowed with natural parents. Zeresh, the mother of no less than ten sons (see below), never displays maternal affection. Ahasuerus has no mother to admonish or advise him.[20] He operates in an exclusive male environment while Vashti remains in an exclusive female one. His is a familiar figure of an oriental despot, a stereotype whose contrived image in the scroll also raises the question of the credibility of his marriage as a marital model for every couple in the empire. The royal council's claim that the relations between the royal couple are imitated in every household needs to be examined. This can be done, in part, through another (gentile) couple, namely Haman and Zeresh.

Marriage Between Gentiles, Model 2: Haman and Zeresh

Like his employer, the "king of kings," Haman "the Agagite" (Esther 3:1) is a short-tempered man (3:5; 5:9) anxious to share his good and bad moments with his wife and friends (5:10). And like his ruler, who considers a private insult a public affront (3:6), Haman embarks on a general anti-Jewish campaign in the wake of a feud with a single Jew. He is also the "baddie" of the tale, a casting that appears to determine his words and movements but, surprisingly, not quite his relations with his wife.

When elevated to a lofty position in the royal administration and twice invited by the queen herself, Haman, sending for his wife and supporters to share his bliss (Esther 5:10), is featured as a king in his own household. His brief speech to the intimate assembly is odd: he reminds them of his wealth and of the number of his sons (5:11), both pieces of information that they, and surely his own wife, would have been presumably privy to. Perhaps the narrator wished to emphasize a notable lack of communication between the spouses, or to anticipate the grim fate of these sons, the only offspring in the entire story (Esther 9:10, 12, 13, 25).[21] Be that as it may, Haman and Zeresh's dwelling is the only "home" outside the palace enclosure where protagonists directly interact.

Ambiguity lingers. On the one hand, Haman is the undoubted master of his household; on the other, he has to remind his wife of their financial and human resources as though she has been unaware of them. She emerges as a perfect female foil of her husband only to end as a prophetess of his decline and doom. Although the scene of premature jubilation takes place in the intimacy of their home, Haman and Zeresh never converse in private. This is a characteristic familiar from the delineation of communication in the royal palace. Unlike Vashti, Zeresh seconds her husband's promotion and acts as a representative of the choir of his followers. In this, she conforms to the expected norms of wifely behavior as outlined in the royal decree of Esther 1:20.

At home, Haman's appreciative audience is also informed of the one thorn left in their patron's flesh, namely the defiant Mordechai. When they consider the moment apt to settle scores, Zeresh, whose words are invariably uttered in conjunction with those of Haman's male supporters, proposes the construction of a tall tree from which to hang Mordechai (Esther 5:14). As audience and redactor are fully aware, this is the tree that will eventually be the hanging pole of her own husband. Happily reassured of support at home, Haman departs for the royal banquet where his lot will not follow the optimistic prognostications of his wife.

Yet, when Mordechai is later elevated, and Haman, humbled, expects sympathy at home (Esther 6:13), neither wife nor supporters appear surprised by the turn of affairs. She and they predict that if Mordechai, the new royal favorite, is a Jew, then Haman's fate is sealed (6:13). Zeresh is proven wrong and redundant, precisely as her husband has been. Haman, in fact, had been apprised of Mordechai's affiliation from the beginning of their rivalry (3:6). Zeresh's guessing was therefore unwarranted. Her husband's demise would be engineered not by his revealed male enemy but by a woman, his concealed enemy.

By far the most ironic-comic aspect of this marital model is the fact that the only intimacy that Haman ever shares with a woman is not with his own wife but with Esther, a woman unrelated to him, a queen, and an enemy who pretends to be a supporter while plotting his downfall. During a banquet which she ostensibly arranges to celebrate Haman's promotion, Esther suddenly informs her husband of Haman's evil designs on her people (Esther 7:6). The king is incensed yet again, but this time on behalf and not against his wife. He is presumably drunk once more as he goes out of the queen's apartment for a walk in the garden.[22] Haman, frightened out of his wits, turns for help to the nearest person with perceived power over the king, namely the queen.

What should have been a festive occasion is once more interrupted by an unexpected turn of events. And what could have been a comedy of errors, with a respectable married man (Haman) stumbling in panic into the bed of a beautiful married woman (Esther) as her husband strolls nearby, ends as a deadly game. The loser, however, is not the one who had anticipated defeat (Esther) but the man whose wife had first rejoiced in his good fortune and then predicted his downfall.

Behind the bedroom farce in Esther's chambers lurk several serious issues. Ahasuerus accuses Haman of an attempt "to conquer" the queen (Esther 7:8). The term is often used in both a military and a sexual context. Ahasuerus's emphasis on the location of the intended "conquest," the nuptial bed, was meant to illustrate the enormity of the transgression. Yet, the possibility of Haman raping Esther was hardly the issue at stake. What

Ahasuerus envisaged as he saw his minister on his wife's bed was a usurpation of his own throne. In other words, the violation of marital boundaries by Haman was tantamount to a perpetration of a general upheaval well beyond issues of gender.

The only glimpse, then, that the Esther story's audience ever gets into the intimacy of a marriage bed is when that bed is polluted by the presence of a nonrelative, an aspirant to the throne (and a gentile to boot).[23] How realistic is the picture of the marital bliss and woes presented by the two gentile couples in Esther? How does each of the gentile liaisons contribute to an understanding of the (inter)marriage of Esther and Ahasuerus and of the presentation of the Jewish family in the text? In both cases (Ahasuerus/Vashti; Haman/Zeresh) the uncompromising loyalty of wives to their spouses is not readily demonstrable. Zeresh's gloating in her husband's fortune is short-lived and she seems to be singularly ignorant of the identity of her husband's real political rival. When Haman is publicly humiliated she predicts his final downfall. Their sons, ostensibly a critical complement of the familial models, are mentioned only to be disposed of. Yet, examples of biblical marital relationships invariably hinge on the presence or absence of male heirs.

As models of familial relations, then, the two gentile couples of Esther provide contradictory conclusions. Neither Zeresh's nor Vashti's relations with their respective spouses are depicted in terms that create perfect role models for the Jewish family or for any family of the realm. The opposite may well be the case. Physical distance and nearness further determine the construction of the dialogues between the gentile spouses. Ahasuerus and Vashti communicate across the vast expanse of the imperial palace through mediators. The landscape underlines the differences of their moral and marital agendas. Haman and Zeresh, communicating in the intimacy of their own home, never talk to each other in private. The narrative is dry and devoid of any hint of intimacy, sexual, social, or political. Husbands and wives occupy a space that is, theoretically, shaped by the former but, in reality, reshaped by the latter.

The Jewish Family

Perhaps the most intriguing aspect of the presentation of Jewish family life in Esther is the absence of conjugal kinship. There is no conventional Jewish couple nor ordinary marital tie. There are no Jewish mothers, wives, or, for that matter, children. Instead, the two Jewish protagonists are cousins by blood and father and daughter by adoption (Esther 2:7). The cousin/father is improbably old; his cousin/daughter is presumably very young and certainly very beautiful. This age difference, as well as the emphasis on the adoptive relationship, hints at a certain prudishness. Esther's adoption is clearly a means of explaining her presence in a single male household. The adoption seems calculated to endow Mordechai with fatherly authority over his ward/daughter, thus legitimizing his later demands and expectations of her.[24]

Mordechai is not only Esther's sole surviving relative but he is also evidently unmarried. Why he is cast as an elderly bachelor remains outside the recorded tale. What the redactor does emphasize is the relationship of mutual obligation between the two. As an adoptive father and a guardian Mordechai has the responsibility of ensuring his ward/daughter's welfare.[25] Yet, he abandons her to her fate in an unfamiliar and potentially hostile environment. To add to it all, when his own behavior becomes a source of trouble to all the Jews, he turns to her, demanding unconditional surrender to his commands. This is precisely what two patriarchs, Abraham and Isaac, had done when confronted with a dilemma and with a threat to their own lives (Gen. 12, 20, 26). In Egypt and Gerar they presented their wives as sisters, thus gaining favor with their host at the potential cost of their wives' marital chastity.[26] Mordechai exposes his ward's most important asset, her virginity, hoping, paradoxically, that she would be compromised.

A father/guardian's chief duty toward his ward was to find her a suitable match. Strictly speaking, this is exactly what Mordechai did. But, of course, by planting Esther in the royal harem, he also bared her body to sexual contacts with a gentile. There seems to be no expressed awareness in the scroll of either Pentateuchal bans on intermarriage (Exod. 34; Deut. 7) or of Deuteronomistic strictures and cautionary tales (Josh. 23; 1 Kings 11). The silence appears eloquent. It was, as is well known, "corrected" in the Greek versions of Esther.

Perhaps the strangest aspect of this first page of the history of the Jewish family in the Diaspora is the apparent contrasting gender strategies that the Jewish protagonists adopt. Esther says nothing about herself, least of all of her kinship with Mordechai and, by implication, of her Judaeanness.[27] Mordechai stands at the gate of the palace, refuses to pay homage to a powerful minister, and informs all and sundry of his true (Judaean) affiliation (Esther 3:4). In other words, Mordechai does precisely the opposite of what he bids Esther to do. Paradoxically, his orders and her dutiful execution of them apparently work well; but his strategy vis-à-vis competitors inaugurates a national disaster for the Jews (3:6b).

Once installed as Ahasuerus's queen, Esther has to thread between two poles, the demands of her family of origin and of her new family. Mordechai appears reluctant to relinquish his rights as guardian and adoptive father to a gentile husband, even though he had, indirectly, engineered the marriage. Ahasuerus naturally expects his new queen to abide by the rules of the palace and not the least by his wishes as her husband and ruler. As long as the interests of both males in her life match, Esther can continue to inhabit a liminal space. The beginning of the relations between the trio, Ahasuerus, his new queen and his new yet undisclosed "father-in-law," is peaceful enough. She proves a loyal subject by relating a plot against her king/husband (Esther 2:22), while carefully acknowledging the role of Mordechai in the process. This delicate balance, however, carries the seeds of tension and conflict.

In the course of an ongoing power struggle between Mordechai and Haman over top palace positions and royal favor, the king's marriage to a Judaean (an affiliation seemingly unbeknownst to him) engenders a complex intertwining of public and private affairs. What makes the events even more exciting is the fact that of the four protagonists, three (Haman, Mordechai, and Esther) are foreigners. Their successes and failures depend solely on the good or ill will of the monarch. For Haman, the Jews constitute an element that cannot be integrated into the Persian landscape. The presentation of his plans (Esther 3:8) is made at a moment when one Jew, Esther, is doing rather well in the palace. Nor does Haman's accusation of Jews as disloyal misfits fit the recent unearthing of an anti-royal plot by the two Jewish protagonists of the tale.

The first meeting between Ahasuerus and Haman elicits a royal decree authorizing the massacre of Jews in the Persian realm. It forms a critical turning point. How this interview affects the relationship between its two Jewish protagonists is the subject of the rest of the scroll. Mordechai, for the time being, is in no position to act. Esther is much better placed, or so it seems. They embark on an indirect dialogue conducted between the queen's quarters and the royal gate through the mediation of a eunuch (presumably gentile). This is the only (indirect) verbal exchange between "daughter" and "father" that the audience ever witnesses. And while the entire capital knows that something is very wrong merely by observing their mourning Jewish neighbors, Esther herself, safe and secure in the palace, is encapsulated in a cocoon of ignorance. Even more ironic is the necessity to present her with a copy of her husband's decree against the Jews (Esther 4:8). Did Mordechai think that she would not believe him without a textual proof?

In famously bitter words Mordechai threatened his cousin/daughter/ward:

Do not imagine that you alone of all the Jews will escape (their fate) by being in the king's house. If you remain silent at this time, relief and deliverance will come from another source, and you and your father's house will perish. Who knows whether it had not been for this purpose that you obtained royalty? (Esther 4:13–14)[28]

Mordechai, who should have known the rules of the palace as well as Esther herself, expects her to risk her life for the sake of the people from whom he had detached her. She, who must have been fully cognizant of the fate of her predecessor, is faced with a difficult choice. Vashti had been punished for refusing to appear before the king; Esther runs the risk of incurring a graver penalty for intruding upon the king's presence without royal summons.

Spectators may have begun to wonder about a Jewish family in which the life of a daughter is of no consequence when communal survival is at stake. Mordechai's reminder of Esther's membership in a paternal household (Esther 4:14) is calculated to recall her obligation to him, the patriarch. Pushing the argument to a logical or, rather, illogical conclusion, Mordechai was suggesting martyrdom to his cousin.

Deciding to throw her lot in with the community in which her membership has been alternately denied and reasserted, Esther assumes the type of authority that had been hitherto the sole prerogative of the men surrounding her. Her response, "if I am lost, so be it" (Esther 4:16b), highlights a moment of personal tragedy when speech and action involve her in the tragic experience projected by the royal anti-Jewish decree. No longer hovering between two identities, Esther's dilemma appears all the more pronounced against the one dimensional presentation of the male protagonists of the plot.

The exchange between Mordechai and Esther in Esther 4:7–17 further implies that Mordechai perceived his "son-in-law" as a man whose demands were secondary to those of the "father." His insistence that her translation into the palace had come about solely "for a purpose" (Esther 4:14) reflects this belief. Since the marriage of Esther and Ahasuerus is the only biblical example of an intermarriage approved by the woman's family, the question of the bride's identity and affiliation must have loomed large. In the only parallel tale of a "mixed marriage" (Gen. 34), the intended bride's family expressed its disapproval of the proposed match (between Dinah and Shechem) by slaughtering the potential gentile groom, his family, and all their subjects (see Chapter 1). To whom, then, did Esther owe her primary affection? Split loyalties are a recurrent theme of the women in the scroll. Men faced no such problem. Their allegiance was to their interests alone.

By endowing Mordechai with continuing paternal power over his married relative (and a queen), Esther's redactor cleverly avoided the thorny subject of the acceptability (or unacceptability) of intermarriage. The very fact that this intermarriage takes place between a Jewish woman allegedly of royal descent and a (gentile) king elevated the debate on intermarriage beyond a level of mixed marriage as projected by Pentateuchal bans. It also provided a curious foil to the Deuteronomistic presentation of Solomon's gentile harem in 1 Kings 11:1–7 (also used by Nehemiah to promote his anti-intermarriage agenda, Neh. 13:26). While marriage between a Jewish monarch and a gentile princess was not exactly the same as one between a gentile king and a Jewish "princess," it is difficult to escape the impression that 1 Kings 11 provided a proof text for the mixed couple in Esther.

As Esther proceeds to intervene with her husband, to undermine Haman, and to redeem both herself and her people, her relations with her adoptive father become more and more formalized. Not a word is exchanged between the two after the indirect dialogue of 4:13–17. Even when Esther professes to the King her affiliation with the Jewish community (7:3–4), only after Haman's fall does she disclose her connection with his own minister (8:1). She continues to act independently while Mordechai gradually succeeds to the position that Haman had occupied. In the end, the cousins are featured as joint lawgivers, but only after Haman is dead does Esther introduce Mordechai as a family member and, in fact, as the king's father-in-law (Esther 8:1).[29]

How functional is this model of the Jewish family, devoid as it is of maternal figures and children? As Esther's guardian and father, Mordechai fails to carry out his most basic responsibilities, including the location of an appropriate match within the community. In fact, only once, when Esther is still a freshwoman, so to speak, in the palace, does Mordechai manifest concern over her well-being (Esther 2:1). His most singular omission of duty as a Jew and as a father is his authorization of a major Pentateuchal transgression. He could have argued that Persians were excluded from the bans on mixed marriages but such an argument was apparently unacceptable, at least in the Persian Yehud of Ezra and Nehemiah (see Chapter 2).

The absence of a conventional Jewish couple from the narrative is remarkable. Patriarchs usually appear with matriarchs, as Genesis tales plainly demonstrate. Young and vulnerable women in need of advice appear with a female guardian, as Ruth does. The omission in Esther appears deliberate. There was evidently no room for a Jewish couple to balance the stereotypes of gentile couples. A Jewish woman, not unlike gentile women, was expected to abide by the rules of her senior male relatives, fathers, brothers, or husbands. The presence of a Jewish couple, furthermore, would have emphasized the problems entailed in the casting of the central couple as a mixed couple.

Intermarriage: Ahasuerus and Esther

The couple meets as she "is taken" (2:16a; cf. 2:8) to the king's palace (or rather his bedchamber) and he "falls in love" with her (2:17a).[30] Romantic as this may sound, the encounter is a result of what must have been a dreary, if not dangerous, national beauty pageant. The verbs also recall another fateful meeting belonging to the foundational tales of Judaism, when Shechem "took" Dinah and then proceeded to fall in love with her (Gen. 34:2–3). Both texts emphasize the passivity of the women. Neither is heard. Neither is consulted.

Dinah's siblings are outraged when they discover that their sister had been violated by an uncircumcised man. They devise a vengeance that, like Haman's anti-Jewish campaign, penalizes all Shechem's subjects for the transgression of a single man. Yet, as far as Ahasuerus is concerned, Esther has neither kin nor ancestry.[31] Any appearance of outraged male relatives on the scene would have been uncalled for. Esther's apparent orphan state makes her all the more dependent on the good (or ill) will of her husband. Her isolation is complete.[32] Ahasuerus's falling in love with her is not counterbalanced by any information about her sentiments toward him. As far as the plot is concerned this was irrelevant. What mattered was merely the fact that by achieving access to the palace Esther was positioned to act in a capacity not ordinarily associated with Jewish virgins of good patriarchal homes.[33]

In spite of a promising beginning and the king's crowning of Esther, the audience is left in the dark about the development of their intimacy.

By her own testimony, she had not seen her husband for at least a month (Esther 4:11a). But as the relationship between herself and Mordechai evolves so does that between the new royal couple. In fact, the marriage of Ahasuerus and Esther is characterized by a dynamism wholly lacking in the static images of the two gentile couples of the tale. Communications between the mixed couple are direct and reciprocal, unlike the commanding position that Mordechai had assumed over his "daughter." Ahasuerus never explicitly dictates to his wife but shows tenderness that Mordechai never displays. In this he conforms to the best-known model of royal intermarriage, that of Solomon and his gentile wives. Solomon, in fact, went further than Ahasuerus. His affection for his wives even extended to the adoption of their cults (1 Kings 11:4–5).

The truth is that, aside from authorizing a wholesale massacre of his wife's community (without, of course, realizing her affiliation), Ahasuerus proves an uncommonly accommodating spouse. From a liaison of silence (based on Esther's reticence about her origins) Esther enters a public dialogue with the king (Esther 5:1) who gladly complies with her seemingly modest requests to entertain him and his favorite minister in the intimacy of her own rooms (5:4, 8). His surge of emotion (5:2; cf. 2:17), however, at the sight of his beautiful wife some five years after their wedding banquet, is difficult to interpret.[34] She was then standing in deference in the yard, conscious of turns of fate, and he was ensconced in his throne, fully aware of his power and position.

Royal couples, as far as the scroll's readers can glean, conducted their relationships mostly in public, each abiding by the court protocol. Their words had to be carefully evaluated. Neither quite meant what he or she said. Ahasuerus had no intention of "granting her half of his kingdom"; Esther had no intention of showering queenly favors on Haman. The banquet that Esther had prepared for the two men becomes the most intimate occasion of the entire drama. The absence of other women, and most notably the minister's own wife, is remarkable. It contrasts with Vashti's all-female banquet and with the positioning of women in the narrative. Even more strikingly, Esther entices, so to speak, her husband to her own quarters, while Vashti refused to leave these very same premises to see her husband.

But perhaps the most interesting aspect of the scroll's construction of marital structures is the (mixed) couple strategies vis-à-vis each other. Esther conceals her true identity; Ahasuerus feigns ignorance when confronted with the repercussions of his own edict (Esther 7:5). Just how ironic this mutual adaptation and concealment is is left for the audience to judge. The queenly banquet proves a turning point for the three participants. Haman, who had come with high expectations, finds himself confronted with an irate queen and king. Ahasuerus, who had presumably anticipated a pleasant evening with a favored wife and minister, witnesses the latter on the bed of the former. The only member of the party to follow a predetermined course is Esther herself as she turns a festive occasion into a political event.

As the scroll charts a path from ignorance to knowledge and from deception to revelation, its familial stereotypes live and act out the consequences of clinging to a partial view of the world and of themselves. They do so largely within the circumference of their own homes, royal or ordinary, and where the males remain largely dominant. In a way, all three female protagonists, confined to their own quarters willingly or unwillingly, represent a subversive threat to male authority. In Esther's case in particular, her double role as a daughter and a wife creates a conflict of interests. It is difficult to escape the notion that the models of Jewish family life and of intermarriage, as well as of gentile couples, are not entirely contradictory. Yet, the text's emphasis on Esther's prime duty to her own kin provides an exception to any perception of unmitigated harmony, as does Vashti's defiance and Zeresh's prognostications of doom.

By juxtaposing two types of marriage, gentile and mixed, the scroll of Esther joined a long-standing debate over intermarriage in ancient Judaism. By converging on the issue of divided loyalties, the redactor placed the Jewish woman in the center of the discussion. The novelty, even within the framework of a comedy of absurdities, cannot be overestimated. Pentateuchal bans and narratives on intermarriage placed a premium on sexual intimacy between Jewish or, rather, Israelite males and gentile women (Num. 25; 1 Kings 11; Ahab and Jezebel; Ruth and Boaz).

With the exception of the Dinah affair, the scroll of Esther provides the only example of a Jewish woman allied to a non-Jew. In both cases, all the Jewish protagonists, male and female alike, are foreigners in a foreign land. But the redactor of Genesis 34 minced no words about the enormity of such a sexual configuration. Esther's redactor, by providing an alternative view of the implications of intermarriage, leaves the issue wide open, or so it seems.

Intermarriage remains, however, one stereotype of familial relations in a Diaspora environment and it is confined to the royal palace. Intimate relations in royal palaces in general carry strategic connotations. Solomon and his foreign, non-Israelite wives usher in the division of the monarchy; Ahasuerus and his foreign, Jewish spouse bring temporary salvation to the Jews. Perhaps the symmetry is intentional. If it is, the tale of Esther and Ahasuerus also highlights the improbability of conducting normal married life in a nonpalatial, ordinary Diaspora context.

Underlying the text of the scroll is a critical transformation of the meaning of belonging to a community in exile. Ironically, the most penetrating comments are put in the mouth of two gentile observers, Haman and Zeresh. The first draws attention to the "strangeness" or alien nature of the Jews (Esther 3:8); the second emphasizes Jewish staying power in adversity (6:13b). Both references confirm the uniqueness of the people, a facet well established in Pentateuchal demands of sexual separation between the Israelites and the local Canaanites (as well as in Ezra's attitude to intermarriage in Persian Yehud and in Jubilees).

Exilic existence proved to be fraught with dangers. It seems as though there was no room for "normal" existence, and least of all for an ordinary family unit. Such, indirectly, was also the message of the exilic prophets who preached a return to the land of Israel as the only way of life for a Jew. Such, paradoxically, was the message of Ezra 9–10 as he advocated the expulsion of foreign wives from the reconstructed community in Yehud where the only "normal" and acceptable life included intimate relations between men and women born and bred in pure Jewish wedlock. To preserve a distinct identity in a regressive Diaspora environment the scroll of Esther manufactured not only unimitative familial paradigms but also the greatest paradox of all, namely intermarriage.[35] Plainly put, only by violating the very law that had been devised to create and perpetuate Jewish identity could the Jewish people survive in the Persian environment conjured up in the scroll. Herein lies the stunning silence of the Esther text.

Integrating Brides into the Family: Aseneth and Joseph

Joseph and Aseneth (J/A) tells the story of a young woman who falls in love with a good-looking man who, however, rejects her.[36] It continues with an account of her search for a new identity to ensure her desirability in his eyes. As it leads to an inevitable happy reunion, J/A also examines what happens to the husband's family once the couple settles to enjoy, presumably, a blissful marriage. Based on a single biblical reference to marriage between Joseph the patriarch and Aseneth the Egyptian (Gen. 41:45), J/A weaves a fanciful exegesis to justify what its author appears to have regarded as an intermarriage between a Jew and a gentile, or rather as a marriage between a Jew and a proselyte of sorts. As such, it offers an instructive complement to the Persian tale of Esther and Ahasuerus. But beyond proposing an ideal conjugal unit in which the religious affiliation of the woman must be adjusted to suit that of the male prior to the wedding, J/A also explores, uniquely, the meaning of "ordinary" family life once this adjustment had been made. What happens, then, when a woman not related to the groom's family in any way whatsoever joins a quarrelsome clan, in this case the founding family of Judaism?

In spite of many elements familiar from ancient Hellenistic romances, not the least narratives of endless trials and tribulations of the heroine before her reunification with her beloved, J/A displays many disquieting features.[37] Its two protagonists have to surmount not the objections of parents and relatives but the impediment of the disparity of cult. And although Aseneth ventures on a long and arduous journey it is accomplished within the narrow confines of her own room rather than across lands and continents, as the heroines of the novels invariably do.[38] Nor is it precisely clear what Aseneth "converts" to from "idolatry" as she seeks to become a worthy bride for Joseph.[39] How does her incorporation into Jacob's family impact familial structures and configurations?

Like the MT Esther, J/A features a beautiful and determined young woman faced with a crisis of identity. In J/A the crisis is self-generated. In both, the heroine's wits, rather than her beauty, are put to the test, as well as her commitment to her past familial links. But J/A is also a sentimental tale of forbidden love, while the MT Esther is not. Esther's sentiments toward her husband or herself were left out of the Hebrew version. Her personal salvation is closely linked with the fate of her people. Aseneth's inner turmoil forms the nucleus of the story and her path to salvation is individual and personal. Her religious identity requires adjustment in order to legitimize her marriage with Joseph the Jew and the position of her children in Israelite history. That of Ahasuerus was not easily adjusted. He had to remain in a position of power and hence, gentile.

As it stands, the story of Joseph and Aseneth is composed of two tales, somewhat uneasily juxtaposed, each reaching a different climax. The first (1–21), and by far the most discussed section of the work, takes place within the domestic confines of Pentephres' domain. It narrates the stormy meeting between Joseph and Aseneth at the home of her parents. She had just rejected her father's idea of marrying her off to Joseph, but then, upon the merest first glance, found herself in love with him and ready to become even his slave. Dismayed by his rejection of her dazzling persona Aseneth willed a curious metamorphosis that involved an angelic being who guided her along an unseen path from polytheism to monotheism, and from idolatry to Joseph's creed. Interspersed with lengthy soliloquies and with dialogues between Aseneth and that elusive divine creature, the first part of J/A inexorably moves toward its happy conclusion with Joseph's acceptance the "new" Aseneth as a worthy bride. The second part (22–29) of J/A assigns a prominent role to the most determined of Aseneth's rejected suitors, the son of the Pharaoh himself. Deciding to get rid of Aseneth's husband so that he could marry the widow, this man launched a scheme that involved conspiracy, betrayal, and abduction. But true to character, the story provides last-minute help for the abducted Aseneth in the shape of Levi and Shimon, Joseph's two brothers, and the couple was once more reunited.

What saves J/A from utter banality is its curious shift of emphasis from the self-vowed virginity of both heroes to a commitment to married life through a unique experience of "conversion." Neither Greek romances nor Christian tales of sexual renunciation with which J/A has been compared, nor any other genre, experience, or sect that have been adduced as keys to the J/A context, provide instructive parallels.[40] The heroines of the romances do their mighty best to preserve their virginity for the man they love and eventually marry; those of Christian hagiography spend a lifetime recovering a lost sense of primordial virginity. Aseneth's sexual integrity is never called into question before her marriage. The issue at stake in J/A is not the heroine's bodily state but her state of mind.

J/A appears to suggest that only by overcoming the impediment of cultic disparity is a union between a man and a woman of different religious affiliation possible. But what about her family of origin and the place of religion in their lives? In a monologue lamenting her fate,[41] Aseneth points out the isolation of a proselyte whose renunciation of faith also entails the severance of family, communal, and social ties.[42] A rebirth as an appropriate bride required the woman to become an orphan (J/A 12), precisely the point at which Esther begins her own career. Aseneth's metamorphosis, with its puzzling images of the "man from heaven," the honeycomb, and the bees,[43] implies that conversion is a self-generated and self-accomplished process. J/A provides no formal external procedure for foreigners who desire to join the community out of love for one of its members.

Aseneth's new identity is never clearly defined. She becomes a "city of refuge."[44] Perhaps the term was intended to convey her potential to transmit her new identity to a large number of "citizens." In the course of her transformation she retains and acquires two associations, virginity and guardianship (of her "city"). Her new persona, then, embraces both males and females just as a city does. In the end, however, Aseneth fails to act as her very own "city of refuge," reverting to her ordinary human guise that requires male protection. She becomes another Dinah rather than an Esther.

In her summary of her own life, articulated in the form of a prayer on the eve of her wedding (and contained in one family of manuscripts), Aseneth recaptures her spiritual journey from an "arrogant and boastful virgin" to a mate worthy of "Joseph the powerful one of God" (21, Burchard). The monologue recalls a Hellenic wedding song, the *hymenaios*. By one interpretation the *hymenaios* conveyed expressions of regret and longing for Hymenaeus, a viginal state in an imminent loss.[45] It reflected a somber aspect of the wedding festivities as it anticipated the departure of the god (Hymenaeus) who symbolized virginity. Aseneth combines in her final prayer for repentance the history of her intact body and a lament for its impure state of the past. Perhaps a deliberate authorial reversal of Greek customs may be suspected in J/A's borrowing of a wedding song to achieve a wholly different purpose.

The first and main part of Joseph and Aseneth is, like the Esther story, a tale of a heroine whose commitment to her people (Esther) and to her faith (Aseneth) is tested through the mirror of a sexual encounter with a man of different creed and milieu. The second part of J/A tests the acceptability of the match by Aseneth's society of origin and by Joseph's family. It depicts an ardent suitor whose passion had not abated and brothers-in-law who were quite willing to help him with murder and abduction. It also recasts Genesis 34 so as to make Shimon and Levi once more the avengers of the family's honor, this time with the gratitude of the abductor's parent.[46] But it also, finally, provides a justification for Aseneth's title of a "city of refuge" by assigning to her the role of a mediator between the warring factions in Joseph's family.

In this picture of married life Joseph is surprisingly absent while his devoted wife undergoes a series of trials and tribulations. Pharaoh's son, who is still evidently in love with Aseneth, plans her abduction with the help of two of Joseph's own brothers. Other brothers, however, display their affinity with Joseph by extricating the abducted Aseneth from the hands of her abductor and their valor by killing thousands of men in the process. In the end, Aseneth becomes a peace broker as she mediates familial harmony among Joseph's strife-torn folk.

Joseph and Aseneth provides insights into two models of family life, Egyptian and patriarchal, each based on marital and credal harmony. The two couples, Aseneth's parents on the one hand and the newlyweds, also relate to different legal cultures. Aseneth's father, a priest, is usually presented with his wife at his side, whether the two are at home, preparing for a guest, or in the fields, tilling their land. She is first seen returning home from the field "of their inheritance," namely property owned by both with, it seems, equal rights of usufruct.[47] From this common heritage the parents bestow fruit on their daughter (4.3), thus supporting her decision to remain in her tower rather than to help them with estate management. As they move between the house, where the daughter is enclosed, to the open field, the parents also witness the mutation of her romance and its happy ending (20.5). Aseneth considers the parental field her own heritage and apparently keeps a watchful eye over it even when married to Joseph.[48] By then, her parents had disappeared from the narrative.

Throughout, Aseneth's mother, wife of Pentephres, remains nameless and voiceless although she is a sharer in the family's duties of hospitality and in the responsibilities of managing properties. The omission is striking. The only female voice actually heard is that of Aseneth. In the crucial dialogues that deal with marriage for Aseneth, only father and daughter participate but the silent presence of the wife/mother is easily inferred. Thus when Joseph's approaching visit had been announced, it was the father who broached to the daughter the subject of marriage, but the mother was right there beside her.[49] And when Joseph agreed, not without a good deal of persuasion on the part of Pentephres, to meet Aseneth, it was the mother who fetched her from her room. Aseneth addresses her father as a "master,"[50] but neither talks nor, obviously, uses such respectful terminology toward her mother. The relationship between mother and daughter, like that between wife and husband in Pentephres' household, is, perhaps, taken for granted. But what legalities did these reflect?

A significant measure of spousal equality may be deduced not only from references to community of property but also to the ubiquitous, if silent, presence of the mother. By endowing Aseneth with a mother the author of J/A took a curious liberty with the biblical text. It may be asked why was a mother a necessary feature of the narrative, all the more since the text sealed her lips. Biblical images of non-Israelite women range from a silent maid, like Hagar, to an outgoing queen, like Jezebel. Among Egyptian women one encounters a daughter of Pharaoh who becomes a wife of King Solomon and a princess who saves an exposed Hebrew baby. None could have been harnessed, even by way of a literary flight of fancy, as a predecessor of the shadowy wife of Pentephres, mother of the rebellious Aseneth. Whatever role the mother played in the family, the most dynamic relationship in the Egyptian family of J/A is that between father and daughter. Pentephres appears bent on finding the best possible match for his beautiful daughter who is, apparently, his only child. He wants her to marry above class and rank. She aims even higher as she rejects the idea of marriage with an eminent official and proposes instead, at least according to one version, to marry the "king's firstborn son."[51]

Aseneth's behavior toward her father is extraordinary by both social and legal criteria. His reaction is equally unusual for he elects to say nothing whatsoever in response to her indignant rejection of marriage with Joseph. When Joseph appears, the father forges a link between the visitor and the family by presenting his daughter as a "sister" of Joseph. Such liberality in the use of familial terminology is well attested, for example, in the Aramaic private letters from the Elephantine archives in Egypt where fathers were addressed as "my lord," precisely the way in which Aseneth first addressed her father,[52] and wives were often called "sisters" or vice versa.[53] And although the conversation is primarily carried between males during Joseph's visit, Joseph's reply addresses both father and mother.[54] When Joseph and Aseneth meet face to face, it is Pentephres who initiates the ritual of hospitality with a call upon his daughter to kiss her "brother."[55]

Perhaps the most peculiar of these pictures of days in the life of an Egyptian family is the one that concludes the first part of the tale. Aseneth, in the absence of both her parents, undergoes a transformative experience. They were evidently still away when Joseph comes back to their home to reenact his first meeting with Aseneth in a diametrically opposed fashion. Instead of rejecting her welcoming kiss he stretches out his hands and embraces her (19); she then invites him into the house; the guest seats himself in her father's seat and orders her maids about; Aseneth volunteers for the menial task of washing his feet, and the couple exchanges kisses (20.1–3). This is the vision that meets the eyes of Aseneth's parents when they return home from their country estate. Nor are they surprised but, in fact, rather elated. After all, Pentephres suggested the match long before. Then the two men discuss formalities with regard to the giving of the bride. Mother and daughter do not appear involved in this discussion, nor is their voice heard when Joseph virtuously states that he will not sleep with his intended bride before their marriage.[56]

When the dutiful Joseph further informs his royal employer of his plan to marry, the king summons daughter and father to the palace, but not the mother (21.1). The couple kisses once more, this time under the eyes of the Pharaoh, who proceeds to give a wedding banquet of seven days. The author of J/A then recorded the first sexual intercourse between Joseph and Aseneth, now married presumably according to Egyptian law, and the prompt birth of their two sons. Whether Aseneth's mother attended the wedding was not disclosed.

The second familial model, that of Joseph and Aseneth, assigns to the woman, both before and after her marriage, a highly prominent place. To be functional, however, this model requires adjustment. Compatibility of creed forms the foundation of this second model but its viability depends on the way in which the wife navigates between members of the groom's clan. Without outrightly rejecting intermarriage, the text insists on conversion of sorts as an indispensable preliminary to any workable alliance between a Jew and a gentile-turned-proselyte. In the absence of shared origins, J/A proposes an intimacy of sexual relations based on shared creed.

What is immediately discernible about the relationship between Aseneth and Joseph is her degree of independence. Having selected her man, she negotiates the terms of the marriage and presents her parents with a fait accompli. In Joseph's family she develops a particularly close relationship with Levi, one of her brothers-in-law who "used to read (letters written in heaven) and interpret them to Aseneth privately."[57] The couple itself is never seen in marital intimacy. They converse once, when Aseneth announces rather than discusses her decision to visit her country estate.[58] Uncharacteristically, she is also made to express fear of traveling alone. Neither wifely apprehension nor the dangers in store for travelers are sufficient to deter Joseph from other plans. But he sends her on her journey with his younger brother, Benjamin, for protection. As readers could guess, Aseneth had ample reason to express anxiety. On her way she is abducted by an erstwhile suitor with the aid of her own brothers-in-law. Her presence, then, in Joseph's family brings discord rather than harmony. In the end, she becomes a mediator of peace, effecting a reconciliation between members of her husband's kin.

Aseneth's children, whose birth is duly recorded, play no role whatsoever in the narrative involving their parents. And while readers become intimately acquainted with Aseneth, first as a virgin bride and then as a wife, Aseneth as a mother remains outside the scope of the narrative. The only motherly figure is that of her own mother.

Since the tale ostensibly takes place in Egypt, it may be asked how the legal cultures of the families depicted in J/A fit into its allegedly biblical framework. The answer is simple—they do not. The relationships that J/A envisaged between Pentephres and his wife as a couple, and between them and their daughter, have no parallel in biblical narratives. And although Aseneth was compared with Sarah, Rebecca, and Rachel, in other words, with Joseph's mother, grandmother, and great-grandmother, it is clear that none of these matriarchs provided a model for Aseneth. On the other hand, the apparent progression from a dutiful and silent wife, such as Aseneth's mother, to a self-willed woman, such as Aseneth, reflects legal developments in Achaemenid and Hellenistic Egypt.

The archives of the island of Elephantine provide invaluable testimony regarding family and conjugal relations in Egypt over several centuries, from the sixth century B.C.E. to Byzantine Egypt in the early seventh century C.E. Both Aramaic (Jewish) and demotic papyri reflect the considerable interest of the bride's family in the welfare of the daughter after her marriage. A demotic papyrus dated to 537 B.C.E. is instructive:

Said the boatman of the bad water Hapertais, son of Djedhor and Taiounakhetou his mother, to the lady Tshenyah, daughter of Pankherei and Tetiseped, her mother. I made you wife in the year. . . . The children whom you will bear to me are the sharers with my children [of previous marriage] of everything which belongs to me together with that which I will acquire, together with the goods of father and mother. If I leave you, I will give you [money and grain].[59]

The prospective bride and groom are identified through both parents, but this could have been legal usage only. Paternal concerns to safeguard the financial interests of the wife and her children in cases of both death and divorce are evident. What is of particular interest is the designation of the man's inheritance as one belonging to both his father and his mother, precisely the way in which the property of Aseneth's parents is presented in J/A. Paternal interests in the future financial security of their daughters is also reflected in a demotic document of 510 B.C.E. in which a father recorded the transfer of his own stipend to his daughter in order to ensure her hold over it even after his death, when the property was to be divided between his son and his daughter: "No man in the world, apart from you, whether father, mother, brother, sister, son, daughter, master, mistress, will be able to exercise control over [the share]."[60] This would have been property that the daughter would retain as hers, whether married, single, or divorced. And this was indeed the case for Aseneth who evidently regarded her parental heritage as hers alone.

Jewish matrimonial contracts of the fifth century B.C.E. from the same locality reflect a similar legal culture. In the family of Mahseiah the father was likewise solicitous of securing the welfare of the daughters, particularly in case of several marriages and, potentially, several claimants, whether husbands or ex-husbands. Mahseiah's father left her a house and its attached land in contemplation of death and with the proviso that no other person could stake a claim to the same property, either in the lifetime of its owner or after his death.[61] In other words, the exclusive right of the daughter over all other potential inheritors, including male members of the father's family, was the deciding factor, even in the case of contestants. This property was, moreover, to be inherited by the daughter's children. The father further stated that he was not going to change his mind, reclaim the property, and hand it over to another:

> The land is yours. Build and/or give it to whomever you love. If tomorrow or the next day I bring against you suit or process and say: "I did not give it to you." I shall give you silver without suit and without process. And the house is your house likewise.[62]

Since the daughter, Mibtahiah, married several times, the precautions proved indispensable. In fact, the father repeated the exclusive rights of his daughter in a document that granted one of these sons-in-law the right to enjoy the usufruct of this property without, however, gaining legal possession over it.[63] When improvements to the house had been introduced at the husband's expense, the latter had the right to gain adequate compensation in case of divorce.

If the Elephantine documents reflect, to a remarkable degree, the legal culture of J/A, the one glaring divergence relates to the marital negotiations. Taken literally, Aseneth and Joseph negotiated their own marriage settlement after she had approached him. In none of the surviving documents was such a direct form of negotiations sanctified before 200 B.C.E. Whatever may have been the reality behind the legalities of the law of the papyri, the hand of a woman, even if widowed, had to be sought from her father, although an adoptive brother could also act as a sponsor. Yet, as a Greek matrimonial contract of the year 310 B.C.E. demonstrates, the voice of the couple itself was beginning to be heard from the day of their nuptials:

Herakleides, a free man, takes Demetria, a free woman as his legitimate wife from her father and from her mother. She is to bring clothing and jewelry. Let him provide Demetria with everything pertaining to a free wife. We (Demetria and Herakleides) shall reside in the same place which the father [of the bride] and Herakleides, deciding together and in joint decision, choose.[64]

A century later, a demotic text reflects one step forward as the bridegroom was directly addressing the bride over the exact inventory of the goods she had brought to the marriage and to which she remained entitled in case of divorce.[65] No longer did a father figure appear as the mediator between his daughter and her future husband. Surprisingly, perhaps, J/A seems to record precisely this transition from the critical role of a father, or a close male relative, in any marital arrangement to that of direct dealings between bride and groom on the eve of the wedding.[66]

Historians of ancient Egypt also remark that from as early as the sixth century B.C.E., the Egyptian woman's own consent was necessary for marriage, at least formally.[67] And while Egyptian sentiments placed a high value on harmonious and faithful marriage, the law did not grant the males the power that classical Greek law, for example, gave to fathers and husbands over daughters and wives. The theme of honor and shame, so prominent in the second part of "Joseph and Aseneth," did not play any role, although an injured husband could pursue a wife's lover at law. There is also no evidence for the use of matchmakers in Egypt, nor is it easy to determine the degree of parental control over the marital choice of their children.

The juridical culture of Hellenistic Egypt, perhaps the temporal context of J/A, was based on a double heritage, Egyptian and Greek. At the law courts both Greek and local laws were applied. But other communities had their own set of legal guidelines as well. The Septuagint, or the Greek Torah, became a sort of civic law (*nomos politikos*) applicable to the Jews of Egypt modified, it may be assumed, by local Jewish customs.[68] And this is, precisely, where the "Jewishness" of J/A is particularly apparent. Although our information on mixed marriages between various population groups in Greco-Roman Egypt is limited, it has been recently argued that the Hellenistic era favored the endogamic tendencies of Greek matrimonial law.[69] But in no case was disparity of cult attested as a matrimonial impediment. In this, Judaism and J/A remain the exception.

Taken in conjunction with the Hebrew Esther, J/A provides an extended commentary on the effects of (inter)marriage and on the presumed functions of a married woman. Neither text casts its heroine primarily as a wife, and both avoid depicting either woman as a mother. Relationships with males other than the husbands form a dominant subtext. To seek, then, a wifely role model in either Esther the Jewess or in Aseneth the proselyte would have been a vain quest. Nor does the marriage of Esther and the king, and of Aseneth and Joseph, depict an ideal state of matrimonial bliss. Aseneth and Esther share their most intimate moments with men other than their wedded husbands. The former owes the preservation of her marital chastity to her brothers-in-law, while Esther owes her own survival in a difficult marriage to her wit and charm. Whatever form of Judaism either Esther or J/A advances, and neither is clear on the subject, the protagonists are identified as members of a community that sees itself as Jewish, and whose marital microcosm emphasizes the discord rather than the harmony that the incorporation of women into their family of marriage entails.[70]

PART II

VISIONS OF RABBINIC ORDER

4

Keeping Adultery at Bay

The Wayward Wife in Late Antiquity

Theologies and Theories of Sexuality: Roman and Rabbinic Perspectives

In the Decalogue no less than two commandments deal, apparently, with adultery. One forbids it, sweepingly stating "thou shalt not commit adultery" (Exod. 20:15).[1] The foundational chart of Judaism also makes it clear that the burden of contemplating adultery lies squarely on male shoulders: "Thou shall not covet the wife of your friend" (Exod. 20:17), together with his other possessions.[2] The Hebrew Bible provides a major deterrent to potential adultery by subjecting suspected adulteresses to a public ordeal (Num. 5, and below). Paradoxically, perhaps, it is a married woman, and not a man, who is cast in the act of covertly craving a body outside the marriage bed.[3] When Jewish men lust, it is after God and not after mortal women.[4]

When did this shift of blame and responsibility occur? Had husbands failed to take care of their belongings? These are not idle questions. They touch at the heart of Jewish perceptions of female-male relations, of the image of the married woman and, above all, of the biblical, postbiblical, and rabbinic concretization of the sacred bond between Israel and God in heterosexual terms.[5] Within this framework the emphasis on wifely fidelity reflects the centrality of the conviction that the issuing from a single seed, be it all Jews out of Abraham's, or Jewish males (and females) out of legitimate paternal seeds, is a primary tenet of belonging.[6] The sacred bond of marriage and of the conjugal act are, therefore, fragments of a larger canvas that excludes unfaithful women. "The body is the multiplier of the divine image as long as the child's mother is the child's father's wife, as long as he can be recognized as the child of a man who was his mother's husband."[7]

Considerable effort was invested in the Hebrew Bible in preventing extramarital liaisons by prescribing an ordeal that women suspected of adultery had to undergo (Num. 5:11–31). At its conclusion the suspicious husband who had initiated the procedure and witnessed it was "cleansed of sin" (Num. 5:31), as though his wife's trial and tribulations had acted as an exonerating agent.[8] A woman who had failed the test led subsequently a life apart from the community, branded forever with infamy; the one who passed it was ready to fall pregnant. Ordeals of this sort, in which the body of a woman was subjected to a test of purity and impurity, enabled a body of men to enact in a specific way based on specific beliefs, and permitted communities to impose settlements on disputes that threatened to lead to dissension.[9] Notable is the absence of a third party from the biblical ordeal—there is no lover, actual or putative.

The biblical ordeal revolves on the application of (bitter) water as an instrument that facilitates the recognition and identification of genuine adulteresses.[10] The centrality of water in determining the quality of male-female sexual relations is echoed in the Mishnaic tractate dealing with marital obligations (*ketubbot*). According to the rabbis the basis of a valid marital contract is the husbandly assumption that the woman with whom one is contracting matrimony is approaching the marriage bed in an intact state of virginity. Yet, the possibility of discovering the opposite had not eluded the rabbis. Thus a situation in which a husband seeks arbitration as soon as he realizes that he had been "cheated" is envisaged. But the issue is not as simple as a broken hymen, for the fresh wife can state that "No sooner you betrothed me I was raped. Your field had been flooded" (M Ket. 1.6). To which her affronted spouse may reply: "This is not the case at all. Rather, it happened before I betrothed you (and not after) and hence I got a bad bargain" (ibid.).[11] With such contrasting and unprovable testimonies the rabbis pondered not on the prescription of an appropriate ordeal for the wife with compromised virginity but on the question of trust. In the recorded rabbinic debate two authorities believed the woman; one, however, claimed that her word had no validity unless she furnished proof of her assertion. The nature of this evidence is left out of the discussion, as is the existence of a presumed lover.

Suspicions of illicit sex or adultery and unreported rape, then, exposed a husband to the same perils that threatened a farmer who observed, helplessly, his precious field flooded with the equally precious but also pernicious commodity of water.[12] Metaphors that assimilated female bodies with fields have a long history in the predominantly agricultural ancient world, as Plutarch's "Advice on Marriage" (*Coniugalia praecepta*, late first/early second century C.E.) shows:

> The most sacred of all sowings is the marital sowing and ploughing for the procreation of children. It is a beautiful epithet which Sophocles applied to Aphrodite when he called her "bountiful-bearing Cytherea." Therefore man and wife ought especially to indulge in this with circumspection, keeping themselves pure from all unholy and unlawful intercourse with others, and not sowing seed from which they are unwilling to have any offspring.[13]

Mishnaic discussions of potential confrontation between a man and a woman over the question of her bodily integrity use earth and water as marriage metaphors of plenty and scarcity and of guilt and innocence. A well-watered field is an ideal landscape that, in due course, yields fruit; a flooded one spells disaster. The biblical "bitter water" was believed to have the power of revealing the concealed. But at the heart of the problem, as the rabbis had seen, rests an unresolved issue—while the loss of virginity was an uncontested fact, the question of timing remained unsolved. In the absence of a third party a resolution ultimately revolved on mutual trust. Less straightforward, however, was a scenario that depicted a husband who suspected his wife of adultery after he had cohabited with her for a while, without having proof of her misdemeanor.

Rabbinic theology of sexuality regarded the pure conjugal union as an actualization of the descent of the divine presence between two partners.[14] One rabbi is reported to say that the Holy One "has greater affection for fruitfulness and increase than for the Temple," perhaps an unlikely comparison, yet a powerful metaphor for the sacred ground that brings men and women together in an act of begetting.[15] Nurtured on such discernment rabbinic rules on sexual conduct, and especially on suspected adultery, mirror the isolation of sex as a discrete area for discussion and regulation.[16] The process of "disembedding sex" from other types of human relationships is clearly reflected in the isolation imposed on a woman who is believed to have fractured the legitimacy of her marital bed.[17]

Both Roman law and rabbinic rulings devote considerable space to the legalities of adultery in general and of suspected adultery in particular. Such attention illustrates how the authorities shifted the codes of honor and shame from their traditional family context to the public, initiating thereby a new discourse of identity in which affiliation, particularly of women, with society was based on compliance with prescribed sexual preferences and performances.[18] Comparisons between Roman and rabbinic legal perspectives in late antiquity on detecting suspected adulteresses are extremely instructive, particularly from the beginning of the third century C.E., when Jewesses are also Roman citizens with the right of appeal from rabbinic arbitrators to Roman courts.[19] In the Roman and rabbinic "commonwealth of fathers" the correct deportment of a woman mirrored the "sanctity of the house and hearth" and by implication the orderliness of society itself.[20] Underlying this ideology is the belief that the soundness of the domicile reflects on the well-being of society, as though a man whose wife is capable of betraying him is, by extension, incapable of governing his fellow men. Adultery in this context meant not only the invasion of one's body and one's domicile but also the violation of the norms that governed the relationship between men.[21]

To conform to the Roman cultural model of masculinity and authority a noble woman, like Lucretia, whose sexual and marital integrity was compromised against her will, had to commit suicide (see Chapter 1).[22] Her death, caused by (forced) adultery, was reckoned the force that ushered in a revolution. This was the tale that encoded in Roman memory the demise of the monarchy and the establishment of the republic around 500 B.C.E. Its popularity in Augustan Rome (31 B.C.E.–14 C.E.), some five centuries later, demonstrates the sway that the notion of intimate links between private and public, the body of a woman and the body politic, continued to exert over Rome's ruling classes.

Lawmakers, however, could hardly expect women and men who committed adultery, willingly or unwillingly but without being caught redhanded, to commit suicide. Theoretically, at least, an extramarital affair could have ended on a happy rather than a sour note, especially if all parties subscribed to the idea that "good is what does good to the largest number, and with which the largest number are pleased."[23] This is precisely the message of the greatest play ever written by Machiavelli (*Mandragola*). The farce, clearly based on the Roman tale of Lucretia, recasts the virtuous matron as an equally upright Florentine woman married not to a Roman noble but to a foolish and aged lawyer. Behind the inevitable tale of adultery lies not a wager between drunken men in the middle of war but the ardent desire of the husband to have a son and heir, and the equal eagerness of another man to provide for it. Both women, the ancient Lucretia and her Machiavellian counterpart and namesake, become objects of passion of a man who is not their wedded husband without their knowledge or collusion. In Machiavelli's play the lover enters the house with the husband's consent and proceeds to the woman's bed after she had drunk a potion that was meant to ensure conception. She, unlike the Roman Lucretia but like Meir of the midrash (above, Introduction), appears to be under the influence of the elixir. Her husband, having discreetly withdrawn for fear of dying since he had been led to believe that the first man to have intercourse with his wife right after she takes the drink would die, obligingly makes room for another in the marital bed. The lover enters the house to realize the fulfillment of his fantasy. All this takes place with the help of a mediator, a friend of the young lover who provides him with the love beverage and with advice on how to win the hearts of chaste married matrons and the confidence of their gullible husbands. In the end everyone gets what they wanted, or seems to. The husband gets the heir he had so desired; the young man's desire is reciprocated; and Lucretia can look to a future in which the death of one husband paves the way to marriage with another.

Unlikely as the plot appears, Roman law assigned considerable space to a discourse of the "husband-pimp" (*leno*), a man who profits from his wife's adultery, ignores her meandering, and even provides a venue for them.[24] In Machiavelli's hands Lucretia, the model of Roman virtue, becomes a woman whose marital loyalty can be easily compromised. But she is also not entirely responsible for her changed conduct. Between a husband besotted with the production of an heir, an ardent lover keen on conquest, a love potion, and a canny adviser, she has little chance. Such ever-present female vulnerability or fickleness, depending on the point of view, appears to have inspired Roman and rabbinic reflections on the suspicious adulteress.[25]

Machiavelli's *Mandragola* presents a cheated husband who elects to live in happy ignorance of his wife's infidelity. But this was an option that the state could not condone. Roman law attempted to address the issue of husbandly collusion through a series of laws that degraded the husband into a "pimp."[26] The emperor Augustus (late first century B.C.E.), whose family legislation intended to regulate sexual behavior in the microcosm of the (noble) Roman household, promoted an agenda of prevention of misconduct through a rhetoric of discipline and harmony.[27] From the first century C.E. onward Christian theologians advanced a marital ideology that espoused chastity within marriage to the extent of extolling sexual renunciation among the married.[28] *Porneia*, fornication or the manifestation of an illicit desire for another's body, became a measure of human weakness.[29] Rabbinic views of sexuality deplored male (and female) abstinence, but the lavish attention paid to issues of purity and impurity in the domains of the body, the community, and the ritual, contributed to a rigorous search for the elusive identity of women who transgressed the boundaries of the permissible.[30]

Between Dinah and Esther, Cozbi and Aseneth, stretched a nebulous region of negativity where a Jewess should not tread. In Roman Palestine, where the descendants of biblical redactors and interpreters dwelt, the spectacle of Roman law inspired Jewish legal compilations that still affect the shape of Judaism. No discussion of the making of Jewesses can, therefore, be complete without a brief excursion into the domain of rabbinic legal reflections. The image of a Jewess in the Mishnah and the Talmuds (Palestinian and Babylonian) stands on biblical shoulders. Indeed, it is incomprehensible without the biblical precedents discussed in the previous chapters. But the rabbis who pondered and prescribed models of feminine conduct were part of a different legal and geopolitical reality. There is no full understanding, I suspect, of the engendering of rabbinic Jewesses in Jewish law or of the elevation of the rhetoric of sexual morality in late antiquity without constant reference to late Roman law. In this chapter I deal with the epitome of negativity, the *sotah* or the woman who is suspected of having sex with a man other than her husband.

In what amounts to a sustained probe into the domicile, Roman law and rabbinic rulings in late antiquity attempted to redraw the landscape of female identity within marriage by detecting suspected adulteresses. The procedures established for detecting adulteresses provide a useful measurement of how society defined its matrons, be they Jewesses or the Roman *materfamilias*. While the discussion of Roman law may appear straightforward, the precise scope, authority and applicability of rabbinic rulings is unclear. By focusing on biblical law that had lost its historical reference point it has been assumed that rabbinic discussions were purely theoretical and that Jewish law was an abstract construct.[31] But this is hardly the case. In fact, the similarities between Roman and rabbinic legal reflections point to a culture of law in which two legal discourses converged to deter and, if necessary, prosecute and punish women suspected of adultery.

Suspecting Adultery

Caught in the act, adultery seemingly presented no problem to ancient legislators as they visited death upon the unfortunate participants.[32] A husband or a father was allowed to kill with impunity the lover and the wife/daughter. Yet, the freedom to kill was not granted without restrictions. The (Roman) state's dispensation of murder to irate male relatives, especially to fathers and husbands of the women concerned, was counterbalanced by specific requirements calculated to act as deterrents.[33] And there was also the chance that the killer would be sued for murder. More complicated yet was the issue of proving a case in which the lovers were not caught in flagrante delicto and witnesses were unavailable. Both Jewish and Roman jurists evinced considerable interest in detecting genuine adulteresses.[34] So similar in some aspects and so detailed is their quest for establishing the identity of the female transgressor in late antiquity that comparisons are inevitable.[35] In fact, the similarities as well as the divergences of Roman and Jewish legal opinions on the crime of adultery invite further probe into possible mutual influences, as well as into the social and economic context that embedded both rabbinic and Roman expressions.[36]

Virtually all modern discussions of adultery in Jewish law have focused on the so-called ordeal of the bitter water, a multistaged ritual already prescribed in the Bible (Num. 5:11–31).[37] Briefly put, a woman suspected of adultery was brought by her husband to the central sanctuary (the Temple) where the husband made a sacrifice known as the "offering of jealousy" as a priest let loose the wife's hair. The priest then administered an oath to the suspected adulteress as well as a concoction of "bitter water" meant to uncover her guilt or to assert her innocence. If she survived the ordeal and was proven innocent, she was then re-enrolled in the commonwealth and was likely to fall pregnant. If the water she drank manifested her guilt, she was doomed to become an object of perpetual public derision and condemnation. It is hardly surprising that these vague regulations generated debates and substantial commentaries which were preserved, in part, in the Mishnah and the two Talmuds.[38] Yet, most of the ancient legal experts who dealt with the issues pertaining to the ordeal had not witnessed it. According to Mishnah Sotah (M Sot.) 9.9, the ordeal was abolished some time in the course of the first century C.E.[39] Although the precise date cannot be established, the centrality of the Temple in the ritual rendered the procedure untenable after 70 C.E.[40] The dispersion of the Jewish communities in the east and the west likewise undermined the practicality of the ordeal of the bitter water in any territory but that of the land of Israel.

The question that has never been asked by modern interpreters of the history of the ordeal of the bitter water is what replaced the ordeal after its abolition.[41] In other words, what legal procedures were available to investigate and prosecute suspected adultery from the end of the first century onward? How was a wayward wife perceived and how did her suspected activities impact the environment of the society that emerged in Palestine after the destruction of the Temple? That the rabbis themselves were aware that times had changed is hinted at in their comments in the Babylonian Talmud (BT) on the credibility of the testimony of the husband concerning the alleged adultery of his wife:

Rabbi Hanina of Sura said: Nowadays a man should not say to his wife, "Do not be secluded with so-and-so," lest we decide according to Rabbi Jose son of Rabbi Judah who said: "A warning [to a wife about her suspected behavior is effective] if given on [the husband's] personal testimony. If she then secluded herself with the man, since we have not now the water for the suspected woman to test her, the husband forbids her to himself for all time. (BT Sot. 2c, Soncino)[42]

One underlying quest of this chapter is a search for the alternative that replaced the pre-70 procedures of detecting adulteresses, assuming that husbands did continue to suspect their wives of adultery and that sexual loyalty was the prime attribute of a Jewess. Since the rabbis formulated and discussed their legal theories and principles in the shade, so to speak, of Roman law, this investigation is further informed by an attempt to explore the possibility of Roman rulings on adultery providing supplements and/or substitutes for rabbinic regulations.[43]

The present discussion is embedded within a postclassical and post-Mishnaic context and draws largely on imperial pronouncements on the one hand, and on talmudic (= amoraic) opinions on the other.[44] Both Jewish and Roman legal exegesis depended on basic texts the authority of which was never doubted or challenged. Roman jurists and emperors invariably harked back to the Augustan legislation on adultery (18 B.C.E.[?] *lex Iulia de adulteriis coercendis*) while the Talmuds based their readings on both the Bible and the Mishnah. Augustus's law had not survived in its original wording. It was, however, never formally repealed and its clauses were often quoted in responses to queries that illustrate the difficulties of applying its theories to realities.[45] Underlying the Augustan adultery laws was the intention to suppress forms of socially unacceptable extramarital sexual relations by wresting arbitration in such matters from the private sphere and punishing violations, for the first time, through a trial in a standing criminal court.[46] In other words, an adulteress, a complaisant husband, and her lover, if members of the elite, became, if proven guilty, public criminals.[47] The rationale of this approach was fairly straightforward:

For many prominent men a wife married too recklessly or kept on too tolerantly has been a source of disgrace; so the loss of reputation within the household has contributed to the ruin of those who enjoyed distinction outside it, and what made it impossible for them to be deemed the greatest of citizens was the fact that they were unsuccessful as husbands.[48]

Methodologically, this study is based on the assumption that Mishnaic aspects of the ordeal of the bitter water that had not directly related to the Temple or to the priesthood did continue to have legal validity. These include preliminaries, such as warnings and witnesses, the husband as an accuser; and the involvement of an alleged lover as a third party in the proceedings.

Preliminaries: Singling Out Adulteresses

Rabbinic rulings provide information or, rather, point to a discourse regarding preliminary steps prior to a court case concerning suspected adultery. The rabbis focused attention on two issues: (1) the reason that moved a husband to accuse his wife of adultery apparently without proof of misbehavior; and (2) the manner of warning or alerting an alleged adulteress to her husband's suspicion. Roman law allowed a husband to prosecute a wife for adultery on the grounds of suspicion alone. So did Jewish. None of the surviving Roman laws, however, provides information about the reasons for such a suspicion nor for any legal or semilegal transaction, in public or in private, between the married couple prior to the court proceedings.

The rabbis who pondered on the motivation of husbands when it came to washing the home's dirty laundry in public had little help from the Scriptures. Numbers refers to "a spirit of jealousy" as an operative factor in revealing what had been concealed (5:11–14). The question the Bible appears to pose is: who could expose the crime or, rather, raise the alarm in the first place? The biblical answer of "a spirit of jealousy" implies a supernatural resource that inspired the husband with suspicion. Tannaitic authorities "translated" this elusive inspiration into a concrete legal procedure that involved a due warning issued by a suspicious husband to his suspected wife in the presence of witnesses, and thus in public (M Sot. 1.1). The requirement presents a legal novelty. What, precisely, had prompted it is unclear but the measure appears designed to prevent baseless accusations and the launching of costly procedures.[49]

So great was the importance attached to this preliminary step that the rabbis even stepped in when a husband was incapable of issuing a warning himself.[50] This was the case of a woman whose husband was deaf, insane, or imprisoned (M Sot. 4.5). The *gemara* that explicates this stipulation touches on several critical issues that illuminate underlying factors in cases of suspected adultery. One such is the desirability of issuing a warning in every instance of suspicion (BT Sot. 25a). Another is the existence of a possible contradiction between court actions (when the husband was deemed incapable) and the presumed will of the husband concerned (BT Sot. 25b). A third is the possibility of a husband's change of heart. In the last case the rabbis had to determine whether the retraction was legally valid (BT Sot. 25b). No resolution was offered in either the second or the third instance other than a general observation to the effect that most husbands would tend to comply with the requirements of a court of law (BT Sot. 25c).

If the sources cited in the Mishnah agreed on the necessity to issue a preliminary warning to an alleged adulteress, the brief Mishnaic allusion generated a lengthy debate which focused on the number of witnesses that had to be used and on the validity of the husband's own testimony. One underlying concern of the debate appears to have been a desire to discern a genuine accusation from a false one.

Resh Lakish said: "What is the meaning of the term 'kinui' ('jealousy,' Num. 5:14)? A matter that introduces hatred between her and others." Consequently he holds that the warning can be [valid] on [the husband's] own testimony. And since not everybody knows that he gave her a warning they say: "What has happened that she separates herself [from others], proceeding to cause hatred against her?" Rabbi Jemar ben Shelemia said in the name of Rabbi Abbaye: "[Kinui means] a matter that introduces hatred between a couple." Consequently he holds that the warning must be [valid only] on the testimony of two witnesses and that everybody should be aware that he issued her a warning. (BT Sot. 2c, Soncino, slightly modified)

Palestinian rabbis struggled with many side issues that arose from the proper implementation of the warning.

[What is, then, the rule about the husband's own testimony?] Does everything depend on him, namely he can warn her in the presence of two witnesses and then assert that she went secretly [with the named man], and as a result to invalidate her right to collect her marriage settlement? Rabbi Yosi said: "Why does she need to hide in the first place?" But this comment is irrelevant. [What matters is] whether everything depends [on the husband's testimony when he asserts] that he has warned with his own mouth and then claims that she went secretly [with the named man] and [on this basis the law court] invalidates her right to collect her marriage settlement. (PT Sot. 1:1, 7b-d)[51]

The first passage provides a rare insight into the effects of a warning conducted in private. The frightened woman, it seems, was driven to shun the entire neighborhood raising thereby even more speculations about her behavior. In both passages the bone of contention is the validity of a warning administered and acted upon by the husband alone. A majority of the rabbis held that even at this early stage of suspicion alone the husband was required to use a witness, and preferably two. One rabbinic assumption was that the husband himself must be above suspicion, not so much in sexual matters as in general uprightness, although the rabbis did not lull themselves into believing that all husbands who were willing to expose their wives' alleged transgressions to the public were themselves invariably innocent of a similar type of behavior.[52]

Several other features of this preliminary step are noteworthy. The warning is directed against an association with a specific man, but it was issued to the suspected wife and not to the alleged lover. The point is significant for this is precisely the aspect that Roman jurists would later consider in their modifications of the Augustan legislation on adultery, reaching a conclusion diametrically opposed to the rabbinic regulation (below). The precise aim of publicizing a husbandly suspicion of adultery remains speculative. One possible answer is that it was meant as a deterrent since the woman was observed by others and presumably had to watch her own steps. But another possibility is that by broadcasting the suspicion the rabbis also prepared the ground for an eventual court case. The latter gains some support from the discussion concerning the law of evidence with regard to a violation of the warning. A husband who wished to divorce his wife on the basis of alleged adultery and to retain her dowry had to base his case on eyewitnesses at both the preliminary stage of warning and at the stage of observing and reporting a transgression. The elaborate discussions of the value of the husband's testimony, when unsupported by witnesses, illustrate the problems entailed in unraveling the early phases of suspected adultery.

Once a warning was issued in the presence of witnesses, it was necessary to determine whether it was subsequently disregarded. A related matter was the resultant nature of the relationship between a suspecting husband and his suspected wife. Rabbinic authorities linked wifely defiance of the warning against association with another man with the continuance of marital intimacy:

> Said Abbaye: By "do not converse with him" (which she flouted) by talking, and by "do not talk to him" (which she flaunted by) concealment, it is meant that this is still nothing. "Do not be concealed with him" and she did talk to him does not make her forbidden to her husband. . . . If she entered with him [i.e., an alleged lover] a house in secret and stayed long enough to commit impurity she is forbidden to her husband. (BT Sot. 5b)

The essence of a transgression is determined, then, by location, circumstances of association, and time. An important component in deciding whether sexual intimacy did take place depended on the rabbis' personal views regarding the temporal frame of sexual intercourse.

> What is a measure of concealment? It is measured in the time necessary to effect an impurity, intercourse, incest[?], or encircling a palm tree, according to Rabbi Ishmael. According to Rabbi Eliezer it is the time required to pour a drink. Rabbi Joshua said that (the time in question is that sufficient) to drink it. According to Ben Azzai (it is the period necessary) to boil an egg; Rabbi Akiva to swallow it; Rabbi Juda ben Bathira to swallow three eggs one after the other; . . . Yet we have not heard what precisely is the (time) measure of the concealment. . . . The question remains unanswered. . . . Each one (of the rabbis) offered a hypothesis (based on his own experience), including the unmarried Ben Azzai! (BT Sot. 4a-b, Soncino)

Whoever recorded these enchanting debates wished to highlight not only the difficulty involved in determining the length of time required to commit adultery but also, and much more so, the general disapproval of any association whatsoever between a Jewish male and a woman to whom he was not married.[53] Nor were these idle speculations for they further touched on the question of what, precisely, constituted an adultery—the mere "concealment" of a suspected couple or an actual intercourse? Talking to a man did not necessarily lead to an adultery, although the fact that such an association was even considered points to the narrow social circles in which a married woman could move.[54] An assignation in a private house (whose?), on the other hand, was clearly a measure of defiance if not of adultery itself.

The involvement of outsiders, either as witnesses or as potential accusers, in the intimacy of marital affairs had been an established feature of both rabbinic and Roman legalities on suspected adultery. In the late first century B.C.E. the emperor Augustus allowed members of the public (*extranei*), whether related to the suspected woman or not, to launch an accusation. The only limitation was that the outsiders' suit had to wait until the husband got his chance since the law reserved for him and for the woman's father the first sixty days from the date of the divorce, conferring then four months on interested parties during which they could act on suspicion of adultery.⁵⁵ Statutory time limits on prosecution for adultery played a prominent role in Roman law but were altogether absent from rabbinic rulings. On the other hand, classical and postclassical Roman law are silent on the type of preliminaries outlined by rabbinic discussions of suspected adultery.

Yet, in the sixth century, well after the redaction of the Palestinian Talmud (ca. 400), Roman legal authorities did address the issue of public admonishing of suspected adultery. In a lengthy novella of 542 C.E., one of several in which Justinian's legal advisers tried to regulate the vast complexity of late ancient family law, the emperor Justinian introduced a legal novelty. He mandated that a husband who suspected another man of having adulterous designs on his wife's chastity had to issue three written warnings to the alleged lover through three men "worthy of trust."⁵⁶ Besides rabbinic regulations I know of no other legal precedent to account for this law. The possibility that such a rule may owe its ideology to rabbinics may not be altogether discarded.⁵⁷

Several other Roman-rabbinic commonalities of pre-trial procedures and concepts can be discerned. One relates to the intentions of the parties to the suspected crime. In other words, was the wife committing adultery deliberately and willfully? The question was further linked with the woman's reputation, her social status, and the status of her children if she was pregnant at the time of the accusation (see below). As far as an admonition was concerned, a wife who disobeyed her husband's public injunctions concerning an association with an alleged lover was clearly guilty of intentional adultery. But even here the rabbis made an effort to deal with the woman's understanding of her crime, ruling that a minor, for example, could not be held accountable as an adulteress.⁵⁸ Classical Roman law defined the offense as committed only if the offender did so with malicious intent and full understanding.⁵⁹ Late Roman law ignored this aspect.

That transgressions could occur unwittingly is illustrated by a petition to the emperor submitted by a woman who married a man without realizing that he already had a wife in another province.⁶⁰ She was afraid lest she be counted an adulteress, but the emperor assured her that a married woman was not guilty of adultery if she had married in all innocence and believed herself to be the sole legitimate wife. The petition originated in Antioch and probably involved a Jewish man who acted lawfully according to Jewish law but was violating Roman law by committing bigamy. The imperial rescript authorized the second wife to appeal to the provincial governor for financial restitution (throwing an interesting light on the economic advantages of polygamy) but no clear penalty was prescribed for the male offender. If indeed he was Jewish, the case reflects a situation in which the Roman authorities exhibited certain reserve in intervening in a legal sphere which condoned polygamous practices.[61]

In his law on adultery Justinian further considered the effects of a formal warning to an alleged lover. Novella 117.15 stipulates that if subsequently that man was seen together with the married woman in question in one of the following private or public venues—her own or his house, a public eating/drinking establishment, or in the "suburbs"—the husband had the right to kill the lover with impunity. The lover's penalty reverts to Augustan provisions but the timing bears no precedents in Roman law since Justinian did not specify whether the killing was done publicly. Contacts between alleged lovers in places other than those specified required a less violent course. The husband had to summon the witnesses involved in the warning preliminaries, then hand the couple over to a judge (or ecclesiastical authorities if the couple had been seen talking in a church) for custody, and only then could he proceed to launch a formal accusation according to law.

Prior to Justinian, then, the question of the relations of suspected lovers after the wife had been observed in apparent violation of the warning had not received juristic attention. Justinian's law added a new dimension to the legal dilemma by focusing on the behavior of the alleged lover. Both systems, Roman and rabbinic, shared a concern regarding the development of a marriage in which a wife has become an object of suspicion. Roman laws, both classical and postclassical, clearly expected a severance of marital ties, since in theory, at least, a husband could not accuse his wife of adultery as long as he remained married to her. The rabbis appeared to vacillate between a temporary suspension of conjugal intimacy and an outright final separation.

The Right to Accuse: Constantinian and Rabbinic Innovations

By the fourth century C.E. the climate that generated accusations of adultery on the basis of suspicion alone was nurtured by imperial legislation that actively promoted the role of the husband as a guardian of his wife's virtue.

Emperor Constantinus Augustus to Evagrius (April 25, 326 C.E.):
Although the crime of adultery is counted among public crimes of which an accusation is commonly conceded to everyone without any other interpretation of the law, nonetheless, lest it would be allowed to all and sundry to sully marriage rashly, it is our pleasure to confer the authority to accuse on close kin and relatives, namely on the cousins and especially the step-brother and brother who are driven to accuse by real shame. . . . The husband above all ought to be the avenger of the marriage bed, since to him former emperors of olden time had granted the right to accuse his wife even on suspicion and not to be bound by the bond of inscription within the statutory time limits. We decree, however, that extraneous persons shall be barred from bringing this accusation. For although the obligations of inscription shall bind every kind of accuser, still some persons use the right of accusation wantonly and ruin marriage by false slander. (CTh 9.7.2)[62]

Thus far legal theories. How these ideologies applied to realities is illustrated by a case of which, exceptionally, we are fully informed. It took place in the north Italian city of Vercelli (or Vercella) around 370 C.E. and the reporter is the famed theologian Jerome:

When the governor of the province was holding his usual round in the city, a poor woman and her lover were brought before him and both were consigned to the penal horrors of a prison. The charge of adultery had been fastened upon them by the husband. Shortly after an attempt was made to elicit the truth by torture and when the blood-stained hook smote the young man's livid flesh and tore furrows in his side, the unhappy wretch sought to avoid prolonged pain by a speedy death. Falsely accusing his own passions, he involved another in the charge . . . leaving an innocent woman no means of self-defense. But the woman, stronger in virtue if weaker in sex, though her frame was stretched upon the rack, and though her hands, stained with the filth of the prison, were tied behind her, looked up to heaven with her eyes, which alone the torturer had been unable to bind. . . . The governor, who had been feasting his eyes on the bloody spectacle, like a wild beast . . . ordered the torture to be doubled. . . . But she has one thing to say: "Beat me, burn me, tear me, if you will. I have not done it. If you will not believe my words, a day will come when this charge shall be carefully sifted. I have One who will judge me." . . . [But], in a fit of passion the governor cried: "Why does it surprise you, bystanders, that a woman prefers torture to death? It takes two to commit adultery and I think it more credible that a guilty woman should deny a sin than that an innocent young man should confess one."

The same sentence was pronounced on both and the condemned pair was dragged to execution. The entire people poured out to see the sight. Indeed, so closely were the gates thronged by the out-rushing crowds that you might have imagined the city itself to be migrating. At the very first stroke of the sword the head of the hapless youth was cut off, and the headless trunk rolled over in its blood. Then came the woman's turn . . .[63]

These are the bare bones of a long and complex narrative which Jerome reconstructed in his very first published letter. His account provides insights into the formation of individual and communal sets of relationships as they focused on the prosecution of the crime of adultery. Through the legal perspective of establishing "the truth" and of disseminating "justice," the Vercellan affair reveals how a society constructed its private and public spaces in an environment dominated by changing sets of moral rights and wrongs, when both Roman and rabbinic laws were converging on the husband as the active promoter of private morality.

Throughout the narrative of the affair the husband makes a single appearance. Having set in motion a legal investigation, he is subsequently absent or, at least, his presence remained unmarked. Once he had approached the governor with his suit, he became irrelevant. Jerome does not supply a reason for the accusation. There need not have been one. Suspicion alone was sufficient to open legal proceedings and to implicate not only a suspected wife but also an alleged lover. Constantine's law granted the husband a crucial role as an accuser. But the accusation had to be submitted within a specific time limit that had not changed since Augustus's days. Within these limits (of sixty days) the husband could pursue his charge without fearing the consequences of false or failed accusation (*calumnia*).[64] In the Vercellan case, the husband, moreover, timed his accusation to coincide with a visit of the governor. Whatever else, the case was deemed of sufficient gravity to be tried not by an ordinary judge but by the highest provincial legal authority. Yet, by charging wife and lover simultaneously and by investigating them under the umbrella of one case, both the governor and the husband were in violation of the law that had prescribed separate investigations and prosecutions.

Two important Constantinian contributions to the traditional criminal process dealing with adultery are noteworthy. One was the narrowing of the circle of accusers to a few male relatives. Another was the latitude given to these men to withdraw the charge at will.[65] By limiting the right to accuse and by investing the husband with the role of the chief accuser, Constantine approached rabbinic views on the matter. Recent analyses of Constantine's legislation on family affairs have emphasized the negligible influence that Christianity had on them.[66] Christian thinkers insisted, for example, on the removal of the double standard which counted only women as objects of an accusation of adultery. If Constantine ignored Christian trends to equalize the guilt of the spouses in any breach of marital fidelity, the source of his innovations needs to be sought elsewhere. Perhaps the emperor's choice reflected direct borrowing from the Bible. Perhaps late Roman legislation on adultery echoed a contemporary mentality that called for the disposition of the fate of suspected adulteresses in the hands of a few relatives, chiefly their husbands.[67] The fact that only rabbinic systems consistently promoted the role of the husband is noteworthy and suggests some form of exchange.

Constantine also granted an accusing husband permission to proceed by virtue of his *ius mariti* (right of the husband) within the statutory time limits (of sixty days) even without a formal accusation (*libelli accusationis*).[68] The provision seems to adhere to the classical prescription that regarded the date of a divorce as the critical time measure for the launching of an accusation against an adulterous wife. Yet, the Theodosian Code (CTh 9.7.2) makes no direct reference to the question of a divorce prior to any legal proceedings.[69] CTh 9.7.1 of 326 ignored altogether the issue of the relations between accusing husbands and accused wives if both belonged to the lower classes. And a Justinianian interpolation of CTh 9.7.2 conceded outright that a husband could charge his wife with adultery without first divorcing her.[70] This addition implies that by the time the Justinianian commission on collecting and editing imperial laws was at work, the understanding was that a divorce no longer constituted a required preliminary. How the "husband's time" was counted remains unexplained.

Late Roman law also introduced adultery as one of three legitimate grounds for a divorce. Constantine's surviving regulations on divorce exhibit a departure from the latitude that previous laws had granted to both sides regarding unilateral divorces. In 331 the emperor penalized divorce with celibacy and loss of dowry for the husband and with exile and forfeiture of dowry for the wife, unless the latter was found guilty of adultery, poisoning, or prostitution.[71] But a wife could not divorce her husband for suspected or proven infidelity. This law further introduced a disparity in the treatment of husbands and wives, a discrimination that had no legal antecedents in Roman or ecclesiastical (canon) law.[72] Once more, only rabbinic views offer a viable contemporary parallel (see below).

The gap between legal theories and practicalities reflects the difficulties faced by any court trying to substantiate an accusation of adultery without direct evidence or witnesses. As long as suspicion alone was a legal ground to open a criminal case of adultery, the result of a public prosecution could have been fatal. In this light it is perhaps hardly surprising that religious leaders, like Augustine in early fifth-century North Africa, strongly urged their male parishioners not to expose their wives to the public if they suspected them of adultery, but instead to contend with their private penance.[73] Augustine's urgent requests convey the risks that women, innocent or guilty of adultery, faced if accused by their own husbands. That he had to voice his concern in public shows how tempting a law like CTh 9.7.2 would have appeared to a Christian man who, although he could legally obtain divorce on the grounds of adultery, was nonetheless admonished by the church not to remarry during in the lifetime of his first spouse.

Both emperors and rabbis, then, regarded husbands and not wives as the guardians of marital chastity. Husbands possessed full powers over the body of their wives not only by having exclusive access to it but also by being invested with the authority to prosecute the violation of her body by another. In a case of suspected adultery the guilt of the wife had to be established by her own confession, primarily to enable the husband to remarry and legally claim her dowry. The lover, as happened at Vercelli, merely attested the woman's guilt, but his confession was insufficient to establish it.[74]

Rabbinic debates over husbandly motivation demonstrate a like awareness of the role of the male in the family as a guardian of female morality.[75] The absence of all other males, besides the husband, as parties to potential prosecution is, however, remarkable and, to the best of my knowledge, has no legal antecedents in the Greco-Roman legal sphere.[76] Such an exclusive focus on the suspecting husband, largely dictated by the demands of the biblical narrative, led to a debate on the reliability of the spousal testimony, a discussion wholly absent from late Roman law:

Rabbi Judah said: "A husband is to be trusted [when he suspects his wife of adultery]. If he is trusted when she is menstruating and is under kareth [i.e., when the law imposes a heavy penalty on the husband for sexual intercourse with his wife], he is to be trusted all the more when she is straying and is merely forbidden [without penalty for the husband for violating terms]." This is not the case. The rabbis argued that when a wife is menstruating the fear of kareth renders the husband trustworthy. But in the case of suspected adultery, the lack of penalty make him untrustworthy. (BT Sot. 7a, Soncino)

Between the public admonition and the trial a local court used to assign two rabbinic disciples to accompany the couple on their way to Jerusalem.

The rationale behind the appointment of this escort was to examine the sincerity of the husband's motives.

Come and hear: They assign to him [the husband] two disciples of the sages lest he cohabits with her on the journey [to Jerusalem]. Should you maintain that if a husband retracts his warning the warning is retracted, and he may withdraw it and cohabit with her? Why are disciples of the sages specified [if this is the case]? Because they are learned men so that if he [the husband] wishes to cohabit with her, they say to him: Withdraw your warning and cohabit with her. (BT Sot. 25a, Soncino, modified)

Whether rabbinic "courts" continued to allocate disciples to couples in late antiquity is not specified. Since the basic issue was an examination of the husband's behavior after he had voiced his suspicion of his wife in public, it is plausible that this type of precaution continued to be valid. Be that what it may, the passages offer a neat summary of the problems attendant on elevating a husband to the rank of sole accuser. Jewish law attempted to prevent a rapprochement between the couple, and to ensure the consistency of the husbandly stand by observing not only the suspected wife but also the suspecting husband. The rabbis realized that without substantial penalties (such as the Roman *calumnia*, which made an accuser liable to the same penalties as the accused if the accusation proved unsubstantiated) there was no legal deterrent to prevent false or rash accusations.

According to the Mishnah (Sot. 1.2), a defiant wife "is forbidden to her husband" although there is no reference to a divorce as such. If the husband died she was not allowed to contract levirate marriage (ibid.). The Babylonian Talmud appears to take this as a reference to a divorce (Sot. 5b), while the Palestinian appears to regard the prohibition as implying the discontinuance of sexual relations between the suspected wife and her suspecting husband.[77] While the husband's right to effect a divorce is not contested, the precise cause seems to be a matter of some controversy. Unless a reliable report was available, divorce was inadvisable. If a suspecting husband opted for a divorce on the basis of a mere rumor and without further evidence, he had no right to his wife's dowry.

The introduction of divorce so early in rabbinic proceedings of suspected adultery appears to reflect the influence of classical Roman law which required divorce prior to any court accusation for adultery. The operative rationale behind this requirement was that a married woman as such could not have been sued for adultery. The rabbis, to whom the biblical account did not provide guidance on this score, considered first a temporary separation. Some, however, also supported a permanent solution in the shape of a divorce (M Sot. 6.1). Such an endorsement also entailed considerations of a financial settlement (see below).

If a suspected adulteress was pregnant at the time of her accusation, considerations of the status of her offspring became critical (M Sot. 4.1). One rabbinic opinion maintained that if she was pregnant by her former husband she did not receive her marriage settlement; another, that her husband could take her back after two years (M Sot. 4.1), precisely the period prescribed by Justinian for reunification between a couple after a trial for suspected adultery. As yet another tannaitic source found children of suspected adulteresses legitimate altogether.[78] This verdict was followed by the Palestinian Talmud on the ground that, "A married woman who plays the whore, the children are credited to her husband because with him occurred the majority of acts of intercourse" (PT Sot. 1.7 [17a]).[79]

Like their Roman counterparts, the rabbis were concerned with the establishment of correct paternity. But both Roman jurists and rabbinic courts preferred to exclude considerations of suspected adultery from legal discussions of the status and inheritance of illegitimate children. There are, however, stories that hint at the depth of the dilemma of a husband who, tacitly ignoring his wife's meandering, risked the inheritance of his natural children.

> A certain man heard his wife say to her daughter: Why do you not observe more secrecy in your amours? I have ten children and only one is from your father. When the man lay on his deathbed, he said to his children: I leave all my property to my one son. They did not know which of them he meant so they consulted Rabbi Bana'ah. (BT Baba Batra 58a, Soncino)[80]

Far-fetched as the tale appears, it drives home a simple point—if a husband elected to retain an adulterous wife, there were far-reaching consequences that he had to take into account.

The reputation of a suspected adulteress formed, then, a common bond of concern to both Roman and rabbinic legal experts. In 290, for example, the emperors Diocletian and Maximian ruled that a man is not guilty of adultery if the woman involved was known to "behave like a prostitute" in public (CJ 9.9.22). In 326 Constantine gave full expression to the legal concept that accusations of suspected adultery had to investigate the status, rank, and character of the accused woman. Considerations relating to social status of a suspected adulteress were in general absent from rabbinic rulings on suspected adultery. Public accessibility to the body of a woman, such as a serving maid in an inn, entailed the legal validity or invalidity of a case against her. In late antiquity Roman law insisted that the reputation of a married woman was intimately associated with her social status. The growing emphasis of late Roman laws on the reputation of the accused woman reflects the convergence of both systems, Jewish and Roman, on the body of a woman as a locus of the reputation of her husband. Roman law also weighed the role of an alleged lover, a factor on which the rabbis hardly ever commented.

The "Other": Lovers and Aftermath

On the whole, lovers or male adulterers remain elusive in rabbinic discussions of the "straying wife." The absence of a presumed lover from the elaborate biblical and Mishnaic discussions of the ordeal of the bitter water and from any of the other legal proceedings is remarkable and, it seems, uniquely Jewish. The presence of a partner in the suspected adulteress's crime remains a deduction based on the elaborate descriptions of the ordeal. An equivocal reference of the Mishnah to the effect that "as the water test her so they test him" (M Sot. 5.1), ignited a rabbinic controversy with regard to the identity of "him." Some thought it referred to the husband; others to the lover, others yet to both men.[81]

Lovers, however, could surface after a trial as, potentially, future husbands. The question then revolved on the propriety of an alliance between a woman who had been prosecuted as a suspected adulteress (especially if condemned) and her alleged lover. The Mishnah asserted (in a rare pun) that: "As she is forbidden to her husband so she is forbidden to her lover" (M Sot. 5.1). Mishnaic authorities concluded that the woman had been twice defiled and hence twice forbidden, and the Babylonian Talmud concurred, suggesting that the woman was forbidden to both her husband and her alleged lover, particularly to the latter, as long as her husband was alive (BT Sot. 19a).

The Palestinian Talmud provides an interesting insight into the links in the triangle of husband-wife-lover:

If the husband divorced her, what is the law regarding the lover being permitted to marry her? Surely it is not possible to say that, as he deliberately had sexual relations with her he is now permitted to marry her! If he did it inadvertently and she did it deliberately, it is obvious that she is prohibited to have sexual relations with her husband. If the husband divorced her it is not possible to say that she goes forth from the husband's [into her lover's] house. How do we know that the matter depends solely on her [in case she acted intentionally and her lover innocently]? Simeon bar Ba in the name of Rabbi Yohanan said: ". . . If she did the deed deliberately, she is forbidden. If inadvertently, she is permitted."[82]

The question of intent here is associated with the aftermath of a trial and an anticipated divorce. But how the rabbis proposed to establish the intent of the lover is far from clear. One story hints at a belief that the paramour's behavior vis-à-vis the suspecting husband could prove his innocence or his guilt:

A certain adulterer visited [the house] of a certain woman. Her husband arrived and the adulterer fled and concealed himself behind a curtain[?]. Now cress was lying there and a snake was feeding itself on it. The master of the house [= the husband] was about to eat from this cress unknown to his wife, but the adulterer warned: Do not eat from it because a snake has tasted it!

Raba said: In this case the wife is permitted [to her husband]. Had he [the adulterer] committed some forbidden act, it would have been fine for him to let the husband eat and die, as it is written: "For they have committed adultery, and blood is on their hands" (Ezek. 23:37). Is this not obvious?

Yet, one might think that he [the alleged lover] had indeed committed a forbidden act. As to his warning, that came because he did not wish to let the husband die that the woman may be to him like "stolen waters are sweet as is bread eaten in secret and therefore taste all the better" (Prov. 9:17). Thus we are informed [to the contrary]. (BT Ned. 91b, Soncino, modified)[83]

Although the lover acted gallantly toward the suspicious husband his motives were correctly questioned. One side asserted that saving the husband's life proved the innocence of the lover (in other words, that nothing adulterous took place). Another side, however, claimed that the interchange proved the opposite since the death of the husband would have deprived the affair of its excitement.

Perhaps the absurdity of the incident depicted above highlights the futility of rigid notions concerning an innocuous association between married women and men other than their husbands. The point is underscored in talmudic versions of a famed Hellenistic romantic tale in which a case of a gravely ill man came for arbitration. This man had fallen in love with a woman, become sick, and when his doctors advised that the only way to save him was to allow him to be with that woman, the matter was referred to the rabbis.[84] They ruled against the dying man's desire, a verdict that was taken to mean that the object of his passion was a married woman.[85]

In the absence of allowances for bilateral divorce or for a divorce by mutual consent, as ingrained in classical Roman law, a rabbinic ban on remarriage in general, and specifically with an alleged lover, was hardly likely to have been effective without a penalty. The rabbis addressed this deficiency by imposing financial disadvantages on both sides. A husband who rushed to divorce his suspected wife without, seemingly, sufficient proof had to give up the marriage settlement.[86] A wife who did not heed preliminary warnings concerning her suspected behavior could have been divorced without regaining her marriage portion. Divorce as such had been easy enough for any Jewish male who could use a variety of reasons to justify the measure, from the most trivial (such as a wife's spoiling a dish) to a suspicion of indecency (unchastity, sexual impropriety).[87] Suspected adultery clearly fell under the latter, making rabbinical efforts to define the essence and procedures regarding suspected adultery even more remarkable.

Classical Roman law treated a couple of suspected lovers as equally guilty and subjected the lover to the same ordeal as his alleged mistress. Unlike Jewish law, it also provided for legal actions against the lover. The ideology of punitive measures against the lover is well reflected in Musonius's words: "The adulterer wrongs the husband of the woman whom he corrupts,"[88] precisely the sentiment echoed by Jewish sources who, however, preferred to consign the lover to hell.

Both systems, Roman and rabbinic, faced the problem of establishing the identity of a lover who was not caught in flagrante delicto. There were, however, apparently enough accusers willing to point a finger not only at their suspected wives but also at their suspected paramours. By issuing warnings to the suspected adulteress, as rabbinic rules required, the identity of the lover remained concealed. By issuing warnings to the suspected lover, the emperor Justinian focused attention on the most elusive party in the triangle.

Jerome's tale of the adultery in northern Italy (see above) indicates a growing rigidity with regard to both suspects. Late Roman law encouraged a speedy trial so that a person "may be punished if guilty or absolved if innocent" (CTh 9.3.1 of 320). At Vercelli, according to Jerome, the suspected couple was tortured in order to elicit "the truth." Once the alleged lover admitted to guilt "he left an innocent person no chance of denial." But when the suspected wife was put to torture she defied expectation and in the process, as Jerome states, she demonstrated "a courage superior to her sex."[89] Her strategy of innocence was to recall her past life, her reputation, and her moral commitments. She relied on the court audience who would have known her previously, on her alleged lover whom she tried to shame by denying his confession, and on her link with the church. In other words, her denial of a sin (adultery) and her assertion of (Christian) piety were the two sources of her appeal to justice.

Execution was by no means the only prescribed legal penalty for suspected adultery. Given, however, the climate of righteous morality in the fourth century, a government official like the governor in the story could afford to interpret imperial laws in a manner most detrimental to the objects of inquiry. Throughout the tale of adultery at Vercelli there is an awareness of the role of the authorities as a moral arbiter. In the absence of precise guidelines to dictate the conduct of criminal investigations, the state left its judges considerable scope for determining the severity of the crime once an accusation had been made. The law also granted considerable latitude to seek confessions of crimes, especially in the case of adultery.

Emperors Constantius and Constans Augusti to Catullinus:
You ought to punish with a severity equal to its wickedness any crime of adultery reported to your court and proven after an investigation had been held. In such crimes it must be observed hereafter that when adultery is proved by clear evidence, a frustrate appeal must not be admitted, since for an equal and similar reason the judge must sew up alive in a leather sack and burn the sacrilegious violators of marriage as though they were manifest parricides. (CTh 11.36.4)[90]

Fourth-century legal rhetoric on adultery, then, consigned both adulterers to a torturous death.[91] But in reality convicted adulterers met a variety of penalties, including temporary exile. Sentences were issued by judges according to various criteria, not the least the rank and class of the accused. An imperial novella of 459 chastised a judge who imposed too light a penalty on a convicted adulterer.[92] The emperor even granted the public the right to kill any adulterer who was apprehended at large. Such strictness may have remained largely ineffective. In 556 Justinian provided details regarding the fate of the property of condemned lovers besides consigning adulteresses to a nunnery (Nov. 134.10).

Roman law, like rabbinic regulations, also envisaged a situation in which the lovers did marry each other. In such a case, however, the adulterer could not validly make her his heir nor could she make him hers.[93]

Besides financial penalties, then, there were few other deterrents to stand in the way of a couple who had survived an accusation of suspected adultery.

Within classical Greek, Roman, and Jewish discourses of adultery, extant Athenian discussions provide an interesting point of departure that emphasizes the far-reaching moral revolution that affected Roman and Jewish ideology of adultery. There was no classical Greek term that corresponds to "adulteress." There is, however, a word that refers to a man who engages in illicit sexual intercourse (*moichos*, or "adulterer").[94] Classical Athenian law of adultery did not aim at the legal enforcement of moral or religious notions of proper sexual conduct.[95] It provided for the summary arrest of the adulterer as a man who perpetrates evil (*kakourgos*) by penetrating a domicile at night and by sowing the seeds of shame, dishonor, and blood feud. And it dealt with justifiable homicide, that is, the killing of a lover by a husband.

The Hebrew Bible provides for a summary execution of lovers caught in the act and enables suspicious husbands to put their wives before a public tribunal. But there are no specific examples to illustrate the application of these provisions. Dinah's brothers slay her suitor, alleging that he had treated her as a prostitute. But the penalty is one that the Hebrew Bible prescribes for an adulterer caught in the act. Phineas kills Zimri and Cozbi as though he had caught them in the act, but the adultery they may have committed did not involve illicit sexual relations but a betrayal of Yahweh. A rabbinic midrash asserts that the covenant of circumcision was placed on the genitals so that the fear of God would restrain males from sin.[96] But the closeness of the right kind of procreation and adultery is evident in biblical perceptions of adultery as an improper expression of human sexual desire and in the discussion on the duty of procreation. The Mishnah exempts a woman from this obligation (M Yeb. 6.6). One dissenting opinion claimed that both men and women were expected to obey the injunction of "to be fertile and increase" (Gen. 1:28).[97] Strictly speaking, however, even if Jewish law does not obligate women to bear children, the bodily state of married women becomes a topic of significant concern.

At the end of the first century B.C.E. the emperor Augustus "had invented an odd crime: the extent and complexity of writing on this law [the Julian law on adultery] are in striking contrast with Roman treatment of offences against clearly identified victims, such as rape and theft. In the Roman context, the Julian Law is surely anomalous."[98] Augustan legislation on marriage and adultery also focused on the upper classes where the interplay of sex and politics became the essence of the degradation of the adulteress and the potential criminalization of her complaisant husband.[99] And it added to the legal vocabulary the offense known as *domum praebere*, namely the provision of a house (or a venue) for committing adultery, a concept that reflects an aristocratic bias by assuming that potential defendants live in a *domus* (aristocratic dwelling).[100]

Lex Iulia de adulteriis coercendis and its successive modifications set out to prevent casual relationships entered into by free women who were considered respectable.[101] Rabbinic discussions of the *sotah* (straying wife) demonstrate a similar concern even after the destruction of the Temple removed a central spatial feature from the process of exposing concealed adulteresses. Within a context witnessing the intensification of the rhetoric of morality in late antiquity and against shared male perceptions of female chastity it is possible to discern areas of overlapping rabbinic and Roman rulings. The desire to promote legitimate marriages and legitimate paternity formed two guiding principles in both systems. Yet, some rabbinic and Roman rulings are both unique and exceptional and suggest direct or indirect borrowings.[102] What, precisely, replaced the biblical and Mishnaic rules on the treatment of suspected adulteresses is difficult to ascertain. It seems likely that in late antiquity the rabbis continued to adhere to the notion of public exposure and trial of a suspected adulteress. They could do so through the mechanism of Roman law. As a result, a procedure that combined earlier rabbinic rules with Roman notions came into being. By requiring a set of preliminaries the rabbis (and later Justinian) may have tried to introduce an additional mechanism of settling domestic dissension within the local community. Public trials were seen as a last resort. But once this course was adopted, the chances of suspected adulteresses in late antiquity to survive either the trial or the humiliation, as Augustine noted, were slim.

Beyond legal strictures, Roman or rabbinic, the most effective way to instill the fear of adultery in women was public exposure, shaming, and humiliation. The point is beautifully illustrated in a rabbinic commentary on Deuteronomy:

A certain king issued a decree to the effect that anyone who eats unripe figs grown during the Sabbatical year shall be paraded (in disgrace) in the arena. Now, a woman from a noble family proceeded to gather such figs and ate them. As they were parading her around the arena she said to the king: I beg of you, my king, let my offense be publicly proclaimed so that the citizens would not say: She seems to have been caught in the act of adultery or witchcraft! If they see figs wrapped around my neck they will know that it is because of them that I am being paraded.[103]

In rabbinic discourses of late antiquity the image of the suspected adulteress becomes a power icon of the forbidden. To remain a Jewess, and hence a harmonizing member of the community, a married woman must remain within the domestic precincts of the legitimate marriage bed. If she does not, the complications are unimaginable, not the least the production of disqualified Jews. Worse, she is like an animal, controlling neither her sexuality nor her honor.[104] Paradoxically, the regulation of sexual behavior through public scrutiny rather than through familial channels of honor and shame also designated or, perhaps, elevated adultery into a freely chosen activity between legal persons.[105] The creation of a Jewess in terms of negative sexual associations remains, however, a traditional feature of Judaism.

5

The Harmony of the Home in Late Antiquity

Jewish, Roman, and Christian Perspectives on Intermarriage

In the community of the Garden of Eden, at least according to Gen. 2:20, the harmony of nature and the first human (male) was guaranteed only with the advent of the first woman.[1] Boredom, too, was dispelled. With Eve came understanding and learning capabilities, conferred on the human couple through the intervention of a serpent. But her appearance on the idyllic scene also heralded morality, mortality, and exile. As a result of her eagerness to acquire sagacity, Eve the wisdom-bearer to humanity, had to be demoted to the status of a wife and child-bearer. Her successors had to be put under a marriage yoke lest they display similar rebelliousness and recalcitrance. What, however, if Eve ate alone? The prospect had to be monitored through the invention of marriage, or of organized coupling.

Strictly speaking, to perpetuate itself the human race needs men for a split of a second. Other than the act of dissemination, the early and crucial stages of human conception and development have nothing to do with men and everything to do with women. By creating marriage and family, Judaism, as other societies in antiquity, mediated between men and women and shaped their social relations.[2] One critical stage in the institutionalization of women through marriage is reflected in the words that Lā'mech, son of Methusha-el, son of Mehujael, son of Irad, son of Enoch, son of Cain, addressed to his two wives:

Ada and Zila, listen to my voice; wives of Lā'mech, lend your ears to my words: I killed a man who had wounded me, and a boy who had beaten me. If Cain is avenged sevenfold. Lā'mech's revenge is seventy-seven-fold. (Gen. 4:23–24)

This domestic conversation to which we hear no reply aspires to inform wives about the psyche of their spouses. It also conveys a threat, for it implies that wives are potentially rivals, rather than lovers, and that, like enemies, they can be squashed for slight reasons.

Between the tender expression of Adam in Gen. 2:23 as he beholds the nascent Eve that had just been fashioned out of his rib, and the threatening declaration of Lā'mech to Ada and Zila, delivered after they had given birth to two sons and one daughter, stands a genealogy of a human race that gradually dispensed with female agents. If in Gen. 4:1–2, as in 4:17, births are recorded in a correct biological manner, with intercourse, conception, and the acknowledgment of the role of woman in the process, in Gen. 4:18 men, rather than women, are bearers of exclusive parentage. When Lā'mech takes two women in the first reported polygyny, the text still refers to them by name and as mothers of specifically named children. Even the longest and most detailed genealogy of the early generations of humanity (Gen. 5) is punctuated by listing the birth of "sons and daughters" to each of Adam and Eve's successors. Basically, men bear men and all is well until only daughters are born (Gen. 6:1) and then a series of "mixed marriages" takes place between "daughters of men" and "sons of gods" and the whole scheme of tracing the history of the human race is confused beyond repair.

When Noah and his sons leave the ark, the history of ancient Israel begins with a long list of productive men who somehow manage to generate more men (Gen. 10) and to restore the balance of reproduction with the birth of more "sons and daughters" (Gen. 11). At the dawn of the fateful encounter between God and Abraham endogamy is officially born with a series of alliances between half-brothers and sisters, uncles and nieces (Gen. 11:29–30). And until the birth of twelve sons and one daughter, the survival of the fledgling founding family of Judaism depends solely on procuring the right brides, all members of the close-kin family.

Throughout the history of Judaism marriage has been designated as the epicenter of the making of a Jewess. Whatever moments in the life of Jewesses were deemed worthy of recording, childhood and adolescence were singularly absent from their biographies. From the moment of birth, the female course of existence inexorably led to a union with the male half. In the ideal land of women that ancient Jewish writings delineate the bond that attaches a Jewess to her father and her brothers is duly and dutifully transferred to her husband (and his brothers). Any deviation is deemed adulterous, a transgression, and a grievous source of pollution. Of all the negative icons that crowd the road of women to legitimate and lasting membership in the Jewish community, that of a woman who marries outside the male group of birth and faith proved the most potent.

Marriage and family, although based on biological foundations, emerge in Judaism, as elsewhere in the ancient world, as legal and social constructs.[3] The paradox lies in the fact that the origins of marital unions are marked by separation. Already in Gen. 2:24 the dismantling of the family of the husband is accepted as a detachment necessary for the construction of a new family unit. The trauma of leaving home to join a strange man in a strange bed that women must sustain has never been appreciated or recorded. It was left to a sensitive poet, like the Roman Catullus, to penetrate the sentiments of a bride about to be taken out of her mother's protection to the home of her newly wed husband:

> Open the locks of the gate
> The virgin-bride is here . . .
> See how the wedding torches lit the shining tresses? . . .
> Overpowering shyness detains her. . . .
> As she listens to all this she weeps
> Since she must leave . . .
> Proceed, freshly wed bride . . .
> And listen. . . .
> Your husband would not lightly indulge in evil adultery
> Nor embark on disgraceful course
> Desiring to lie away from your tender arms . . .
> But in your bosom he will be entwined . . .
> And you, just married wife,
> That which your husband seeks do not deny
> Lest he seek it elsewhere.[4]

Marriage was the means to establish boundaries to resolve social tensions.[5] Marital impediments were intended to prevent a clash of marital strategies and interests. In Judaism a correct genealogy was an issue of enormous importance, especially after the Judaean aristocracy settled in Babylonian exile. At virtually every point in biblical annals mixed marriages acquired a connotation far beyond the actual sexual union of a woman and a man. The Pentateuch transmits two ordinances banning marriage with Canaanites (Exod. 34; Deut. 7:3–4). They convey an understanding that should Israelite men choose gentile women, these women might harbor the seeds of apostasy and idolatry. Yet an astounding number of apparent transgressions are recorded in the Bible without criticism or commentary. This is not the place to trace the vicissitudes of the biblical bans on intermarriage or the history of marriage and family in Judaism. Here I wish to examine the development and deployment of legal rhetoric of undesirable matches in late antiquity, from the Mishnah (redacted ca. 200 C.E.) to the late fourth century, when civil and theological discourses combined for the first time in recorded human history to preserve the harmony of the domestic community through outlawing marriage outside prescribed religious/ethnic boundaries.

Although the topic of mixed marriages in late antiquity has been discussed often enough in modern scholarship, particularly in conjunction with conversion to Judaism, no work has examined the ideological interrelations of Jewish, Christian, and Roman attitudes to intermarriage between Jews and Christians.[6] Even less has been said about the realities behind the repeated prohibitions on mixed (religious) marriages in late antiquity.[7] As Christianity became an established religion, a rhetoric of morality, Jewish, Christian, and imperial Roman, aspired to create a society based on tight institutional control of sex and on the strength of marital fidelity.

Neither rabbis nor Christian leaders favored the intimacy of marital bonds between Jews and Christians, unless the "other" converted through prescribed channels. Rabbinic objections were based on a long exegetical tradition that could be traced back to the Pentateuch where Israelites/Jews were invariably pitted against non-Israelites/gentiles. But they were also something of an anomaly in a Greco-Roman environment in which no marital impediment was anchored in either ethnic or religious disparity. Christian objections to marriage between believers and nonbelievers were founded exclusively on disparity of cult. In the fourth century the three nomic spheres of rabbinic legal exegesis, Christian canons, and Roman law converged to act against mixed marriages.[8] One result was a brief but sweeping civil (Roman) prohibition that categorically forbade intermarriage between Jews and Christians. In various reincarnations this ban had an extraordinarily long life in medieval and early modern legislative history, playing a significant role in the formation of both Jewish and Christian communal identity, and in the definition of Jewessness.[9]

The first extensive discussions of mixed marriage took place among rabbinical schools in late ancient Palestine. Their opinions are, in part, recorded in the Mishnah and the two Talmuds, the Palestinian (redacted at the beginning of the fifth century) and the Babylonian (redacted at least a century later).[10] It is thus within a context of an exclusively Eastern Jewry, in Palestine and Babylonia (Persia), that rabbinic reflections on the subject were formulated. By contrast, the first recorded ban on Jewish-Christian marriage in ecclesiastical rulings originated within a western context, in Spain. And the first general Roman ban on the same subject was issued from Thessalonica (Macedonia) to the top Eastern official in the empire, the Praetorian prefect of the Orient (*praefectus praetorio per Orientem*), a civil dignitary in charge of a vast geographical entity which included the province of Palestine. In spite of the varieties of geography and mental outlooks, rabbinical, episcopal, and Roman agencies coalesced to ban marriage outside the Jewish and Christian faiths.

Such apparent unanimity of legal opinions also raises a question about the relations between legal theories and realities, as well as about the establishment of Jewish and Christian marital ceremonies. Here it must be stated that the precise scope and effectiveness of rabbinical strictures is far from evident, even in their home province of Palestine. Recent research has not only acknowledged the varieties of Judaism in the Diaspora in late antiquity, but it has also cast doubt on the unanimity of Judaism projected by rabbinic writings, as well as on general adherence to rabbinic precepts.[11] The so-called Babatha archives from the province of Arabia (early second century) hint at the limits of the rabbinic legal sphere on the very frontiers of Palestine, while marriage contracts of the same period from the Judaean desert demonstrate that not all Jews in Palestine married according to the rabbinic formula of "the Law of Moses and Israel."[12] On the other hand, a Greco-Aramaean marriage contract (*ketouba*) from Egyptian Antinopolis not only reflects Jewish-rabbinical marital formulas, but is also inscribed in Hebrew characters.[13] If the rabbinical orbit in the heart of late ancient Judaism was apparently circumscribed, the application of rabbinic legalism to the rest of the Mediterranean Diaspora, where local Jewish officials held sway, remains an open question.[14] Nor is it clear to what degree the church developed and disseminated a typically Christian type of marriage. Since marriage was a much older institution than the church, the differentiation of a Christian understanding of marriage and the desecularization of marital institutions took centuries and began with a series of prohibitions.[15] In the absence of civil legal hindrances, the validity of any type of marriage across religious boundaries did not rely on either a ceremony or a certificate but rather on mutual consent and affection.[16]

What is, therefore, the precise meaning of the term "mixed marriage"? In classical Roman law mixed marriages were those that a Roman citizen could not contract for reasons ranging from military service to disparities of class, rank, and citizenship.[17] Late Roman law retained the prescribed categories of classical law while introducing harsher penalties for violations of marital bans. It also introduced two novel concepts, ethnic and religious, banning marriages between "Romans" and "barbarians" on the one hand, and between Jews and Christians on the other.[18]

An investigation into the ideological roots of the prohibitions on Jewish-Christian marriage is merely a first step in the re-creation of the human landscape in which modules of community interactions operated to engender meanings of Jewessness. Such an inquiry can provide insights into the notions of cohesion, communal and individual identity, and distinctiveness which prevailed at the time, as well as into the invisible but highly intimate forms of contact between Jews and Christians, women and men. The limitations of this investigation are obvious. We cannot chart with any approximation the relations between individual family units affected by this marital prohibition and by the structures of government, religion, and kinship groups in their environment. Nor can we follow decision-making processes that would have led to strategies of choices of spouses.[19] We can, however, appreciate the laws and the institutions that governed the harmony of the domestic community and how they changed in late antiquity.[20]

Why Not Marry a Goy?

At a risk of a gross oversimplification of the intricacies of rabbinic opinions as gleaned from the Mishnah and the Talmuds, it seems necessary to clarify at the start that the issue of mixed marriage in rabbinic Judaism is intimately linked with that of conversion (*giur*) and, by implication, with that of the faith and status of the children born in such unions.[21] There is, however, no straightforward consensus either among Mishnaic or talmudic authorities on any of these issues, nor is it possible to trace with any certainty the modifications which the ascent of Christianity must have introduced into rabbinic thinking about mixed marriages. Recent discussions of rabbinic views on intermarriage have focused on attempts to trace the principle of matrilineal succession and on marriage with converts.[22] These are important aspects of the rabbinic debate but they hardly represent its entire scope or complexity. No attention has been paid to a curious but telling rabbinic reticence on Christians, rather than gentiles in general, as potential marital partners. The terminology of rabbinic debates on marriage with non-Jews remains tannaitic (first and second centuries C.E.) even though the amoraic period (third to sixth centuries C.E.) witnessed growing awareness of Christians and Christianity.²³

A useful starting point for an exploration of rabbinic views on intermarriage is a quotation from a Mishnaic tractate devoted to betrothals (*kiddushin*).²⁴

1. In cases in which there is [valid] betrothal not attended by a disqualifying feature [of one of the prospective spouses], the issue follows the male. What are these? These concern [marriage] between a [female member] of priestly, Levite and Israelite families and a priest, a Levite or an Israelite.

2. In cases in which there is [valid] betrothal attended by a disqualifying feature [of one of the prospective spouses], the issue follows the disqualified [parent]. What are these cases? These concern [marriage] of a widow to a great priest, of a divorcée and *halusa* to an ordinary priest, of a *mamzeret* and *netina* to an Israelite, and of an Israelite woman to a mamzer and *natin*.

3. [In case of] an [Israelite woman] who cannot [be validly] betrothed to a certain party but can [validly] be betrothed to others, the issue [of this marriage] is a mamzer. Who is that? An [Israelite] man who [has intercourse] with a woman who is proscribed by the Torah's rules on incest.

4a and b. If a woman cannot have [valid] betrothal with any Israelite male, her child follows her. And who is this? A child of a slave and of a non-Jewish woman. (M Kidd. 3.12)

The terminology requires explanation. Betrothals (*kiddushin*), the subject of this passage and, indeed, the topic of the entire tractate, marks a critical stage in the relations between a man and a woman and a commitment to a lifelong partnership. The process entailed assurances regarding the (qualifying) status of the prospective spouses and was often attended by some type of economic or financial transaction. Mishnaic marriage terminology employs three technical terms to describe the process of affiliation between a man and a woman: *erusin* (first step in which an intent to marry in the future is declared, usually by the parents), *kiddushin* (the actual betrothal), and *nissu'in* (the consummation of the previously described process).²⁵ A "disqualification" (*avera*) relates to forbidden liaisons and to prohibited sexual partners. Thus a *halusa*, for example, is a woman who is released from levirate ties but is still forbidden in marriage to a priest, while a child of incestuous relations (i.e., consanguineous unions) is also disqualified from marrying a number of people belonging to various fully qualified categories.[26] *Natin* or *netina* (naturalized residents) are biblical terms which designated unacceptable marital partners in the days of Ezra-Nehemiah (ca. 400 B.C.E.). Their employment in this specific text (and elsewhere) is a demonstration of rabbinic attachment to biblical terminology (as is the use of the term "Israelite") rather than a reflection of contemporary groups.[27] In fact, the entire passage is marked by archaic biblical terminology which should alert the readers to its idealistic, if not utopian character. When the Mishnah was redacted there was no longer a great priest, and "Israelites" was a term which even the later biblical books, like Esther, had no longer used.

At first glance it appears that the main subject of M Kidd. 3.12 is the status of children born of any conceivable type of forbidden marriages. But this is only one of several aspects discussed in this complex passage. Its main aim is to chart marital territories of eligible and ineligible partners. In this, the passage as a whole provides a tight ring-composition with two broad generalizations (1 and 4) and two specific prohibitions (2 and 3). In visual terms, this passage draws ever narrower circles of exclusion by moving from the widest range of valid marital possibilities through decreasing valid relations to those between two categories of women with whom no valid betrothal is possible and who are, by implication, altogether disqualified. But the passage also juxtaposes different types of exclusionary factors, from genealogy (or "citizenship" in Roman legal terms) to social, familial and marital status (free/bonded, consanguinity, and so on) which, legally speaking, require careful distinctions. It also serves as a lively reminder that endogamy is not only a convention aimed at excluding complete outsiders but one that can also target undesirable insiders.[28]

Purity of descent or genealogy is the basis of valid marital relations and a critical component in the determination of the precise affiliation of the offspring of this union to the community. Thus M Kidd. 3.12(1) insists that Jews who do not labor under any restrictive disqualification have the right to contract valid marriage with Jews of similar background and to produce more Jews who in their turn will have access to a similarly wide circle of marital partners. In spite of this wide range of endogamous relations, 3.12(1) also hints at preference for inner endogamy, with priestly families retaining the purity of their genealogy by marrying into other priestly families, and similarly for Levites. Underlying all these is the principle of eligibility. In 3.12(2) the rabbis impose restrictions on marriage between "qualified" partners and a category which they considered "deficient." Here the issue is twofold, one focusing on disqualification by marriage and another on exclusion by birth. In the first place, a tighter marital circle is drawn around priests who are exhorted to avoid marrying a woman who had been married before, as though her first marriage carries an element of impurity into her second. Another recommendation discourages marriage between a full-fledged member of the community and two inferior categories, namely Jews whose birth was either illegitimate or outside the community (mamzer and *natin*). In all these cases the issue follows the status of the inferior partner, thus perpetuating the circle of marital exclusivity and disqualifying these children from assuming the rank of their "superior" parent.

A third strand of rabbinic ideals of endogamy relates to a comparable circle of marital exclusion as the discussion turns to Jews who fall under the prohibition of incestuous unions. The insertion of this strand into a discussion of valid betrothals is curious. It emphasizes the ability of members of this group to marry anyone outside it but seems to recall that in a case of transgression the issue of this union will suffer from permanent disability. Genealogy and descent, then, become once more the decisive criteria of the legal ability to contract valid marriage and to confer full legitimacy on children. Yet, the comment does not appear to undermine the validity of such marriages, if they did occur. Instead, it penalizes them by disqualifying their issue from full marital eligibility. Strictly speaking, this phrase forms an extension of M Kidd. 3.12(2) by focusing on one type of forbidden union. It is worth noting that tannaitic midrashim also often associate incest with sex with gentiles, as though to highlight the undesirability of this type of union.[29]

Beginning with fully eligible members of the community this Mishnaic passage ends with ineligible matrimonial partners as the discussion also turns from the boundaries of endogamy to exogamy. In the fourth part of M Kidd. 3.12 neither birth nor marital status forms a marital impediment but new categories of status (free/bonded) and affiliation (Jew-gentile) underlie the boundaries of Jewish marriage. Basically, a Jewish male who "marries" a slave or a "foreigner" cannot guarantee the entry of his children to the Jewish community. Rather, such a union ensures their permanent exclusion as well as that of their mothers. By linking marriage between freemen and slaves on the one hand, and marriage between insiders and outsiders on the other, the rabbis clearly demonstrated their disapproval of both categories. Such an association of gentiles with slaves as ineligible marital partners for Jewish men also hints at either rabbinic ignorance of Roman legal categories that would not juxtapose two such disparate groups or, more likely at a deliberate move on the part of the rabbis to emphasize their disastrous consequences.

Yet, they also left a few questions unanswered. What type of slaves are those forbidden in marriage? Why is the Mishnah reticent about unions between Jewish women and slaves or gentiles? Before turning to rabbinic texts which attempted to correct and to contest these lacunae, it is necessary to ask what, precisely, is the purpose of these rulings on marital circles. These questions further involve an investigation of the nature of this text. Is this a legal text which reflects practical or ideological concerns? Does it incorporate specific responses to specific practical issues and queries? Were these rulings meant to serve as guidelines to be implemented, or as a school text, or were they a rhetorical expression of ideology? Moreover, who had the authority to enforce such rules and, when transgressed, to execute a punishment? The passage is recorded anonymously, as are many Mishnaic rulings. Whether this anonymity reflects consensus or a contested view, a minority opinion, an ancient ruling, rules without an established or known source, is an open question.[30] No penalty is prescribed for the offending parties besides the limitations imposed on their children. Such restrictions were clearly intended to serve as a preventive measure as well as a threat.

Nor can this passage be fully understood without the corresponding formulas which deal with the validity of (Jewish) divorce. Mishnah Gittin provides a list of men whom a divorced woman cannot (re)marry (M Git. 9.2). Unlike M Kidd. 3.12, which only specifies a divorcée as an ineligible partner of a priest, the divorce formula (M Git. 9.2) permits a soon-to-be divorced woman to marry, theoretically at least, any man except her own father, her father-in-law, her brother and brother-in-law, a slave, an idolater, and men (presumably priests) with whom she cannot contract valid betrothal. No penalty is imposed on future transgressions nor is the status of the children of such forbidden unions threatened. The same passage also deems invalid a bill of divorce which states that the divorced woman can marry anyone but a few stated categories. The list of exceptions reads precisely like the one in M Kidd. 3.12(2). In fact, the one significant lexical difference resides in the employment of the term "gentile," alternately called "idolater" (*oved/et kokhavim*) in Gittin but "a foreigner" (*nokhrit*) in Kiddushin. Since, as Jacob Neusner has maintained, the tractate Kiddushin is possibly "secondary and derivative," it seems likely that its list of matrimonial circles combines the information provided in Gittin with lists pertaining to levirate marriage (M Yeb. 2.4).[31] If this is the case, the change in terminology that refers to marriage outside the Jewish community may signify an editorial adaptation based on an intent to include all non-Jews, polytheists, and monotheists alike, in the prohibition on intermarriage. Indeed, the place of M Kidd. 3.12 in the text of the tractate, between rules on incestuous marriages and on the status of children born to a slave woman, hints at an attempt to group together two basically separate topics, namely the validity of marriage between certain categories of Jews and the status of children born of inferior or disqualified classes of potential marital partners.

Ultimately, such Mishnaic opinions present several problems. Not only did they not represent a unanimous rabbinic front on so important an issue as marriage, but they failed to invalidate marriages which had taken place in spite of these strictures and rulings on exclusion. Moreover, the rabbis had only limited authority to enforce separation besides their ability to impose a sentence of excommunication and, of course, to threaten the status of the offspring. This said, it seems clear that as long as there was, at least, another legal system (namely Roman law) which condoned the types of unions that the rabbis condemned, the validity of certain types of marriage could not be undermined.

Roman law insisted that there was no *conubium* (or legal marriage, *matrimonium iustum*) with slaves, precisely the ruling of M Kidd. 3.12(4a).[32] Moreover, even within this category an association between free men and slave women was less of a problem for the Roman legislator than was one between free women and slaves. The former is precisely what M Kidd. 3.12 discusses; the latter it ignores. Marriage across the boundaries of status were also considered (in Roman legal eyes) a legal breach, particularly when members of the upper class contemplated marriage with freedwomen or actresses. The clearest marital frontiers prior to 212 were drawn across the lines of citizenship, between citizens and non-citizens, and here, as in rabbinic rulings, the issue revolved on whether those involved also had the capacity to contract legal marriage (*conubium*). If they did, the children of such mixed-status marriage followed the father whether he was a citizen or not; if they did not, the children followed the mother if she was a foreigner and the father if she was a citizen. In rabbinic terms this meant that the children followed the status of the "inferior" partner.

The Mishnah's curt comment on unions between Jews and gentiles already received differing opinions in the Tosefta, another tannaitic composition, where the subject of the discussion centered on Jewish women who unite with slaves or with gentiles to produce, according to one opinion, a mamzer, and according to another, a child who is not a mamzer but whose status is not defined.³³ Equally questioning are the amoraic comments preserved in the Babylonian and the Palestinian Talmuds, each attempting to adopt, adapt, and explicate the Mishnaic rules in its own terms and for its own audiences. BT Kidd. 66–68 questions every aspect of M Kidd. 3.12 by positing opposing views and by seeking a ruling on, and confirmation of them. Thus, for example, it questions the Mishnaic principle of "valid betrothal, no disqualification, and issue following the father," by postulating a case of marriage between a proselyte and a mamzer. According to the Mishnah the offspring of such a union should be, like the father, a proselyte, but another rabbinic opinion regarded the issue as a mamzer, and hence as following the status of the mother. This is not the place to enlarge on this complicated debate, but its focusing on proselytes reflects the tenor of the entire exegesis of M Kidd. 3.12 in the Babylonian Talmud. In other words, the shifting of parameters from the matrimonial horizons of the Mishnah to those of the Talmuds, with their emphasis on proselytes, may reflect a process of adaptation to contemporary circumstances.

Commenting on M Kidd. 3.12 (4) the Babylonian Talmud distinguishes, unlike the Mishnah, between slaves on the one hand and gentiles on the other, claiming that the former are "Canaanites" and thus disqualified marital partners whose issue follows the status and identity of the mother. To justify the Mishnaic ban on intermarriage with gentiles, the Babylonian Talmud enlarges the discussion to both Jewish men and women.

How do we know [that betrothal is invalid] with a freeborn gentile woman (*nokhrit*)? Scripture says: *Neither shall you make marriage with them* (Deut. 7:3). Hence her betrothal is invalid. How do we know that her issue is like her [in status]? Rabbi Johanan said on the authority of Rabbi Simeon b. Yohai: because Scripture says: *For he will turn away your son from following me* (Deut. 7:4). Your son by an Israelite woman is called your son, but your son by an idolatress (*ovedet kokhavim*) is not called your son but her son. Rabina said: This proves that thy daughter's son by an idolater (*oved kokhavim*) is called your son. Shall we say that Rabina holds that if an idolater or a [non-Jewish] slave who has intercourse with a daughter of Israel produces a mamzer? [No.] Granted that he is neither fit (*kasher*) nor mamzer (bastard) but unfit (*pasul*) [to marry a priest].

Now, the [biblical] verse refers to the seven nations (*goyim*). How do we know it of other nations? Scripture says: *For he will turn away your son* (Deut. 7:4), which includes all who may turn [him] away. That is well according to Rabbi Simeon who interprets the reason of Scripture. But on the view of [other] Rabbis, what is the reason? Scripture says: *And after that thou shalt go in unto her and be her husband* (Deut. 21:13), whence it follows that before that *kiddushin* [betrothal] with her is invalid (*lo tafsu*).[34]

Besides a well-known rabbinic tendency to anchor Mishnaic rulings in biblical quotations,[35] the Babylonian Talmud interpretation of M Kidd. 3.12(4b) supports the Mishnaic claim of invalid betrothals between a Jew and a gentile not only by endowing the Deuteronomic ban on intermarriage with the widest possible sphere of application but also by adducing verses which, in fact, appear to undermine this insistence. The Deuteronomic ban on intermarriage forbade all intermarriage with seven named peoples, but the fear of idolatry, the reason for which this ban was pronounced, continued to haunt the rabbis. It was, then, perfectly acceptable to recruit Deut. 7:3–4 not only to oppose all intermarriage but also as a reminder of the danger inherent in these unions. And it is precisely to bring home this menace that the rabbis emphasized the so-called matrilineal principle, namely the production of more Jews if the mother is Jewish, but the production of more gentiles if the mother is a gentile.

Thus far talmudic exegesis confirms and expands the thrust of the Mishnah. But the employment of Deut. 21:13 as scriptural support of the invalidity of betrothal between a Jewish man and a gentile is problematic. The subject of the Deuteronomic verse is the relations between free (Israelite male) and bonded (beautiful war captive) whose union is perceived as a valid marriage.[36] The unnamed rabbis who opposed Rabbi Simeon's reference to Deut. 7:4 in conjunction with the identity of the gentiles as forbidden marital partners appear to claim that since Deut. 21:13 does not refer to betrothal at all its silence can be taken to mean that betrothal between Jews and gentiles, in general, is always invalid. The fact of the matter is that Deuteronomy makes no distinction between betrothal and marriage and the verse cited has no relevance to the subject of marriage between a free Jewish man and a free gentile. Rather, the employment of Deut. 21:13 obfuscates the issue and still leaves unexplained the reason for invalidating betrothal between a Jewish man and a gentile who are both free. What is clear, however, is the continuous fear of apostasy, a fear which also accounts for the talmudic focus on proselytes as marital partners.[37]

Another curious aspect of BT Kidd. 68b is its use of terminology to designate gentiles. The Mishnah, in this case, uses the term "foreigner" (*nokhrit*) while the Babylonian Talmud specifies "idolaters" (worshipers of the stars, *ovdei kokhavim*). Since neither Deuteronomy nor this Mishnah employs the term, it may be asked whether the Babylonian editor adapted the biblical and Mishnaic terms to the environment in which these rules were to be operative, or whether the passage merely displays a rhetorical array of words that describe the same object. "Worshipers of the stars" or "of idols" appear elsewhere in the Mishnah, and the selection of this term to apply to intermarriage may indicate both a desire to conform to a widespread Mishnaic use as well as to conditions prevailing in Babylon.[38] Above all, the use of "idolaters" to designate non-Jews in this *gemara* was driven by a clear-cut dichotomy between monotheists and polytheists, the kind of distinction that made sense in late ancient Persia. It is hardly surprising, therefore, that the Palestinian amoraim discarded the Mishnaic "foreigner" (*nokhria*) in favor of the biblical "goy" (PT Kidd. 64c-d). This last, at least in the Bible, designated both the Israelite group and non-Israelite groups but later came to denote non-Jews. By selecting so wide an appellation the redactor of the Palestinian Talmud emphasized the ambiguity that surrounded the issue of the validity of intermarriage and at the same time the all-embracing sphere of application of biblical and Mishnaic marital bans to all non-Jews, idolaters, and/or Christians. While reproducing the same rabbinic debate over the status of a child of (supposedly invalid) marriage between Jewish men and gentile women, the Palestinian Talmud adds a tale of a rabbi who authorized the circumcision (and on the Sabbath!) of a son born to a gentile woman by her Jewish husband (PT Kidd. 64d). Needless to say, although this rabbi was severely reprimanded, the validity of this marriage was not contested, nor the parental attempt to incorporate their (non-Jewish, according to the Mishnah) child into the Jewish community.[39]

That marital bans had different scopes and purposes at different periods seems obvious. The author of Deut. 7:3–4 aimed the prohibition at intermarriage with the numerically superior local tribes of Canaan. Here the possibility of leaving Judaism is given as the reason for this ban, and daughters, whether Jewish or non-Jewish, are regarded as the main agent of conversion. Rabbinic discussions enlarged the field of contact from the more formal betrothal and marital bonds to informal sexual contacts, strongly condemning both as detrimental to the welfare of the Jewish people.[40] Yet, as numerous talmudic references to non-Jews (*goyim*) show, contacts between Jews and gentiles were too frequent to allow for complete isolation, desirable as such a state may have been in the eyes of the rabbis.⁴¹ To lessen the attraction of non-Jewish women for Jewish males, the rabbis likened the former to animals and compared such an association with the eating of forbidden food and even with sacrilege.⁴² The underlying anxiety remained the fear of apostasy and the production of non-Jews, and the problem resided in the religious identity of the children born of mixed-religion marriages.⁴³ Several passages in both the Babylonian and the Palestinian Talmuds imply that a son of a non-Jewish mother is not Jewish and not even his father's son.⁴⁴

A striking Mishnaic omission in the discussion of intermarriage relates to the option of conversion as a palliative and, by extension, as a validating act. Rabbinic opinions on proselytism are complex, ambiguous, and do not lend themselves to easy categorization.⁴⁵ One talmudic view regarded timing as the critical criterion for validation of marriage between a convert and a Jew.

If a man said to a woman, "you become betrothed to me and after that I shall become a proselyte," or "after that you will become a proselyte" . . . her betrothal is not valid. (M Kidd. 3.5)

A mere promise to convert, then, was insufficient to validate the betrothal. If the marriage went ahead prior to the completion of the conversion, the status of the children was in doubt even though their fate is not discussed in this passage.⁴⁶ Two scenes are envisaged here: one postulates a non-Jewish male proposing to a Jewish woman, the other a Jewish male proposing to a non-Jewish woman. Conversion for the sake of marriage or love had to be accomplished before the betrothal and the marriage took place. If the marriage went ahead prior to the completion of the conversion process, the children would have followed the status of the mother, as Kidd. 3.12 specified with reference to marriage between a Jewish man and a gentile woman (*nokhrit*). The fate of the children born of an alliance between a Jewish woman and a gentile is not discussed either in Kidd. 3.5 or in 3.12.⁴⁷

A certain readiness to convert to Judaism for love had also been acknowledged by the rabbis who, nevertheless, remained firm supporters of those who converted "for the sake of heaven" rather than for any other reason.⁴⁸ Talmudic exegesis of M Kidd. 3.5 (above), which required conversion before betrothal, also focused on conversion as a juridical process. As long as the prospective spouses did not become Jews, the gentile status of the groom or of the bride rendered the marriage null (BT Kidd. 63a).

Such opinions also reflect the intricacies of conversion to Judaism and the process's transformation from a privately conducted informal one (as delineated, for example, in "Joseph and Aseneth"), to the more formal process under rabbinical supervision.

Since the issue of mixed marriage is inextricably linked to conversion both to and from Judaism, it is necessary to inquire about the realities behind its legal theories.[49] Rabbinic sources, unfortunately, rarely lend themselves to precise dates and numbers. Assuming that in spite of rabbinic strictures, or perhaps because of their ambiguity on several aspects of mixed marriage, apostasy did follow marriage with non-Jews, at least in some cases, it is nonetheless difficult, if not impossible, to gauge its spread either chronologically or numerically. Any discussion of apostasy, whether as a result of intermarriage or not, is further complicated by the ambiguity of rabbinic opinions on whether apostates remain Jews forever, and by a certain reluctance to deal with the problem of apostasy.[50] General rabbinic antipathy, however, can be easily deduced from the vehemence of the so-called "Benediction of the sectarians (*minim*)."[51] Popular reactions to the presence of apostates in the community can also be gauged from Roman laws of the fourth and fifth centuries which tried to protect apostates from the wrath of their former coreligionists.[52]

Nor can the precise extent of conversion to Judaism as a result of intermarriage be determined. Although there is now some consensus that the Jews never proselytized actively, there is sufficient information about interest in, sympathy with, and conversion to Judaism in late antiquity to show that a certain degree of communal interactions did occur. Synagogal services, for example, were open to non-Jews.[53] It is also likely that "by the third century some Jews had begun to see proselytizing as a religious duty."[54] Perhaps, as Martin Goodman has claimed, the Jews acquired some missionary zeal from the success of the Christians.[55] But the question of proselytism, as far as mixed marriages are concerned, goes beyond the presence or absence of an orchestrated promotion.

It is equally difficult to trace the historicity of the development of rabbinical views on conversion to Judaism, and specifically as a result of a desire to marry a Jew. By one reading, there was a certain hardening of rabbinic positions on converts in general during the talmudic period (ca. 220 to 550).[56] But even here there is no consensus, and various rabbis are reported to either favor or reject converting gentiles. In its most extreme expression, attributed to Helbo, a Palestinian amora of the late third century, rabbinic opinion held that "proselytes are as injurious to Israel as a scab."[57] Yet, a pupil of Helbo, Brachia, used the same biblical phrase to adduce, somewhat theoretically if not euphemistically, that descendants of proselytes can become priests in the Temple.[58] The question is whether there was a general antagonism to all proselytes or to certain types of proselytes.[59] Goodman notes that all the comments which imply approval of proselytizing are ascribed to Palestinian rabbis of the third and early fourth centuries.[60]

How frequent or infrequent were, in fact, nonsanctified unions between Jews and gentiles in late antiquity? Repeated biblical and postbiblical prohibitions may lead one to suppose that they were not rare. Even the Mishnah, where references are few and scattered, refers without a comment to its own distinction between the levirate obligations of children born of valid and of invalid marriages.[61] All it states is that those born of the latter (who according to M Kidd. 3.12 are in any case not Jews but according to the Talmud are *mamzerim*) were exempt from the duty of the levirate:

If a man has any kind of brother, such a brother imposes on his brother's wife the duty of levirate marriage, and he counts as his brother in every respect unless he was the son of a bondwoman or a gentile woman. (M Yeb. 2.5)

Besides tannaitic (Mishnaic) disapproval of mixed marriages, another disincentive to marriage between Jews and non-Jews prior to 212 was a disparity in civic status. *Conubium*, or valid marriage between Roman citizens and foreigners, existed only upon grant of special permission from the civil authorities.[62] Jews were, by definition, *peregrini*, or foreigners. If the mother was a Roman citizen and the father a foreigner, even with *conubium* the children remained foreigners. One, of course, could enter a marriage without being aware of the status of the potential partner, either because of false pretenses or promises. Both Roman and Mishnaic law envisaged such situations.[63]

Whether or not Roman law influenced rabbinic opinions on marriage is debatable but not unlikely.[64] At present, suffice it to note the similarities of approach. The fact that both the Mishnah and the Palestinian Talmud were written and redacted under Roman rule should be borne in mind. The nearest equivalent in Roman legal terminology of intermarriage to Jewish-gentile marriage is the Roman ruling on marriage between a noncitizen female (without *conubium*) and a Roman male citizen, a union that produced another foreigner. Here, in fact, resides a significant contradiction between Roman and Jewish legal opinions. Prior to 212 if neither Jew nor gentile were Roman citizens their marriage was conducted along the rulings of *ius gentium*. At the same time, if a Jewish groom was also non-citizen while his gentile bride happened to be one, with or without *conubium*, their child (by Roman law) followed the status of the foreign father. By Jewish law, that child followed the status of the mother. In their eagerness to prevent intermarriage the rabbis ignored the issue of citizenship and merely affirmed that a union between a Jewish man and a gentile woman had no contractual validity and could not produce more Jews. Whether by deeming such unions undesirable the rabbis also desired to highlight ethnic or religious differences is an open issue.[65]

Rabbinic disapproval of mixed marriage across both status and religious/ethnic lines must be assessed, therefore, against the larger context of different operative legal systems. While Roman law acknowledged the disparity of status as a marital impediment, the disparity of cult (or even of ethnicity) was wholly foreign to the classical Roman idea of marriage. Thus, although the Mishnaic injunction on the nullity of betrothal (and marriage) between Jews and gentiles had a long and distinguished ancestry in Jewish writings,[66] it was reformulated in an area controlled by Rome and where Roman law, at least nominally, held sway.[67] Since the Roman government allowed groups within the empire to abide by their own customs as long as they did not infringe on Roman jurisdiction, it can be further assumed that when mixed-religion marriage took place without conversion, the couple had to marry according to local or Roman law.[68] Otherwise, the rabbinical assimilation of free-bonded marriage to marriage between a Jew and a gentile rendered both null and void.

In spite of rabbinic condemnations, the possibility of intimacy between a Jewess and a gentile was not altogether discounted. BT San. 57b provides an elaborate discourse on adultery between a gentile and a betrothed or married Jewess and on the rules, Roman or rabbinic, that apply to such situations. Since it seems that the rabbis did not have the official authority to execute the penalties that they prescribed, it can be assumed that the discussion served to illustrate the gravity of any sort of intimate interaction between Jews and gentiles, particularly between Jewish maidens and gentile males.[69] The issue of adultery between Jews and gentiles had far-reaching repercussions. It contributed to ongoing polemics not only against extramarital liaisons but also against intermarriage. Moreover, the very possibility of adultery outside the community prompts a question about the roots of this discourse. Are we dealing with another rabbinic theory which envisaged an unlikely case merely to discuss various forms of punishments, or did the debate echo Roman legislation on adultery and on marriage between Jews and Christians? Since Roman law on Jewish-Christian intermarriage equated, rather oddly, mixed-religion marriage with adultery, it is likely that rabbinic discussion of adultery outside the faith indeed reflected this equation without, however, going so far as to discuss this specific type of mixed marriage.

The most resounding talmudic silence with regard to mixed marriage and to its attendant problems is the absence of specific references to Jewish-Christian marriage. This is particularly striking in view of the growing likelihood of such a match, not only from the first century onward but even more so from the early fourth century onward, both in Palestine and the Roman imperial Diaspora.[70] Christians were naturally included in the category of gentiles, and hence, perhaps, did not merit a specific mention. Not once were Christians envisaged as potential non-Jewish partners in marriage. Yet, the appearance of both canonic and Roman bans on Jewish-Christian marriage even before the redaction of either the Palestinian or the Babylonian Talmud renders rabbinic silence curious and possibly deliberate, and invites speculations regarding Jewish customs in the Diaspora. Did members of the Jewish communities in the Roman Empire follow rabbinical precepts? Was it rather fragmentation and regionalism that distinguished internal Jewish affairs in late antiquity?

Since the chances of mixed marriages were considerably higher in a Diaspora context than in a Palestinian one, this is not an idle question. The arguments for lack of links between the two are largely arguments from silence. Thus, in a recent analysis of Diaspora synagogues, Louis Feldman remarked that "The lack of reference to Jerusalem and to the hope of rebuilding the Temple, which had been so central in Jewish life, is extremely surprising in view of the fact that apparently funds were collected for the Temple each year from every Jew even after the destruction of the Temple."[71] Shaye Cohen believes that any links between the patriarch (Nasi) in Palestine and the Diaspora communities cannot antedate the fourth century.[72] Once more, the question is how much can be deduced from silence. For just as there are scant allusions to Jerusalem within a Diaspora context, there are equally scant allusions in the Talmuds to Diaspora communities in provinces like Spain, Gaul, and Britain.[73] At this point, it is necessary to turn briefly to non-Jewish sources to further probe into the phenomenon of mixed-religion marriage.

Early Christianity and Marital Peripheries

If rabbinic legal thought introduced the element of religion as a weighty component in the consideration of marriage, early Christian thought did the same with regard to separation. While acknowledging the possibility of mixed-religion marriage, 1 Cor. 7:12–15 also circumscribed the freedom of a believer to leave the nonbelieving spouse.

If any brother has an unbelieving wife, and she is content to live with him, let him not put her away. And the wife that has an unbelieving husband, who is content to live with her, let her not put away her husband. For the unbelieving husband is sanctified in the wife, and the unbelieving wife is sanctified in the brother. Otherwise your children would be unclean whereas now they are holy. But if the unbeliever departs, let him depart; the brother or the sister is under no bondage in such cases, for God has called you unto peace.

The prohibition seems to imply a preexisting marriage in which one spouse underwent conversion and baptism while the other remained non-Christian. In this case, the believing spouse sanctified the relationship, thus changing, at least theoretically, the legal reality of Roman (civil) law which never considered divorce on the ground of religious disparity. Yet, Paul also conceded that if the nonbeliever preferred separation, divorce was valid and, by implication, second marriage as well. He thus provided for what has been called "the Pauline privilege" which allowed the converted spouse to dissolve the marriage under certain conditions, once more in contravention of both Jewish and Roman law. In spite of the neat symmetry of this unusual message, its vagueness, not unlike that of rabbinical sentences on the same topic, has resulted in a lengthy historical and legal debate.[74]

A marriage, then, which upon conversion and baptism of one spouse turned into a mixed Jewish-Christian marriage, remained a valid agreement. Rabbinic discussions of mixed marriage did not confront the question of conversion after the marriage, perhaps an indication that apostatized or not, a Jew remained a Jew. Thus, even if in the course of married life one spouse converted to Christianity, the marriage probably remained valid.[75] The exception which Paul proposed allowed for a divorce but did not undermine the validity of the marriage itself. Nor did Paul question the precise religious affiliation of the Christian's spouse. Like the rabbis, Paul discussed mixed marriage in general terms without envisaging a specifically Jewish partner.

Theologians of the early church, like Cyprian and Tertullian, both

Africans, regarded intermarriage between Christians and pagans as *stuprum*, namely an illicit sexual liaison with virgins or with widows.[76] Conciliar discussions of mixed marriages were more specific. In the collection of canons from the Spanish council of Elvira, the first to have survived in the history of Christianity, the issue of marriage outside the (Christian) faith figures prominently.[77] Although the precise date of the council is uncertain, it is pre-Constantinian and thus reflecting the crystallization of Christian thinking on the subject prior to the legalization of Christianity and to the engagement of Roman law with the subject of mixed marriages.[78]

Among canons dealing with relations between Jews and Christians, one specifically forbids mixed marriages:

If heretics should be unwilling to cross over to the catholic church they are not to have catholic girls given to them in marriage. Nor shall catholic girls be given to Jews or to heretics, since there can be no alliance between the faithful and the unfaithful (2 Cor. 6:15). If parents act against this prohibition, they shall be kept out for five years.[79]

Here, indeed, is the very first prohibition specifically relating to marriage between Jews and (catholic) Christians. Nor is it, as is obvious from this canon, the only one imposing restrictions on the marital circle of "catholic" women. The bishops assembled at Elvira issued two canons against marital links between pagans and Christians, and especially between Christian women and pagan priests, and a third canon banning marriage between "heretics" and "Catholics."[80] Different reasons and different penalties were assigned to each type of the banned unions, depending on the real or perceived gravity of the transgression.[81] Episcopal attitudes to mixed Christian-Jewish marriage within the Elviran context can be gauged from the relatively mild penalty imposed on the parents of transgressors.[82] The Elvira bans also introduced a new dimension into the Pauline discussion of mixed marriage. Instead of envisaging marriage in which one partner became Christian and/or an eventual separation and remarriage, the bishops exhorted believers to avoid mixed marriages altogether. In this, they echoed the strategy which the rabbis had adopted in their attempt to retain the purity of Jewish identity.

Following Pauline strictures, the Elviran bans justify the prevention of mixed marriage on the basis of the absence of religious compatibility. A fear of the other spouse converting to Judaism or relapsing to paganism is implied but not stated. The very first canons of the council (1–4) punish those who continued to sacrifice to idols even after conversion as well as those who apostatized. In the case of mixed marriages, the threat of excommunication, however, was pronounced on the parents of the catholic bride and not on the woman herself. By imposing penalties on the parents of a Christian bride, the Elviran ban on mixed marriage acknowledged familial authority over the choice of spouses for their daughters.

In classical Roman law the woman's consent, as a contracting party in a marriage, was essential, but reality, of course, was often different and parental choice and approval were vital.[83] Since, moreover, the initial negotiations over marriage involved dowry, the bishops at Elvira had an additional motive to disapprove of mixed marriages.[84] Dowries could mean the transfer of property from Christian to non-Christian hands, a prospect which they clearly did not relish. Yet, apart from threatening with excommunication, the bishops at Elvira could not undermine the legal validity of marriage between Jews and Christians, if such a union had occurred. What they did try, once more not unlike the rabbis, was to link conversion to "catholicism" with marriage, at least in the case of heretics, and by implication in the case of Jews.[85] Moreover, there was always hope, as Paul had expressed, that the believer might influence the other person.

Intimate relations between Jews and Christians, at least in the mirror of Spain of the Elviran council, also extended to extramarital liaisons. Canon 78 of the council of Elvira declared that:

Should any of the faithful, although married, commit adultery with a Jewish or a pagan woman, he will be banned from communion. If someone else detects [this adultery], the prescribed penance having been completed, he [the adulterer] may join the Sunday communion after five years.[86]

Here, the disparity of creed and status explains the vehemence of the bishops who imposed perpetual exclusion on a transgressor. By doing so, they condemned not only the very existence of these ties but also their secrecy and informality. Although adultery featured prominently on the agenda at Elvira this is the only reference to extramarital liaisons outside the "catholic" fold. Strictly speaking, as the bishops must have known, a married man was hardly considered an adulterer on the basis of religious disparity between himself and his sexual partner. The bishops applied, however, possibly deliberately, the wrong legal term to sex between married Christian males and non-Christian women, permitting the wife to leave the transgressing spouse but not to remarry until he died.[87]

The originality of the Elviran concept of adultery as sexual relations between free and bonded and/or between Christian males and Jewish or pagan women is particularly striking in its peculiar mixture of Pauline and Roman legal precepts. Following the Pauline idea of the equality of sexual guilt, the Spanish bishops held men liable for adultery, even in cases where Roman law did not recognize criminality.[88] But they also adopted and adapted ideas of Roman jurists on the liability of adultery. Interpreting the Augustan legislation on adultery, the jurist Marcian enlarged the term "adultery" to embrace marriage between a guardian and his ward.[89] On the other hand, unlike Roman law, the church was willing to grant forgiveness to a man who had repeatedly committed adultery if he repented on his deathbed.[90]

Other canons touching on relations between Jews and Christians in early-fourth-century Spain show that not only beds but also foods were shared among Christians and Jews. Spanish landowners who evidently believed in the power of Hebrew and/or Aramaic incantations invited Jews to grace their fields with Jewish benedictions.[91] The spread of Jewish settlements along the Spanish Mediterranean is well attested by inscriptions which have been found in Majorca, Ibiza, Adra (Abdera), Elche (Ilici), Tortosa (Dertosa), Tarragona (Tarraco), and Villamesías (north of Merida). From these inscriptions it seems that members of these communities used Hebrew/Aramaic names (such as Shmuel, son of Haggai of Majorca), and that their wealth and local prominence drew attention, if not crusades of conversion.[92] The forced conversion of the Jewish community of Magona (Minorca) in 418, engineered by the local bishop, provides the first example of this type of confrontation between Christian and Jewish communities in the empire, and supplies invaluable insights into the strategies of mass conversion to Christianity used by the church in Spain.[93] An anti-Semitic streak in Spanish Christianity may be also discerned in the earliest surviving Christian literary compositions, and particularly in Juvencus's poetry.[94] In the middle of the fourth century, Elvira, the seat of the first recorded ecclesiastical council, had a bishop whose staunch allegiance to Nicene (catholic) Christianity and hostility to the Jews were much admired.[95]

In situations in which Christian parents had more daughters than eligible husbands, the choice between a pagan, a heretic, and a Jew was not always clear-cut. Jewish husbands may have been more desirable than either pagan or heretic spouses. Jewish brides, on the other hand, did not enter the considerations of the bishops at Elvira. Either the possibility of a Christian man marrying a Jewish woman was very remote or the bishops were aware that such a marriage often led to conversion to Judaism and, possibly, to the alienation of the children from the father's faith. On the whole, the evidence is both too scanty and too ambiguous to assist in determining the precise tapestry of relationships between Jews and Christians circa 300 in Spain. Its very ambiguity underlines both friendships and rivalries as well as assimilation and separatist tendencies on both sides. The very inclusion of "Jewish" canons in Elvira shows that the bishops were not as complaisant as their folk when it came to eating and sleeping with Jews. In this light, the efforts made at Elvira to redefine the "catholic" community of Spain through the marginalization of other groups (pagans, heretics, and Jews), and by penalizing straying members, echo rabbinical regulations on precisely the same issues.

The absence of eligible Jewish brides and the presence of Jewish lovers in the canons remains a striking illustration of the complexities of the social landscape in which intimate relations were intertwined with public morality. Whether or not Jewish parents kept a tight control over the choice of husbands for their daughters is an issue open to conjecture, as is the readiness of Jewish women to engage in extramarital sex with Christians. Perhaps the reticence about marriage between Jewish women and Christian men relied on the strength of Jewish convictions, communal authority, and familial strategies. It may be assumed that both the Jewish and Christian establishments exerted considerable pressure on anyone contemplating an undesirable match. Yet, neither these preventive measures nor the penalties pronounced had the power to nullify a "mixed" marriage that had taken place as long as disparity of cult was not enshrined as an impediment in civil law.

Banning Jewish-Christian Marriage: Roman Legal Perspectives

The decisive formulation of *disparitas cultus* as matrimonial impediment in civil law was introduced in 388 by the emperor Theodosius I.[96] It is not, however, without its problems, nor was it the first attempt of the Roman government to intervene in the marriage market. As early as 326 (or 339), a law referred to a "shameful association" between Christian female weavers and Jewish men, but its vehement anti-Jewish rhetoric effectively conceals the precise nature of the Jewish-Christian connection.[97] In the early 370s an imperial constitution banned Roman-"barbarian" marriage.[98] By introducing an ethnic slant into marital impediments, this ban paved the way to the introduction of religion as another marital barrier.

The 388 ban on intermarriage between Jews and Christians belongs to a series of imperial laws which dealt with Jewish affairs in late antiquity.[99] While the quantity of "Jewish" laws dating to the fourth and the fifth centuries implies sustained imperial efforts to define the status of the Jewish community in the Roman Empire, mixed marriages constituted only one among several matters that required imperial attention and intervention besides voluntary apostasy and proselytism, circumcision of Christian slaves, and the internal jurisdiction of Jewish courts. In its edited version, the imperial prohibition regarding marriage between Jews and Christians is succinct. It represents the first general civil ban of marriage on the grounds of religious disparity:

Let no Jew accept a Christian woman in marriage, nor should a Christian man contract marriage with a Jewish woman. For if anyone should commit something of this sort, the crime of adultery will be considered to have taken place, and the freedom of accusing will be granted also to members of the public. (CTh 3.7.2 = 9.7.5 = CJ 1.9.6)[100]

The law appears twice in the Theodosian Code, once in a section (3.7) devoted to marriage in general (*de nuptiis*), and once in a section (9.7) devoted to the Augustan legislation on adultery (*ad legem Juliam de adulteriis*). Modern interpreters of this ban have regarded it as an attempt to curtail proselytism, and as a measure against Jewish polygamy which contradicted marital impediments imposed by Roman law.[101] It has also been suggested that this law represents a drive toward religious and political unity of the empire through an assertion of Christian matrimonial unity (*concordia fidei*).[102] All three hypotheses are reasonable, but only up to a point. To begin with, there are enough Roman laws on proselytism without resorting to the bedroom to add as yet another deterrent. This factor renders doubtful the relevance of the ban to the issue of proselytism. Then, there is a specific law banning polygamy (which had already been banned by Diocletian in 285, CJ 5.5.2), as well as laws that repeatedly insist on entrusting internal communal affairs to the Jewish authorities and not to Roman judicial bodies. As part of the Roman-Christian rhetoric on family values and marriage in late antiquity, the 388 ban on Jewish-Christian intermarriage is, therefore, unique and requires different explanation.

Addressed to Cynegius, the Praetorian prefect of the East (whose domain included Palestine), the law (CTh 3.7.2/9.7.5) introduced two novelties into existing imperial legislation on mixed marriages. One is the application of the ban to all mixed marriages (here clearly defined as *matrimonium iustum*) between Jews and Christians, regardless of sex, class, and rank. The second is the equation of such marriages with adultery. The former signaled the conclusion of a long process of rabbinic and episcopal reflections on the subject. The latter enabled such marriages to be dissolved, since Roman law never provided for a divorce on the ground of the disparity of cult.

Although at present, it seems impossible to recover the precise circumstances which had prompted the ban on Jewish-Christian marriage in 388, it is not unlikely that both Christian and Jewish ideologies had exercised some influence on its formulation. Particularly striking is the introduction of the issue of adultery as a component of the ban. Jewish, imperial, and ecclesiastical strictures on adultery have a long history.[103] Imperial legislation on adultery from Augustus onward aimed at preserving the integrity of the (aristocratic) family through penalizing extramarital affairs of married women and by making adultery a public offense.[104] Under Constantine, the public was excluded from the circle of potential accusers but the right of the husband to accuse a woman on the basis of suspicion alone was reinforced. The emperor even encouraged male relatives of a suspected adulteress to bring an accusation against her by granting them the right to withdraw their suit if they could not prove it at court.

Adultery also became, under Constantine, one of three lawful grounds for divorce, alongside prostitution and magic. If a husband wished to divorce his wife on any of these three grounds (and could prove it), he was also entitled to her dowry as well as to marry a second time.[105] The penalties for adultery ranged from exile and confiscation of property to death, depending on the rank of the offender and the presence of other serious crimes.[106] Moreover, although women were by legal definition culpable of adultery, their partners, as well as male adulterers were occasionally punished and, at times, as severely as wayward women.[107] Declaring as adulterous legal marital alliances between Christians and Jews enabled their families and even the public to resort to laws on adultery in order to undermine the validity of the marriage. To be precise, the equation of such marriage with adultery did not nullify it. But it put it within a category which had been repeatedly denounced by emperors, bishops, and rabbis, and it facilitated divorce.

The 388 ban on Jewish-Christian marriage, then, introduced several novelties. It pronounced a legally married couple as adulterous; it made their marriage a public criminal offense; and it clearly made the disparity of cult a weighty consideration in marital arrangements. Mixed-religion marriage became a moral offense, precisely the same stigma which both rabbis and bishops had attached to it. By approving public accusations of adultery the state made such marriages into an affair which could be prosecuted at court. And it wrested these marriages out of their intimate and private familial context and put them in the harsh limelight of the public arena.[108]

It is difficult to determine whether the Roman ban on mixed marriage had been issued in response to the prompting of Christian theologians, or at requests of zealous prefects, or urgings of Jewish leaders. Its very issuance served to undermine the legal validity of the marriage itself. It also made such unions a dangerous proposition. Yet, the efficacy of the law remains an open question. It was taken by both the editors of the *Breviarium Alarici* of 506, with significant modifications, and by the editors of the Justinian Code (CJ 1.9.6), and had a remarkable afterlife in both canonic and civil legislation.[109] But cases that illustrate the precise working of the law are not available. Perhaps, then, for a while at least, rabbinic, episcopal, and imperial strictures against marriage outside the faith did prevent such misalliance or at least combined to shroud these in silence.

From birth to death the tales of the past provide an ancient and venerable mode of illustrating the turning points that accompany the life of a Jew. Marriage and learning loom large, when the two are compatible.[110] But women also provide a forceful reminder of mortality and of the torment of sexuality and not only of comfort and fertility. Through the law of marriage that distributes or, rather, redistributes women, one by one, into masculine households, men bring women back into the human order of society, that is, into the domicile. To maintain reproduction within a closed circuit so as to ensure legitimate offspring it is necessary to monitor the upbringing and development of women from daughters to wives and thence to mothers. In a remarkably homogeneous discourse about women, "foreign" women pose an inextricable problem. If to be a Jew is the only condition that defines membership in the community there is no way to become one other than by already being a Jew.

Rabbinic discourses about intermarriage are, understandably, complex. To produce Judaism, the rabbis had to keep a strict watch over the purity and fecundity of the community. When birth becomes a criterion for exclusion, lineage determines the equality of origins and an equal share in privileges and responsibilities. A Jew must be born not only of a Jewish father but also of a mother whose father is a Jew. This had been the assumption of the founders of the Second Temple commonwealth. In Ezra-Nehemiah the foreign women become an anonymous group, threatening by its very presence in a sanctified land and by its power of procreation. By contrast, foreign men who meddle in patriarchal marital arrangements, like Shechem, appear as individuals incapable of self-control and hence of membership in a community that strives to make men masters of their own natural urges.

According to Genesis's order of creation Jews "descend" from God in a tale of origins without reproduction and outside the confines of all sexuality. To mediate lineage, however, Jewesses are essential. The matrilineal principle does not elevate the Jewish mother to a position of an arbiter of status. It affirms here inextricability within the circle of marriage and maternity. Within this domestic frame, "foreign" women remain an emblem of all that can go wrong, a heretic element in an orthodoxy in matters of birth and belonging that characterizes rabbinic, Roman, and Christian perceptions of communal affiliation in late antiquity.

Between Pentateuchal strictures on marriage outside the elected group and the Roman ban on ethnically or religiously mixed matrimony stands a conviction that membership is determined not through the individual but through specific forms of socialization. A Jewess allied with a gentile incorporates all that was forbidden, from sex outside the sect to the possibility of apostasy and alienation. (Inter)marriage is tantamount to the crossing of multiple boundaries, all resulting in violations of accepted norms. Roman law defined a partner in a mixed marriage as an adulterer or an adulteress. Christian bishops imposed excommunication on parents who approved such matches and branded any illicit sex outside the sect as adultery. The parents of a Jewess who marries a man of her choice, and particularly a gentile, mourned her as though she has crossed the threshold that separated life from death. Having engendered a Jewess they buried her in the prime of her life. Her wedding turned into her funeral that marked her departure from the religion of her birth.

Marriage entails maternity. This is one underlying motive of the various discourses of marital eligibility and ineligibility in late antiquity. Wrong marriages breed children with doubtful status and confuse the boundaries of the family. In Genesis 34 and Numbers 25 the possibility of progeny as a result of an incorrect alliance is eliminated through death. Ezra forcibly removes "foreign" women whose fertility threatens the integrity of the community. To be born a Jew becomes an imperative for legal definition of "citizenship." In promoting the correct parentage and projecting a domicile with the right kind of woman, Christian, Roman, and rabbinic discourses of identity and marriage in late antiquity also promoted "the security of the male for all times."[111] Women become women only as spouses of Jews, Christians, or Romans.

Conclusion

*To Die like a Woman? To Live like a Woman?
Is There a Jewess in Judaism?*

> In a society that reserves politics for men—such as the privilege of representing the paradigm of humanity—it is the feminine that discriminates because the task of gathering the imprint of all the hesitations, problems, and patterns of compromise always reverts to the feminine.
>
> —Nicole Loraux, *Children of Athena*, 249

A classic deathbed scene guides readers of Genesis 48–49 through the dying moments of a venerable patriarch in his Egyptian home. Old, frail, and virtually blind, Jacob is pleasantly surprised to receive a visit from his powerful son, Joseph, accompanied by the latter's two young sons. Overjoyed, Jacob expresses his pleasure through blessings. But he, like Isaac before him, fails to recognize the correct identity of each child, bestowing on the younger the blessings due to primogeniture. Jacob then summons all his sons to listen to their respective destinies. Finally he issues orders regarding the desired topography of his burial—he is to be buried in the family burial ground in Canaan, next to Abraham, Sarah, his grandmother, Isaac, Rebecca, his mother, and Leah, his wife (Gen. 49:30–31).

This is clearly an ideal. To judge by the irenic spectacle, an Israelite hero who has enjoyed singular divine favor in his lifetime dies in old age, at home, and surrounded by his numerous progenies. Greek heroes, by contrast, if loved by the gods, die young and in battle. An Israelite male model is buried according to his wishes, together with his ancestors and with his (senior) wife.

One element is conspicuously missing from the elaborate scene of Jacob's demise. No women are present at his deathbed, neither wives, nor concubines, daughters or daughters-in-law, or granddaughters. Yet, women do make an appearance on the stage of patriarchal death, somewhat obliquely and through verbal allusions rather than visual attendance. Jacob's dying words recall the memory of the deceased matriarchs whom he is about to join in the familial graveyard where select members, male and female, had been buried. He mentions, twice, the events that embroiled his daughter, Dinah, in premature and forced widowhood without, however, referring to her by name (Gen. 48:22; 49:5–7). And he recalls the death of his beloved wife, Rachel:

When I came from Padan, Rachel, to my sorrow, died in the land of Canaan, on the way, when there was still some distance to go to Ephrath. And I buried her there on the way to Ephratha, that is Bethlehem. (Gen. 48:7, RSV)

This is a touching but select tribute. In the confrontation between life and death that underlies Jacob's text, the death of Rachel is made to fit the dignity of the patriarch's departing words. But in the clash between birth and death, as they meet in the body of a dying woman, Rachel's demise presents a startling contrast with that of Jacob. She dies in an agony that men cannot share, untimely and away from the domicile.

Gen. 35:16–19 is terse:

They left Beit El and still had a way to go before reaching Ephratha when Rachel was seized with labor pains. She had a difficult labor. And when she was experiencing difficult labor the midwife said to her: Do not fear for this [baby], too, is a son. And when she was dying, Rachel named him "Son of my Sorrow" with her dying wish. But his father renamed him "Son of my Strength" [Benjamin]. And Rachel died and was buried on the road to Ephratha, namely Bethlehem.

Rachel's labor, repeatedly characterized as difficult, drives home a closed world of women in which pain mixes with joy, and sorrow with satisfaction. When motherhood finally comes to her it entails a personal transformation and a tragedy. Rachel, the daughter and wife, becomes a prophet of the mother's self-destruction when she issues an ultimatum to her husband to provide her with sons or to bear the responsibility for her death (Gen. 30:1). He demurs and Yahweh arbitrates. She gives birth to her firstborn, Joseph, naming him "The one who will add more sons" (Gen. 30:22–24). But the redacted text, chillingly, registers the fulfillment of Rachel's ardent longing for a second son right after it records the birth of Dinah who never becomes a mother (Gen. 30:21). And it anticipates Rachel's fate by inserting the tale of Dinah (Gen. 34), a fractured virgin forced into childless "widowhood," before it describes Rachel's death (Gen. 35).

The birth of Benjamin implements Rachel's politics of nomenclature. She becomes the mother of sons and pays with her life for the acquisition of full membership in the household community. Her death in labor provides a tragic illustration of the female "horizon of fertility."[1] Rachel is also a disturbing figure (see Introduction). In Genesis she disrupts established patterns of patriarchal matrimonial preferences. Her hand is sought in marriage before her older sister is engaged. Although second to Leah in age, order of marriage, seniority, and fertility, Rachel is Jacob's beloved wife. She also hastens a conflict between her father and her husband and she is the embodiment of the belief that "to belong" means to be a mother. Her ultimate removal from the family burial emphasizes her final displacement. In the symmetrical arrangement of patriarchs and matriarchs in death there is no room for a subversive wife.

Ironically, it is also possible through speculative calculations to measure the cycle of Rachel's life in implements of seven, a much-favored number. Her virginity is prolonged by seven years as her cunning father imposes celibacy on her by shrewd dealings. As a married woman she witnesses the birth of seven children to her husband by her sister before producing one of her own. And she dies, one may assume, when Joseph turns seven years old. The seven symbolism continues to play a critical role in the life of her son, Joseph, in Egypt, where he becomes the king's favorite soothsayer, employing with efficacy a talent he had inherited from his mother. Underlying this transparent strategy of numerology appears a redactional desire to idealize the grim tale of the rebellious Rachel by "fitting" it into a familiar pattern that begins with the story of the creation itself.

Rachel's final moments expose her vulnerability. She is hit in the most fragile part of the female body and dies through the womb. Having endeavored to join the ranks of mothers she loses her motherhood at the moment of proving her reproductive capacity. When men seek to kill women, as Phineas does when he chases Cozbi into her domicile (above Chapter 1), they do so by wounding their motherhood. Underlying this form of violence is an issue of control not only of specifically female functions but of the entire female realm.

Yet, in inner biblical interpretation the supreme appellation of a "mother in Israel" is reserved not for women with a proven maternity record or for those ardently desiring motherhood but for women, like Deborah, who lead Israelite males to victory in battle (Judg. 5:7b).[2] The female saviors of the people of Israel—Deborah, Jael, and Esther—happen to be wives. None is accredited with children. Nor, for that matter, does one meet either Deborah's or Jael's husband. Their marital status may mean little more than "not virgins." They are mothers of all Israel and not just of individual Jews. By a similar process of mental stripping and redressing Rachel becomes a figure of national motherhood and mourning in Jeremiah (see Introduction).

In the process of patriarchal generation that Genesis lays out, the paradox of procreation finds its sublime expression in the lingering description of Jacob's last words. His final discourse confirms the intimate bond between father and sons, dispensing altogether with mothers (= wives), daughters, and sisters. Yet, Rachel's death brings home both the continuity and the rupture of patriarchal patterns of succession. As long as the production of males depends on the wombs of women men become mortal at the very moment of their birth. Circumcision reverses the pattern, for with it men carry the sign of the covenant in their own flesh.[3] In this scheme of procreation and recreation women introduce "the ultimate division between humankind and God."[4] They remain the foreigners.

Giving birth and dying in Pentateuchal matriarchal narratives ordinarily occurs at home.[5] By placing the scene of Rachel's demise outdoors and away from home Genesis 35 confronts two realities, the domicile where typically female activities such as childbirth normally take place, and the outside world, where men conduct their dealings. Paradoxically, Rachel's violent death out of the domicile recalls the way men often die, while Jacob's peaceful death in bed ought to, but does not, hint at the manner in which women should die.

Although the domicile harbors female activities that are crucial for mankind, it also conceals and silences. In the book of Genesis the matriarch's departing words and last moments remain on the whole unrecorded. While exploring the myriad ways in which men die, whether timely or untimely, peacefully or violently, by their own hands or at the hands of another, the Hebrew Bible rarely provides balanced accounts of the contrasting ways in which women die or ought to die. Perhaps this reticence reflects historical reasons that viewed the proper place of a woman in the seclusion of her home and far away from the public eye.[6]

On rare occasions, when the death of women is described in some detail, these women invariably die violently, untimely, and unnaturally. Such is the lot of Cozbi, a Midianite princess, and of Jezebel and her daughter, two queens, one Sidonian, the other semi-Israelite. The last pages of the Book of Judges record the murderous gang rape of an unnamed woman on the way from her father's home to that of her "husband" (Judg. 19). To this brief list it is possible to add the wife of Lot who is petrified, and the daughter of Jephthah who is slaughtered by her own father. Even more forbiddingly, Dinah "dies," textually, while she is still alive as does Tamar (2 Sam. 13), both pawns in deadly male games.

Biblical excursions into the darkest recesses of female lives realign male communal communications. As she dies Rachel names her son, as do other mothers in the Bible. But Jacob wrests the maternal privilege to launch a new politics of naming that emphasizes the place of males in the process of creation. Issues of sterility and fertility are usually settled directly between women and Yahweh through an unwritten dialogue that dispenses with males as arbiters of reproductive powers. But the affair of Dinah, the "rape" of Cozbi, and the controversy over the "foreign" wives from Yehud reestablish an exclusive mode of communication between males and Yahweh. In these tales, Dinah's brothers, Phineas, and Ezra appoint themselves spokespersons and executioners of a divine will to which they alone are privy.

In the process of engendering women the Hebrew Bible provides contradictory messages. When it penetrates the domicile it unravels wives, like Esther, whose sole communication with their husbands is over "national" politics, or concerned spouses, like Jezebel, who is willing to engage in murder in order to ensure the harmony of her marriage and her husband's peace of mind. But how far is a Jezebel from an Esther?[7] Their tales offer the only glimpses ever provided into the activities generated in the marital intimacy of the royal bedchamber.

In Esther, the only "Jew" so identified, is Mordechai. His female relative, by extension one presumes, is a Jewess. But Esther is no ordinary Jewess. She is entered into a marriage of which the Hebrew Bible usually disapproves and she does not have children, Jewish or otherwise. Her body embodies the disruption of the Jewish family in spite of her role as a savior of the Jews. She, and Mordechai, as well as Haman, are all strangers in a strange land where their survival and their modes of action depend on the hospitality and benevolence of a frivolous king. Dinah's tale reveals a similar pattern. She leaves, temporarily, the territory allocated to her father by virtue of hospitality only to discover that she has forfeited the "Jewish" or Israelite identity that she had acquired through the clan. Her penalty is childlessness, precisely the state that drove Rachel to despair. In the annals of Yehud, however, it is the motherhood of the "foreign" women that endangers the nascent covenantal community.

Women's experiences with marriage, divorce, rape, birth, and death, as narrated and redacted in the Hebrew Bible, contribute to the production and promotion of powerful negative images. Rather than delineating an ideal or idealized paths to follow as channels of identity, they emphasize the Jewess's perpetual alienation. Virgins with intact or with threatened virginity, married women with children or without, devoted or unhappy wives, all represent problems and compromises for "male paradigms of humanity."[8]

I started this study by asking who is or was a Jewess? I am tempted to wander away into wondering whether there was ever such an entity. In classical Athens there was no term for a "female citizen" (*Athenaia*) to parallel the word for a male citizen (*Athenaios*), just as there was none to describe an "adulteress" (see Chapters 3 and 4).[9] Athenian tragedy, like that of Hippolytus and Phaedra, indulged male fantasies in invoking an existence for which women were altogether dispensable. The rabbinic midrash on the Seventh Commandment (prohibition of adultery) conjured up the same illusion (see Introduction). Athenian comedy, by contrast, like Aristophanes' *Lysistrata*, envisioned women dominating the sacred center of the city through the temporary reacquisition of a state primordial virginity.[10] The midrashic Rachel under the bed, in a similar *tour de force*, is a virgin experiencing vicariously and surreptitiously the state of matrimony and intercourse (see Introduction).

Linguistically speaking, there *are* female Israelites and female Hebrews, or the equivalent of male Israelites and Hebrews, in the Hebrew Bible. One such is Shelomit, who marries an Egyptian man and gives birth to a blasphemer (Lev. 24:10–11). Her story is brief and ominous. Her son sows dissension in the camp and becomes a model of negativity. The incident does not inspire emulation. On the other hand, midwives are "Hebrew" females (Exod. 1:15), especially when they save Hebrew male babies from extinction. Do female "Hebrews," then, carry the promise of life while a female "Israelite" that of death? Hardly. Midwives do not bestow identity; mothers do, at least they give names. In naming mothers do not so much convey their own identity as the legitimacy of birth by virtue of being a daughter and a wife of a Jew. Midwives mediate the birth of Jews; mothers ensure or undermine the correct genealogy. A Jewess is thus a vital component in an elaborate construction of the correct community in which women belong to something other than themselves.

It would be otiose to argue that Jewish texts of antiquity, be they biblical, postbiblical, or rabbinic, are primarily androcentric. This has been maintained often enough. It is a fair assumption that such texts advance a model of orthodoxy for thinking about Jewish birth and provide rules that cast Jewesses as merely the name given to virgins who are also daughters of Jews, or to married women who are also the wives of Jews.[11] What I have tried to trace here are the limits of patriarchy in the subtexts and the ways in which it is possible to penetrate the remarkably homogeneous discourse about women in order to recover "truths" no longer clearly stated.[12] For in living with women and speaking about them the "truth" can be often lost.[13]

A primary encounter with Genesis 34, the text of the Dinah affair, has often focused on rape and revenge. A reading of the subtext or the pre-redacted "original" version, however, reveals a culture in which the encounter of Shechem and Dinah had little to do with rape and much to do with reciprocity between males, and with women as potential mediators of a peaceful coexistence between Jews and gentiles. Between "recollection" and elaboration Dinah forfeits her position in the household. She is de-communalized, or de-Israelitized, doomed to live in the margins of society, neither a bride, nor a widow or a mother. In this light, the identity of a Jewess (or female Israelite) is like a cloth that can be acquired, adopted, and adapted but also removed and discarded.

To drive home the horrors of leaving the paternal domicile Dinah meets with seduction and Cozbi meets with death. Esther is allowed to leave a Jewish home and to marry a gentile in order to save her people while the "foreign" wives of Yehud are driven out of the familial (Jewish) domicile in order to confirm their husbands' patriotism. Somewhere in the elusive chronology that links the Hebrew Bible to rabbinic writings in late antiquity there are glimpses of growing rigidity and lesser compromises. Jubilees consigns nonconforming daughters who contemplate marriage with gentiles to a funeral pyre. This may be an effective way to kill a Jewess but not necessarily a feasible mode of dealing with the emotions of women. By contrast, the story of Joseph and Aseneth indulges the heart of a woman. Aseneth the Egyptian can declare her love, be rejected, and then, mysteriously and somewhat unaccountably, gain acceptance. Even here there are problems. Not every Egyptian woman is likely to become a privileged host of an administering angel in the privacy of her bedroom. Not many are likely to convince their intended husbands that the experience has prepared them for marriage. Jubilees' Dinah and Aseneth of "Joseph and Aseneth" are two poles of female behavior. But Aseneth the "proselyte" wife introduces dispute into the domicile, just as Jubilees' Dinah the daughter carries defilement that can contaminate all of Israel.

Dinah's biblical father, Jacob, barely speaks in Genesis 34. In Jubilees, the father of Dinah's spiritual "daughters" becomes an object of a harangue that forges a bond of accountability between fathers and daughters. She is to be burned; he is to be stoned, subjected to the fate of biblical blasphemers. In rabbinic perspectives the father-daughter attachment becomes a burden of inescapable male responsibility:

A daughter is a vain treasure to her father. On her account he has sleepless nights. During her minority period he fears lest she be seduced. When she matures he is fearful lest she commits adultery (or: plays the harlot). And when she reaches maturity he is afraid lest she remains without a husband. When she gets married he is worried lest she does not have sons, and when she grows old he fears lest she dabbles in magic (or: witchcraft). (Ben Sirah 42:9–10)

But the rabbis said: It is not possible for the world to exist without males and without females. Happy is he whose children are all males and woe to him whose children are female. (BT San. 100b, Soncino)

The text contains familiar components. It casts Jewesses as an extension of a Jew, overlooking mothers and wives. It represents the life cycle of women as a chain of negativities, and women as a constant threat to males' peace of mind. Underlying the text is a question of application—if one's own daughter poses a constant problem, how is a Jew to view all other Jewesses?

"Like mother, like daughter" is a familiar rabbinic adage with ancient roots.[14] It features in a coda to the tale of Akiva and Rachel which records the nuptials of their daughter with Ben Azzai, a famed sage.[15] These intimate mother-daughter links generate uneasiness and images of the woman as the "other." When the coda links Rachel's daughter with Ben Azzai, it breeds significant problems. Elsewhere Ben Azzai is considered celibate for the sake of the Torah, as the following so poignantly illustrates:

[Ben Azzai said:] "Anyone who does not engage in procreation commits murder and nullifies the image of God".... Rabbi Eleazar ben Azariah said to him: "Ben Azzai, instruction is edifying when preached by those who practice it." Some, however, preach well but do not act properly, while others act properly but do not preach well. Ben Azzai preaches well but does not act properly. Ben Azzai said to him: "What shall I do? My soul craves the Torah; so let the world endure through the efforts of others."[16]

The passion of Ben Azzai has nothing to do with women. Yet his selection, of all the available sages, as Akiva's (putative) son-in-law may be interpreted as a "triumph of domestication."[17] The model of relationship set by Akiva's Rachel is, then, passed on to her daughter in order to "vanquish" the love that a man bears for the Torah. Yet, nowhere do rabbinic discourses state that a Jewess has the power to transform a man from a Torah lover into a lover of herself. When rabbinic texts talk of love of a husband for his wife it is not physical attraction but mutual respect, as long as she knows her place in the domicile and in society.[18] If a relationship between marriage (wife) and learning (Torah) harbors conflict, no Jewess can win. If she tries, she requires a notable champion or she may die in the process.

Only rarely do biblical and rabbinic texts capture the fears of women as they face the uncertainties of marriage, sterility, fertility, and death in childbirth. Something of the constant terror that the inexorable cycle of women's life contained is expressed in magical formulas where the imagination could give vent to realities. Only there it is possible to sense not the worries that beset fathers as they watch their daughters mature but the anxieties that propel women to search for supranatural cures for sterility and for assurances regarding their ability to complete terms of pregnancy, to bring harmony to the domicile, to sleep well, to love and be loved, to hate, and to forget.[19] Around the Mediterranean such concerns underline the commonalities of women's experiences, as numerous late ancient Coptic spells show:

If I stay at this house where I am, and remain inside with my mother, my heart will be at rest and shall bear a living child. [20]

Besides such forbidding prospects women could also become helpless objects of passions of men who resorted to erotic spells and potions to win their hearts:

Fill her heart with every fiery desire
And every longing and every passion and every form of love . . .
To bring her to N. son of N. . . .
Until you disturb all the reason in her heart
So that she is unable to eat or drink

> Or remain in any place
> Until she arises and goes on her feet
> And comes to N. son of N.
> And he satisfies his desire[21]

Rabbinic texts of late antiquity express fear of adultery and of marrying outside the community, but do not explain how and why lovers and wives, Jewesses and gentiles, get together in the first place. Nor do they suggest why, in spite of so many strictures, women were willing to take the risk of losing their communal identity. Aided by Roman law and the tightening of Christian-Roman morality, the rabbis consigned suspected adulteresses and women involved with non-Jews to a realm beyond the pale of the community. The Bible employs a rhetoric of ordeal to expose a suspected adulteress to the shame of public gaze, believing in the miraculous power of the revelation of potions. Rabbinic and Roman discourses of suspected adultery use the rhetoric of trial and threats of penalty to induce fear and prevention.

Paradoxically, Jewesses do not appear to desire their own husbands.[22] Legitimacy rather than love is the dominant theme of rabbinic marital ideology. To control women who desired men other than their husbands the rabbis could use the power of public pressure, as the story of the fig-gatherer shows (see Chapter 4). To regulate marriage outside the community they had to resort to Roman law. By a remarkable coincidence, Roman law, Christian theology, and rabbinic ideology congealed their visions of communal cohesion in the fourth century on the basis, partly, of banning women (first, and then men) who defied prescribed marital boundaries.

"What is a man (*enosh*)?" the Bible asks (Ps. 8:5), and replies: "He is a little less than divine" (Ps. 8:6). This conviction runs through Jewish texts of antiquity. But where does it leave a woman? "I have never called my wife my wife but always 'my house'" (BT Shab. 118). The domicile then *is* a Jewess. She has no existence outside it. In the *Lysistrata* married women daydream of living at home without men.[23] Judaism does not allow room for so far-fetched a fantasy.

In the environment that engendered and shaped the Judaism(s?) of the Hebrew Bible and rabbinic texts, Jews formed a minority, "a people apart," as Haman asserts. The scroll of Esther illustrates the precariousness of this existence. The vision of the destroyed Temple of 70 C.E., the fountainhead of rabbinic theology, constantly reinforces a sense of temporality that bred a remarkably diverse discourse of masculinity.[24] In rabbinic law heroes are men who become masters of learning (Akiva); in rabbinic lore heroes are men who learn what knowledge and self-awareness are (Meir). Such quests do not require women. Yet, the domicile provides an anchor of male existence. Jewesses, like shadows, are intimations of the spectrum of the experiences of men.

Exploring the function of women as potential loci of crisis and discord the characters, constructs, and discourses discussed here only hint at the essence of gender harmony. In the course of the lengthy period surveyed, from biblical episodes purporting to have taken place in patriarchal Canaan, in itself perhaps a myth, to Roman Palestine in late antiquity, Judaism's search for orthodoxy narrowed the margins of meaning. Rabbinic and Roman "codification of knowledge" produced legal rhetoric that shifted the burden of morality from men to women.[25] New codes of conduct, Jewish, Christian, and Roman, focused on a wife who did not guard the boundaries of her body and on women who married outside the communal perimeters. Legal ideas and social expectations combined to draw the contours of a large and negative region beyond the domicile in which no Jewess should dare to dwell.

Notes

Introduction

1. Cf. N. B. Joseph, "The Feminist Challenge to Judaism: Critique and Transformation," in *Gender, Genre, and Religion*, ed. M. Joy and E. K. Neumaier-Dargyay (Waterloo, 1995), 47–70, esp. 48, where the central premise of contemporary feminist Judaism and its transformative key are based on the premise that women *are* Jews (my italics). See also J. Plaskow, *Standing Again at Sinai: Judaism from a Feminist Perspective* (San Francisco, 1990); and E. Umansky, "Females, Feminists, and Feminism: A Review of Recent Literature on Jewish Feminism and a Creation of Feminist Judaism," *Feminist Studies* 14 (1998): 349–65.

2. M. Bal, *Lethal Love: Feminist Literary Readings of Biblical Love Stories* (Bloomington, Ind., 1986), 50.

3. Neither L. H. Schiffman, *Who Was a Jew?* (Hoboken, N.J., 1985), nor S. J. D. Cohen, *The Beginnings of Jewishness* (Berkeley, Calif., 1999), draws distinctions between gender affiliation with Judaism. But see Cohen, "Why Aren't Jewish Women Circumcised?" *Gender and History* 9 (1997): 560–78, on inherent inferiority of female Jewishness vis-à-vis male Jewishness. See also the useful comments of H. Eilberg-Schwartz, *God's Phallus and Other Problems for Men and Monotheism* (Boston, 1994), passim, on gendered symbols and the links between gendered images, conceptions of men and women, sexuality, desire, and the body. In my study the question addressed is not so much "how a male God is problematic for men's conceptions of self," as has been fully and provocatively explored in *God's Phallus*, nor the ways in which a masculine image of God undermined female experience (*God's Phallus* and H. Eilberg-Schwartz, ed., *People of the Body: Jews and Judaism from an Embodied Perspective* [Albany, N.Y., 1992], passim), but rather how the female body is perceived to function in society and how gender/sex ideology contributes to the formation of national identity. It is closer to what D. Novak calls "the socialization of human sexuality" ("Some Aspects of the Relationship of Sex, Society and God in Judaism," in *Contemporary Ethical Issues in the Jewish and Christian Traditions*, ed. F. E. Greenspahn [Hoboken, N.J., 1986], 140–66, p. 150 for quote) but does not follow the underlying assumption that institutions inform us of individuals. Rather the opposite may be the case.

There are now several important studies on the gendering of rabbinic Judaism, including J. R. Baskin, "The Separation of Women in Rabbinic Judaism," in *Women, Religion and Social Change*, ed. Y. Y. Haddad and E. B. Findly (Albany, N.Y., 1985), 3–18; J. R. Baskin, ed., *Jewish Women in Historical Perspective* (Detroit, Mich., 1991); C. E. Fonrobert, *Menstrual Purity: Rabbinic and Christian Recon-

structions of Biblical Gender (Stanford, 2000); J. Hauptman, *Rereading the Rabbis: A Woman's Voice* (Boulder, Colo., 1998); L. A. Hoffman, *Covenant of Blood: Circumcision and Gender in Rabbinic Judaism* (Chicago, 1996); J. Lassner, *Demonizing the Queen of Sheba: Boundaries of Gender and Culture in Postbiblical Judaism and Medieval Islam* (Chicago, 1993); M. B. Peskowitz, *Spinning Fantasies: Rabbis, Gender and History* (Berkeley, Calif., 1997); M. Peskowitz and L. Levitt, eds., *Judaism Since Gender* (New York, 1997); J. R. Wegner, *Chattel or Person? The Status of Women in the Mishnah* (New York, 1988).

On biblical gender premises, see J. Ochshorn, *The Female Experience and the Nature of the Divine* (Bloomington, Ind., 1981), esp. 181 f. (sex roles and the relation of power to gender).

4. For a useful overview see S. J. D. Cohen and E. L. Greenstein, eds., *The State of Jewish Studies* (Detroit, Mich., 1990). Cf. L. Davidman and S. Tenenbaum, eds., *Feminist Perspectives on Jewish Studies* (New Haven, Conn., 1994).

5. Second Temple period has been conventionally described as ca. 500 B.C.E. to 70 C.E., thereafter Judaism begins its "late antiquity," a period that in non-Jewish studies begins about 250. See P. Brown, *The World of Late Antiquity* (London, 1971). There are numerous studies that provide coverage of select periods, each expressing the author's view of periodization. S. J. D. Cohen's *From the Maccabees to the Mishnah* (Philadelphia, 1987), and L. L. Grabbe's *Judaism from Cyrus to Hadrian* (Minneapolis, 1992) and *Judaic Religion in the Second Temple Period: Belief and Practice from the Exile to Yavneh* (London, 2000) are three from a huge crop.

6. Jubilees, 2 Maccabees, and Josephus provide the exceptions and paradigms of rejection. They have been transmitted through the church. A. Momigliano, *Essays on Ancient and Modern Judaism*, trans. M. Masella-Gayley, ed. S. Berti (Chicago, 1994).

7. J. Neusner, *Self-Fulfilling Prophecy: Exile and Return in the History of Judaism* (Boston, 1987), passim, on the diversity of Judaism(s).

8. M. Haran, *The Biblical Canon* (in Hebrew; Jerusalem, 1996). The question of mechanisms of canonization was the subject of the fall term of 1999 at the Institute for Advanced Studies at the Hebrew University of Jerusalem, directed by G. Stroumsa and M. Finkelberg, at which some of the ideas raised here were discussed. See also M. Weiss, *The Bible from Within: The Method of Total Interpretation* (Jerusalem, 1984), 1–73 on the last century of biblical criticism.

9. A lengthy but immensely readable introduction is provided by D. H. Akenson, *Surpassing Wonder: The Invention of the Bible and the Talmuds* (New York, 1998).

10. On feminist biblical hermeneutics or codes of interpretation, see M. Bal, *Murder and Difference: Gender, Genre, and Scholarship on Sisera's Death* (Bloomington, Ind., 1988), to mention but one example.

11. In the area of biblical studies these questions periodically open a can of worms. For current controversies, see N. P. Lemche, *The Israelites in History and Tradition* (London and Louisville, Ky., 1998) where every stage, from the Exodus to the Exile is analyzed as a foundation myth. See also L. L. Grabbe, ed., *Can a History of Israel Be Written?* (Sheffield, 1997). More on the exile, or "exile" as a formative or foundational driving force in shaping biblical and ancient Judaism in L. L. Grabbe, ed., *Leading Captivity Captive: The Exile as History and Ideology* (Sheffield, 1998).

12. R. S. Kraemer, "Jewish Women in the Diaspora World of Late Antiquity" in Baskin, *Jewish Women in Historical Perspective*, 43–67, and B. Brooten, *Women Leaders in the Ancient Synagogue* (Chico, Calif., 1982), to mention but two of the studies that emphasize diversity and difference in women's lives, in spite of E. P. Sanders, "Common Judaism and the Synagogue in the First Century," in *Jews, Christians, and Polytheists in the Ancient Synagogue*, ed. S. Fine (London, 1999), 1–17, which insists on a "global" vision of Judaism. On the typical Diaspora institution of the *archisynagogoi*, T. Rajak and D. Noy, "*Archisynagogoi*: Office, Title, and Social Status in the Greek-Jewish Synagogue," *Journal of Roman Studies* 83 (1993): 75–93, for which there appear no parallels in Palestine.

13. W. Horbury, "Suffering and Messianism in Yose ben Yose," in *Suffering and Martyrdom in the New Testament*, ed. W. Horbury and B. McNeil (Cambridge, 1981), 143–82, esp. 176–80 on commonalities and divergencies between Yose's piyyutim and rabbinic midrashim with regard to the presentation of Israel's relations with God and, above all, p. 178 on Yose's lack of emphasis on the Oral Torah. I am grateful to Professor Horbury for drawing my attention to this important article. On piyyut as a historical source for Jewish history in late antiquity, see Y. Yahalom, *Poetry and Society in Jewish Galilee of Late Antiquity* (in Hebrew, Tel Aviv, 1999).

14. Best known is, perhaps, Jacob Neusner's voluminous commentary on the Mishnah's *Nashim* (women). See J. Neusner, *A History of the Mishnaic Law of Women* (Leiden, 1980).

15. In *Zakhor: Jewish History and Jewish Memory* (Seattle, Wash., 1982), 24, Y. H. Yerushalmi summarizes rabbinic notions of chronology as an ongoing response to the biblical challenge of becoming holy people. See the comments of P. Vidal-Naquet, *The Jews: History, Memory, and the Present*, trans. D. Ames Curtis (New York, 1996), 57–60, on "the weight of Jewish memory." The Bible itself is one such response, I believe. On rabbinic temporal perceptions, see B. Z. Wacholder, *Messianism and Mishnah: Time and Place in the Early Halakha* (Cincinnati, Ohio, 1978), and L. A. Hoffman, *Beyond the Text* (Bloomington, Ind., 1989), as well as the brief comments of S. Fine, *This Holy Place: On the Sanctity of the Synagogue During the Greco-Roman Period* (Notre Dame, Ind., 1997), 21–23. For a survey of genres in a Greco-Roman context, see R. A. Kraft and G. W. E. Nickelsburg, eds., *Early Judaism and Its Modern Interpreters* (Atlanta, Ga., 1986).

16. Among numerous answers to the question of "why the Bible matters," F. Landy, "On Metaphor, Play, and Nonsense," *Semeia* 61 (1993): 231.

17. See my "From Jezebel to Esther: Images of Queenship in the Hebrew Bible," *Biblica* (forthcoming).

18. Neusner is, therefore, correct in regarding even the considerable space allocated to "women" in rabbinic writings, beginning with the Mishnah, as an attempt to regulate transactions that happen to involve women (*A History of the Mishnaic Law of Women* 5: 13–42 and passim). See also the intelligent reconstructions of Tal Ilan that emphasize the haphazard and sporadic nature of the sources (*Jewish Women in Greco-Roman Palestine* [Tübingen, 1995]; *Mine and Yours Are Hers* [Leiden, 1997]; *Integrating Women into Second Temple History* [Tübingen, 1999]).

19. *Women in Scripture: A Dictionary of Named and Unnamed Women in the Hebrew Bible, the Apocryphal/Deuterocanonical Books, and the New Testament*, ed.

C. Meyers et al. (Boston, 2000), esp. part 3, provides a useful point of departure. Peskowitz's insights into spindles as burial goods (*Spinning Fantasies*, 166 f.) and Brooten's analysis of the epigraphic evidence are refreshing exceptions as is Babatha's archive, which has become a major source of information regarding Jewish marriage (Y. Yadin, J. C. Greenfield, and A. Yardeni, "Babatha's Ketubba," *Israel Exploration Journal* 44 [1994]: 75–101), not to mention administration, taxation, and rural society (B. Isaac, "The Babatha Archive: A Review Article," *Israel Exploration Journal* 42 [1992]: 62–75).

20. See the introductions to the studies listed above in note 3.

21. H. Eilberg-Schwartz, "The Nakedness of a Woman's Voice, the Pleasure in a Man's Mouth: An Oral History of Ancient Judaism," in *Off with Her Head! The Denial of Women's Identity in Myth, Religion, and Culture*, ed. H. Eilberg-Schwartz and W. Doniger (Berkeley, Calif., 1995), 165–84.

22. The following is inspired by N. Loraux, *Tragic Ways of Killing a Woman*, trans. A. Forster (Cambridge, Mass., 1987).

23. Lamentations Rabbah, proem 24, Hebrew text ed. by S. Buber in G. Hasan-Rokem, *The Web of Life: Folklore in Rabbinic Literature* (in Hebrew; Tel Aviv, 1996), 137 (I have not seen the English version of the book). For English translation I have relied on *Midrash Rabbah, Lamentations*, trans. A. Cohen (London, 1939), 48. On the layers of the midrash, L. Zunz, *Die gottesdienstlichen Vorträge der Juden, historische Entwickelt*, 2nd ed. (1892), Hebrew trans. M. A. Jacque (Jerusalem, 1974), 78–79 and passim.

24. On Naomi and Ruth in general, see P. Trible in *Women in Scripture*, 130–31, 146–47.

25. Hasan-Rokem, *Web of Life*, 139.

26. By making her a passive participant the midrash also provides an interesting corrective to a rabbinic image of Leah as the "brazen woman" and the antithesis of the ascetic woman; see PT Sot. 3.4 (19a) with S. E. Weinstein, *Piety and Fanaticism: Rabbinic Criticism of Religious Stringency* (Northvale, N.J., 1997), 128–30.

27. For detailed analyses of the Rachel-Akiva cycle, see S. Valler, *Women and Womanhood in the Stories of the Babylonian Talmud* (in Hebrew; Jerusalem 1993), 56 f., esp. 73–76 for the two BT versions printed side by side, and T. Ilan, *Mine and Yours*, passim, both concluding, as does D. Boyarin, *Carnal Israel* (Berkeley, Calif., 1993), 153–55, that the underlying theme is a conflict between husbandly obligations toward their wives and the duty to learn Torah, coupled with rabbinic sensitivity to the needs of women. Boyarin further regards the cycle as a series of mediating narratives that reconcile the two contradictory needs, but Valler prefers to emphasize the absence of a settlement and rabbinic insistence on the primacy of home and domesticity over learning. For a different interpretation, see below.

28. Boyarin, *Carnal Israel*, further emphasizes the aspect of the woman/ewe who is led and cherished by a male leader/shepherd.

29. See Boyarin, *Carnal Israel*, 134 f., and Valler, *Women and Womanhood*, 56 f.

30. See the illuminating comments of M. Finkelberg, "Royal Succession in Heroic Greece," *Classical Quarterly* 41 (1991): 303–16. I am grateful to Rita Finkelberg for discussing these issues with me.

31. Homer, *Odyssey* 11.404 f. Loeb trans., slightly modified.

32. Recent analyses of Penelope have emphasized her "positiveness," but the text itself remains ambiguous. See, among others, N. F. Rubin, *Regarding Penelope* (Princeton, N.J., 1994); I. Papadopoulou-Belmehdi, *Le chant de Pénélope: Poétique du tissage féminin dans l'Odyssée* (Paris, 1994); the articles gathered by Beth Cohen in *The Distaff Side* (Oxford, 1995), esp. by H. Foley and F. Zeitlin; E. Gregory, "Unraveling Penelope: The Construction of the Faithful Wife in Homer's Heroines," *Helios* 23 (1996): 3–20; W. Hellerman, "Homer's Penelope: A Tale of Feminine Arete," *Échoes du Monde Classique* 39 (1995): 227–50.

33. Her prolonged hesitation may have been linked with fear of adultery. Her insistence on Odysseus's "positive identification" reflects a tacit acknowledgment of her precarious position and of how close she could have come to committing adultery had she been beguiled by a false Odysseus. See S. Murnaghan, *Disguise and Recognition in the Odyssey* (Princeton, N.J., 1987), 141–42.

34. Homer, *Odyssey* 24.191 f., Loeb trans.

35. The expression is coined by N. Loraux, *Mothers in Mourning*, trans. C. Pache (Ithaca, N.Y., 1998), 97–100, where the strength of the sentiment is echoed in the power of anger, an emotion that mourning can breed or vice versa.

36. In the words of N. Loraux, *Mothers in Mourning*, 60, Penelope is a mother but first and foremost a wife.

37. Boyarin, *Carnal Israel*, 154, refers to a coda of the tale in BT Ket. 62b–63a which links Ben Azzai, a rabbinic authority attested elsewhere as unmarried, and the daughter of Akiva and Rachel. Cf., too, Akiva's reputed concern over the neglect of marriageable daughters, with *Carnal Israel*, 156–57. I suspect, however, that the marriage is fictional, like that between Dinah and Job, in which two oppositions are reconciled to create an implausible union.

38. *Midrash Decalogue* (ad Seventh Commandment), in A. Jellinek, *Bet ha-Midrash*, 3rd ed. (Jerusalem, 1967), 81–83 (here cited as basis of my translation). An abbreviated and misleading translation is found in M. Gaster, *The Exempla of the Rabbis* (1924; reprint, New York, 1968), 147. For a fuller and more accurate one, see J. Rosenberg's translation, in *Rabbinic Fantasies*, ed. D. Stern and M. J. Mirsky (New Haven, Conn., 1990), 107–10, based on a text published by G. Hasan-Rokem from the Verona 5407 ms. Where it differs from the text I used, the omissions are pointed out with points of ellipsis. The date of the present form of these aggadic tales is probably Geonic (8th century C.E.?), but I would hazard a guess that they include much earlier material. Cf. the conclusions of M. Kister regarding the versions of "The Fathers according to R. Nathan" in "Legends of the Destruction of the Second Temple in Avot de-Rabbi Nathan," *Tarbiz* 67 (1998/9): 483–529, esp. 519–20, where, in spite of its relative late date, the work appears to preserve earlier traditions, some found only there. Kister, however, refrains from specifying which are the later and which are the earlier traditions, prudently asserting that it is vital to examine every single line and phrase minutely and separately. The most detailed analysis of the complexities of this midrash is that of M. B. Lerner, "On the Midrashim on the Decalogue," in *Talmudic Studies*, ed. Y. Sussmann and D. Rosenthal (Jerusalem, 1990), 1:217–36, suggesting criteria for examining earlier layers but not the one on the Seventh Commandment.

Since the tale is situated in Jerusalem and linked with Rabbi Meir, a well-known tannaitic authority, reputedly the pupil of both Rabbi Ishmael and of Akiva, and belonging to what has been considered the generation of ca. 130–160 (H. L. Strack and G. Stemberger, *Introduction to the Talmud and Midrash*, 2nd ed. [Edinburgh, 1996], 76), it may appear, at first, to firmly place it in the realm of late midrashic imagination. I note, however, that the title of Meir, "talmid" (pupil) (*khakham*, or rather, *khakhamim*), is an appellation that seems to convey his youth and stage of learning rather than a mature authority and a teacher, thus hinting at a date prior to the Bar Kokhba revolt and to the closure of Jerusalem to Jews. For other hints linking the midrashic Meir with his tannaitic namesake, see below.

39. S. Albeck, "The Ten Commandments and the Essence of Religious Faith," in *The Ten Commandments in History and Tradition*, ed. B.-Z. Segal (Jerusalem, 1990), 280–82, in general on the Seventh Commandment. The book does not include a single reference to the midrash on the commandment, as far as I could see in the absence of an index. See below, Chapter 4, on the legal ramifications of suspected adultery.

40. R. Lattimore, "Phaedra and Hippolytos," in *Essays on Classical Literature*, ed. N. Rudd (Cambridge, 1972), 19–20 for the list. On Lucretia, see I. Donaldson, *The Rape of Lucretia* (Oxford, 1982); C. G. Calhoon, "Lucretia, Savior and Scapegoat: The Dynamics of Sacrifice in Livy 1:57–9," *Helios* 24 (1997): 151–69, and below, Chapter 2.

41. On Hippolytus I found particularly useful the work of J. Gregory, *Euripides and the Instruction of the Athenians* (Ann Arbor, Mich., 1991); F. I. Zeitlin, "The Power of Aphrodite: Eros and the Boundaries of the Self in the *Hippolytus*," in *Directions in Euripidean Criticism*, ed. P. Burian (Durham, N.C., 1985), 52–111; C. A. E. Luschnig, *Time Holds the Mirror: A Study of Knowledge in Euripides' Hippolytus* (Leiden, 1988); D. Kovacs, *The Heroic Muse* (Baltimore, Md., 1987), chap. 2 (on rhetoric of heroism in *Hippolytus*).

42. For a recent reconstruction of the first version, see S. Mills, *Theseus, Tragedy, and the Athenian Empire* (Oxford, 1997), 195 f.

43. *Hippolytus*, 688–92, Grene trans.

44. Homer, *Od.* 23.222–24, in H. C. Fredricksmeyer, "Penelope Polutropos: The Crux at *Odyssey.* 23.218–24," *American Journal of Philology* 118 (1997): 490.

45. Cf. the image of the passively tempting beauty of wives, as illustrated in the wife-sisters tales of Genesis, with W. P. Brown, *The Ethos of the Cosmos: The Genesis of Moral Imagination in the Bible* (Grand Rapids, Mich., 1949), 190–93.

46. On these as women's chief attributes, see Loraux, *Tragic Ways*, 21.

47. *Hippolytus*, 603–12, Grene trans.

48. She also externalizes her internal pressures by her suicide. See E. P. Garrison, *Groaning Tears: Ethical and Dramatic Aspects of Suicide in Greek Tragedy* (Leiden, 1995), 65. See also B. E. Goff, *The Noose of Words: Readings of Desire, Violence, and Language in Euripides' Hippolytos* (Cambridge, 1990).

49. This is also why Meir survives. Women usually die in enclosures, thus creating a double prison around their body through death and bolted doors; see Loraux, *Tragic Ways*, 21. Men normally die outdoors, like Hippolytus, if they have to die at all.

50. Cf. D. Biale, *Eros and the Jews: From Biblical Israel to Contemporary America* (New York, 1992).
51. *Hippolytus*, 617–57, Grene trans.
52. *Hippolytus*, 392–409, Grene trans.
53. *Hippolytus*, 617–24, Grene trans.
54. *Hippolytus*, 411–12, trans. in Gregory, *Euripides*, 71.
55. *Hippolytus*, 79–80, trans. in Gregory, *Euripides*, 71.
56. The evidence for Hellenism and the rabbis has been recently reassessed by A. Wasserstein, "Non-Hellenized Jews in the Semi-Hellenized East," *Scripta Classica Israelica* 14 (1995): 111–37, esp. 124, who concludes that most of the Greek that the rabbis had was derivative, not from the Greek but from Aramaic loanwords.
57. That the medieval compiler of the midrash had the famed tanna in mind seems hardly in doubt since every aspect of the tale can be associated with a saying or a deed attributed to the second-century sage in rabbinic sources. For a convenient collection of these citations, see I. Konovitz, *Rabbi Meir: Collected Sayings in Halakha and Aggadah, in the Talmudic and Midrashic Literature* (in Hebrew; Jerusalem, 1967). The Midrash Decalogue clearly alludes to BT Kidd. 81a where Satan appears to Meir in the guise of a woman after Meir was reputed to mock transgressors. The sage was also a well-traveled man.
58. The tanna shares a remarkable number of traits with his legendary namesake of the midrash, not the least the insistence on the identification of a scholar with an "individual," BT Ta'anit 10b. Weinstein, *Piety*, 40 f. on this passage.
59. D. Goodblatt, "The Beruriah Traditions," *Journal of Jewish Studies* 26 (1975): 68–86, records the departure of Rabbi Meir for Babylon on account of "a matter involving his wife" (*maaseh Beruriah*). Ilan, *Integrating Women*, 189 f., regards the tale as a medieval fabrication rather than one based on a lost Babylonian tradition, versus Boyarin (*Carnal Israel*) and R. Adler ("The Virgin in the Brothel and Other Anomalies: Character and Context in the Legend of Beruriah," *Tikkun* 3, no. 6 [1988]: 28–32) who assert its historicity. Leviticus Rabbah 9.9, another midrashic composition, presents Meir as a sage who espoused marital harmony rather than as a disrupter of marriage. In this midrashic instance, a jealous husband orders his wife, who has attended Meir's sermons, to manifest her contempt for both Meir and the Torah by spitting on the former. In spite of her scruples, Meir "volunteers" so that the marriage will not be broken. Underlying this tale is, possibly, also an erotic form of love that the woman feels toward the rabbi (Boyarin, *Carnal Israel*, 188). Be that as it may, such details regarding Meir's career may further serve to identify the hero of the "rape" myth with the rabbinic sage of the second century. On the links between the ancient and the midrashic stories of seduction and adultery involving Meir and Beruriah, Ilan, *Mine and Yours Are Hers*, 71 note 32.
60. In Boyarin, *Carnal Israel*, 190, and with illuminating discussion at 181–96.
61. Rashi on BT AZ 18a, in Boyarin, *Carnal Israel*, 184.
62. Boyarin, *Carnal Israel*, 194; P. Brown, *The Body and Society* (New York, 1988).
63. See the examples given by S. Ashbrook Harvey, "Spoken Words, Voiced Silence: Biblical Women in Syriac Tradition," *Journal of Early Christian Studies* 9 (2001): 105–31.

64. For this expression, see C. Mopsik, "The Body of Engenderment in the Hebrew Bible, the Rabbinic Tradition, and the Kabbalah," in *Fragments for a History of the Human Body*, ed. M. Feher et al., 3 vols. (New York, 1989), 1:54.

65. See the comments of G. A. Yee, "By the Hand of a Woman: The Metaphor of the Woman Warrior in Judges 4," *Semeia* 61 (1993): 99–134, esp. 109 f.

Chapter 1: From Dinah to Cozbi

1. F. van Dijk-Hemmes, "Tamar and the Limits of Patriarchy: Between Rape and Seduction," in *Anti-Covenant: Counter-Reading Women's Lives in the Hebrew Bible*, ed. M. Bal (Sheffield, 1989), 135–56; K. A. Stone, *Sex, Honor, and Power in the Deuteronomistic History* (Sheffield, 1996).

2. H. Gunkel's *Genesis* (1910, 3rd ed.) is still invaluable (now available in an English translation by M. E. Biddle [Macon, Ga., 1997]), 357–65 (on Gen. 34). Among more recent interpretations, S. Lehming, "Zur Überlieferungsgeschichte von Gen 34," *Zeitschrift für die Alttestamentliche Wissenschaft* 70 (1958): 228–50; A. de Pury, "Genèse XXXIV et l'histoire," *Revue biblique* 76 (1969): 5–49; C. Westermann, *Genesis 12–36* (London, 1985), 532–45; and N. Wyatt, "The Story of Dinah and Shechem," *Ugarit Forschungen* 22 (1991): 433–58.

3. D. N. Freedman, "Dinah and Shechem, Tamar and Amnon," *Austin Seminary Bulletin* 105 (1990): 51–63, and L. Bechtel, "What If Dinah Is Not Raped?" *Journal for the Study of the Old Testament* 62 (1994): 19–36, constitute a rare exception. Feminist readers have invariably focused on a rape (implied in the verb *inah*) and on the omission of Dinah's reactions to it. D. N. Fewell and D. M. Gunn, *Gender, Power, and Promise* (Nashville, Tenn., 1993), 81. Even the brilliant analysis of M. Sternberg, *The Poetics of Biblical Narrative* (Bloomington, Ind., 1985), 445–74, assumes that a rape functioned as the centrifugal power and the projector of the varying attitudes that he explores. The reservations of Fewell and Gunn, "Tipping the Balance: Sternberg's Reader and the Rape of Dinah," *Journal of Biblical Literature* 110 (1991): 193–211, do not contest this centrality. See also Sternberg's reply, in *Journal of Biblical Literature* 110 (1991): 212.

4. N. M. Sarna, *Genesis: The Traditional Hebrew Text with New JPS Translation*, The JPS Torah Commentary (Philadelphia, 1989), and M. M. Caspi, "The Story of the Rape of Dinah: The Narrator and the Reader," *Hebrew Studies* 26 (1985): 25–45, cast the Shechemites as the villains of the piece and the Israelites as the justified avengers. The view is hardly original. Ancient Jewish commentators already did their best to present Shimon and Levi as honorable characters. See J. L. Kugel, "The Story of Dinah in the Testament of Levi," *Harvard Theological Review* 85 (1992): 1–34, and *The Bible as It Was* (Cambridge, Mass., 1997), 233–44; C. Werman, "Jubilees 30: Building a Paradigm for the Ban on Intermarriage," *Harvard Thelogical Review* 90 (1997): 1–22.

5. S. A. Geller, "The Sack of Shechem: The Use of Typology in Biblical Covenant Religion," *Prooftexts* 10 (1990): 1–15, finds Genesis 34 a "repellent" foundation myth; Y. Amit, "Implicit Redaction and Latent Polemic in the Story of the Rape of Dinah" (in Hebrew), in *Texts, Temples, and Traditions: A Tribute to Mena-*

hem Haran (Winona Lake, Ind., ed. M. V. Fox et al., 1996), 11*-28*, reads it as a tool in the Ezra-Nehemiah campaign against intermarriage.

6. This is not to say that I underestimate the degree of sexual violence to which women had been (and are) subjected. For a recent debate on semantics (namely rape versus seduction and/or abduction) in classical literature, see Z. M. Packman, "Call It Rape: A Motif in Roman Comedy and Its Suppression in English-Speaking Publications," *Helios* 20 (1993): 42–55.

7. See J. E. Grubbs, "Abduction Marriage in Antiquity: Law of Constantine and Its Social Context," *Journal of Roman Studies* 79 (1989): 59–83, for successful application of this methodology to the exploration of late Roman law and society. See also J. A. Pitt-Rivers, *The Fate of Shechem: or The Politics of Sex: Essays in the Anthropology of the Mediterranean*, Cambridge Studies in Social Anthropology, no. 19 (Cambridge, 1977), 145–71, suggesting the centrality of marriage rules as a moral issue.

8. I have not seen an analysis of guest-friendship relations within the biblical framework. But this is clearly the setting of the relations between Abraham and Abimelech, Abraham and the three divine emissaries, Lot and the angels at Sodom, the last episode (Gen. 19) providing a near exact replica of Judg. 19, as has been often observed.

9. A. Wallace-Hadrill, ed., *Patronage in Ancient Society* (London, 1989), dealing primarily with Rome.

10. See R. P. Saller, *Personal Patronage under the Early Empire* (Cambridge, 1982), 1, as well as T. Johnson and C. Dandeker, "Patronage: Relation and System," in Wallace-Hadrill, *Patronage*, 224.

11. In spite of Sarna, *Genesis*, 144, and I. N. Rashkow, *The Phallacy of Genesis: A Feminist-Psychoanalytical Approach* (Louisville, Ky., 1993), 67. There is nothing in the biblical narrative to indicate that father-daughter relations were invariably tense and based on fear of transgression lest the latter cross into forbidden territory. Rebecca provides a striking illustration (Gen. 24:15 ff.) of the rules applied to unmarried daughters as she happily chats with a complete stranger outdoors, receives valuable gifts from him, and offers the hospitality of her "mother's home" without prior consultation with any males.

12. The term *inah* has a wide range of connotations. See P. Gordon and H. C. Washington, "Rape as a Military Metaphor in the Hebrew Bible," in *A Feminist Companion to the Latter Prophets*, ed. A. Brenner (Sheffield, 1995), 313. It is applied, for example, to rules governing the treatment of a beautiful war captive in Deut. 21:10–14. See T. Frymer-Kensky, "Law and Philosophy: The Case of Sex in the Bible," *Semeia* 45 (1989): 100 n. 9, and Frymer-Kensky, *In the Wake of the Goddesses: Women, Culture, and the Biblical Transformation of Pagan Myth* (New York, 1992), 274 n. 34; also C. Pressler, *The View of Women Found in the Deuteronomic Family Laws* (Berlin, 1993), 12.

13. Gunkel, *Genesis*, 34.

14. Sternberg, *Poetics*, 2.

15. Pitt-Rivers, *Fate of Shechem*, 156.

16. This appears to have been the most misunderstood aspect of the entire affair.

17. Cf. the rabbinical discussion on the time period it takes to have sexual intercourse in their effort to determine whether adultery had taken place or not, BT Sot. 4a, and below Chapter 4.

18. The use of "daughter," rather than "sister," is explained in various ways. Sternberg, *Poetics*, regards it as a deliberate substitute reflecting on Jacob's failure to act according to parental expectations and on his sons appropriating their father's role. More likely the employment of "daughter" in 34:17 is a direct result of the reference to a general set of marriage alliances between "our daughters" and "your daughters" in 34:16. A switch to "a sister" would have undermined the force of 34:16 and would have introduced a jarring note.

19. The availability of these women has never been discussed—where, in fact, were they supposed to come from?

20. S. Treggiari, *Roman Marriage* (Oxford, 1991), 4–5, for passage. The translation is hers with my modifications.

21. Fewell and Gunn, "Tipping the Balance," 210.

22. Deuteronomy does not consider the ethnic identity or the religious affiliation of the rapist.

23. Indeed, in the Mishnah (Kidd. 1.1) a marriage can be effected, theoretically at least, by sexual intercourse alone.

24. CTh 9.24.1: *Si quis nihil cum parentibus puellae ante depectus invitam eam rapuerit vel volentem abduxerit patrocinium ex eius responsione sperans, quam propter vitium levitatis et sexus mobilitatem atque consili a postulationibus et testimoniis omnibusque rebus iudiciariis antiqui penitus arcuerunt, nihil ei secundum ius vetus prosit puellae responsio, sed ipsa puella potius societate criminis obligetur. . . . Et si voluntatis assensio detegitur in virgine, eadem qua raptor severitate plectatur, cum neque his impunitas praestanda sit, quae rapiuntur invitae, cum et domi se usque ad coniunctionis diem servare potuerint et, si fores raptoris frangerentur audacia, vicinorum opem clamoribus quaerere seque omnibus tueri conatibus. . . . Raptor autem indubitate convictus si appellare voluerit, minime audiatur. . . . Participes etiam et ministros raptoris citra discretionem sexus eadem poena praecipimus subiugari.* English translation in Grubbs, "Abduction Marriage," 60, and in C. Pharr, *The Theodosian Code* (Princeton, N.J., 1952); the translation here is mine. For an analysis of this law, based, in part, on anthropological data, see J. E. Grubbs, "Abduction Marriage" and *Law and Family in Late Antiquity: The Emperor Constantine's Marriage Legislation* (Oxford, 1995), 183 f.

25. See C. Sourvinou-Inwood, "The Young Abductor of the Locrian Pinakes," *Bulletin of the Institute of Classical Studies* 20 (1973): 12–21, for insights into pictorial imagery of the emotions involved in mythical abduction.

26. Among recent works on this notion in Archaic Greece, see M. W. Blundell, *Helping Friends and Harming Enemies* (Cambridge, 1989); D. Konstan, *Friendship in the Classical World* (Cambridge, 1997), 33 f.; J. T. Fitzgerald, ed., *Greco-Roman Perspectives on Friendship* (Atlanta, Ga., 1997), each with further bibliography. The Greek notion of *xenia* approximates the one that Genesis outlines, as seen through the works of Hesiod and Theognis. See also the contradictory accounts of the seizure of the Shechem (the territory) given in Gen. 48:22 (where Jacob is featured as capturing the place from the Amorites), and in Gen. 34 (where Shimon and Levi are the conquerors).

27. Pace Sternberg.

28. On the common authorship of the Dinah and the Tamar tales, see Freedman, "Dinah and Shechem."

29. K. Stone, "Concubine (Secondary Wife) of a Levite," in *Women in Scripture*, ed. C. Meyers et al. (Boston and New York, 2000), 248–50.

30. I doubt if Pitt-Rivers's notion of sexual hospitality (*Fate of Shechem*, 158–59) applies here.

31. In the third, the idea that all Israel had originally been in sibling relations need not be forgotten.

32. CJ 9.13.1 (Krueger): *qui eis [i.e., to the abductors, raptores] auxilium tempore invasionis praebuerint . . . convicti interficiantur*.

33. CJ 9.13.1; see also Grubbs, "Abduction Marriage," 78.

34. This is just one of several anachronisms in the Jacob Genesis narrative. Another is the very insertion of Dinah's story into the place it now occupies — Gen. 33:18 records the arrival of Jacob and his clan from Padan Aram to Shechem. Gen. 35:9 brings Yahweh and Jacob together once more in Padan Aram (although the narrator made a laudable effort to gloss over the apparent discrepancy with a hint that the revelation at Gen. 35:10–12 had occurred in the past).

35. Fitzgerald, *Greco-Roman Perspectives*, 21–24.

36. W. Donlan, "Pistos, Philos, Hetairos," in *Theognis of Megara: Poetry and the Polis*, ed. T. J. Figueira and G. Nagy (Baltimore, Md., 1985); Fitzgerald, *Greco-Roman Perspectives*, 29.

37. Once more sexual symbolism, if one wishes to follow this line of analysis.

38. E. Fuchs, "Structure and Patriarchal Functions in the Biblical Betrothal Type-Scene: Some Preliminary Notes," *Journal of Feminist Studies in Religion* 3 (1987): 7–13, for preliminary observations indeed. I trust that there is no longer need to reassert the patriarchal biases of the biblical narrative in general. I doubt her conclusions regarding the distinctiveness of the three types of betrothal (Gen. 24, 29, and Exod. 2:16–21) and their manifestation of a "steady development . . . towards deemphasizing the status and significance of the bride" (p. 12).

39. 1.21, trans. R. Warner.

40. B. F. L. Fair, *The Impediment of Abduction* (Washington, D.C., 1944); J. A. Brundage, *Love, Sex, and Christian Society in Medieval Europe* (Chicago, 1987), s.v. "abduction," "elopement," "rape," and "*raptus*." The impediment was late in coming since, presumably, the church relied on civil procedures to penalize abductors and, at any rate, could do little to prevent abduction marriages as long as they were viable alternatives to controlled procedures.

41. To the best of my knowledge none of the commentaries on Numbers deals with this episode in the manner it is dealt with here. See, among others, G. B. Gray, *A Critical and Exegetical Commentary on Numbers*, International Critical Commentary (New York, 1903); J. H. Greenstone, *The Holy Scriptures. Numbers* (Philadelphia, 1939); B. Maarsingh, *Numbers: A Practical Commentary*, Text and Interpretation, (Grand Rapids, Mich., 1987); E. W. Davies, *Numbers*, New Century Bible Commentary (Grand Rapids, Mich., 1995); D. T. Olson, *Numbers*, Interpretation (Louisville, Ky., 1996); J. Milgrom, *Numbers*, The JPS Torah Commentary (Philadelphia, 1990); D. M. Douglas, *In the Wilderness: The Doctrine of Defilement in the Book of Numbers* (Sheffield, 1993); K. D. Sakenfeld, *Journeying*

with God, International Theological Commentary (Grand Rapids, Mich., 1994). For much of what follows, see my "The Rape of Cozbi (Numbers XXV)," *Vetus Testamentum* 51 (2001): 69–80.

42. See G. B. Gray, *A Critical and Exegetical Commentary on Numbers*, for a final redactional date between Ezekiel and Ezra. The latter is more likely.

43. For introductory remarks, S. J. D. Cohen, "The Prohibition of Intermarriage: From the Bible to the Talmud," *Hebrew Annual Review* 7 (1983): 23–39, reprinted with revisions in Cohen, *The Beginnings of Jewishness: Boundaries, Varieties, Uncertainties* (Berkeley, Calif., 1999), 241–62. There is no full treatment of this important subject.

44. G. Knoppers, "Sex, Religion, and Politics: The Deuteronomist on Intermarriage," *Hebrew Annual Review* 14 (1994): 121–42.

45. On procreation as a central theme in priestly redactional perspectives, see H. Eilberg-Schwartz, *The Savage in Judaism* (Bloomington, Ind., 1990), 192, 196, and passim, esp. with regard to priestly reproductive policies.

46. See G. Wenham, *Numbers: An Introduction and Commentary*, Tyndale Old Testament Commentaries (Downers Grove, Ill., 1981) on Zimri/Cozbi in the role of animals as sacrificial atonement.

47. See the illuminating comments of A. Feldherr, "Livy's Revolution: Civic Identity and the Creation of the Res Publica," in *The Roman Cultural Revolution*, ed. T. Habinek and A. Schiesaro (Cambridge, 1997), 136–57, esp. 146 ff.

48. Livy, 1.57, English translation in Livy, *Early History of Rome: Books I–V of the History of Rome from Its Foundation*, Penguin Classics, trans. A. de Selincourt (Harmondsworth, 1971). Unless otherwise stated, all translations of Livy are from this Penguin edition.

49. P. K. Joplin, "Ritual Work on Human Flesh: Livy's Lucretia and the Rape of the Body Politic," *Helios* 17 (1990): 61.

50. Ibid., 62. Cf. S. R. Joshel, "The Body Female and the Body Politic: Livy's Lucretia and Verginia," in *Pornography and Representation in Greece and Rome*, ed. A. Richlin (Oxford, 1991), 112–30.

51. Livy 1.59.1, in Feldherr, "Livy's Revolution," 149. Cf. C. W. Newlands, "The Rape of Lucretia in Ovid's Fasti," *Augustan Age* 8 (1988): 36–48, on the turning of a female elegiac model into a Roman matron in the Livian mold. The paradigm proved powerful.

52. Feldherr, "Livy's Revolution," 152.

53. Cf. Feldherr, "Livy's Revolution," 156, on Brutus's oath as an action of Roman citizenship.

Chapter 2: Patriarchy and Patriotism

1. For a recent useful general survey, see R. W. Klein, "The Books of Ezra and Nehemiah" in *The New Interpreter's Bible*, vol. 3 (Nashville, Tenn., 1999), 663–851. On the historical implications of the text, especially on the definitions of who was a Jew, see L. H. Schiffman, "At the Crossroads: Tannaitic Perspectives on the Jewish-Christian Schism," in *Jewish and Christian Self-Definition*, ed. E. P. Sanders

et al. (Philadelphia, 1981), 2:115–56, esp. 121 (on the formation of the matrilineal principle in the mid–fifth century B.C.E.). But see S. J. D. Cohen, "The Matrilineal Principle," in *Beginnings of Jewishness*, 263–307, for a different opinion. See also K. Koch, "Ezra and the Origins of Judaism," *Journal of Jewish Studies* 19 (1974): 173–97. On a recent reevaluation of the idea of exile or, rather, "exile" in Ezra, see B. Becking, "Ezra's Re-enactment of the Exile," in *Leading Captivity Captive: The Exile as History and Ideology*, ed. L. L. Grabbe (Sheffield, 1998), 40–61. What follows is based on my "The Silent Women of Yehud: Notes on Ezra 9–10," *Journal of Jewish Studies* 51 (2000): 3–18.

2. The question of the chronology of Ezra and of Nehemiah has been hotly debated. For a recent hypothesis, A. Demsky, "Who Came First, Ezra or Nehemiah? The Synchronistic Approach," *Hebrew Union College Annual* 65 (1994): 1–20, arguing for 445 B.C.E. as the date of Nehemiah's appearance in Yehud, and 443 for Ezra's. The recent archaeological discoveries on Mount Gerizim appear to support this conclusion; see Y. Magen, "Mt. Gerizim—A Temple City" (in Hebrew) *Qadmoniot* 120 (2000): 74–118, esp. 116, on finds that attest the construction of a Samaritan temple on Mount Gerizim in the first half of the fifth century B.C.E. (and indirectly refute Josephus's testimony concerning its late date).

3. For an excellent evaluation of women in general in the Ezra/Nehemiah narrative(s), see T. C. Eskenazi, "Out from the Shadows: Biblical Women in the Postexilic Era," *Journal for the Study of the Old Testament* 54 (1992): 25–43, esp. 36 f.

4. Among recent commentaries, I found Lester L. Grabbe's *Ezra-Nehemiah*, Old Testament Readings (London and New York, 1998) particularly stimulating and provocative. See also the standard commentaries of W. Rudolph, *Esra und Nehemia samt 3 Esra*, Handbuch zum Alten Testament 29 (Tübingen, 1949); J. M. Myers, *Ezra-Nehemiah*, Anchor Bible 14 (Garden City, N.Y., 1965); R. G. Coggins, *The Books of Ezra and Nehemiah*, Cambridge Bible Commentary on the New English Bible (Cambridge, 1976); A. H. J. Gunneweg, *Esra*, Kommentar zum Alten Testament (Gütersloh, 1985, 1987); H. G. M. Williamson, *Ezra, Nehemiah*, Word Biblical Commentary 16 (Waco, Tex., 1985); J. Blenkinsopp, *Ezra-Nehemiah*, Old Testament Library (Philadelphia, 1988); D. J. Clines, *Ezra, Nehemiah and Esther*, New Clarendon Bible (reprint, Grand Rapids, Mich., 1992); M. A. Throntveit, *Ezra-Nehemiah*, Interpretation (Louisville, Ky., 1992); M. Breneman, *Ezra, Nehemiah, Esther*, New American Commentary, vol. 10 (Nashville, Tenn., 1993); and J. W. H. Van Wijk-Bos, *Ezra, Nehemiah* and *Esther*, Westminster Bible Companion (Louisville, Ky., 1998). For overviews regarding the text's chronology and its compositional problems, S. Japhet, "Composition and Chronology in the Book of Ezra-Nehemiah," in *Second Temple Studies*, vol. 2, *Temple and Community in the Persian Period*, ed. T. C. Eskenazi and K. H. Richards (Sheffield, 1994), 189–216; A. Gelston, "The End of Chronicles," *Journal for the Study of the Old Testament* 10 (1996): 53–60. On the period within the larger canvas of Second Temple history, J. Blenkinsopp, "Interpretation and the Tendency to Sectarianism: An Aspect of Second Temple History," in Sanders et al., *Jewish and Christian Self-Definition*, 2:1–26, esp. 4–13, with a review of previous opinions. This is not the place to enter the debate on the unity or rather the distinct nature of Ezra, Nehemiah, and Chronicles. For the purpose of this study, Ezra is regarded as a separate and autonomous unit.

5. Useful analyses of Ezra 9–10 include the numerous articles of D. L. Smith-Christopher, including "Between Ezra and Isaiah: Exclusion, Transformation, and Inclusion of the 'Foreigner' in Post-Exilic Biblical Theology," in *Ethnicity and the Bible*, ed. M. G. Brett (Leiden, 1996), 117–42; and T. C. Eskenazi and E. P. Judd, "Marriage to a Stranger in Ezra 9–10," and H. C. Washington, "The Strange Woman of Proverbs 1–9 and Post-Exilic Judaean Society," both in Eskenazi and Richards, *Second Temple Studies*, 2:266–85 and 217–42 respectively. See also L. L. Grabbe, "Triumph of the Pious or Failure of the Xenophobes? The Ezra-Nehemiah Reforms and Their Nachgeschichte," in *Jewish Local Patriotism and Self-Identification*, ed. S. Jones and S. Pearce (Sheffield, 1998), 50–65, for interesting observations.

6. W.-M. Johnson, "Ethnicity in Persian Yehud: Between Anthropological and Ideological Criticism," *Society of Biblical Literature*, Seminar Papers (1995): 182, on the identity of the otherwise unidentified "officials" as returnees seeking to re-establish their status in the administration of Yehud.

7. On the inversion of the root *erev*, designating in Exod. 12:38 the multi-ethnic composition of the Egyptian generation and in Ezra 9:1 a negative activity of ethnic mixing, see P. Hanson, *The People Called: The Growth of Community in the Bible* (San Francisco, 1986), 299.

8. Cf. Eskenazi, "Out from the Shadows," 34 on the presence of foreign women as a problem for which their absence becomes the sole remedy.

9. Cf. *zera kodesh* (holy seed) of Ezra 9:2 with Esther 6:13, describing Mordechai, through a foreign woman, as a man "of Jewish seed," and below, Chapter 3.

10. And, of course, against biblical tales such as that of Ruth and Esther.

11. Among particularly useful studies on the Roman side are A. Feldherr, *Spectacle and Society in Livy's History* (Berkeley, Calif., 1998); G. B. Miles, *Livy: Reconstructing Early Rome* (Ithaca, N.Y., 1995); and the articles in T. N. Habinek and A. Schiesaro, *The Roman Cultural Revolution* (Cambridge, 1997).

12. Nor, for that matter, was the ethnic homogeneity of the returnees a foregone conclusion as Becking, "Ezra's Reenactment," 45, asserts on the basis of non-Israelite names in the list of returnees. I find, however, J. G. McConville's proposal (*Ezra, Nehemiah* and *Esther* [Edinburgh, 1985], 70, with J. M. Sprinkle, "Old Testament Perspectives on Divorce and Remarriage," *Journal of the Evangelical Theological Society* 40 [1997]: 537–38) that the denounced intermarriage with pagans followed first marriages with Jewish women somewhat improbable. Had it been the case, surely the accusers would have used it as an example of an even greater abomination, as Malachi 2 does.

13. Clines, *Ezra*, 122.

14. See the illuminating comments of Florence Dupont on the visual context of public speech, "Recitatio and the Reorganization of the Space of Public Discourse," in Habinek and Schiesaro, *Roman Cultural Revolution*, 44–45.

15. On the centrality of the Temple in the Ezraic community, see J. Weinberg, *The Citizen-Temple Community* (Sheffield, 1992), passim.

16. In general, S. J. D. Cohen, "Prohibition of Intermarriage," *Hebrew Annual Review* 7 (1983): 23–39.

17. H. Maccoby, "Holiness and Purity: The Holy People in Leviticus and

Ezra-Nehemiah," in *Reading Leviticus. A Conversation with Mary Douglas*, ed. J.-F. A. Sawyer (Sheffield, 1996), 153–70.

18. W. Kornfeld, "L'adultère dans l'orient antique," *Revue biblique* 57 (1950): 92–109; E. Neufeld, *Ancient Hebrew Marriage Laws* (London, 1944), 11–26.

19. See Knoppers, "Sex, Religion, and Politics," 121–41, for an excellent analysis of this historiographical motif.

20. E. Lipinski, "Marriage and Divorce in the Judaism of the Persian Period," *Transeuphratene* 4 (1991): 63–71.

21. Cf. Ezekiel 44 for a similar anti-gentile attitude.

22. Van Wijk-Bos, *Ezra, Nehemiah, and Esther*, 44.

23. Cf. the distinctions between "goyim" and "am" of the land, in Weinberg, *Citizen-Temple Community*, 62–74.

24. Hence the avoidance of the term *gerot* in order to place the women outside the law of hospitality, Van Wijk-Bos, *Ezra, Nehemiah, and Esther*, 44–45, and, more generally, C. van Houten, *The Alien in Israelite Law* (Sheffield, 1991), passim.

25. On the identity of these women as "Judahites," namely Jews whose Jewishness was not quite acceptable to the Babylonian migrants, see Eskenazi and Judd, "Marriage to a Stranger," 268. On the use of the term "foreigner" as generic rather than in a specific sense, see Washington, "Strange Woman," esp. 231 f. See also H. Ringgren, "The Marriage Motif in Israelite Religion," in *Ancient Israelite Religion: Essays in Honor of Frank Moore Cross*, ed. P. D. Miller et al. (Philadelphia, 1987), 421–28, esp. 427 on "foreign women" in wisdom literature as a metaphor in the polemics over the ceremony of *hieros gamos*; as well as the useful observations of R. S. Kraemer, "The Other as Woman: An Aspect of Polemic Among Pagans, Jews and Christians in the Greco-Roman World," in *The Other in Jewish Thought and History: Constructions of Jewish Culture and Identity*, ed. L. J. Silberstein and R. L. Cohn (New York, 1994), 121–43 for a later period but with a number of universal truths.

26. See F. Kearley, "Difficult Texts from Ezra, Nehemiah, and Esther (Ezra 10)," in *Difficult Texts of the Old Testament Explained*, ed. W. Winkler (Hurst, Tex., 1982), 288–300.

27. Contra M. Fishbane, *Biblical Interpretation in Ancient Israel* (Oxford, 1985), 117, who also insists, incorrectly to my mind, on treating the Moabites, Ammonites, and Egyptians as falling under similar disabilities.

28. Needless to say, the question of why conversion was not proposed has been often asked. See, among others, Y. Kaufmann, *The Religion of Israel, from its Beginnings to the Babylonian Exile* (in Hebrew; Tel Aviv, 1956), 296–301, on the absence of an institution for religious conversion, and the articles gathered in Cohen, *Beginnings of Jewishness*.

29. W. F. Luck, *Divorce and Remarriage: Recovering Biblical Law* (San Francisco, 1987), 57–67; and D. I. Brewer, "Deuteronomy 24:1–4 and the Origins of the Jewish Divorce Certificate," *Journal of Jewish Studies* 49 (1998): 230–43. Klein, *New Interpreter's Bible*, 737 (above, note 1) maintains that it was their very foreignness that constituted the objection.

30. In spite of Sprinkle's assertion ("Old Testament Perspectives," 537) of the use of Deuteronomy's divorce law.

31. See also the comments of various authors in *Women, War and Metaphor* in *Semeia* 61 (1993).

32. E. Stehle, "Venus, Cybele, and the Sabine Women: The Roman Reconstruction of Female Sexuality," *Helios* 16 (1989): 143–64, esp. 150.

33. Dionysius of Halicarnassus 2.30.2, in another version of the Sabine affair.

34. Joplin, "Ritual Work on Human Flesh," 56–57, on the Roman presentation.

35. Trans. in R. Brown, "Livy's Sabine Women and the Ideal of Concordia," *Transactions of the American Philological Association* 125 (1995): 291–319.

36. On the difficulties, involved in interpreting the concluding phrase, see S. I. Feigin, "Some Cases of Adoption in Israel," *Journal of Biblical Literature* 50 (1931): 186–200. I find, however, his suggestion that the children of Ezra 10:44 were the pagan children of the foreign women from previous marriages implausible. Indeed, reconstructions of previous marriages, either to Jewish women or to non-Jewish, appear unwarranted.

37. In Miles, *Livy*, 203.

38. Miles, *Livy*, 204.

39. *Fasti* 3.221–24, in Miles, *Livy*, 201.

40. Among numerous recent studies, see M. Albani et al., eds., *Studies in the Book of Jubilees* (Tübingen, 1997); and B.-Z. Wacholder, "Jubilees as the Super Canon: Torah-Admonition Versus Torah-Commandment," in *Legal Texts and Legal Issues*, eds. M. J. Bernstein et al. (Proceedings of the Second Meeting of the International Organization for Qumran Studies, Cambridge, 1995; published in honor of J. M. Baumgarten, Leiden, 1997), 195–211.

41. Date not established, but ranges between 175–164 B.C.E., the reign of Antiochus IV, and 128 B.C.E., E. J. Christiansen, *The Covenant in Judaism and Paul: A Study of Ritual Boundaries as Identity Markers* (Leiden and New York, 1995), 67.

42. Jubilees' Ethiopian text was edited and translated by R. H. Charles, rev. C. Rabin in *The Apocryphal Old Testament*, ed. H. F. D. Sparks (Oxford, 1913, 1984), 1–139, and by J. C. VanderKam, *The Book of Jubilees* (Corpus Scriptorum Christianorum Orientalium, Scriptores Aethiopici 87–88, Louvain, 1989), with the fragments in Hebrew, Greek, Latin, and Syriac. See also the translation of O. S. Wintermute in *The Old Testament Pseudepigrapha*, 2 vols., ed. J. H. Charlesworth (Garden City, N.Y., 1983–85), 2:35–142.

43. Jubilees is one example of the culture of exegesis of the Second Temple era. The Qumran scrolls are another; see M. Kister, "A Common Heritage: Biblical Interpretation at Qumran and Its Implications," in *Biblical Perspectives: Early Use and Interpretation of the Bible in Light of the Dead Sea Scrolls*, ed. M. E. Stone and E. G. Chazon (Leiden, 1998), 101–11. I am limiting my discussion, deliberately, to canonized rather than esoteric texts or texts transmitted through the Christian church. Jubilees and later Joseph and Aseneth (below, Chapter 3), two exceptions to my rule, provide striking examples of the flexibility and expandability of canonic biblical characters and views. See also above, Introduction.

44. See, in general, J. C. Endres, *Biblical Interpretation in the Book of Jubilees* (Washington, D.C., 1987), with detailed juxtaposition of the biblical and pseudepigraphical texts. Wintermute's translation also provides scriptural quotations.

45. On the calendar, see A. Jaubert, "Le calendrier de Jubilés et de la secte de Qumrân: ses origines bibliques," *Vetus Testamentum* 3 (1953): 250–64; J. C. VanderKam, "The Origin, Character, and Early History of the 364-Day Calendar: A Reassessment of Jaubert's Hypothesis," *Catholic Biblical Quarterly* 41 (1979): 390–411; P. R. Davies, "Calendrical Change and Qumran Origins: An Assessment of VanderKam's Theory," *Catholic Biblical Quarterly* 45 (1983): 80–89; and J. C. VanderKam, "Das chronologische Konzept des Jubilaenbuches," *Zeitschrift für die alttestamentliche Wissenschaft* 107 (1995): 80–100.

On the "heavenly tablets," see M. Himmelfarb, "Torah, Testimony, and Heavenly Tablets: The Claim to Authority of the Book of Jubilees," in *A Multiform Heritage*, ed. R. A. Kraft (Atlanta, Ga., 1999), 19–29. I cannot read Ethiopic, the language in which the fullest version of Jubilees has been transmitted. I find, however, A. Cahana's translation into Hebrew extremely useful (*Hasefarim hahisoniim* = the *Pseudepigrapha of the Old Testament*, I [reprint, Jerusalem, 1978]). The first recorded phrase of "heavenly tablets" seems to appear in 3:10, with regulations relating to the period of purification of mothers after the birth of a male child.

46. Here is my translation, based on Cahana's Hebrew: "Should a woman or a daughter prostitute herself she will be burnt by fire, nor should they be led astray after their eyes and hearts. And they shall not take a wife out of the daughters of Canaan but rather eliminate the seed of Canaan from the land." Cf. Wintermute, "Jubilees," in Charlesworth, *The OT Pseudepigrapha*: "And when any woman or girl fornicates among you you will burn her with fire, and let them not fornicate with her after their eyes and hearts and let them not take wives from the girls of Canaan because the seed of Canaan will be rooted out of the land."

47. See VanderKam, *Book of Jubilees*, 116, on the grammatical difficulties of this phrase.

48. VanderKam, *Book of Jubilees*, 160, notes that all the other translators of 25:3 prefer "from your father's family and clan" (including Cahana), which he considers corrupt and poorly attested. Gen. 28:2 supports VanderKam, as does Jub. 25:3, which continues with the exhortation: "but you shall take a wife from my father's house." However, there is a neat symmetry in Jub. 25:3 between the "will of the mother" and "the family of the father" (VanderKam) (if such is the phrase) which is not entirely out of keeping with Jubilees' sense of the text. Of course, Isaac and Rebecca were themselves related, nor was it forgotten that the original ban on marrying locals had been issued by Abraham (Gen. 24:3–4), who orders his *maiordomus* to seek a bride for Isaac in his country and from among his kindred.

49. B. H. Amaru, "The First Woman, Wives, and Mothers in Jubilees," *Journal of Biblical Literature* 113/14 (1994): 609–26, esp. 609 and 623 f. with tables detailing the types of family relations between the couples of the first twenty generations.

50. J. C. VanderKam, *The Book of Jubilees*, translated "the spirit of righteousness"; Wintermute, "the spirit of truth"; and Cahana, "a holy spirit or the spirit of the holy." Since the latter is a familiar term, I opted, with Cahana, to translate this way.

51. On Jubilees' moral agenda, see C. Hayes, "Intermarriage and Impurity in Ancient Jewish Sources," *Harvard Theological Review* 92 (1999): 3–36.

52. E. Qimron and J. Strugnell, eds., *Qumran Cave 4: Miqṣat Ma'aśé Ha-Torah* (hereafter MMT), vol. 10 of *Discoveries in the Judean Desert* (Oxford, 1994).

53. MMT B 75–81. On these lines, see Hayes, "Intermarriage," 34 f. and M. Kister, "Studies in 4Q *Miqṣat Ma'aśé Ha-Torah* and Related Texts: Law, Theology, Language, and Calendar" (in Hebrew), *Tarbiz* 68 (1999): 317–71, esp. 343 f. on which I base my remarks.

Chapter 3: From Esther to Aseneth

1. The same cannot be said for rabbinic literature which contains extensive discussions regarding a wide range of premarital, marital, and postmarital matters, from sisters-in-law to wayward wives and from divorce to betrothal as can be gleaned from the titles of the various Mishnaic and talmudic tractates of the order "Nashim" (women) and from its arrangement. For adulterous wives and for married women in the wrong unions, see below.

2. A full bibliography is clearly out of place here. In addition to bibliographies in all the standard commentaries (including L. B. Paton, *A Critical and Exegetical Commentary on the Book of Esther*, The International Critical Commentary [New York, 1908]; C. A. Moore, *Esther*, Anchor Bible 7B [Garden City, N.Y., 1971]; D. J. A. Clines, *Ezra, Nehemiah and Esther*, New Century Bible Commentary [Grand Rapids, Mich., 1984]; and the more recent J. D. Levenson, *Esther: A Commentary*, Old Testament Library [Louisville, Ky., 1997] and W. H. J. Van Wijk-Bos, *Ezra, Nehemiah and Esther*, Westminster Bible Companion [Louisville, Ky., 1998], and the important contributions of M. V. Fox), see the bibliographical overview of L. R. Klein, "Esther's Lot," *Currents in Research: Biblical Studies* 5 (1997): 111–45, to which I would add A. M. Rodriguez, *Esther: A Theological Approach* (Berrien Spring, Mich., 1995); S. Talmon, "Was the Scroll of Esther Known Among the Congregation of Those Who Came into the New Covenant?" (in Hebrew), *Eretz Israel* 25 (1996): 377–82; J. R. Russell, "Zoroastrian Elements in the Book of Esther," *Irano-Judaica* 2 (1990): 33–40; M. Wechsler, "Shadow and Fulfillment in the Book of Esther," *Biblia Sacra* 154 (1997): 275–84; and M. Wechsler, "The Purim-Passover Connection: A Reflection of Jewish Exegetical Tradition in the Peshitta Book of Esther," *Journal of Biblical Literature* 117 (1998): 321–35. See also the raging debate, in Hebrew, between A. Oppenheimer and B. Bar-Kochva in *Zion* 1995, 1996, and 1997, over the history of the feast of Purim as reconstructed in J. Tavori, *Jewish Feasts in the Period of the Mishnah and the Talmud* (Jerusalem, 1995).

3. On the family, in general, see the articles gathered in L. G. Perdue et al., *Families in Ancient Israel* (Louiville, Ky., 1997), with contributions by C. Meyers, J. J. Blenkinsopp, and J. R. Collins.

4. This peculiar exegetical mode also makes it rather difficult to determine the precise genre of the book. Scholarly opinions have envisioned Esther as a novella, a short story, a romance, a fiction, a fictionalized history, a work of wisdom literature, a folktale, a tale of a Jew in a foreign court (a Diaspora story), a festival etiology, or a lection. For a summary of recent views, see Klein, "Esther's Lot," 121 f.

5. This is, understandably, no mean task when deliberate and ironic inversions may be suspected throughout the scroll. The layered text (Esther 1–8, the core; 9–10, later addition) raises the possibility of inner-exegesis. Thus, Esther 9:27, where the ritual of Purim is shared by Jews and "others," is intended to interpret Esther 8:17 with its statement of a general "conversion" to Judaism. In other words, 9:28 explains just what being a Jew entailed, at least in Esther's Persia.

6. Although Esther 1:5 refers to a general banquet for all the inhabitants of Susa including, presumably, the Jewish community in the city, the tale does not dwell on this incongruity. The point, however, has not escaped the pen of a Purim piyyut of late antiquity which designates Mordechai as the only Jew who had not eaten and hence in the feast, the only person deserving to be called a "Jew." See M. Sokoloff and J. Yahalom, *Jewish Palestinian Aramaic Poetry from Late Antiquity* (in Hebrew; Jerusalem, 1999), 187.

On the significance and nuances of public feasting as promoter of social bonding, and as temporary leveler or reinforcer of class distinctions, and as well as an expression of prestige economy, see M. J. Herskovits, *Economic Anthropology* (New York, 1952), 461–83. For an analysis of banqueting in the Greek world, see P. S. Pantel, *La cité au banquet: Histoire des repas publics dans les cités grecques* (Rome, 1992).

7. Public appearances of royal Persian women, so far as can be ascertained from historical sources, were requested and expected on occasions such as military campaigns, hunts, and the court's seasonal moves between capitals. Whether they were also required to make a public appearance during a major (male?) feast is difficult to ascertain. See A. Kuhrt, *The Ancient Near East* (London, 1995), 683.

8. Note the curious difference between the Masoretic text (MT) and the Greek Septuagint (LXX), with the former (2:1) showing Ahasuerus as "recalling" or "remembering" his condemned wife (*zakhar*), and the latter casting him as precisely the opposite (3:1: "having forgotten," *tou mnemoneuein tes Oustin*).

9. The motif of obedience-disobedience in Esther has been frequently noted; see, among others, B. Wyler, "Esther: The Incomplete Emancipation of a Queen," in *A Feminist Companion to Esther, Judith, and Susanna*, ed. A. Brenner (Sheffield, 1995), 144; and K. Jackoski, "Holy Disobedience in Esther," *Theology Today* 45 (1989): 403–14.

10. T. K. Beal, "Tracing Esther's Beginnings" in *A Feminist Companion to Esther, Judith, and Susanna*, ed. A. Brenner (Sheffield, 1995), 94, on the link between male power in individual households and the maintenance of power in the larger order of things.

11. Josephus, *Jewish Antiquities* 11:195, claims that the king was in love with Vashti but had to separate from her as the law demanded. But this is more of an excuse to account for Esther's appearance than for the marital model which the text proposes.

12. Knoppers, "Sex, Religion, and Politics," 121–42 passim, for the theme of sex outside the sect and historical turning points in Israelite history.

13. The passage (Neh. 13:23–27) is difficult. Clines (*New Century Bible Commentary*, 246–47) notes the absence of the phrase "the language of each people" in the LXX, as well as an internal contradiction that records marriage with three

types of gentiles but linguistic problems stemming only from marriage with Ashdodites. A redactional hand solicitous of forging a link between 1 Kings 11:1-2 and the Judaean situation in the days of Nehemiah is evidently at work, as can be inferred from the insertion of *tradita* recalling both Deut. 23:4 and the Pentateuchal bans on intermarriage (Exod. 34 and Deut. 7). Since older traditions contained no reference to Ashdodites, Nehemiah added his own touch by enlarging the scope of the *tradita* to include these women. Fishbane, *Biblical Interpretation*, 124 n. 51, regards the reference to Ammonites and Moabites as a "tendentious addition."

14. The date of Esther has never been fixed within clear chronological boundaries. Modern opinions have opted for dates ranging from the fifth/fourth century B.C.E. (Persian) to the second (Hellenistic). If I am correct in reading echoes of Ezra-Nehemiah in Esther, namely in seeing the former as providing a hermeneutic precedent for the latter, the scroll clearly postdates Ezra-Nehemiah, but by how much it is difficult to tell. A late, rather than early date is more feasible, in my mind.

15. Marriage in the Achaemenid court was largely dictated by political considerations and kings often married close female relatives. Nor was polygyny unusual. The ranking of royal wives is unclear but those of Persian origins may have ranked above the others. H. Sancisi-Weerdenburg, "Exit Atossa: Images of Women in Greek Historiography on Persia," in *Images of Women in Antiquity*, ed. A. Cameron and A. Kuhrt (London, 1983), 20-83. See also M. Brosius, *Women in Ancient Persia, 559-331 B.C.E.* (Oxford, 1996).

16. Murders were not unknown in the Persian palace, however, including those of queens. On the poisoning of Stateira, wife of Artaxerxes II, by Parysatis, a female rival, see F. Jacoby, *Die Fragmente der Griechische Historiker* (FGH) (Berlin 1923–   ), 688 Frag. 27, with Kuhrt, *Ancient Near East*, 683.

17. The similarities between the Esther narrative and the Joseph one have been often noted; see K. Butting, "Esther: A New Interpretation of the Joseph Story in the Fight against Anti-Semitism and Sexism," in *Ruth and Esther: A Feminist Companion to the Bible*, second series, ed. A. Brenner (Sheffield, 1999), 239-48. But I am not aware of a comparison between the two gentile couples of the Genesis and Esther tales. In general, see S. T. Hollis, "The Woman in Ancient Examples of the Potiphar's Wife Motif, K2111," in *Gender and Difference in Ancient Israel*, ed. P. L. Day (Minneapolis, Minn., 1989), 28-42.

18. Exod. 34:16; Deut. 7:4. See the comments of Knoppers, "Sex, Religion, and Politics."

19. The sympathy so clearly evinced by modern interpreters is, perhaps, out of place in this context.

20. Unlike Aeschylus's Xerxes, for example, whose mother, Atossa, is by far the most dominant figure in the play (*The Persians*).

21. The chapter may well be a late redactional touch, as Clines and others have argued.

22. It is noticeable that the king does not manifest any surprise at his consort's revelation of identity but only rage. Clearly the identification of Esther with the doomed people of the decree had not been the point of concealment.

23. Compounded by his proposal to don royal insignia (Esther 6:8) and by his initial demand for deference due only to monarchs and to gods.

24. The words used to describe the legal-adoptive relations between the cousins (Esther 2:7; 2:20) recall the term used in Neh. 10:1 to describe the rallying of the exilic community behind Nehemiah's reforms. The echo may be deliberate.

25. Paternal responsibilities toward daughters are beautifully summarized in Eccl. 42:9 ff.

26. B. L. Eichler, "On Reading Genesis 12:10–20," in *Tehillah Le-Moshe: Biblical and Judaic Studies in Honor of Moshe Greenberg* (Winona Lake, Ind., 1997), 23–38; in general, N. Steinberg, "Kinship and Gender in Genesis," *Biblical Research* 39 (1994): 45–56.

27. I am echoing here, and elsewhere, S. J. D. Cohen, "Iudaios, Judaeus, Judaean, Jew," in *Beginnings of Jewishness*, 69–106, esp. 82, where he defines *Yehudim* as members of the tribe of Judah or as "people of the kingdom of Judah," a definition based on geographic or ethnic affiliation.

28. T. K. Beal, *The Book of Hiding: Gender, Ethnicity, Annihilation, and Esther* (New York, 1997), 72–73, contains the interesting suggestion that Mordechai was alluding to the vengeance of the Jews on Esther.

29. Whether the relations between Esther and Mordechai also signify the emergence of a new type of identity based on the accident of birth rather than on a shared exilic experience (as in the case of Ezra-Nehemiah) is another issue. C. Moore (in *Anchor Bible Dictionary*, ed. D. N. Freedman, 6 vols. [New York, 1992], 2:635) views the Hebrew Esther's "Jewish nationalism" as an agenda based on birth. Pentateuchal bans on intermarriage were formulated in the shade of a constant threat of apostasy and idolatry. Neither features in Esther. The silence, like others in the text, may have been deliberate. It is left to the readers to figure out to what extent religious or credal differences were of weight in the relationship of the mixed couple. The king himself showed no discrimination, other than one based on purely aesthetic preferences, although the text implies that it was advisable to hide Esther's precise (Jewish) identity. The ruse was primarily needed to advance the plot. Whether Esther conveys approval or disapproval of intermarriage must be examined through a scrutiny of the couple itself.

30. On this and other sexual vocabulary, see A. Brenner, *The Intercourse of Knowledge* (Leiden, 1997), esp. 13–18.

31. On concealment as an integral part of Esther's plot, see W. T. McBride, "Esther Passes: Chiasm, Lex Talio, and Money in the Book of Esther," in *Not in Heaven: Coherence and Complexity in Biblical Narrative*, ed. J. Rosenblatt and J. C. Sitterson (Bloomington, Ind., 1991), 220. See also J. Derby, "The Paradox in the Book of Esther," *Jewish Bible Quarterly* 23 (1995): 115–19.

32. Cf. the case of the beautiful captive of Deuteronomy 21 in Pressler, *View of Women*, 10 and passim. See also A. Rofé, "Family and Sex Laws in Deuteronomy and the Book of the Covenant," *Henoch* 9 (1987): 136; and D. Stern, "The Captive Woman: Hellenization, Greco-Roman Erotic Narrative, and Rabbinic Literature," *Poetics Today* 19 (1998): 91–127.

33. Cf. Yael, a married woman, and Judith, a widow—women with sexual experience prior to their encounters with gentile males. Ruth, likewise, had been married.

34. Beal, *Book of Hiding*, 76, compares the scene with the one between Ruth

and Boaz on the threshing floor (Ruth 3). There are certainly several commonalities, but the stakes, as well as the motivation, are singularly different.

35. To apply Knoppers's terminology.

36. The original language of J/A, by a majority of scholarly consensus, is Greek. One text (= short recension) was published in M. Philonenko, *Joseph et Aséneth: Introduction, texte critique, traduction, et notes*, Studia Post-Biblica 13 (Leiden, 1968), 128–221, for text and translation, and 110–23 for an appendix on the afterlife of the motives of J/A in Christian and Islamic romances. For a provisional edition of the longer recension, see C. Burchard, "Ein vorläufiger griechischer Text von Joseph und Aseneth," *Dielheimer Blätter zum Alten Testament* 14 (1979): 2–53 and 16 (1982): 37–39, repr. in C. Burchard, *Gesammelte Studien zu Joseph und Aseneth* (Leiden, 1996), 161–209, with a massive up-to-date bibliography at the end. Each version was also translated into English, the shorter in H. F. D. Sparks, ed., *The Apocryphal Old Testament* (Oxford, 1984), 473–503; and the longer in J. H. Charlesworth, *The Old Testament Pseudepigrapha* (New York, 1985), 202–47, with ample notes and introduction, all by Burchard. The primacy of the longer one, argued by Burchard and usually accepted by others, has been recently rejected by R. S. Kraemer, *When Aseneth Met Joseph: A Late Antique Tale of the Biblical Patriarch and His Egyptian Wife, Reconsidered* (Oxford, 1998). When possible, I have referred to both versions. Neither, to my mind, represents a now lost original. See also the internet bibliography on the website http://www.ac.uk/theology/goodacre/Aseneth.

Dated to somewhere between 100 B.C.E. and 100 C.E., the work may, in fact, be earlier. See G. Bohak, *Joseph and Aseneth and the Jewish Temple in Heliopolis* (Atlanta, Ga., 1996), with arguments that do not settle the question of date. The argument for a *terminus post quem* of 100 B.C.E. usually revolves on the use of the LXX by the author. Since the Pentateuch was translated in the early third century and there were certainly older translations than the LXX as we know it, this is not a critical objection. For a summary of the problems concerned with the LXX text and transmission, see E. Tov, "The Septuagint," in *Mikra: Text, Translation, Reading and Interpretation of the Hebrew Bible in Ancient Judaism and Early Christianity*, Compendia Rerum Iudaicarum ad Novum Testamentum, section 2, ed. M. J. Mulder and H. Sysling (Assen/Maastricht and Philadelphia, 1988), 161–88. For a summary of modern scholarship regarding all these vexing issues, see R. D. Chesnutt, *From Death to Life: Conversion in Joseph and Aseneth* (Sheffield, 1995), 20–93.

37. For comparisons with Hellenistic and early Christian novelistic and ascetic literature, see Kraemer, *When Aseneth Met Joseph*.

38. Even if the journeys of the Greek heroines are interpreted as mystical and spiritual (as R. Merkelbach has done in *Roman und Mysterium in der Antike* [Munich, 1962]), such an interpretation does not account for Aseneth's road—in fact, it takes away the edge from it.

39. It is hardly surprising that the "conversion" of Aseneth has been interpreted as initiation into a mystical sect, such as the elusive Therapeutae (who are described in Philo, *On the Contemplative Life*; see M. Delcor, "Un roman d'amour d'origine thérapeute: Le livre de Joseph et Asenath," *Bulletin de Littérature Ecclésiastique* 63 [1962]: 3–27), a reading that limits the description to a narrow audience but perhaps not altogether unacceptable. But valid objections have been raised, in-

cluding C. Burchard, "The Present State of Research on Joseph and Aseneth," in C. Burchard, *Gesammelte Studien*, 308 (originally in *New Perspectives on Ancient Judaism*, vol. 2, ed. J. Neusner et al. [Lanham, Md., 1987]); Kraemer's *When Aseneth Met Joseph* maintains that J/A could have described conversion to Christianity and possibly to Christian asceticism. The most widely accepted scholarly notion is that Aseneth typified a convert to Judaism.

40. For a useful survey of all such attempts, Chesnutt, *From Death to Life*, and Kraemer, *When Aseneth Met Joseph*, and the criticism of A. Schweitzer who long ago condemned the methodology of amalgamating heterogeneous elements from diffuse sources of uneven value (*Paul and His Interpreters* [London, 1912], 192–93, cited in Chesnutt, 219).

41. J/A 11, Burchard; cf. 12.7.

42. On the experience of conversion in liminal terms, see R. C. Douglas, "Liminality and Conversion in Joseph and Aseneth," *Journal for the Study of the Pseudoepigrapha* 3 (1988): 31–42.

43. E. M. Humphrey, *The Ladies and the Cities: Transformation and Apocalyptic Identity in Joseph and Aseneth, 4 Ezra, the Apocalypse, and the Shepherd of Hermas* (Sheffield 1995), sees the bees bearing a "corporate importance" (38), which shows Aseneth, as "mother of converts" (44), nourishing all other bees (namely proselytes), through the honeycomb on her lips.

44. Modern explanations of this term have ranged from a metaphor recalling the biblical cities of asylum to one representing Christ and the church. But such analogues fail to relate this specific allusion to the rest of the tale. To be identified, metaphorically, as a city, implies that Aseneth acquired the power to bestow civic identity. But an affiliation between a female and a city is problematic, as the association between the goddess Athena and the city of Athens demonstrates: see N. Loraux, *The Children of Athena: Athenian Ideas about Citizenship and the Division between the Sexes*, trans. C. Levine (Princeton, N.J., 1993), 116. One notes that there are no *Iudaiai*, namely female Jewish citizens, in J/A, just as there are no *Athenaiai* but only *Athenaioi*, male citizens of the city of Athens. In Aristophanes' *Thesmophoriazousai*, the chorus, all females, just like Aseneth's attendants, sings the praises of the goddess: "Pallas, the friend of choruses, the virgin free from all yokes, the guardian of our city" (1136–42, cited in Loraux, *Children*, 140).

45. G. Sissa, *Greek Virginity*, trans. A. Goldhammer (Cambridge, Mass., 1990), 106–7, who objects to this interpretation.

46. The rehabilitation of the two brothers is a well-known feature of the Pseudepigrapha; see above, Chapter 1.

47. 3.7, Philonenko; 3.5, Burchard, *argon tes kleronomias auton*; cf. 4.3, 16.2, 20.5, 24.14, 26.1, Philonenko.

48. 16.2, *ton argon kleronomias mou*; 24.14; 26.1.

49. 4.5, Philonenko.

50. *Kyrios*, possessor; 8.1, Philonenko.

51. J/A 4.11, Burchard.

52. J/A 4.5, Burchard.

53. B. Porten et al., *The Elephantine Papyri in English* (Leiden, 1996), 75–76. References are to the papyri as given in this collection.

54. 7.11, Philonenko.
55. 8.3, Philonenko.
56. 20.8, Philonenko.
57. 22.8, Philonenko.
58. 26.1, Philonenko.
59. Porten, C27.
60. Porten, C28.
61. Porten, B25.
62. Porten, B25.
63. Porten, B26.
64. Porten, D2, slightly abbreviated.
65. Porten, C33, 198 B.C.E.

66. Women giving themselves in marriage are attested in Egypt already in the third century, J. M. Modrzejewski, "Les documents du désert de Judée à la lumière des papyrus d'Égypte," paper delivered at Bar Ilan University's conference on the documents of the Judaean Desert, June 1998.

67. P. W. Pestman, *Marriage and Matrimonial Property in Ancient Egypt* (Leiden, 1961); C. J. Eyre, "Crime and Adultery in Ancient Egypt," *Journal of Egyptian Archaeology* 70 (1984): 92–105; G. Robins, *Women in Ancient Egypt* (Cambridge, Mass., 1993); and G. Robins, *The Art of Ancient Egypt* (Cambridge, Mass., 1997). The following comments on Egyptian women are based on R. S. Bagnall, *Egypt in Late Antiquity* (Princeton, N.J., 1993), 188 f.

68. J. M. Modrzejewski, "La Septante comme nomos: Comment la Tora est devenue une 'loi civique' pour les Juifs d'Égypte," *Annali di scienze religiose* 2 (1997): 143–58. See, however, the comments of V. A. Tcherikover and A. Fuks on papyrus no. 128 (*Corpus papyrorum Judaicarum*, vol. 1) of 218 B.C.E. in which a woman (Helladote) claims that she has been wronged by her husband, Jonathan the Jew, who had agreed "in accordance with the law of the Jews" to marry her but evidently changed his mind. The editors comment (p. 238) that this is the only instance in the Greek papyri of Jewish national law being applied to the legal life of members of the Jewish community in matrimonial matters.

69. Modrzejewski, "Qu'est-ce que le droit hellénistique?"

70. This is not the place to explore in detail either the arguments about the precise date of J/A, which is likely to remain elusive, or the question of proselytism in the period of its composition. That J/A aims to enhance the status of converts has been already noted (Chestnutt, *Anchor Bible Dictionary*; and Chestnutt, *From Death to Life*) although the process of conversion does not conform to rabbinic precepts (G. G. Porton, *The Stranger Within Your Gates: Converts and Conversion in Rabbinic Literature* [Chicago, 1994], 132 f., versus S. J. D. Cohen, "Conversion to Judaism in Historical Perspective: From Biblical Israel to Post-Biblical Judaism," *Conservative Judaism* 36 [1983]: 31–45.)

Chapter 4: Keeping Adultery at Bay

1. On the ambiguity of the language of this commandment, see Albeck, "Ten Commandments," 281.

2. A view somewhat "remedied" by the aggadic tale quoted in the Introduction about the temptation of Rabbi Meir.

3. This is, of course, Potiphar's wife, Genesis 39. Whether it preceded the Exodus prohibition is immaterial for the present argument. She is also a gentile.

4. According to rabbinic interpretation of Exodus 24; see Eilberg-Schwartz, *God's Phallus*, 189–90.

5. On the latter, see Eilberg-Schwartz, *God's Phallus*, 97 f., emphasizing the appropriation of the role of the married wife by Israelite males.

6. Mopsik; "Body of Engenderment," 54.

7. Ibid., 55.

8. The word *avon* is difficult. It can also be translated as "guilt" or "iniquity." B. D. Haberman, "The Suspected Adulteress: A Study of Textual Embodiment," *Prooftexts* 20 (2000): 15, reads the phrase as cleansing the husband of false accusation.

9. Whether the action of the ordeal itself stemmed from a specific belief about the supernatural remains unclear. See P. Brown, "Society and the Supernatural: A Medieval Change," *Daedalus* (Summer 1975): 140. See also C. M. Radding, *A World Made by Men: Cognition and Society, 400–1200* (Chapel Hill, N.C., 1985), 14.

10. On women-water in connection with purity and menstruation, see R. R. Wasserfall, ed., *Women and Water: Menstruation in Jewish Life and Law* (Hanover, N.H., 1999). On water and sexuality in Jewish writings, see J. Cohen, *"Be Fertile and Increase, Fill the Earth and Master It": The Ancient and Medieval Career of a Biblical Text* (Ithaca, N.Y., 1989), 83–84.

11. On this passage see also N. Margalit, "Not by Her Mouth Do We Live: A Literary/Anthropological Reading of Gender in Mishnah Ketubbot Chapter 1," *Prooftexts* 20 (2000): 61–86.

12. Cf. M Ket. 3.4–5, which describes marriage after rape as a state in which the husband "drinks from an earthen pot"—in other words, man has to put up with whatever blemishes his wife may have without being able to divorce her. On women, as earth, women and earth see the magnificent reflections of N. Loraux, *Born of the Earth: Myth and Politics in Athens*, trans. S. Stewart (Ithaca, N.Y., 2000), passim, esp. the encounter with Bachofen.

13. *Coniugalia praecepta* 144a-b, trans. in P. duBois, *Sowing the Body: Psychoanalysis and Ancient Representations of Women* (Chicago, 1988), 39. On the agenda of the work, see V. Wohl, "Scenes from a Marriage: Love and *Logos* in Plutarch's *Coniugalia praecepta*," *Helios* 24 (1997): 170 f.

14. BT Sot. 17a; see Mopsik, "Body of Engenderment," 56.

15. PT Ket. 5.6; see Mopsik, "Body of Engenderment," 56.

16. Cf. D. Milligan, *Sex Life* (London and Boulder, Colo., 1993), passim.

17. For the expression, see T. Habinek, "The Invention of Sexuality in the World-City of Rome," in T. Habinek and A. Schiesaro, *The Roman Cultural Revolution* (Cambridge, 1997), 27.

18. Cf. J. Weeks, *Sex, Politics and Society: The Regulation of Sexuality since 1800* (rev. ed., London, 1989), passim.

19. I am using the term "arbitration" because the subject of rabbinic "courts" is, to my mind, far from clear. That the rabbis themselves used their authority to act as judges for their flocks goes without saying. But the precise range of their

jurisdiction within the larger framework of Roman law is unclear. I suspect that in many cases they acted as arbiters rather than as official judges. See the remarks of C. Hezser, *The Social Structure of the Rabbinic Movement in Roman Palestine* (Tübingen, 1997), 275 f. and 461 f., and compare the widespread resort to arbitration rather than to provincial courts in late antiquity, as discussed by J. Harries, *Law and Empire in Late Antiquity* (Cambridge, 1999), passim.

20. H. Arendt, "What Is Authority?" in *Between Past and Future* (Cleveland and New York, 1963), 120–21, quoted in H. F. Pitkin, *Fortune Is a Woman: Gender and Politics in the Thought of Niccolò Machiavelli* (Berkeley, Calif., 1984), 49–50, on the Romans.

21. The point is particularly evident in Athenian legislation on adultery that focuses largely on the husband and the lover. See D. Cohen, *Law, Sexuality, and Society: The Enforcement of Morals in Classical Athens* (Cambridge, 1991), 98 f.

22. See also Calhoon, "Lucretia, Savior and Scapegoat," 151–69.

23. Machiavelli, *Mandragola*, 3.4, quoted in Pitkin, *Fortune Is a Woman*, 30, the source for what follows.

24. D 4.4.37.1, quoted in T. A. J. McGinn, *Prostitution, Sexuality, and the Law in Ancient Rome* (New York, 1998), 172.

25. Cf. the discussion that led to Beruria's "fall," above, Introduction.

26. Note, however, that although the complaisance of a husband was classified as a criminal offense the activity of actual pimps was not subjected to criminal procedures nor are there specific penalties prescribed. McGinn, *Prostitution*, 171–72 and note 236.

27. See McGinn, *Prostitution*, 140 f. for a comprehesive analysis of the Augustan *lex Iulia de adulteriis coercendis*.

28. P. Brown, *The Body and Society*; D. Elliott, *Spiritual Marriage: Sexual Abstinence in Medieval Wedlock* (Princeton, N.J., 1993).

29. A. Rousselle, *Porneia: On Desire and the Body in Antiquity*, trans. F. Pheasant (New York, 1996), passim.

30. See Weinstein, *Piety and Fanaticism*, 65 f., on ascetic behavior. On issues of purity in general, see J. Klawans, *Impurity and Sin in Ancient Judaism* (Oxford, 2000); M. Poorthuis and J. Schwartz, eds., *Purity and Holiness: The Heritage of Leviticus* (Leiden, 2000); J. Neusner, *Purity in Rabbinic Judaism* (Atlanta, Ga., 1994); H. Maccoby, *Ritual and Morality: The Ritual Purity System and Its Place in Judaism* (Cambridge, 1999). On female bodily purity, see C. E. Fonrobert, *Menstrual Purity: Rabbinic and Christian Reconstructions of Biblical Gender* (Stanford, Calif., 2000).

31. Fonrobert, *Menstrual Purity*, 23.

32. Lev. 20:10; Deut 22:22; with the comment of Origen, *Ad. Rom.* 6.7 (PG 14.1073), who claims that the Jews (of his time?) did not have the right to stone adulteresses, a surprising claim in view of his famed observation on patriarchal powers of life and death in the third century; both probably must be taken with a grain of salt. See L. I. Levine, "The Jewish Patriarch (Nasi) in Third Century Palestine," *Aufstieg und Niedergang der Römischen Welt* II.19.2 (1979): 662. The power to kill a lover caught in the act had already been restricted in the late Roman republic. On the abolition of the right to kill a wife taken in flagrante delicto, *Collatio*, 4.3.1, in P. E. Corbett, *The Roman Law of Marriage* (Oxford, 1930), 135.

33. Corbett, 127–46, and Treggiari, *Roman Marriage: Iusti Coniuges from the Time of Cicero to the Time of Ulpian* (Oxford, 1991), 275 f., for the Roman side.

34. For a useful overview of late Roman legislation on adultery, see J. Beaucamp, *Le statut de la femme à Byzance 4e-7e Siècle*, 2 vols. (Paris, 1990, 1992), 1:139–69. Concrete examples from the papyri which she examines are few and far between and the only clear piece of evidence relates to an in flagrante case (1992), 2:78. On the only case that illustrates in some detail the application of law to practice see below.

35. Among existing scholarship on Roman and Jewish law, see Boaz Cohen. *Jewish and Roman Law: A Comparative Study*, 2 vols. (New York, 1966), esp. 1.279 f. on betrothal and dowry, and 1.377 f. on divorce. R. Yaron, *Gifts in Contemplation of Death in Jewish and Roman Law* (Oxford, 1960). See below, Chapter 5.

36. The subject of the mutual influence of Jewish and Roman law on each other has generated considerable debate; opinions vary from minimal to substantial interaction. See, among others, D. Daube, "Jewish Law in the Hellenistic World," in *Jewish Law in Legal History and the Modern World*, ed. B. S. Jackson (Leiden, 1980), 45–60, esp. 58. For what follows see my "Revealing the Concealed: Rabbinic and Roman Legal Perspectives on Detecting Adultery," *Zeitschrift der Savigny-Stiftung für Rechtsgeschichte: Romanistische Abteilung* 116 (1999): 112–46.

37. On the difficulties of interpreting the biblical injunctions in this passage, see M. Fishbane, "Accusations of Adultery: A Study of Law and Scribal Practice in Numbers 5:11–31," *Hebrew Union College Annual* 45 (1974): 25–45, esp. 35. Fishbane discerns a treatment of two different cases of adultery, one substantiated by probability, the other merely based on suspicion. More recently, A. Bach, "Good to the Last Drop: Viewing the Sotah (Numbers 5:11–31) as the Glass Half Empty and Wondering How to View It Half Full," in *The New Literary Criticism and the Hebrew Bible*, ed. J. C. Exum and D. J. A. Clines (Valley Forge, Pa., 1993), 26–55. Previously published articles on Num. 5:11–31 are now conveniently assembled in *Women in the Hebrew Bible*, ed. A. Bach (New York, 1999), 461–522 (articles by T. Frymer-Kensky, J. Milgrom, J. Sasson, M. Fishbane, and A. Bach).

38. For a useful introduction to rabbinic literature, see the bibliographical essay of B. M. Bokser, "An Annotated Bibliographical Guide to the Study of the Palestinian Talmud," and the descriptive one by D. Goodblatt, "The Babylonian Talmud," both in *Aufstieg und Niedergang der Römischen Welt* II.19.2 (1979): 139–256 and 257–336 respectively. There is no scientific edition of either text. For a more recent overview, B. M. Bokser, "Talmudic Studies," in Cohen and Greenstein, *State of Jewish Studies*, 80–112, with ample bibliography.

39. See below on the abolition. The reasons supplied in the Mishnah (Sot. 9.9), and elaborated upon in the Talmuds (BT Sot. 47c), to account for the abolishment of the ritual include the multiplicity of cases of adultery and the equality of guilt of both men and women. Both are dubious. (See Ilan, *Jewish Women in Greco-Roman Palestine*, 137–39.) Moreover, the former was hardly limited to Jewish communities. Cf. the family legislation of Septimius Severus (193–211 C.E.), about which the historian Dio Cassius (*Roman History* 77.16.4) reports that instead of stemming adultery it generated no fewer than three thousand indictments, a huge number with which the judiciary was incapable of dealing.

Yet no Roman emperor proposed an abolition of the legal procedures involving suspicion of adultery. Nor is there an indication in any of the ample rabbinic discussions on relations between the two sexes that they came to view married males who committed adultery (with unmarried partners) with severity equal to the one applied to married women. For lovers, see below.

40. On rabbinic discussions of the ordeal as "totally academic," see R. Biale, *Women and Jewish Law* (New York, 1984), 188. In general on rabbinic teachings relating to extra-Temple rites, see B. M. Bokser, "Rabbinic Responses to Catastrophe: From Continuity to Discontinuity," *Proceedings of the American Academy for Jewish Research* 50 (1983): 37–61; W. S. Green, "Reading the Writing of Rabbinism," *Journal of the American Academy of Religion* 51 (1983): 191–206; and A. J. Avery-Peck, "Law and Society in Early Judaism: Legal Evolution in the Mishnaic Division of Agriculture," *New Perspectives on Ancient Judaism* 1 (1987): 67–87, esp. 84–87.

41. Nor, for that matter, have issues relating to rank, class, and socioeconomics of the group targeted by the Mishnaic elaborations of the biblical ordeal been examined. It is hardly conceivable, for example, that a procedure so taxing and time-consuming as a journey to Jerusalem, a period of sojourn in the city, and the willingness of a husband to expose his wife to public humiliation could have been undertaken by every man who suspected his wife of adultery. Since, moreover, the issue at stake appears invariably to have been the retention or the loss of the wife's dowry, the suspicion that the ordeal was primarily planned for aristocratic plaintiffs must be voiced and explored. But this falls outside the scope of the present study.

42. Cf. M Git. 8.5 on dating a bill of divorce to a year "after the destruction of the Temple," and M Sot. 9.12 also referring to the destruction of the Temple as the beginning of an accursed and lean era.

43. On the extent of rabbinic jurisdiction within Roman Palestine, see A. M. Rabello, "Jewish and Roman Jurisdiction," in *An Introduction to the History and Sources of Jewish Law*, ed. N. S. Hecht et al. (Oxford, 1996), 141–67. On rabbinic legal authority, through rabbinic eyes, J. Roth, *The Halakhic Process: A Systematic Analysis* (New York, 1986), 115–33 and passim.

44. On definitions of the former, see S. Corcoran, *The Empire of the Tetrarchs: Imperial Pronouncements and Government, 284–324* (Oxford, 1996), passim. On the halakhic differences between the Palestinian and the Babylonian Talmuds, due perhaps to two versions of the Mishnah, and on their susceptibility to historical analysis, see C. E. Hayes, *Between the Babylonian and Palestinian Talmuds* (New York and Oxford, 1997), 7 ff. and passim.

45. Rousselle, *Porneia*, 85. See also M. H. Crawford, *Roman Statutes* (London, 1996), 2:781–860 (on the *lex Iulia de adulteriis coercendis*), with bibliography.

46. McGinn, *Prostitution*, 140–41.

47. Ibid., 194 and for what follows on the Augustan law.

48. Pliny, *Panegyricus* 83.4, trans. in McGinn, *Prostitution*, 191.

49. Perhaps, too, the preliminaries were designed to solve a legal paradox that on the one hand allowed a woman to recover her marriage settlement if her husband divorced her without actual proof of misconduct, and on the other hand dealt with precisely the lack of such proof through the biblical ordeal of the bitter water. See Wegner, *Chattel or Person?* 92.

50. On rabbinic courts in general, see E. B. Quint and N. S. Hecht, *Jewish Jurisprudence*, vol. 2 (Chur, 1986), passim.

51. The translation is of J. Neusner et al., *The Talmud of the Land of Israel*, vol. 27 (Chicago, 1984), 13–14 (hereafter Neusner).

52. A. Destro, *The Law of Jealousy: Anthropology of Sotah* (Atlanta, Ga., 1989), 62; Ilan, *Jewish Women*, 138.

53. M. L. Satlow, *Tasting the Dish: Rabbinic Rhetorics of Sexuality* (Atlanta, Ga., 1995), 127–28, on "sexual interpretation" of this passage. On the circle of permissible social contacts and physical mobility of women according to rabbinic ideas, see M Ket. 7.4–5 (visits to father's house and to houses of mourning or feasting are at stake in a case of potential divorce).

54. Jewish men were constantly exhorted to avoid talking and even eye contact with women in general and were promised hell (Gehenna) if they had intercourse with married women (BT Sot. 4a; BT BM 58b; in Satlow, *Tasting*, 141; M Avot 1.5, in Ilan, *Jewish Women*, 126–27). Pressure of upbringing should have thus been a sufficient deterrent for any man who contemplated a sexual liaison with a married woman. A rabbinic debate even suggests that female education should consist of familiarity with precisely the passages relating to penalties imposed on adulteresses (M Sot. 3.5, Ilan, *Jewish Women*, 139).

55. D 48.5.2.8, 12.7–13, 15.2, in Treggiari, *Roman Marriage*, 287.

56. *Novella*, 117.15.

57. U. Manthe, "Beiträge zur Entwicklung des antiken Gerechtigkeitsbegriffes II: Stoische Würdigkeit und die iuris praecepta Ulpians," *Zeitschrift der Savigny-Stiftung für Rechtsgeschichte: Romanistische Abteilung* 114 (1997): 1–26, esp. 16 ff.

58. PT 1.2 (Neusner, p. 20). See also Hauptman, *Rereading the Rabbis*, 77 f., esp. 86–87 with BT Ket. 51b.

59. Treggiari, *Roman Marriage*, 279, with D 48.5.40 *praefatio*; *Collatio*. 5.2.2; CJ 9.9.20. The issue of intent, in general, is important. Neither Jewish nor Roman law held a person accountable for intention alone (D 48.19.18: *cogitationis poenam nemo patitur*). The rabbis realized that at the heart of criminal action lies intent. Thus coveting someone else's possessions (including a wife) could lead to a sin and a crime (*Mekhilta de Rabbi Ishmael* ad Exod. 20:17) as cited in B. S. Jackson, "Liability for Mere Intent in Early Jewish Law," in *Essays in Jewish and Comparative Legal History* (Leiden, 1975), 202–34, esp. 215, 218.

60. CJ 9.9.18. pr. (258 C.E.): *Eum qui duas simul habuit uxores sine dubitatione comitatur infamia. in ea namque re non iuris effectus, quo cives nostri matrimonia contrahere plura prohibentur, sed animi destinatio cogitatur.*

61. Cf. M Git. 8.5 on rabbinic attitudes to a woman who married two men but whose divorce writ from her first husband was deemed invalid due to scribal error. The woman had to leave her two husbands and to forfeit her marriage portion. On this passage, see Wegner, *Chattel*, 65.

62. Cf. CJ 9.9.29, with R. A. Bauman's comments in "The 'leges indiciorum publicorum' and Their Interpretation in the Republic, Principate, and Late Empire," *Aufstieg und Niedergang der Römischen Welt* II.13 (1980): 231–32 on the Justinianian modifications of this constitution. English translations of this constitu-

tion are also found in Pharr, *The Theodosian Code* (Princeton, N.J., 1952) and in J. E. Grubbs, *Law and Family in Late Antiquity: The Emperor Constantine's Marriage Legislation* (Oxford, 1995), 208–9.

63. Jerome, Epistula 1, quoted with modifications from *St. Jerome: Letters and Selected Works*, in *Nicene and Post-Nicene Fathers*, ed. P. Schaff and H. Wace, 2nd ser., vol. 6 (1975). The date is between 350 and the early 370s, the latter more likely. The analysis of Jerome's letter is largely based on H. Sivan, "Le corps d'une pécheresse, le prix de la piété: La politique de l'adultère dans l'Antiquité tardive," *Annales* (1998): 231–53.

64. If an accusing husband remained married to the woman he accused he was further liable to prosecution on grounds of *lenocinium* (pimping; CJ 9.9.17). The law allowed, however, for a change of heart (see below). It also granted the husband sixty days within which to press charges (after the divorce) by the "right of the husband" (*ius mariti*) or, in the case of a father, by the "right of the father" (*ius patris*) (Treggiari, *Roman Marriage*, 287). But temporal injunctions were not as clear-cut as they first appear. The limit of sixty days was reinforced in an imperial rescript of 223 (CJ 9.9.6), after which the right to accuse was transferred to strangers. These unknown accusers were further encouraged by an exemption from a charge of *calumnia* or their own liability in case of false accusation. Another law of 223 reminded the public that any accusation against a man for adultery must be made within five years from the date the act was committed (CJ 9.9.5, but an exception was granted by CJ 9.9.21 of 290 to men in public service).

65. On the difficulties of interpretation, see Bauman, "Leges iudiciorum publicorum," 215 no. 343 and 214 ff. on this law, and R. Bonini, *Ricerche di diritto giustinianeo* (Milan, 1968), 151 ff.

66. Grubbs, *Law and Family*, 253 f., but see the comments of Averil Cameron, "Ascetic Closure and the End of Antiquity," in *Asceticism*, ed. V. L. Wimbush et al. (New York and Oxford, 1995), 147–61 on the mentality and moral ambiance that bred new attitudes to sex.

67. Bauman, "Leges," 232, observes that the husband appears in CTh 9.7.2 "almost as an afterthought." But this seems unlikely since the husband is central to this ideology of morality.

68. E. Volterra, "Per la storia dell'*accusatio adulterii iure mariti vel patris*," in *Scritti giuridici*, ed. M. Talamanca, vol. 1 (Naples, 1991), 219–78, esp. 269 ff. on CJ 9.7.2 and 253 on CJ 9.9.16.1.

69. I am not certain that Bauman, "Leges," 214 ff. (following M. A. de Dominicis, "Sulle origini romanocristiane del diritto del marito ad accusare constante matrimonio la moglie adultera," *Studia et documenta historiae iuris* 16 [1950]: 221 f.), is correct in assuming that an accusation could be launched *stante matrimonio*. This remained a gray area until Justinian.

70. CTh 9.7.2 = CJ 9.9.29.2; see Grubbs, *Law and Family*, 210: *in primis maritum genialis tori vindicem esse oportet, cui quidem ex suspicione ream coniugem facere licet, vel eam, si tantum suspicatur, penes se detinere non prohibetur.*

71. CTh 3.16.1; see A. Arjava, *Women and Law in Late Antiquity* (Oxford, 1996), 177 f.

72. Arjava, *Women and Law*, 184.
73. *De adulterinis coniugiis*. 2.8–17, cited in Arjava, *Women and Law*, 197. See also Grubbs, *Law and Family*, 253.
74. Jerome, Epistula 1.
75. Also reflected in rabbinic discussions of the rebellious wife (*moredet*). See S. Riskin, *Women and Jewish Divorce: The Rebellious Wife, the Agunah, and the Right of Women to Initiate Divorce in Jewish Law. A Halakhic Solution* (Hoboken, N.J., 1989), 3–46.
76. A law of Theodosius I (CTh 9.7.7 = CJ 9.9.32) of 392 seems to imply that even after Constantine's legislation, outsiders were not always excluded, in light of a reference to an "established case" (*accusatione fundata*) brought either by the "right of a husband" (*iure mariti*) or the "right of strangers or outsiders" (*iure extranei*, omitted from the CJ) within the prescribed time limits.
77. PT Sot. 1.2, (7e) (Neusner, 23).
78. T Yeb. 12.8, in Satlow, *Tasting*, 138.
79. I follow here the translation of Satlow, *Tasting*, 138. Cf. McGinn, *Prostitution*, 156 f. on adulteresses as prostitutes and on the consignment of adulteresses to brothels, a practice assigned to Augustus but only attested when it was allegedly abolished by Theodosius in 389 C.E. to make way for other penalties (Socrates, *Historia ecclesiastica* 5.18, cited in McGinn, 171). Justinian preferred to see adulteresses consigned to nunnery (Nov. 134.10). See below.
80. See the translation provided by J. Z. Abrams, *The Women of the Talmud* (Northvale, N.J., and London, 1995), 78–79, which I follow.
81. BT Sot. 27b-28a; see Satlow, *Tasting*, 179–81. On consigning lovers to hell, BT Sot. 4b.
82. PT Sot. 5.1 (Neusner's translation, pp. 130–31).
83. On this passage, see Satlow, *Tasting*, 143–44. On the significance of serpents in general, see B. Mundkur, *The Cult of the Serpent: An Interdisciplinary Survey of Its Manifestations and Origins* (Albany, N.Y., 1983), esp. 172 ff. on the serpent as a sexual symbol.
84. PT Shab. 14.4 (14d), PT AZ 2.2 (40d); BT San. 75a; see Satlow, *Tasting*, 160–62. For the source of the anecdote, see W. Adler, "Apion's 'Encomium of Adultery': A Jewish Satire of Greek Paedeia in the Pseudo-Clementine Homilies," *Hebrew Union College Annual* 64 (1993): 15–49.
85. Note the use of the same Proverbs phrase (Prov. 9:17) to justify the exclusion.
86. M Sot. 4.5; 6.1; see Wegner, *Chattel*, 92, 211.
87. M Git. 9.10; see Ilan, *Jewish Women*, 142; Wegner, *Chattel*, 46–47. The difficulty of a precise definition of the sole ground for divorce, according to the house of Shammai, resides in the interpretation of the Hebrew term *ervat davar*, the first word meaning nakedness or indecency or lewdness, the latter simply "a matter."
88. "On Sexual Indulgence," 12, cited in Treggiari, *Roman Marriage*, 222.
89. Jerome, Epistula 1.
90. 339 C.E. Cf. the last phrase with CJ 9.9.29.4, clearly its source of inspiration.

91. "A strange piece of law making," which not only deviated from classical law but also displayed ignorance of Roman legal tradition (Arjava, *Women and Law*, 179, commenting on CTh 3.16.1).
92. *Novella Majoriani* 9.
93. D 34.9.13, cited in Treggiari, *Roman Marriage*, 385.
94. D. Cohen, *Law, Sexuality*, 99.
95. Ibid., 123.
96. Midrash Tadshe 8, quoted in J. Cohen, *Be Fertile*, 96.
97. Ibid., 141.
98. Treggiari, *Roman Marriage*, 298.
99. McGinn, *Prostitution*, 194.
100. Ibid., 240–42.
101. Rousselle, *Porneia*, 85.
102. The exact ways in which legal opinions permeated other legal spheres are difficult to pinpoint. There are stories which appear apocryphal about Roman officers who attended rabbinic academies, and we still have letters of eminent rhetors, like Libanius, to the patriarch in Tiberias at the end of the fourth century that indicate close intellectual contacts. For further information, see L. H. Feldman, *Jew and Gentile in the Ancient World: Attitudes and Interactions from Alexander to Justinian* (Princeton, N.J., 1993), passim.
103. Sifre Deut. 26, trans. in R. Hammer, *Sifre: A Tannaitic Commentary on the Book of Deuteronomy* (New Haven, Conn., 1986), 47. On the passage, see the comments of S. D. Fraade, "Sifre Deuteronomy 26 (ad Deut 3:23): How Conscious the Composition?" *Hebrew Union College Annual* 54 (1983): 271–77, and M. L. Satlow, "Shame and Sex in Late Antique Judaism," in Wimbush et al., *Asceticism*, 538.
104. S. J. D. Cohen, "The Origins of the Matrilineal Principle in Rabbinic Law," *Association for Jewish Studies Review* 10 (1985): 19–53, rep. in S. J. D. Cohen, *Beginnings of Jewishness*, 263–307, esp. 301.
105. Habinek, "Invention of Sexuality," 2.

Chapter 5: The Harmony of the Home in Late Antiquity

1. My comments on Genesis are inspired by the collection of essays gathered and edited by R. Ravitzki, *Female Readers from the Beginning: Creative Women Write on the Book of Genesis* (in Hebrew; Tel Aviv, 1999).
2. On the relations between the family and society in general, see the provocative remarks of F. Mount, *The Subversive Family: An Alternative History of Love and Marriage* (New York, 1992).
3. F. Heymann, review of *Sexuality and the Family in History*, ed. I. Bartal and I. Gafni (Jerusalem, 1998), *Bulletin du Centre de recherche français de Jerusalem* 5 (1999): 55.
4. *Carmen* 61.76–85, 91, 97 f., 147 f.
5. I. Gafni, "The Institution of Marriage in Rabbinic Times," in *The Jewish Family: Metaphor and Memory*, ed. D. Kraemer (New York, 1989), 13–30.
6. See S. J. D. Cohen, "Prohibition of Intermarriage," 23–39, esp. 28 n. 8

on the need for a full collection of rabbinic and non-rabbinic evidence bearing on marriage and other sexual liaisons between Jews and Christians. P. L. Reynolds, *Marriage in the Western Church: The Christianization of Marriage during the Patristic and Early Medieval Periods* (Leiden and New York, 1994), neglects mixed marriages altogether. For much of what follows see my "Rabbinics and Roman Law: Jewish-Gentile/Christian Marriage in Late Antiquity, *Revue des études juives* 156 (1997): 59–100.

7. Among the few exceptions, see N. R. M. de Lange, "Jews and Christians in the Byzantine Empire: Problems and Prospects," in *Christianity and Judaism*, ed. D. Wood, Studies in Church History 29 (Oxford, 1992), 15–32.

8. Questions concerning the contacts, familiarity, and mutual influences of Jewish, Christian, and Roman legal ideas on each other are immensely complex and have not been fully investigated. Basic is B. Cohen, *Jewish and Roman Law*, on a few but not all aspects. See also Rabello, "Jewish and Roman Jurisdiction," 141–67. Rabbinic familiarity with Roman law has been questioned by B. S. Jackson, "On the Problem of Roman Influence on the Halakhah and Normative Self-Definition in Judaism," in Sanders et al., *Jewish and Christian Self-Definition*, 2:157–203, who minimizes such influences as does Grubbs, *Law and Family in Late Antiquity*, passim, esp. 317 ff. (on Christian influences on Roman moral legislation). On Roman and Jewish law see also the numerous contributions of David Daube, now assembled in *The Collected Works of David Daube*, vol. 1, *Talmudic Law*, ed. C. M. Carmichael (Berkeley, Calif., 1992). Roman familiarity with Jewish law is reflected, to a degree, in numerous laws issued in the fourth and the fifth centuries, conveniently assembled by A. Linder, *The Jews in Roman Imperial Legislation* (Detroit and Jerusalem, 1987).

9. For medieval developments, see J. A. Brundage, "Intermarriage Between Christians and Jews in Medieval Canon Law," *Jewish History* 3 (1988): 25–40; W. Pakter, *Medieval Canon Law and the Jews* (Ebelsbath, 1988); and L. I. Newman, "Intermarriage between Jews and Christians during the Middle Ages," *Jewish Institute Quarterly* 2 (1926): 2–8 and 21–28.

10. The literature on these sources is vast; see, for example, N. S. Hecht et al., *Introduction to the History and Sources of Jewish Law*.

11. L. I. Levine has been an eloquent spokesperson for a minimalist rabbinical orbit; see "The Sages and the Synagogue in Late Antiquity: The Evidence of the Galilee," in *The Galilee in Late Antiquity*, ed. L. I. Levine (New York and Jerusalem, 1992), 201–22.

12. Y. Yadin, J. C. Greenfield, and A. Yardeni, "Babatha's Ketubba," *Israel Exploration Journal* 44 (1994): 75–99.

13. It has the singular advantage of being precisely dated to 417 C.E., and may well reflect the culmination of the process of the consolidation of Jewish marital formulas in the Diaspora. C. Sirat et al., *La Kétouba de Cologne: Un contract de mariage juif a Antinoopolis* (Opladen, 1986).

14. Rajak and Noy, *"Archisynagogoi,"* esp. 82, 84.

15. Reynolds, *Marriage in the Western Church*, xvii–xix.

16. Grubbs, *Law and Family*, 55.

17. Treggiari, *Roman Marriage*, 45–50.

18. CTh 3.14.1 (Roman-barbarian) and 3.7.2 (Jewish-Christian). See below for both.

19. These are questions now asked by family historians; see T. K. Hareven, "The History of the Family and the Complexity of Social Change," *American Historical Review* 96 (1991): 95–124.

20. As D. Herlihy has suggested in "Family," *American Historical Review* 96 (1991): 1–16, esp. 5.

21. In general, see L. M. Epstein, *Marriage Laws in the Bible and Talmud* (Cambridge, Mass., 1942). On conversion to Judaism, see L. H. Schiffman, *Who Was a Jew?* (Hoboken, N.J., 1985); and S. J. D. Cohen, "Crossing the Boundaries and Becoming a Jew," *Harvard Theological Review* 82 (1989): 13–133, reprinted in *Beginnings*, 140–74.

22. S. J. D. Cohen, "The Origins of the Matrilineal Principle in Rabbinic Law," *Association for Jewish Studies Review* 10 (1985): 19–53. A shorter version of this article with twenty replies, each contesting a different aspect of Cohen's interpretation, appeared in *Judaism* (1985). G. G. Porton, *The Stranger Within Your Gates*, 155 ff. See also M. I. Gruber, "Matrilineal Determination of Jewishness: Biblical and Near Eastern Roots," in *Pomegranates and Golden Bells: Studies in Honor of J. Milgrom*, ed. D. P. Wright et al. (Winona Lake, Ind., 1995), 437–43.

23. R. T. Herford, *Christianity in the Talmud and Midrash* (London, 1903; reprint, New York, 1975), remains basic. J. Neusner, "Stable Symbols in a Shifting Society: The Delusion of the Monolithic Gentile in Documents of Late Fourth Century Judaism," in *To See Ourselves as Others See Us: Christians, Jews, "Others" in Late Antiquity*, ed. J. Neusner and E. S. Frerichs (Chico, Calif., 1985), 373–96, on the lack of rabbinic distinction between Christians and pagans and between pagan Rome and Christian Rome.

24. The following is my translation. It reflects my understanding of the text and I have deliberately kept it as literal as possible.

25. Wegner, *Chattel or Person?* 222 n. 38 and passim.

26. Satlow, *Tasting the Dish*, 19 f., provides a useful overview of these forbidden categories.

27. J. Baumgarten, "The Exclusion of 'Netinim' and Proselytes in 4Q Florilegium," *Revue de Qumran* 8 (1972): 87–96. There seems to be a certain affinity between the *netinim* and the Athenian *nothoi* which, at one point, denoted children of mixed marriage between Athenian males and foreign women. See A. Diller, *Race Mixture among the Greeks Before Alexander* (Urbana, Ill., 1937), 91–100.

28. Cf. T Hull. 2.20–21, which forbids marriage with *minim* (Jewish sectarians or "heretics").

29. Satlow, *Tasting*, 80–81, also noting differences of interpretation of incest between the Babylonian and the Palestinian Talmuds.

30. Cohen, "Origins of the Matrilineal Principle," claims that anonymity reflects an established and generally accepted ruling but the matter is considerably more complex. See A. Guttman, "The Problem of the Anonymous Mishnah," in *Origins of Judaism*, vol. 9, *The Literature of Formative Judaism: The Mishnah and the Tosefta*, ed. J. Neusner (New York and London, 1990), 129–43.

31. J. Neusner, *The Philosophical Mishnah* (Atlanta, Ga., 1988), 1:143.

32. *Pauli Sententiae* 2.19.6: "*Inter servos et liberos matrimonium contrahi non potest, contubernium postest*"; *Tituli Ulpiani* 5.5: *Cum servis nullum est conumbium.* Quoted in Treggiari, *Roman Marriage*, 53. Roman law was, in fact, much harsher with regard to marriage between free women and their slaves than between free men and servile women.

33. T Kidd. 4.16, see Satlow, *Tasting*, 85.

34. BT Kidd. 68b, Soncino, modified; cf. BT Yeb. 23a.

35. D. W. Halivni, *Midrash, Mishnah, and Gemara: The Jewish Predilection for Justified Law* (Cambridge, Mass., 1986), passim.

36. See the discussion of D. Stern, "The Captive Woman," 91–127 with citations and bibliography.

37. Cf. BT AZ 36b, where the debate over intermarriage entails a denunciation of both marriage and of informal sexual contacts, as well as of mere familiarity between Jews and gentiles.

38. M Ket. 2.9; M Ned. 3.11; M Git. 1.5, 2.5, 4.9, 8.5. G. G. Porton, *Goyim: Gentiles and Israelites in Mishnah and Tosefta* (Atlanta, Ga., 1988), does not discuss Mishnaic terminology.

39. Satlow, *Tasting*, 86–96, discusses these passages and their rhetoric of exclusion and inclusion; see also 97–118, on rabbinic rhetoric of threat to discourage liaisons between Jewish women and gentiles.

40. S. Stern, *Jewish Identity in Early Rabbinic Writings* (Leiden and New York, 1994), 163.

41. For a fascinating analysis of one aspect of this complex issue, see S. D. Fraade, "Navigating the Anomalous: Non-Jews at the Intersection of Early Rabbinic Law and Narrative," in *The Other in Jewish Thought and History: Constructions of Jewish Culture and Identity*, ed. L. J. Silberstein and R. L. Cohn (New York, 1994), 145–65. See also Porton, *Goyim*.

42. Sifre on Deut. 21:10 f., and BT Kidd. 21b, in S. Stern, *Jewish Identity*, 165–68.

43. Targum Pseudo-Jonathan to Lev. 18:21 in S. Stern, *Jewish Identity*, 160, with. G. Vermes, "Leviticus 18.21 in Ancient Jewish Bible Exegesis," in *Studies in Aggadah, Targum, and Jewish Liturgy in Memory of Joseph Heinemann* (Jerusalem, 1981), 108–24. On the origins of the determination of lineage through the mother, see S. J. D. Cohen, "Prohibition of Intermarriage," 34–35.

44. PT Yeb. 2.6; BT Yeb. 17a, 23a; BT Kidd. 68b, with S. Stern, *Jewish Identity*, 162. The non-Jewish mother was even suspected of adultery since her marriage was not valid (T Ket. 1.3, cited in Stern, *Jewish Identity*, 162).

45. See Porton, *Stranger*, for a recent treatment. See also S. J. D. Cohen, "The Rabbinic Conversion Ceremony," *Journal of Jewish Studies* 41 (1990): 177–203, reprinted in *Beginnings*, 198–238.

46. This passage, incidentally, also throws more ambiguity on the "matrilineal principle" for if the mother is Jewish, as is the case here, whether or not her betrothal was valid would have been irrelevant.

47. L. H. Silberman, "Reprobation, Prohibition, Invalidity: An Examination of the Halakhic Development Concerning Intermarriage," in *Judaism and Ethics*, ed. D. J. Silver (New York, 1970), 196 n. 15 refers to a long debate about the

status of a Jewish mother and a gentile father. He infers from the same Mishnaic passage that such a child is a mamzer. Yet, this is hardly the case and the continuous talmudic debate on the issue shows that it was impossible to interpret in a clear way the Mishnaic references to mixed religious marriage. T Kidd. 4.16 discusses intercourse between a Jewish woman and a slave (*eved*) or gentile (*goy*). One opinion regarded the child of such a union as a mamzer, the other disagreed.

48. Two recent books (in Hebrew) on conversion to Judaism provide a general framework for the debate: A. Sagi and Z. Zohar, *Conversion to Judaism and the Meaning of Jewish Identity* (Jerusalem, 1994), esp. 20–26 on "negative" and "positive" motives; and M. Finkelstein, *Proselytism: Halakhah and Practice* (Ramat Gan, 1994). See also M. Samet, "Conversion to Judaism in the Early Centuries C.E.," in *Jews and Judaism in the Second Temple, Mishnah, and Talmud Periods: Studies in Honor of S. Safrai*, ed. I. Gafni et al. (in Hebrew; Jerusalem, 1993), passim.

49. B. J. Bamberger, *Proselytism in the Talmudic Period* (Cincinnati, 1939), is still valuable on the issue.

50. J. Katz, "Although He Sinned He Is Still Israel" (in Hebrew), *Tarbiz* 27 (1957–58): 203–17, and J. Katz, *Exclusiveness and Tolerance* (New York, 1962), passim. Clarification is still lacking.

51. "And for the apostates, let there be no hope" (Palestinian version), Schechter, *Jewish Quarterly Review* 10 [1898]: 656–57). The bibliography is vast.

52. Linder, *Jews in Roman Imperial Legislation*, 79–80. The relevance of Roman law as a historical source for Jewish history in late antiquity has been questioned by L. V. Rutgers, "Attitudes to Judaism in the Greco-Roman Period: Reflections on Feldman's *Jew and Gentile in the Ancient World*," *Jewish Quarterly Review* 85 (1995): 361–95.

53. E. Will and C. Orrieux, *Proselytisms juif? Histoire d'une erreur* (Paris, 1992), with a review by S. J. D. Cohen, *Gnomon* 18 (1996): 273–75.

54. M. Goodman, *Mission and Conversion* (Oxford, 1994), 148.

55. Ibid., 152.

56. Samet, "Conversion," 336.

57. BT Kidd. 70b, a pun on Isa. 14:1; BT Nid. 13; BT Yeb. 47b; see Samet, "Conversion," 336, who comments on the frequency of this utterance in the Babylonian Talmud and its absence from the Palestinian Talmud, in spite of Helbo's Palestinian provenance.

58. Exodus Rabba 19.4, cited in Samet, "Conversion," 336.

59. Bamberger, *Proselytism in the Talmudic Period*.

60. Goodman, *Mission and Conversion*, 150.

61. Meg. 4.9, San. 9.6, and Kidd. 3.5 and 3.12 are the sum total of Mishnaic direct and indirect references to mixed marriages.

62. *Tituli Ulpiani* 5.3–5: *Conubium est uxoris iure ducendae facultas. Conubium habent cives Romani cum civibus Romanis; cum Latinis autem et peregrinis ita, si concessum sit. Cum servis nullum est conubium.* Quoted in Treggiari, *Roman Marriage*, 43.

63. See Treggiari, *Roman Marriage*, 46 for Roman.

64. S. J. D. Cohen, "Origins of the Matrilineal Principle," opts for Roman influence; others oppose, primarily on the ground of the hatred displayed by the rabbis toward the Romans (all in *Judaism* [1985]). The issue is complex and Roman

influence cannot be ruled out on an emotional basis, nor can commonalities based on *ius gentium* be discarded. On rabbinic-Roman relations, see M. Hadas-Lebel, *Jerusalem contre Rome* (Paris, 1990), esp. 195 f. on awareness of Roman power, 245 f. on enmity and loyalty, and 351 f. on rabbinic moral judgments of Rome.

65. Recent research has chosen to emphasize ethnic aspects of intermarriage, see Porton, *Goyim* and *Stranger*. I doubt if it is possible to draw any sharp boundaries of ethnicity and religion in Judaism, as the two are inextricably linked and practically indistinguishable. For a social-scientific theory of religion which integrates anthropological and psychological approaches, see A. Mol, *Identity and the Sacred* (New York, 1976). I suspect that the issue is largely semantic. More critical is the fact that by allowing conversion to Judaism the rabbis themselves appear to negate any "ethnic" approach.

66. Exod. 34:11 f.; Deut. 7:2-4; Num. 25:1 f.; Deut. 23:4; Josh. 23:11 f; Ezra 9:10; Neh. 10:13, Jub. 30.

67. Epstein, *Marriage Laws*, 174-76 on the novelty of Jewish law with regard to declaring a marriage invalid. Silberman, "Reprobation, Prohibition, Invalidity," 188 on the rabbinic distinction between prohibition and invalidity as the new and central change in the development of rabbinic views on mixed-religion marriages.

68. D. Novak, "The Marital Status of Jews Married Under Non-Jewish Auspices," in *Jewish Law Association Studies*, vol. 1, *The Touro Conference Volume*, ed. B. S. Jackson (Chico, Calif., 1985), 61-77, esp. 63-64.

69. Ambrose, Epistula 40, complains about Jews ignoring Roman law and abiding by their own laws. His testimony, however, is suspicious. It is included in a highly tendentious letter to the emperor Theodosius on the burning and looting of the synagogue in Callinicum. Nor do Ambrose's numerous disparaging remarks on the Jews lend credibility to his observations. Daube, *Collected Works*, on Origen's *Ad Africanum* 14, which refers to an illegal exercise of the death penalty by Jewish authorities, an appropriation of civil jurisdiction which the Roman government ignored. The harshness of rabbinical opinions is based on Deut. 22:23-24 and on Hosea 4:14, both insisting that a betrothed woman who was unfaithful to her intended should be treated as an adulteress. Jerome's translation of Hosea employs the terms *fornicatio* to describe sexual liaisons of a virgin and *adulterium* to describe that of a *sponsa* (betrothed woman); see Reynolds, *Marriage in the Western Church*, 325.

70. Obviously less of a problem in Babylonia. Yet, the majority of rabbinical opinions quoted in the Babylonian Talmud on these matters belong to Palestinian tannaim and amoraim. On Christianity in the Talmud, see Herford, *Christianity*; on Jewish-Christian relations in Palestine, G. Stemberger, *Juden und Christen im Heiligen Land: Palästina unter Konsantin und Theodosius* (Munich, 1987). The works of G. Alon and M. Avi-Yonah on Palestine in late antiquity remain valuable.

71. L. Feldman, in *Sacred Realm*, ed. S. Fine (New York, 1996), 65.

72. S. J. D. Cohen, "Pagan and Christian Evidence on the Ancient Synagogue," in *The Synagogue in Late Antiquity*, ed. L. I. Levine (Philadelphia, 1987), 170 f., and now Levine, *The Ancient Synagogue: The First Thousand Years* (New Haven, Conn., 1999), passim.

73. A. Neubauer, *La géographie du Talmud* (1868; reprint, Hildesheim, 1967).

74. Brundage, "Intermarriage between Christians and Jews in Medieval Canon Law," 28, on the vagueness of the Pauline message on mixed marriage even in its original context, resulting in two opposite interpretations, Augustinian and Ambrosiastrian. See also R. J. Smith, "The Status of Mixed Marriages in the Corinthian Community," in *Marriage Studies: Reflections in Canon Law and Theology*, ed. T. P. Doyle (Washington, D.C., 1980), 3:46–53; and J. T. Noonan, *Power to Dissolve: Lawyers and Marriages in the Courts of the Roman Curia* (Cambridge, Mass., 1972), 342–43.

75. The issue is, admittedly, far from clear.

76. Cyprian *De lapsis* VI; Tertullian *Ad uxorem*. II.3: *fideles gentilium matrimonia subeuntes stupri reos esse constat et arcendos ab omni communicatione fraternitatis*.

77. S. Laeuchli, *Power and Sexuality: The Emergence of Canon Law at the Synod of Elvira* (Philadelphia, 1972), 30 f.

78. M. Meigne, "Concile ou collection d'Elvire," *Revue d'histoire ecclésiastique* 70 (1975): 361–87, argues that the council was actually a collection of canons composed over the fourth century. He accordingly assigned only canons 1–21 to the council itself and the rest either to 314–325 C.E. or to the late fourth century. But see the reservations of E. Griffe, "Le concile d'Elvire et les origines du célibat ecclésiastique," *Bulletin de la littérature ecclésiastique* 77 (1976): 123–27.

79. Canon 1 (Mansi): *Haeretici si se tansferre noluerint ad ecclesiam catholicam, nec ipsis catholicas dandas esse puellas; sed neque Judaeis neque haereticis dare placuit. eo quod nulla possit esse societas fideli cum infideli. si contra interdictum fecerunt parentes, abstineri per quinquennium placit*. Translation is based on A. Linder, *The Jews in the Legal Sources of the Early Middle Ages* (Detroit and Jerusalem, 1997), 483 and on Laeuchli.

80. Canon 15: *propter copiam puellarum, gentilibus minime in matrimonium dandae sunt virgines christianae, ne aetas in flore tumens in adulterio animae resolvatur*. (On account of the large number of young women, Christian virgins must not be given in marriage to pagans, lest [their] age bursting in bloom resolves in adultery of the soul. [Trans. based on Laeuchli]). Canon 17 forbids marriage between Christian women and pagan priests.

81. E. Vodola, *Excommunication in the Middle Ages* (Berkeley, Calif., 1986), passim, on threats and realities of the process.

82. Parents who countenanced marriage between their daughters and pagan priests were punished with perpetual excommunication, canon 17.

83. Treggiari, *Roman Marriage*, 147.

84. Arjava, *Women and Law*, 52 f. with bibliography.

85. Canon 39 in fact facilitates conversion from paganism to catholicism in case of sickness; canon 51 hints at a similar option in the case of heretics and even of the desire of previously heretical priests to continue to serve in the priesthood in their newly adopted "orthodoxy."

86. *Si quis fidelis, habens uxorem, cum Judaia vel gentili fuerit moechatus, a communione arceatur. quod si alius eum detexerit post quinquennium, acta legitima poenitentia, poterit dominicae sociari communioni*. Linder, *The Jews in the Legal Sources*, 483–84 for text and translation. My translation in the text is loosely based on Laeuchli and Linder.

87. Canon 9, although a confusion with regard to the application of the terms *adulterium* and *stuprum* existed even in imperial laws, as Papinian states (D 48.5.6).
88. Jerome, Epistula 77.3, crystallized the theological stand on this by discrediting imperial legislation.
89. D 48.5.7–9.
90. Elvira, canon 47.
91. Canon 50 (food); 49 (blessings).
92. D. Noy, *Jewish Inscriptions of Western Europe*, 2 vols. (Cambridge, 1993–95), no. 188, dating to the fourth or fifth century.
93. Severus, *Epistula de virtutibus* (PL 20.731–46 = PL 41.821–32), with E. Demougeot, "L'évêque Sévère et les juifs de Minorque au V siècle," in *Majorque, Languedoc, et Roussillon de l'Antiquité à nos jours* (Montpellier, 1982), 13–34; E. D. Hunt, "St. Stephen in Minorca: An Episode in Jewish-Christian Relations in the Early Fifth Century," *Journal of Theological Studies* 33 (1982): 106–23. For edition and commentary, see S. Bradbury, *Severus of Minorca: Letter on the Conversion of the Jews* (Oxford, 1996).
94. For an Elviran provenance for Juvencus, J. Fontaine, *Isidore de Seville et la culture classique dans l'Espagne wisigothique* (Paris, 1959), 1:8 n. 3. The council was presided over by Ossius of Cordova who had close contacts with the court of Constantine. V. C. de Clerq, *Ossius of Cordova: A Contribution to the History of the Constantinian Period* (Washington, D.C., 1954).
95. E. Schulz-Flügel, *Gregorius Eliberritanus: Epithalamium sive Explanatio in Canticis Canticorum* (Freiburg, 1994), 20 f. for testimonia.
96. CTh 3.7.2 = 9.7.5 and below.
97. CTh 16.8.6.
98. CTh 3.14.1. See H. Sivan, "Why Not Marry a Barbarian? Marital Frontiers in Late Antiquity," in *Shifting Frontiers in Late Antiquity*, ed. R. W. Mathisen and H. Sivan (Aldershot, 1996), 136–45.
99. Linder, *Jews in Roman Imperial Legislation*.
100. *Ne quis Christianam mulierem in matrimonio Iudaeus accipiat, neque Iudaeae Christianus coniugium sortitiatur. Nam si quis aliquid huiusmodi admiserit, adulterii vicem commissi huius crimen obtinebit, libertate in acusandum publicis quoque vocibus relaxata.*
101. Gothofredus for the first. See G. L. Falchi, "La legislazione imperiale circa i matrimoni misti fra Cristiani ed Ebrei nel IV secolo," and A. M. Rabello, "Il problema dei matrimoni fra Ebrei e Cristiani nella legislazione imperiale e in quella della chiesa (IV–VI secolo)," both in *Atti dell'Accademia Romanistica Constantiniana* 2 (1988): 203–11, esp. 207 and 213–24 respectively.
102. M. Bianchini, "Disparità di culto e matrimonio orientamenti del pensiero cristiano e della legislazione imperiale nel IV secolo," *Serta historica antiqua* (1986): 233–46, esp. 245.
103. Adultery in Roman law, Grubbs, *Law and Family*, and Arjava, *Women and Law*, for recent accounts, each with a comprehensive bibliography. On the adulterous wife in Judaism, see Desoto, *Law of Jealousy*, and above, Chapter 4.
104. CJ 9.9.2 f. (Antonine); 9.9.19 f. (Diocletian).
105. CTh 9.40.1 and 11.36.1 of 313/4; 9.38.1 of 322.

106. Grubbs, *Law and Family*, 221.
107. Ammianus Marcellinus 28.1.
108. We do not know of a case thus prosecuted. But the danger of exposing "adultery" to the public by opening a lawsuit is clearly reflected in the episode described by Jerome, Epistula 1; see above, Chapter 4.
109. BA 3.7.2 and 9.4.4, F. Arvizu, "La femme dans le Code d'Euric," *Revue historique de droit français et étranger* 62 (1984): 391–405. See Silberman, "Reprobation," for a general survey up to the nineteenth century.
110. The following comments are based on Loraux, *Children*.
111. The expression is borrowed from Loraux, *Children*, 11.

Conclusion

1. For the expression, Loraux, *Children*, 241.
2. R. Adler, "'A Mother in Israel': Aspects of the Mother Role in Jewish Myth," in *Beyond Androcentrism: New Essays on Women and Religion*, ed. R. M. Gross (Missoula, Mont., 1977), 237–55 emphasizing the institutional power of Deborah and the background of national crisis.
3. M. Fox, "The Sign of the Covenant: Circumcision in the Light of the Priestly '*ôt* Etiologies,'" *Revue biblique* 81 (1974): 557–96, on circumcision as a mnemonic sign to remind the Israelites of their commands, and as marriage and fertility rite. For an overview of the P (exilic and postexilic) ideology, evidently the guiding principle of Pentateuchal redactional attitude to circumcision, marriage, and procreation, see J. Cohen, *Be Fertile*, 46 f.
4. Loraux, *Children*, 242.
5. Cf. 1 Sam. 4:19–22, which patently echoes the story of Rachel in Bethlehem along, I believe, less sophisticated lines. Here, war and peace are clearly juxtaposed with birth and death. News of the death of her husband (Phineas) and of her father-in-law (Eli) induce an early labor in the former's wife. She dies in childbirth, as her attendants exhort her with the words that the midwife had used to console Rachel: "Do not be afraid since you have given birth to a son" (1 Sam. 4:20). The name she gives her child commemorates the defeat of the Israelites and the demise of her relatives.
6. Cf. Loraux, *Tragic Ways of Killing a Woman*, vii–x. Even on stage Greek drama narrated rather than displayed the dying moments of women.
7. For full presentation, see my "From Jezebel to Esther: Images of Queenship in the Hebrew Bible," *Biblica* (forthcoming).
8. Loraux, *Children*, 249.
9. Ibid., 247, on Athenian notions of citizenship.
10. Ibid., 147 ff., on *Lysistrata*.
11. Cf. ibid., 120, on Athenian orthodoxy.
12. What Boyarin, *Carnal*, 240 f., views as the texts' imperfect hegemony.
13. Loraux, *Children*, 106.
14. Cf. ibid., 85 f.
15. BT Ket. 62b–63a; see above, Introduction.

16. T Yeb. 8.7, S. Lieberman, *The Tosefta* (*Nashin*) (reprint, New York, 1995), translation based on Boyarin, *Carnal Israel*, 134. For evidence on Ben Azzai's marital status, see Cohen, *Be Fertile*, 112 n. 171.

17. As Boyarin, *Carnal*, 154, argues.

18. M. L. Satlow, "'One Who Loves His Wife Like Himself': Love in Rabbinic Marriage," *Journal of Jewish Studies* 49 (1998): 67–86.

19. J. Naveh, *On Sherd and Papyrus: Aramaic and Hebrew Inscriptions from the Second Temple, Mishnaic and Talmudic Periods* (in Hebrew; Jerusalem, 1992), 151. See also J. Naveh and S. Shaked, *Aramaic and Hebrew Incantations of Late Antiquity* (Jerusalem, 1992).

20. Trans. in *Ancient Christian Magic: Coptic Texts of Ritual Power*, ed. M. Meyer and R. Smith (San Francisco, 1994), no. 65, 125.

21. Ibid., no. 77, 162.

22. Satlow, "One Who Loves," 75.

23. Aristophanes, *Lysistrata*, 217, cited in Loraux, *Children*, 162.

24. I do not subscribe to M. L. Satlow's minimalization of rabbinic masculinity regarding self-restraint and self-control ("'Try to Be a Man': The Rabbinic Construction of Masculinity," *Harvard Theological Review* 89 [1996]: 19–40). I agree, however, that it is acquired, as is wisdom.

25. C. Hezser, "The Codification of Legal Knowledge in Late Antiquity: The Talmud Yerushalmi and Roman Law Codes," in *The Talmud Yerushalmi and Graeco-Roman Culture*, ed. P. Schäfer (Tübingen, 1998), 581–641.

Bibliography

Abrams, J. A. *The Women of the Talmud*. Northvale, N.J., and London, 1995.
Adler, R. *Engendering Judaism: An Inclusive Theology and Ethics*. Philadelphia, 1998.
———. "'A Mother in Israel': Aspects of the Mother Role in Jewish Myth." In *Beyond Androcentrism: New Essays on Women and Religion*, ed. R. M. Gross, 237–55. Missoula, Mont., 1977.
———. "The Virgin in the Brothel and Other Anomalies: Character and Context in the Legend of Beruriah." *Tikkun* 3, no. 6 (1988): 28–32.
Adler, W. "Apion's 'Encomium of Adultery': A Jewish Satire of Greek Paedeia in the Pseudo-Clementine Homilies." *Hebrew Union College Annual* 64 (1993): 15–49.
Akenson, D. H. *Surpassing Wonder: The Invention of the Bible and the Talmuds*. New York, 1998.
Albani, M., et al., eds. *Studies in the Book of Jubilees*. Tübingen, 1997.
Albeck, S. "The Ten Commandments and the Essence of Religious Faith." In *The Ten Commandments in History and Tradition*, ed. B.-Z. Segal. Jerusalem, 1990.
Amaru, B. H. "The First Woman, Wives, and Mothers in Jubilees." *Journal of Biblical Literature* 113 (1994): 609–26.
Amit, Y. "Implicit Redaction and Latent Polemic in the Story of the Rape of Dinah" (in Hebrew). In *Texts, Temples and Traditions: A Tribute to Menahem Haran*, ed. M. V. Fox et al., 11*-28*. Winona Lake, Ind., 1996.
Arendt, H. "What Is Authority?" In H. Arendt, *Between Past and Future*. Cleveland, Ohio, 1963.
Arjava, A. *Women and Law in Late Antiquity*. Oxford, 1996.
Arvizu, F. "La femme dans le Code d'Euric." *Revue historique de droit français et étranger* 62 (1984): 391–405.
Ashbrook Harvey, S. "Spoken Words, Voiced Silence: Biblical Women in Syriac Tradition." *Journal of Early Christian Studies* 9 (2001): 105–31.
Avery-Peck, A. J. "Law and Society in Early Judaism: Legal Evolution in the Mishnaic Division of Agriculture." *New Perspectives on Ancient Judaism* 1 (1987): 67–87.
Bach, A. "Good to the Last Drop: Viewing the Sotah (Numbers 5:11–31) as the Glass Half Empty and Wondering How to View It Half Full." In *The New Literary Criticism and the Hebrew Bible*, ed. J. C. Exum and D. J. A. Clines, 26–55. Valley Forge, Pa., 1993.
———, ed. *Women in the Hebrew Bible*. New York, 1999.
Bagnall, R. S. *Egypt in Late Antiquity*. Princeton, N.J., 1993.
Bal, M. *Lethal Love: Feminist Literary Readings of Biblical Love Stories*. Bloomington, Ind., 1986.

———. *Murder and Difference: Gender, Genre and Scholarship on Sisera's Death*. Bloomington, Ind., 1988.

Bamberger, B. J. *Proselytism in the Talmudic Period*. Cincinnati, Ohio, 1939.

Baskin, J. R. "The Separation of Women in Rabbinic Judaism." In *Women, Religion and Social Change*, ed. Y. Y. Haddad and E. V. Findley, 3–18. Albany, N.Y., 1985.

———, ed. *Jewish Women in Historical Perspective*. Detroit, Mich., 1991.

Bauman, R. A. "The 'Leges iudiciorum publicorum' and Their Interpretation in the Republic, Principate, and Late Empire." *Aufstieg und Niedergang der Römischen Welt* II.13 (1980): 103–233.

Baumgarten, J. "The Exclusion of 'Netinim' and Proselytes in 4Q Florilegium." *Revue de Qumran* 8 (1972): 87–96.

Beal, T. K. *The Book of Hiding: Gender, Ethnicity, Annihilation, and Esther*. New York, 1997.

———. "Tracing Esther's Beginnings." In *A Feminist Companion to Esther, Judith, and Susanna*, ed. A. Brenner, 87–110. Sheffield, 1995.

Beaucamp, J. *Le statut de la femme à Byzance, 4e-7e siècle*. 2 vols. Paris, 1990, 1992.

Bechtel, L. "What If Dinah Is Not Raped?" *Journal for the Study of the Old Testament* 62 (1994): 19–36.

Becking, B. "Ezra's Re-enactment of the Exile." In *Leading Captivity Captive: The Exile as History and Ideology*, ed. L. L. Grabbe, 40–61. Sheffield, 1998.

Biale, D. *Eros and the Jews: From Biblical Israel to Contemporary America*. New York, 1992.

Biale, R. *Women and Jewish Law: An Exploration of Women's Issues in Halakhic Sources*. New York, 1984.

Bianchini, M. "Disparità di culto e matrimonio orientamenti del pensiero cristiano e della legislazione imperiale nel IV secolo." *Serta historica antiqua* (1986): 233–46.

Blenkinsopp, J. *Ezra-Nehemiah*. Old Testament Library. Philadelphia, 1988.

———. "Interpretation and the Tendency to Sectarianism: An Aspect of Second Temple History." In *Jewish and Christian Self-Definition*, ed. E. P. Sanders et al., 2:1–26. Philadelphia, 1981.

Blundell, M. W. *Helping Friends and Harming Enemies*. Cambridge, 1989.

Bohak, G. *Joseph and Aseneth and the Jewish Temple in Heliopolis*. Atlanta, Ga., 1996.

Bokser, B. M. "An Annotated Bibliographical Guide to the Study of the Palestinian Talmud." *Aufstieg und Niedergang der Römischen Welt* II.19.2 (1979): 139–256.

———. "Rabbinic Responses to Catastrophe: From Continuity to Discontinuity." *Proceedings of the American Academy for Jewish Research* 50 (1983): 37–61.

———. "Talmudic Studies." In *The State of Jewish Studies*, ed. S. J. D. Cohen and E. L. Greenstein, 80–112. Detroit, 1990.

Bonini, R. *Ricerche di diritto giustinianeo*. Milan, 1968.

Boyarin, D. *Carnal Israel: Reading Sex in Talmudic Culture*. Berkeley, Calif., 1993.

Bradbury, S. *Severus of Minorca: Letter on the Conversion of the Jews*. Oxford, 1996.

Breneman, M. *Ezra, Nehemiah, Esther*. New American Commentary, vol. 10. Nashville, Tenn., 1993.

Brenner, A. *The Intercourse of Knowledge*. Leiden, 1997.

Brewer, D. I. "Deuteronomy 24:1–4 and the Origins of the Jewish Divorce Certificate." *Journal of Jewish Studies* 49 (1998): 230–43.
Brooten, B. *Women Leaders in the Ancient Synagogue*. Chico, Calif., 1982.
Brosius, M. *Women in Ancient Persia, 559–331 B.C.* Oxford, 1996.
Brown, P. *The Body and Society*. New York, 1988.
———. "Society and the Supernatural: A Medieval Change." *Daedalus* 104 (1975): 133–51. Reprinted in *Society and the Holy in Late Antiquity*, 302–32. London, 1982.
———. *The World of Late Antiquity*. London, 1971.
Brown, R. "Livy's Sabine Women and the Ideal of Concordia." *Transactions of the American Philological Association* 125 (1995): 291–319.
Brown, W. P. *The Ethos of the Cosmos: The Genesis of Moral Imagination in the Bible*. Grand Rapids, Mich., 1949.
Brundage, J. A. "Intermarriage Between Christians and Jews in Medieval Canon Law." *Jewish History* 3 (1988): 25–40.
———. *Love, Sex, and Christian Society in Medieval Europe*. Chicago, 1987.
Burchard, C. "Ein vorläufiger griechischer Text von Joseph und Aseneth." *Dielheimer Blatter zum Alten Testament* 14 (1979): 2–53 and 16 (1982): 37–39.
———. *Gesammelte Studien zu Joseph und Aseneth*. Leiden, 1996.
Butting, K. "Esther: A New Interpretation of the Joseph Story in the Fight Against Anti-Semitism and Sexism." In *Ruth and Esther: A Feminist Companion to the Bible*, ed. A. Brenner, 239–48. Sheffield, 1999.
Cahana, A. *The Pseudepigrapha of the Old Testament* (in Hebrew). Reprint, Jerusalem, 1978.
Calhoon, C. G. "Lucretia, Savior and Scapegoat: The Dynamics of Sacrifice in Livy 1.57–59." *Helios* 24 (1997): 151–69.
Cameron, Av. "Ascetic Closure and the End of Antiquity." In *Asceticism*, ed. V. L. Wimbush et al., 146–61. New York, 1995.
Caspi, M. M. "The Story of the Rape of Dinah: The Narrator and the Reader." *Hebrew Studies* 26 (1985): 25–45.
Charles, R. H. "Jubilees." In *The Apocryphal Old Testament*, ed. H. F. D. Sparks, 1–139. Oxford, 1913; rev., Oxford, 1984.
Charlesworth, J. H., ed. *The Old Testament Pseudepigrapha*. 2 vols. Garden City, N.Y., 1985.
Chesnutt, R. D. *From Death to Life: Conversion in Joseph and Aseneth*. Sheffield, 1995.
Christiansen, E. J. *The Covenant in Judaism and Paul: A Study of Ritual Boundaries as Identity Markers*. Leiden and New York, 1995.
Clines, D. J. *Ezra, Nehemiah and Esther*. New Clarendon Bible. Reprint, Grand Rapids, Mich., 1992.
Coggins, R. G. *The Books of Ezra and Nehemiah*. Cambridge Bible Commentary on the New English Bible. Cambridge, 1976.
Cohen, Beth, ed. *The Distaff Side: Representing the Female in Homer's Odyssey*. Oxford, 1995.
Cohen, Boaz. *Jewish and Roman Law: A Comparative Study*. 2 vols. New York, 1966.
Cohen, D. *Law, Sexuality and Society. The Enforcement of Morals in Classical Athens*. Cambridge, 1991.

Cohen, J. *"Be Fertile and Increase, Fill the Earth and Master It": The Ancient and Medieval Career of a Biblical Text.* Ithaca, N.Y., 1989.
Cohen, S. J. D. *The Beginnings of Jewishness: Boundaries, Varieties, Uncertainties.* Berkeley, Calif., 1999.
———. "Crossing the Boundary and Becoming a Jew." *Harvard Theological Review* 82 (1989): 13–33. Reprinted in *The Beginnings of Jewishness*, 140–74.
———. *From the Maccabees to the Mishnah.* Philadelphia, 1987.
———. "Iudaios, Judaeus, Judaean, Jew." In *The Beginnings of Jewishness*, 69–106.
———. "The Origins of the Matrilineal Principle in Rabbinic Law." *Association for Jewish Studies Review* 10 (1985): 19–53. Reprinted in *The Beginnings of Jewishness*, 263–307.
———. "Pagan and Christian Evidence on the Ancient Synagogue." In *The Synagogue in Late Antiquity*, ed. L. I. Levine, 151–81. Philadelphia, 1987.
———. "The Prohibition of Intermarriage: From the Bible to the Talmud." *Hebrew Annual Review* 7 (1983): 23–39. Reprinted with revisions in *The Beginnings of Jewishness*, 241–62.
———. "The Rabbinic Conversion Ceremony." *Journal of Jewish Studies* 41 (1990): 177–203. Reprinted in *The Beginnings of Jewishness*, 198–238.
———. "Why Aren't Jewish Women Circumcised?" *Gender and History* 9 (1997): 560–78.
Cohen, S. J. D., and E. L. Greenstein, eds. *The State of Jewish Studies.* Detroit, 1990.
Corbett, P. E. *The Roman Law of Marriage.* Oxford, 1930.
Corcoran, S. *The Empire of the Tetrarchs: Imperial Pronouncements and Government, 284–324.* Oxford, 1996.
Crawford, M. H. *Roman Statutes.* 2 vols. London, 1996.
Daube, D. *The Collected Works of David Daube.* Vol. 1, *Talmudic Law.* Ed. C. M. Carmichael. Berkeley, Calif., 1992.
———. "Jewish Law in the Hellenistic World." In *Jewish Law in Legal History and the Modern World*, ed. B. S. Jackson, 45–60. Leiden, 1980.
Davidman, L., and S. Tenenbaum, eds. *Feminist Perspectives on Jewish Studies.* New Haven, Conn., 1994.
Davies, E. W. *Numbers.* New Century Bible Commentary. Grand Rapids, Mich., 1995.
Davies, P. R. "Calendrical Change and Qumran Origins: An Assessment of VanderKam's Theory." *Catholic Biblical Quarterly* 45 (1983): 80–89.
de Clerq, V. C. *Ossius of Cordova: A Contribution to the History of the Constantinian Period.* Washington, D.C., 1954.
de Dominicis, M. A. "Sulle origini romanocristiane del diritto del marito ad accusare 'constante matrimonio' la moglie adultera." *Studia et documenta historiae iuris* 16 (1950): 221–53.
de Lange, N. R. M. "Jews and Christians in the Byzantine Empire: Problems and Prospects." In *Christianity and Judaism*, ed. D. Wood, 15–32. Studies in Church History 29. Oxford, 1992.
Delcor, M. "Un roman d'amour d'origine thérapeute: Le livre de Joseph et Asenath." *Bulletin de Littérature Ecclésiastique* 63 (1962): 3–27.
Demougeot, E. "L'évêque Sévère et les juifs de Minorque au Ve siècle." In *Majorque, Languedoc, et Roussillon de l'Antiquité à nos jours*, 13–34. Montpellier, 1982.

Demsky, A. "Who Came First, Ezra or Nehemiah? The Synchronistic Approach." *Hebrew Union College Annual* 65 (1994): 1–20.
Derby, J. "The Paradox in the Book of Esther." *Jewish Bible Quarterly* 23 (1995): 115–19.
Destro, A. *The Law of Jealousy: Anthropology of Sotah*. Atlanta, Ga., 1989.
Diller, A. *Race Mixture Among the Greeks Before Alexander*. Urbana, Ill., 1937.
Donaldson, I. *The Rape of Lucretia*. Oxford, 1982.
Donlan, W. "Pistos, Philos, Hetairos." In *Theognis of Megara: Poetry and the Polis*, ed. T. J. Figueira and G. Nagy. Baltimore, Md., 1985.
Douglas, M. D. *In the Wilderness: The Doctrine of Defilement in the Book of Numbers*. Sheffield, 1993.
Douglas, R. C. "Liminality and Conversion in Joseph and Aseneth." *Journal for the Study of the Pseudoepigrapha* 3 (1988): 31–42.
DuBois, B. *Sowing the Body: Psychoanalysis and Ancient Representations of Women*. Chicago, 1988.
Dupont, F. "Recitatio and the Reorganization of the Space of Public Discourse." In *The Roman Cultural Revolution*, ed. Habinek and Schiesaro. Cambridge, 1997.
Eichler, B. L. "On Reading Genesis 12:10–20." In *Tehillah Le-Moshe: Biblical and Judaic Studies in Honor of Moshe Greenberg*, ed. M. Cogan, B. L. Eichler, and J. H. Tigay, 23–38. Winona Lake, n.d., 1997.
Eilberg-Schwartz, H. *God's Phallus and Other Problems for Men and Monotheism*. Boston, 1994.
———. "The Nakedness of a Woman's Voice, The Pleasure in a Man's Mouth: An Oral History of Ancient Judaism." In *Off with Her Head! The Denial of Women's Identity in Myth, Religion and Culture*, ed. H. Eilberg-Schwartz and W. Doniger, 165–84. Berkeley, Calif., 1995.
———. *The Savage in Judaism: An Anthropology of Israelite Religion and Ancient Judaism*. Bloomington, Ind., 1990.
———, ed. *People of the Body: Jews and Judaism from an Embodied Perspective*. Albany, N.Y., 1992.
Elliott, D. *Spiritual Marriage. Sexual Abstinence in Medieval Wedlock*. Princeton, N.J., 1993.
Endres, J. C. *Biblical Interpretation in the Book of Jubilees*. Washington, D.C., 1987.
Enker, A. N. "Error Juris in Jewish Criminal Law." *Journal of Law and Religion* 11 (1994–95): 23–62.
Epstein, L. M. *Marriage Laws in the Bible and Talmud*. Cambridge, Mass., 1942.
Eskenazi, T. C. "Out from the Shadows: Biblical Women in the Postexilic Era." *Journal for the Study of the Old Testament* 54 (1992): 25–43.
Eskenazi, T. C., and E. P. Judd. "Marriage to a Stranger in Ezra 9–10." In *Second Temple Studies: Temple and Community in the Persian Period*, ed. T. C. Eskenazi and K. H. Richards, 2:266–85. Sheffield, 1994.
Eyre, C. J. "Crime and Adultery in Ancient Egypt." *Journal of Egyptian Archaeology* 70 (1984): 92–105.
Fair, B. F. L. *The Impediment of Abduction*. Washington, D.C., 1944.
Falchi, G. L. "La legislazione imperiale circa i matrimoni misti fra Cristiani ed Ebrei nel IV secolo." *Atti dell'Accademia Romanistica Constantiniana* 2 (1988): 203–11.

Feigin, S. I. "Some Cases of Adoption in Israel." *Journal of Biblical Literature* 50 (1931): 186–200.
Feldherr, A. "Livy's Revolution: Civic Identity and the Creation of the Res Publica." In *The Roman Cultural Revolution*, ed. T. Habinek and A. Schiesaro, 136–57. Cambridge, 1997.
———. *Spectacle and Society in Livy's History*. Berkeley, Calif., 1998.
Feldman, L. "Diaspora Synagogues: New Light from Inscriptions and Papyri." In *Sacred Realm: The Emergence of the Synagogue in the Ancient World*, ed. S. Fine, 48–94. New York, 1996.
———. *Jew and Gentile in the Ancient World: Attitudes and Interactions from Alexander to Justinian*. Princeton, N.J., 1993.
Fewell, D. N., and D. M. Gunn. *Gender, Power and Promise*. Nashville, Tenn., 1993.
———. "Tipping the Balance: Sternberg's Reader and the Rape of Dinah." *Journal of Biblical Literature* 110 (1991): 193–211.
Fine, S. *This Holy Place: On the Sanctity of the Synagogue During the Greco-Roman Period*. Notre Dame, Ind., 1997.
———, ed. *Sacred Realm: The Emergence of the Synagogue in the Ancient World*. New York, 1996.
Finkelberg, M. "Royal Succession in Heroic Greece." *Classical Quarterly* 41 (1991): 303–16.
Finkelstein, M. *Proselytism: Halakhah and Practice* (in Hebrew). Ramat Gan, 1994.
Fishbane, M. "Accusations of Adultery: A Study of Law and Scribal Practice in Numbers 5:11–31." *Hebrew Union College Annual* 45 (1974): 25–45.
———. *Biblical Interpretation in Ancient Israel*. Oxford, 1985.
Fitzgerald, J. T., ed. *Greco-Roman Perspectives on Friendship*. Atlanta, Ga., 1997.
Fonrobert, C. E. *Menstrual Purity: Rabbinic and Christian Reconstructions of Biblical Gender*. Stanford, Calif., 2000.
Fontaine, J. *Isidore de Séville et la culture classique dans l'Espagne wisigothique*. Paris, 1959.
Fox, M. V. "The Sign of the Covenant: Circumcision in the Light of the Priestly 'ôt Etiologies.'" *Revue biblique* 81 (1974): 557–96.
Fraade, S. D. "Navigating the Anomalous: Non-Jews at the Intersection of Early Rabbinic Law and Narrative." In *The Other in Jewish Thought and History: Constructions of Jewish Culture and Identity*, ed. L. J. Silberstein and R. L. Cohn, 145–65. New York, 1994.
———. "Sifre Deuteronomy 26 (ad Deut. 3:23): How Conscious the Composition?" *Hebrew Union College Annual* 54 (1983): 271–77.
Fredricksmeyer, H. C. "Penelope Polutropos: The Crux at *Odyssey* 23.218–24." *American Journal of Philology* 118 (1997): 487–97.
Freedman, D. N. "Dinah and Shechem, Tamar and Amnon." *Austin Seminary Bulletin* 105 (1991): 51–63.
Freedman, H., and M. Simon, eds. *Lamentations*. Trans. A. Cohen. In vol. 7 of *Midrash Rabbah*. London, 1939.
Frymer-Kensky, T. *In the Wake of the Goddesses: Women, Culture and the Biblical Transformation of Pagan Myth*. New York, 1992.

———. "Law and Philosophy: The Case of Sex in the Bible." *Semeia* 45 (1989): 89–102.
Fuchs, E. "Structure and Patriarchal Functions in the Biblical Betrothal Type-Scene: Some Preliminary Notes." *Journal of Feminist Studies in Religion* 3 (1987): 7–13.
Gafni, I. "The Institution of Marriage in Rabbinic Times." In *The Jewish Family: Metaphor and Memory*, ed. D. Kraemer, 13–30. New York, 1989.
Garnesey, P. *Social Status and Legal Privilege in the Roman Empire*. Oxford, 1970.
Garrison, E. P. *Groaning Tears: Ethical and Dramatic Aspects of Suicide in Greek Tragedy*. Leiden, 1995.
Gaster, M. *The Exempla of the Rabbis*. 1924. Reprint, New York, 1968.
Geller, S. A. "The Sack of Shechem: The Use of Typology in Biblical Covenant Religion. *Prooftexts* 10 (1990): 1–15.
Gelston, A. "The End of Chronicles." *Journal for the Study of the Old Testament* 10 (1996): 53–60.
Goff, B. E. *The Noose of Words: Readings of Desire, Violence and Language in Euripides' Hippolytos*. Cambridge, 1990.
Goodblatt, D. "The Babylonian Talmud." *Aufstieg und Niedergang der Römischen Welt* II.19.2 (1979): 257–336.
———. "The Beruriah Traditions." *Journal of Jewish Studies* 26 (1975): 68–86.
Goodman, M. *Mission and Conversion*. Oxford, 1994.
Gordon, P., and H. C. Washington. "Rape as a Military Metaphor in the Hebrew Bible." In *A Feminist Companion to the Latter Prophets*, ed. A. Brenner, 308–25. Sheffield, 1995.
Grabbe, L. L. *Ezra-Nehemiah*, Old Testament Readings. London and New York, 1998.
———. *From the Exile to Yavneh*. London, 2000.
———. *Judaic Religion in the Second Temple Period: Belief and Practice from the Exile to Yavneh*. London, 2000.
———. *Judaism from Cyrus to Hadrian*. London, 1992.
———. "Triumph of the Pious or Failure of the Xenophobes? The Ezra-Nehemiah Reforms and Their Nachgeschichte." In *Jewish Local Patriotism and Self-Identification in the Graeco-Roman Period*, ed. S. Jones and S. Pearce, 50–65. Sheffield, 1998.
———, ed. *Can a History of Israel Be Written?* Journal for the Study of the Old Testament Supplement Series 245. Sheffield, 1997.
———. *Leading Captivity Captive: The "Exile" as History and Ideology*. Sheffield, 1998.
Gray, G. B. *A Critical and Exegetical Commentary on Numbers*. International Critical Commentary. New York, 1903.
Green, W. S. "Reading the Writing of Rabbinism." *Journal of the American Academy of Religion* 51 (1983): 191–206.
Greenstone, J. H. *The Holy Scriptures: Numbers*. Philadelphia, 1939.
Gregory, E. "Unraveling Penelope: The Construction of the Faithful Wife in Homer's Heroines." *Helios* 23 (1996): 3–20.
Gregory, J. *Euripides and the Instruction of the Athenians*. Ann Arbor, Mich., 1991.

Griffe, E. "Le concile d'Elvire et les origines du célibat ecclésiastique." *Bulletin de la littérature ecclésiastique* 77 (1976): 123–27.
Grubbs, J. E. "Abduction Marriage in Antiquity: A Law of Constantine and Its Social Context." *Journal of Roman Studies* 79 (1989): 59–83.
———. *Law and Family in Late Antiquity: The Emperor Constantine's Marriage Legislation*. Oxford, 1995.
Gruber, M. I. "Matrilineal Determination of Jewishness: Biblical and Near Eastern Roots." In *Pomegranates and Golden Bells: Studies in Honor of J. Milgrom*, ed. D. P. Wright et al., 437–43. Winona Lake, Ind., 1995.
Gunkel, H. *Genesis*. 1910, 3rd ed. Trans. M. E. Biddle. Macon, Ga., 1997.
Gunneweg, A. H. J. *Esra*. Kommentar zum Alten Testament. Gütersloh, 1985, 1987.
Guttman, A. "The Problem of the Anonymous Mishna." In *Origins of Judaism*, vol. 9, *The Literature of Formative Judaism: The Mishnah and the Tosefta*, ed. J. Neusner, 129–43. New York and London, 1990.
Haberman, B. D. "The Suspected Adulteress: A Study of Textual Embodiment." *Prooftexts* 20 (2000): 12–42.
Habinek, T. "The Invention of Sexuality in the World-City of Rome." In *The Roman Cultural Revolution*, ed. T. Habinek and A. Schiesaro, 23–43. Cambridge, 1997.
Habinek, T., and A. Schiesaro, eds. *The Roman Cultural Revolution*. Cambridge, 1997.
Hadas-Lebel, M. *Jerusalem contre Rome*. Paris, 1990.
Halivni, D. W. *Midrash, Mishnah, and Gemara: The Jewish Predilection for Justified Law*. Cambridge, Mass., 1986.
Hammer, R. *Sifre: A Tannaitic Commentary on the Book of Deuteronomy*. New Haven, Conn., 1986.
Hanson, P. *The People Called: The Growth of Community in the Bible*. San Francisco, 1986.
Haran, M. *The Biblical Canon* (in Hebrew). Jerusalem, 1996.
Hareven, T. K. "The History of the Family and the Complexity of Social Change." *American Historical Review* 96 (1991): 95–124.
Harries, J. *Law and Empire in Late Antiquity*. Cambridge, 1999.
Hasan-Rokem, G. *The Web of Life: Folklore in Rabbinic Literature* (in Hebrew). Tel Aviv, 1996.
Hauptman, J. *Rereading the Rabbis: A Woman's Voice*. Boulder, Colo., 1998.
Hayes, C. E. *Between the Babylonian and Palestinian Talmuds: Accounting for Halakhic Difference in Selected Sugyot from Tractate Avodah Zarah*. New York and Oxford, 1997.
———. "Intermarriage and Impurity in Ancient Jewish Sources." *Harvard Theological Review* 92 (1999): 3–36.
Hecht, N. S., et al. *Introduction to the History and Sources of Jewish Law*. Oxford, 1996.
Helleman, W. "Homer's Penelope: A Tale of Feminine Arete." *Échos du Monde Classique. Classical Views* 39 (1995): 227–50.
Herford, R. T. *Christianity in the Talmud and Midrash*. London, 1903; reprint, New York, 1975.
Herlihy, D. "Family." *American Historical Review* 96 (1991): 1–16.

Herskovits, M. J. *Economic Anthropology*. New York, 1952.
Heymann, F. Review of *Sexuality and Family in History*, ed. I. Bartal and I. Gafni (Jerusalem, 1998). *Bulletin du Centre de recherche français de Jérusalem* 5 (1999): 55.
Hezser, C. "The Codification of Legal Knowledge in Late Antiquity: The Talmud Yerushalmi and Roman Law Codes." In *The Talmud Yerushalmi and the Graeco-Roman World*, ed. P. Schäfer, 581–64. Tübingen, 1998.
———. *The Social Structure of the Rabbinic Movement in Roman Palestine*. Tübingen, 1997.
Himmelfarb, M. "Torah, Testimony, and Heavenly Tablets: The Claim to Authority of the Book of Jubilees." In *A Multiform Heritage*, ed. R. A. Kraft, 19–29. Atlanta, Ga., 1999.
Hoffman, L. A. *Beyond the Text*. Bloomington, Ind., 1989.
———. *Covenant of Blood: Circumcision and Gender in Rabbinic Judaism*. Chicago, 1996.
Hollis, S. T. "The Woman in Ancient Examples of the Potiphar's Wife Motif, K2111." In *Gender and Difference in Ancient Israel*, ed. P. L. Day, 28–42. Minneapolis, Minn., 1989.
Horbury, W. "Suffering and Messianism in Yose ben Yose." In *Suffering and Martyrdom in the New Testament*, ed. W. Horbury and B. McNeil, 143–82. Cambridge, 1981.
Humphrey, E. M. *The Ladies and the Cities: Transformation and Apocalyptic Identity in Joseph and Aseneth, 4 Ezra, the Apocalypse and the Shepherd of Hermas*. Journal for the Study of the Pseudepigrapha Supplement Series 17. Sheffield, 1995.
Hunt, E. D. "St. Stephen in Minorca: An Episode in Jewish-Christian Relations in the Early Fifth Century." *Journal of Theological Studies* 33 (1982): 106–23.
Ilan, T. *Integrating Women into Second Temple History*. Tübingen, 1999.
———. *Jewish Women in Greco-Roman Palestine*. Tübingen, 1995.
———. *Mine and Yours Are Hers: Retrieving Women's History from Rabbinic Literature*. Leiden, 1997.
Isaac, B. "The Babatha Archive: A Review Article." *Israel Exploration Journal* 42 (1992): 62–75.
Jackoski, K. "Holy Disobedience in Esther." *Theology Today* 45 (1989): 403–14.
Jackson, B. S. "Liability for Mere Intent in Early Jewish Law." In *Essays in Jewish and Comparative Legal History*, 202–34. Leiden, 1975.
———. "On the Problem of Roman Influence on the Halakhah and Normative Self-Definition in Judaism." In *Jewish and Christian Self-Definition*, ed. E. P. Sanders et al., 2:157–203. Philadelphia, 1981.
Japhet, S. "Composition and Chronology in the Book of Ezra-Nehemiah." In *Second Temple Studies*, ed. T. C. Eskenazi and K. H. Richards, 2:189–216. Sheffield, 1994.
Jaubert, A. "Le calendrier de Jubilés et de la secte de Qumrân: Ses origines bibliques." *Vetus Testamentum* 3 (1953): 250–64.
Jellinek, A., ed. *Bet ha-Midrash*, 3rd ed. Jerusalem, 1967.
Johnson, T., and Dandeker, C. "Patronage: Relation and System." In *Patronage in Ancient Society*, ed. A. Wallace-Hadrill, 219–42. London, 1989.

Johnson, W.-M. "Ethnicity in Persian Yehud: Between Anthropological and Ideological Criticism." *Society of Biblical Literature Seminar Papers* (1995): 177–86.
Joplin, P. K. "Ritual Work on Human Flesh: Livy's Lucretia and the Rape of the Body Politic." *Helios* 17 (1990): 51–70.
Joseph, N. B. "The Feminist Challenge to Judaism: Critique and Transformation." In *Gender, Genre and Religion*, ed. M. Joy and E. K. Neumaier-Dargyay, 47–70. Waterloo, 1995.
Joshel, S. R. "The Body Female and the Body Politic: Livy's Lucretia and Verginia." In *Pornography and Representation in Greece and Rome*, ed. A. Richlin, 112–30. Oxford, 1991.
Katz, J. "Although He Sinned He Is Still Israel" (in Hebrew). *Tarbiz* 27 (1957–58): 203–17.
———. *Exclusiveness and Tolerance*. New York, 1962.
Kaufmann, J. *The Religion of Israel from Its Beginnings to the Babylonian Exile* (in Hebrew). Tel Avi, 1956.
Kearley, F. "Difficult Texts from Ezra, Nehemiah, and Esther (Ezra 10)." In *Difficult Texts of the Old Testament Explained*, ed. W. Winkler, 288–300. Hurst, Tex., 1982.
Kister, M. "A Common Heritage: Biblical Interpretation at Qumran and Its Implications." In *Biblical Perspectives: Early Use and Interpretation of the Bible in Light of the Dead Sea Scrolls*, ed. M. E. Stone and E. G. Chazon, 101–11. Leiden, 1998.
———. "Legends of the Destruction of the Second Temple in Avot de-Rabbi Nathan" (in Hebrew). *Tarbiz* 67 (1998–99): 483–529.
———. "Studies in 4Q *Miqṣat Ma'aśe Ha-Torah* and Related Texts: Law, Theology, Language, and Calendar" (in Hebrew). *Tarbiz* 68 (1999): 317–71.
Klawans, J. *Impurity and Sin in Ancient Judaism*. Oxford, 2000.
Klein, L. R. "Esther's Lot." *Currents in Research: Biblical Studies* 5 (1997): 111–45.
Klein, R. W. "The Books of Ezra and Nehemiah: Introduction, Commentary, and Reflections." In *The New Interpreter's Bible*, 3:661–851. Nashville, Tenn., 1999.
Knoppers, G. "Sex, Religion and Politics: The Deuteronomist on Intermarriage." *Hebrew Annual Review* 14 (1994): 121–42.
Koch, K. "Ezra and the Origins of Judaism." *Journal of Jewish Studies* 19 (1974): 173–97.
Konovitz, I. *Rabbi Meir: Collected Sayings in Halakha and Aggadah, in the Talmudic and Midrashic Literature* (in Hebrew). Jerusalem, 1967.
Konstan, D. *Friendship in the Classical World*. Cambridge, 1997.
Kornfeld, W. "L'adultère dans l'orient antique." *Revue biblique* 57 (1950): 92–109.
Kovacs, D. *The Heroic Muse*. Baltimore, Md., 1987.
Kraemer, R. S. "Jewish Women in the Diaspora World of Late Antiquity." In *Jewish Women in Historical Perspective*, ed. J. R. Baskin, 43–67. Detroit, Mich., 1991.
———. "The Other as Woman: An Aspect of Polemic Among Pagans, Jews, and Christians in the Greco-Roman World." In *The Other in Jewish Thought and History: Constructions of Jewish Culture and Identity*, ed. L. J. Silberstein and R. L. Cohn, 121–43. New York, 1994.
———. *When Aseneth Met Joseph: A Late Antique Tale of the Biblical Patriarch and His Egyptian Wife, Reconsidered*. Oxford, 1998.

Kraft, R. A., and G. W. E. Nickelsburg, eds. *Early Judaism and Its Modern Interpreters*. Atlanta, Ga., 1986.
Kugel, J. L. *The Bible as It Was*. Cambridge, Mass., 1997.
———. "The Story of Dinah in the Testament of Levi." *Harvard Theological Review* 85 (1992): 1–34.
Kuhrt, A. *The Ancient Near East*. 2 vols. London, 1995.
Laeuchli, S. *Power and Sexuality: The Emergence of Canon Law at the Synod of Elvira*. Philadelphia, 1972.
Landy, F. "On Metaphor, Play, and Nonsense." *Semeia* 61 (1993): 219–37.
Lassner, J. *Demonizing the Queen of Sheba: Boundaries of Gender and Culture in Postbiblical Judaism and Medieval Islam*. Chicago, 1993.
Lattimore, R. "Phaedra and Hippolytus." In *Essays on Classical Literature*, ed. N. Rudd, 19–20. Cambridge, 1972.
Lehming, S. "Zur Überlieferungsgeschichte von Gen 34." *Zeitschrift für die Alttestamentliche Wissenschaft* 70 (1958): 228–50.
Lemche, N. P. *The Israelites in History and Tradition*. London and Louisville, Ky., 1998.
Lerner, M. B. "On the Midrashim on the Decalogue" (in Hebrew). In *Talmudic Studies*, ed. Y. Sussmann and D. Rosenthal, 1:217–36. Jerusalem, 1990.
Levenson, J. D. *Esther: A Commentary*. Old Testament Library. Louisville, Ky., 1997.
Levine, L. I. *The Ancient Synagogue: The First Thousand Years*. New Haven, Conn., 1999.
———. "The Jewish Patriarch (Nasi) in Third Century Palestine." *Aufstieg und Niedergang der Römischen Welt* II.19.2 (1979): 649–88.
———. "The Sages and the Synagogue in Late Antiquity: The Evidence of the Galilee." In *The Galilee in Late Antiquity*, ed. L. I. Levine, 201–22. New York and Jerusalem, 1992.
Lieberman, S. *The Tosefta*. New York, 1995.
Linder, A. *The Jews in Roman Imperial Legislation*. Detroit, Mich., and Jerusalem, 1987.
———. *The Jews in the Legal Sources of the Early Middle Ages*. Detroit, Mich., and Jerusalem, 1997.
Lipinski, E. "Marriage and Divorce in the Judaism of the Persian Period." *Transeuphratene* 4 (1991): 63–71.
Livy. *Early History of Rome: Books I–V of the History of Rome from Its Foundation*. Trans. A. de Selincourt. Harmondsworth, 1971.
Loraux, N. *Born of the Earth: Myth and Politics in Athens*. Trans. S. Stewart. Ithaca, N.Y., 2000.
———. *The Children of Athena: Athenian Ideas About Citizenship and the Division Between the Sexes*. Trans. C. Levine. Princeton, N.J., 1993.
———. *Mothers in Mourning*. Trans. C. Pache. Ithaca, N.Y., 1998.
———. *Tragic Ways of Killing a Woman*. Trans. A. Forster. Cambridge, Mass., 1987.
Lowry, S. "The Extent of Jewish Polygamy in Talmudic Times." *Journal of Jewish Studies* 9 (1958): 115–38.
Luck, W. F. *Divorce and Remarriage: Recovering Biblical Law*. San Francisco, 1987.

Luschnig, C. A. E. *Time Holds the Mirror: A Study of Knowledge in Euripides' Hippolytus*. Leiden, 1988.

Maarsingh, B. *Numbers: A Practical Commentary*. Text and Interpretation. Grand Rapids, Mich., 1987.

Maccoby, H. "Holiness and Purity: The Holy People in Leviticus and Ezra-Nehemiah." In *Reading Leviticus: A Conversation with Mary Douglas*, ed. J. F. A. Sawyer, 153–70. Sheffield, 1996.

———. *Ritual and Morality: The Ritual Purity System and Its Place in Judaism*. Cambridge, 1999.

Magen, Y. "Mt. Gerizim: A Temple-City" (in Hebrew). *Qadmoniot* 120 (2000): 74–118.

Manthe, U. "Beiträge zur Entwicklung des antiken Gerechtigkeitsbegriffes II: Stoische Würdigkeit und die iuris praecepta Ulpians." *Zeitschrift der Savigny-Stifung für Rechtsgechichte: Romanistische Abteilung* 114 (1997): 1–26.

Margalit, N. "'Not by Her Mouth Do We Live': Literary/Anthropological Reading of Gender in Mishnah Ketubbot ch. 1." *Prooftexts* 20 (2000): 61–86.

McBride, W. T. "Esther Passes: Chiasm, Lex Talio, and Money in the Book of Esther." In *Not in Heaven: Coherence and Complexity in Biblical Narrative*, ed. J. Rosenblatt and J. C. Sitterson, 67–72. Bloomington, Ind., 1991.

McConville, J. G. *Ezra, Nehemiah and Esther*. Edinburgh, 1985.

McGinn, T. A. J. *Prostitution, Sexuality and the Law in Ancient Rome*. New York, 1998.

Meigne, M. "Concile ou collection d'Elvire." *Revue d'histoire ecclésiastique* 70 (1975): 361–87.

Merkelbach, R. *Roman und Mysterium in der Antike*. Munich, 1962.

Meyer, M., and R. Smith, eds. *Ancient Christian Magic: Coptic Texts of Ritual Power*. San Francisco, 1994.

Midrash Decalogue (ad Seventh Commandment). In *Bet ha-Midrash*, 3rd ed., ed. A. Jellinek. Jerusalem, 1967.

Miles, G. B. *Livy: Reconstructing Early Rome*. Ithaca, N.Y., 1995.

Milgrom, J. *Numbers*. The JPS Torah Commentary. Philadelphia, 1990.

Milligan, D. *Sex Life*. London and Boulder, Colo., 1993.

Mills, S. *Theseus, Tragedy and the Athenian Empire*. Oxford, 1997.

Modrzejewski, J. M. "Les documents du Désert de Judée à la lumière des papyrus d'Égypte." Paper delivered at Bar Ilan University's conference on the documents of the Judaean Desert, June 1998.

———. "La Septante comme nomos: Comment la Tora est devenue une 'loi civique' pour les Juifs d'Égypte." *Annali di scienze religiose* 2 (1997): 143–58.

Mol, A. *Identity and the Sacred*. New York, 1976.

Momigliano, A. *Essays on Ancient and Modern Judaism*. Trans. M. Masella-Gayley, ed. S. Berti. Chicago, 1994.

Moore, C. A. *Esther*. Anchor Bible 7B. Garden City, N.Y., 1971.

Mopsik, C. "The Body of Engenderment in the Hebrew Bible, the Rabbinic Tradition and the Kabbalah." In *Fragments for a History of the Human Body*, ed. M. Feher et al., 1:48–73. New York, 1989.

Mount, F. *The Subversive Family: An Alternative History of Love and Marriage*. New York, 1992.
Mundkur, B. *The Cult of the Serpent: An Interdisciplinary Survey of Its Manifestations and Origins*. Albany, N.Y., 1983.
Murnaghan, S. *Disguise and Recognition in the Odyssey*. Princeton, N.J., 1987.
Myers, J. M. *Ezra-Nehemiah*. Anchor Bible 14. Garden City, N.Y., 1965.
Naveh, J. *On Sherd and Papyrus: Aramaic and Hebrew Inscriptions from the Second Temple, Mishnaic and Talmudic Periods* (in Hebrew). Jerusalem, 1992.
Naveh, J., and S. Shaked. *Aramaic and Hebrew Incantations of Late Antiquity*. Jerusalem, 1992.
Neubauer, A. *La géographie du Talmud*. 1868; reprint, Hildesheim, 1967.
Neufeld, E. *Ancient Hebrew Marriage Laws*. London, 1944.
Neusner, J. *A History of the Mishnaic Law of Women*. Leiden, 1980.
———. *The Philosophical Mishnah*. Atlanta, Ga., 1988.
———. *Purity in Rabbinic Judaism*. Atlanta, Ga., 1994.
———. *Self-Fulfilling Prophecy: Exile and Return in the History of Judaism*. Boston, 1987.
———. "Stable Symbols in a Shifting Society: The Delusion of the Monolithic Gentile in Documents of Late Fourth Century Judaism." In *To See Ourselves as Others See Us: Christians, Jews, "Others" in Late Antiquity*, ed. J. Neusner and E. S. Frerichs, 373–96. Chico, Calif., 1985.
Neusner, J., et al. *The Talmud of the Land of Israel*. Chicago, 1984.
Newlands, C. W. "The Rape of Lucretia in Ovid's Fasti." *Augustan Age* 8 (1988): 36–48.
Newman, L. I. "Intermarriage Between Jews and Christians During the Middle Ages." *Jewish Institute Quarterly* 2 (1926): 2–8 and 21–28.
Noonan, J. T. *Power to Dissolve: Lawyers and Marriages in the Courts of the Roman Curia*. Cambridge, Mass., 1972.
Novak, D. "The Marital Status of Jews Married Under Non-Jewish Auspices." In *Jewish Law Association Studies*. Vol. 1, *The Touro Conference Volume*, ed. B. S. Jackson, 61–77. Chico, Calif., 1985.
———. "Some Aspects of the Relationship of Sex, Society and God in Judaism." In *Contemporary Ethical Issues in the Jewish and Christian Traditions*, ed. F. E. Greenspahn, 140–66. Hoboken, N.J., 1986.
Noy, D. *Jewish Inscriptions of Western Europe*. 2 vols. Cambridge, 1993–95.
Ockshorn, J. *The Female Experience and the Nature of the Divine*. Bloomington, Ind., 1981.
Olson, D. T. *Numbers*. Interpretation. Louisville, Ky., 1996.
Packman, Z. M. "Call It Rape: A Motif in Roman Comedy and Its Suppression in English-Speaking Publications." *Helios* 20 (1993): 42–55.
Pakter, W. *Medieval Canon Law and the Jews*. Ebelsbath, 1988.
Pantel, P. S. *La cité au banquet: Histoire des repas publics dans les cités grecques*. Rome, 1992.
Papadopoulou-Belmehdi, I. *Le chant de Pénélope: Poétique du tissage féminin dans l'Odyssée*. Paris, 1994.

Paton, L. B. *A Critical and Exegetical Commentary on the Book of Esther*. The International Critical Commentary. New York, 1908.
Perdue, L. G., et al., eds. *Families in Ancient Israel*. Louiville, Ky., 1997.
Peskowitz, M. B. *Spinning Fantasies: Rabbis, Gender and History*. Berkeley, Calif., 1997.
Peskowitz, M. B., and L. Levitt, eds. *Judaism Since Gender*. New York, 1997.
Pestman, P. W. *Marriage and Matrimonial Property in Ancient Egypt*. Leiden, 1961.
Pharr, C. *Theodosian Code and the Novels and the Sirmondian Constitutions: A Translation with Commentary, Glossary, and Bibliography*. Princeton, N.J., 1952.
Philonenko, M. *Joseph et Aséneth: Introduction, texte critique, traduction, et notes*. Studia Post-Biblica 13. Leiden, 1968.
Pitkin, H. F. *Fortune Is a Woman: Gender and Politics in the Thought of Niccolò Macchiavelli*. Berkeley, Calif., 1994.
Pitt-Rivers, S. *The Fate of Shechem or The Politics of Sex: Essays in the Anthropology of the Mediterranean*. Cambridge Studies in Social Anthropology, no. 19. Cambridge, 1977.
Plaskow, J. *Standing Again at Sinai: Judaism from a Feminist Perspective*. San Francisco, 1990.
Poorthuis, M., and J. Schwartz, eds. *Purity and Holiness: The Heritage of Leviticus*. Leiden, 2000.
Porten B., et al. *The Elephantine Papyri in English*. Leiden, 1996.
Porton, G. G. *Goyim: Gentiles and Israelites in Mishnah and Tosefta*. Atlanta, Ga., 1988.
———. *The Stranger Within Your Gates: Converts and Conversion in Rabbinic Literature*. Chicago, 1994.
Pressler, C. *The View of Women Found in the Deuteronomic Family Laws*. Berlin, 1993.
Pury, A. de. "Genèse XXXIV et l'histoire." *Revue Biblique* 76 (1969): 5–49.
Qimron, E., and J. Strugnell, eds. *Qumran Cave 4: Miqṣat Ma'aśé Ha-Torah*. Discoveries in the Judean Desert 10. Oxford, 1994.
Quint, E. B., and N. S. Hecht. *Jewish Jurisprudence*. 2 vols. Chur, 1986.
Rabello, A. M. "Jewish and Roman Jurisdiction." In *An Introduction to the History and Sources of Jewish Law*, ed. N. S. Hecht et al., 141–67. Oxford, 1996.
———. "Il problema dei matrimoni fra Ebrei e Cristiani nella legislazione imperiale e in quella della chiesa (IV–VI s.)." *Atti dell'Accademia Romanistica Constantiniana* 2 (1988): 213–24.
Radding, C. M. *A World Made by Men: Cognition and Society 400–1200*. Chapel Hill, N.C., 1985.
Rajak, T., and D. Noy. "*Archisynagogoi*: Office, Title, and Social Status in the Greco-Jewish Synagogue." *Journal of Roman Studies* 83 (1993): 75–93.
Rashkow, N. *The Phallacy of Genesis: A Feminist Psychoanalytical Approach*. Louisville, Ky., 1993.
Ravitzki, R., ed. *Female Readers from the Beginning: Creative Women Write on the Book of Genesis* (in Hebrew). Tel Aviv, 1999.
Reynolds, P. L. *Marriage in the Western Church: The Christianization of Marriage During the Patristic and Early Medieval Periods*. Leiden and New York, 1994.
Ringgren, H. "The Marriage Motif in Israelite Religion." In *Ancient Israelite Reli-*

gion: Essays in Honor of Frank Moore Cross, ed. P. D. Miller et al., 421–28. Philadelphia, 1987.

Riskin, S. *Women and Jewish Divorce: The Rebellious Wife, the Agunah, and the Right of Women to Initiate Divorce in Jewish Law: A Halakhic Solution.* Hoboken, N.J., 1989.

Robins, G. *The Art of Ancient Egypt.* Cambridge, Mass., 1997.

———. *Women in Ancient Egypt.* Cambridge, Mass., 1993.

Rodriguez, A. M. *Esther: A Theological Approach.* Berrien Spring, Mich., 1995.

Rofé, A. "Family and Sex Laws in Deuteronomy and the Book of the Covenant." *Henoch* 9 (1987): 131–59.

Roth, J. *The Halakhic Process: A Systematic Analysis.* New York, 1986.

Rousselle, A. *Porneia: On Desire and the Body in Antiquity.* Trans. F. Pheasant. New York, 1996.

Rubin, N. F. *Regarding Penelope.* Princeton, N.J., 1994.

Rudolph, W. *Esra und Nehemia samt 3 Esra.* Handbuch zum Alten Testament 29. Tübingen, 1949.

Russell, J. R. "Zoroastrian Elements in the Book of Esther." *Irano-Judaica* 2 (1990): 33–40.

Rutgers, L. V. "Attitudes to Judaism in the Greco-Roman Period: Reflections on Feldman's *Jew and Gentile in the Ancient World.*" *Jewish Quarterly Review* 85 (1995): 361–95.

Sagi, A., and Z. Zohar. *Conversion to Judaism and the Meaning of Jewish Identity* (in Hebrew). Jerusalem, 1994.

Sakenfeld, K. D. *Journeying with God.* International Theological Commentary. Grand Rapids, Mich., 1994.

Saller, R. P. *Personal Patronage under the Early Empire.* Cambridge, 1982.

Samet, M. "Conversion to Judaism in the Early Centuries CE" (in Hebrew). In *Jews and Judaism in the Second Temple, Mishnah and Talmud Periods: Studies in Honor of Shmuel Safrai*, ed. I. Gafni et al., 316–43. Jerusalem, 1993.

Sancisi-Weerdenburg, H. "Exit Atossa: Images of Women in Greek Historiography on Persia." In *Images of Women in Antiquity*, eds. A. Cameron and A. Kuhrt, 20–83. London, 1983.

Sanders, E. P. "Common Judaism and the Synagogue in the First Century." In *Jews, Christians and Polytheists in the Ancient Synagogue*, ed. S. Fine, 1–17. London, 1999.

Sarna, N. M. *Genesis: The Traditional Hebrew Text with New JPS Translation.* The JPS Torah Commentary. Philadelphia, 1989.

———. *Understanding Genesis.* New York, 1986.

Satlow, M. L. "'One Who Loves His Wife Like Himself': Love in Rabbinic Marriage." *Journal of Jewish Studies* 49 (1998): 67–86.

———. "Shame and Sex in Late Antique Judaism." In *Asceticism*, ed. V. L. Wimbush et al., 535–43. New York, 1995.

———. *Tasting the Dish: Rabbinic Rhetorics of Sexuality.* Atlanta, Ga., 1995.

———. "'Try to Be a Man': The Rabbinic Construction of Masculinity." *Harvard Theological Review* 89 (1996): 19–40.

Schechter, S. "Genizah Specimens." *Jewish Quarterly Review* 10 (1898): 654–59.

Schiffman, L. H. "At the Crossroads: Tannaitic Perspectives on the Jewish-Christian Schism." In *Jewish and Christian Self-Definition*, ed. F. P. Sanders et al., 2:115–56. Philadelphia, 1981.

———. *Who Was a Jew?* Hoboken, N.J., 1985.

Schulz-Flügel, E. *Gregorius Eliberritanus: Epithalamium sive Explanatio in Canticis Canticorum*. Freiburg, 1994.

Silberman, L. H. "Reprobation, Prohibition, Invalidity: An Examination of the Halakhic Development Concerning Intermarriage." In *Judaism and Ethics*, ed. D. J. Silver, 179–98. New York, 1970.

Sirat, C., et al. *La Kétouba de Cologne: Un contract de mariage juif à Antinoopolis*. Opladen, 1986.

Sissa, G. *Greek Virginity*. Trans. A. Goldhammer. Cambridge, Mass., 1990.

Sivan, H. "Le corps d'une pécheresse, le prix de la piété: La politique de l'adultère dans l'Antiquité tardive." *Annales: Histoire, Sciences Sociales* (1998): 231–53.

———. "Why Not Marry a Barbarian? Marital Frontiers in Late Antiquity." In *Shifting Frontiers in Late Antiquity*, ed. R. M. Mathisen and H. S. Sivan, 136–45. Aldershot, 1996.

Smith, R. J. "The Status of Mixed Marriages in the Corinthian Community." In *Marriage Studies: Reflections in Canon Law and Theology*, ed. T. P. Doyle, 3:46–53. Washington, D.C., 1980.

Smith-Christopher, D. L. "Between Ezra and Isaiah: Exclusion, Transformation, and Inclusion of the 'Foreigner' in Post-Exilic Biblical Theology." In *Ethnicity and the Bible*, ed. M. G. Brett, 117–42. Leiden, 1996.

Sokoloff, M., and J. Yahalom. *Jewish Palestinian Aramaic Poetry from Late Antiquity* (in Hebrew). Jerusalem, 1999.

Sourvinou-Inwood, C. "The Young Abductor of the Locrian Pinakes." *Bulletin of the Institute of Classical Studies* 20 (1973): 12–21.

Sparks, H. F. D., ed. *The Apocryphal Old Testament*. Oxford, 1984.

Sprinkle, J. M. "Old Testament Perspectives on Divorce and Remarriage." *Journal of the Evangelical Theological Society* 40 (1997): 529–50.

Stehle, E. "Venus, Cybele, and the Sabine Women: The Roman Reconstruction of Female Sexuality." *Helios* 16 (1989): 143–64.

Steinberg, N. "Kinship and Gender in Genesis." *Biblical Research* 39 (1994): 45–56.

Stemberger, G. *Juden und Christen im Heiligen Land: Palästina unter Konstantin und Theodosius*. Munich, 1987.

Stern, D. "The Captive Woman: Hellenization, Greco-Roman Erotic Narrative, and Rabbinic Literature." *Poetics Today* 19 (1998): 91–127.

Stern, D., and M. J. Mirsky, eds. *Rabbinic Fantasies: Imaginative Narratives from Classical Hebrew Literature*. New Haven, Conn., 1990.

Stern, S. *Jewish Identity in Early Rabbinic Writings*. Leiden and New York, 1994.

Sternberg, M. *The Poetics of Biblical Narrative*. Bloomington, Ind., 1985.

Stone, K. A. *Sex, Honor, and Power in the Deuteronomistic History*. Sheffield, 1996.

Strack, H. L., and G. Stemberger. *Introduction to the Talmud and Midrash*. 2nd ed. Edinburgh, 1996.

Talmon, S. "Was the Scroll of Esther Known Among the Congregation of Those

Who Came into the New Covenant?" (in Hebrew). *Eretz Israel* 25 (1996): 377–82.

Tavori, J. *Jewish Feasts in the Period of the Mishnah and the Talmud* (in Hebrew) Jerusalem, 1995.

Throntveit, M. A. *Ezra-Nehemiah*. Interpretation. Louisville, Ky., 1992.

Tov, E. "The Septuagint." In *Mikra: Text, Translation, Reading and Interpretation of the Hebrew Bible in Ancient Judaism and Early Christianity*, Compendia Rerum Iudaicarum ad Novum Testamentum, section 2, ed. M. J. Mulder and H. Sysling, 161–88. Assen/Maastricht and Philadelphia, 1988.

Treggiari, S. *Roman Marriage. Iusti Coniuges from the Time of Cicero to the Time of Ulpian*. Oxford, 1991.

Umansky E. "Females, Feminists and Feminism: A Review of Recent Literature on Jewish Feminism and a Creation of Feminist Judaism." *Feminist Studies* 14 (1998): 349–65.

Valler, S. *Women and Womanhood in the Stories of the Babylonian Talmud* (in Hebrew). Jerusalem, 1993.

VanderKam, J. C. *The Book of Jubilees*. Corpus Scriptorum Christianorum Orientalium, Scriptores Aethiopici 87–88. Louvain, 1989.

———. "Das chronologische Konzept des Jubilaenbuches." *Zeitschrift für die alttestamentliche Wissenschaft* 107 (1995): 80–100.

———. "The Origin, Character, and Early History of the 364-Day Calendar: A Reassessment of Jaubert's Hypothesis." *Catholic Biblical Quarterly* 41 (1979): 390–411.

van Dijk-Hemmes, F. "Tamar and the Limits of Patriarchy: Between Rape and Seduction." In *Anti-Covenant: Counter-Reading Women's Lives in the Hebrew Bible*, ed. M. Bal, 135–56. Sheffield, 1989.

Van Houten, C. *The Alien in Israelite Law*. Journal for the Study of the Old Testament Supplement Series 107, 238–53. Sheffield, 1991.

Van Wijk-Bos, J. W. H. *Ezra, Nehemiah and Esther*. Westminster Bible Commentary. Louisville, Ky., 1998.

Vermes, G. "Leviticus 18.21 in Ancient Jewish Bible Exegesis." In *Studies in Aggadah, Targum, and Jewish Liturgy in Memory of Joseph Heinemann*, 108–24. Jerusalem, 1981.

Vidal-Naquet, P. *The Jews: History, Memory and the Present*. Trans. D. Ames Curtis. New York, 1996.

Vodola, E. *Excommunication in the Middle Ages*. Berkeley, Calif., 1986.

Volterra, E. "Per la storia dell'*accusatio adulterii iure mariti vel patris*." In *Scritti giuridici*, ed. M. Talamanca, 1: 219–78. Naples, 1991.

Wacholder, B.-Z. "Jubilees as the Super Canon: Torah-Admonition Versus Torah-Commandment." In *Legal Texts and Legal Issues*, ed. M. J. Bernstein et al., 195–211. Proceedings of the second meeting of the International Organization for Qumran Studies, Cambridge, 1995; published in honor of J. M. Baumgarten. Leiden, 1997.

———. *Messianism and Mishnah: Time and Place in Early Halakha*. Cincinnati, Ohio, 1978.

Wallace-Hadrill, A., ed. *Patronage in Ancient Society*. London, 1989.
Washington, H. C. "The Strange Woman of Proverbs 1–9 and Post-Exilic Judaean Society." In *Second Temple Studies*, ed. T. C. Eskenazi and K. H. Richards, 2:217–42. Journal for the Study of the Old Testament Supplement Series 175. Sheffield, 1994.
Wasserfall, R. R., ed. *Women and Water: Menstruation in Jewish Life and Law*. Hanover, 1999.
Wasserstein, A. "Non-Hellenized Jews in the Semi-Hellenized East." *Scripta Classica Israelica* 14 (1995): 111–37.
Watermute, O. S. "Jubilees" in *The Old Testament Pseudepigrapha*, ed. J. H. Charlesworth, 2:35–142. Garden City, N.Y., 1983–85.
Wechsler, M. "The Purim-Passover Connection: A Reflection of Jewish Exegetical Tradition in the Peshitta Book of Esther." *Journal of Biblical Literature* 117 (1998): 321–35.
———. "Shadow and Fulfillment in the Book of Esther." *Biblia Sacra* 154 (1997): 275–84.
Weeks, J. *Sex, Politics, and Society: The Regulation of Sexuality Since 1800*. Rev. ed., London, 1989.
Wegner, J. R. *Chattel or Person? The Status of Women in the Mishnah*. New York, 1988.
Weinberg, J. *The Citizen-Temple Community*. Sheffield, 1992.
Weinstein, S. E. *Piety and Fanaticism: Rabbinic Criticism of Religious Stringency*. Northvale, N.J., 1997.
Weiss, M. *The Bible from Within: The Method of Total Interpretation*. Jerusalem, 1984.
Wenham, G. *Numbers: An Introduction and Commentary*. Tyndale Old Testament Commentaries. Downers Grove, Ill., 1981.
Werman, C. "Jubilees 30: Building a Paradigm for the Ban on Intermarriage." *Harvard Theological Review* 90 (1997): 1–22.
Westermann, C. *Genesis 12–36*. London, 1985.
Will, E., and C. Orrieux. *Prosélytisme juif? Histoire d'une erreur*. Paris, 1992.
Williamson, H. G. M. *Ezra, Nehemiah*. Word Biblical Commentary 16. Waco, Tex., 1985.
Wohl, V. "Scenes from a Marriage: Love and Logos in Plutarch's *coniugalia praecepta*." *Helios* 24 (1997): 170–92.
Women in Scripture: A Dictionary of Named and Unnamed Women in the Hebrew Bible, the Apocryphal/Deuterocanonical Books, and the New Testament. Ed. C. Meyers et al. Boston, 2000.
Wyatt, N. "The Story of Dinah and Shechem." *Ugarit Forschungen* 22 (1991): 433–58.
Wyler, B. "Esther: The Incomplete Emancipation of a Queen." In *A Feminist Companion to Esther, Judith and Susanna*, ed. A. Brenner. Sheffield, 1995.
Yadin, Y., et al. "Babatha's Ketubba." *Israel Exploration Journal* 44 (1994): 75–101.
Yahalom, Y. *Poetry and Society in the Jewish Galilee of Late Antiquity* (in Hebrew). Tel Aviv, 1999.
Yaron, R. *Gifts in Contemplation of Death in Jewish and Roman Law*. Oxford, 1960.
Yee, G. A. "By the Hand of a Woman: The Metaphor of the Woman Warrior in Judges 4." *Semeia* 61 (1993): 99–134.

Yerushalmi, Y. H. *Zakhor: Jewish History and Jewish Memory*. Seattle, 1982.
Zeitlin, F. I. "The Power of Aphrodite: Eros and the Boundaries of the Self in the *Hippolytus*." In *Directions in Euripidean Criticism*, ed. P. Burian, 52–111. Durham, N.C., 1985.
Zlotnick, H. "From Jezebel to Esther: Images of Queenship in the Hebrew Bible." *Biblica*. Forthcoming 2001.
Zunz, L. *Die gottesdienstlichen Vorträge der Juden Historisch Entwickelt*, 2nd ed. 1892. Hebrew trans. M. A. Jacque. Jerusalem, 1974.

General Index

Abduction marriage: biblical, 34, 43–48; Greek, 38, 40, 41, 44; Roman law, 39, 43. *See also* Aseneth; Betrothal; Bride-theft; Dinah; Rape; Women
Abraham: Genesis, 45–48, 51, 85, 133, 161; Jubilees, 70, 73
Adam and Eve, 22, 48, 133
Adultery: biblical and Jewish law, 15, 28, 29, 72, 105–7, 110–17, 122–31, 134, 157–59, 166, 170; Roman law, 107, 117–22, 124–31, 156; Roman literature, 108, 109. *See also* Augustus; Courts; Death; Divorce; Dowry; Gentiles; Hippolytus; Jewesses; Jews; Judah; Lucretia; Marriage; Meir; Morality; Procreation; Prostitution; Seduction; Sex; Testimony
Agamemnon, 12, 40
Ahab (king of Israel), 91
Ahasuerus (king of Persia), 25, 77–81, 83, 84, 86, 87, 89, 90–93. *See also* Esther; Haman
Akiva (sage and rabbi), 9–14, 18, 116, 168–70. *See also* Kalba Savua; Penelope; Rachel
Ambrose (bishop of Milan, 340–97 C.E.), 209 n. 69
Amnon (son of David), 33, 41, 48. *See also* Tamar
Antioch, 117
Aphrodite, 17, 18, 107
Aristotle, 33
Artemis, 17, 18
Aseneth (wife of Joseph; heroine of Joseph and Aseneth), 76–78, 92–102, 146, 167, 168; abduction, 95; Genesis, 92; intermarriage, 94; model Jewess, 28, 102, 110. *See also* Abduction marriage; Bride-theft; Egypt; Family; Gentiles; Joseph; Property
Athens, 24, 166

Augustine (bishop of Hippo, 354–430 C.E.), 122, 130
Augustus (emperor, 27/31 B.C.E.–14 C.E.), 119, 120, 129, 157; legislation on adultery, 109, 112, 116; lex Iulia, 112, 130. *See also* Adultery

Baal, worship of, 52, 54
Babylon, 25, 145; academy in, 16
Balaam, 56
Balak, 56
Baptism, 151
Bastards (*mamzerim*), Jewish law, 138, 140–43, 148. *See also* Birth; Children; Gentiles
Bellerophon, 16
Benjamin (son of Jacob and Rachel; character in Joseph and Aseneth): biblical, 162, 163; Joseph and Aseneth, 98
Beruriah (wife of Rabbi Meir), 23, 24
Betrothal (*kiddushin*), 46, 72, 138, 139, 141, 143; effect on family and clan relationships, 44, 47; Jewish law, 143–49. *See also* Abduction marriage; Dinah; Rabbinic Sources *under* Index of Sources
Bigamy, Roman law, 118
Birth, 9, 13, 50, 64, 70, 98, 133, 134; Jewish law, 140, 164, 166, 167; role and importance of women for, 48, 159, 162, 166. *See also* Bastards; Childbirth; Children; Death
Boaz, 91
Brachia (rabbi), 147
Brides, 12, 59, 60, 62; bride price, 37–39, 46, 47; identity and family, 93, 99, 133, 134, 167; intermarriage, 71, 77, 87, 93–94, 146, 148, 152, 154, 155; Jewish law, 8, 62, 71, 77, 93. *See also* Intermarriage; Jewesses; Marriage; Women
Bride-theft, 34, 39–43, 60. *See also* Abduction marriage; Aseneth; Dinah

Brutus (avenger of Lucretia), 53–56. *See also* Lucretia

Cain, 132
Celibacy, 17, 18; forced, 13, 51, 121, 163. *See also* Chastity; Virginity
Chastity, 17, 73, 109; female, 3, 15, 52, 53, 85, 102, 117, 122, 130; male, 12, 19, 22. *See also* Celibacy; Virginity
Childbirth, death of women in, 4, 162, 164, 169. *See also* Birth; Children; Death; Jewesses; Procreation; Women
Children, 5–7, 10, 12, 14, 27, 28, 35, 38, 41, 50–52, 55, 57, 61, 65–69, 72, 74–76, 82, 85, 88, 93, 97–101, 105, 107, 117, 124, 129, 132, 133, 137–51, 154, 158–69. *See also* Bastards; Birth; Childbirth; Love; Procreation
Clytemnestra (wife of Agamemnon), 12
Codex Justinianus. *See* Roman Legal Sources *under* Index of Citations
Codex Theodosianus. *See* Roman Legal Sources *under* Index of Citations
Collatinus (husband of Lucretia), 52–54
Constantine I (emperor, 306–37 C.E.), 39, 120, 121, 124, 157
Courts: "biblical," 78, 90; Greek, 78, 90, 101; Jewish, 113–15, 121–24, 156; Roman, 108, 112, 121, 128, 157. *See also* Adultery; Divorce; Dowry; Esther; Remarriage; Roman Legal Sources *under* Index of Citations
Cozbi (Midianite princess), 26, 33, 49–52, 54–56, 110, 129, 163, 165, 167. *See also* Levi; Phineas; Rape; Shimon; Zimri
Cynegius (Praetorian prefect), 156
Cyprian (bishop of Carthage), 151
Cyrus (king of Persia), 58, 59

David (king of Israel and Judah), 6, 33, 41
Death, 3, 5, 7, 11, 17, 43, 49, 56, 72, 99, 100; atonement, 50, 119, 126; biblical law, 72, 106, 113; Jewish law, 16, 19, 22; penalty for rape in biblical law, 35, 36; suicide, 19, 53, 108. *See also* Adultery; Birth; Childbirth; Widows; Women;
Deborah (judge), 163, 164
Delilah, 3
Diaspora, 2, 76, 77, 85, 91, 92, 136, 150

Digest. *See* Roman Legal Sources *under* Index of Citations
Dinah (daughter of Jacob and Leah): biblical, 1, 26, 28, 33, 34, 50, 52, 59, 63, 92; —, abduction of, 42–47, 66; —, fate of, 1, 26; —, rape of, 26, 34–40, 48, 52, 56, 66, 89; Jubilees, 2, 27, 58, 69–72, 168. *See also* Abduction marriage; Betrothal; Bride-theft; Family; Gentiles; Guest-friendship; Hospitality; Intermarriage; Levi; Rape; Shimon; Virginity
Diocletian (emperor, 284–305 C.E.), 124, 156
Dionysius of Halicarnassus, 188 n. 33
Divorce: biblical law, 65, 68, 76, 79; canon law, 151, 156; grounds for, 12, 121, 157; Jewish law, 100, 122–27, 141, 156, 157; Roman law, 115, 117, 121, 122, 127, 151, 157. *See also* Adultery; Courts; Elephantine Papyri; Esther; Ezra; Intermarriage; Marriage; Property
Dowry, 20, 153; canon law, 153; Jewish law, 27, 115, 122, 123; Roman law, 121–23, 157. *See also* Adultery; Courts; Family; Gifts; Marriage; Property

Eden, 132
Egypt, 50, 55, 69, 77, 81, 85, 92, 96–98, 101, 136, 161, 163. *See also* Aseneth; Elephantine Papyri; Joseph
Elephantine Papyri. *See* Divorce; Egypt; Marriage; Mibtahiah; Property; Pseudepigrapha, Qumran, Elephantine Papyri, and New Testament *under* Index of Citations
Eliezer (rabbi), 9, 116
Elopement, 35
Elvira, Council of (307 C.E.?), 151–54, 210 nn. 79–80, 85, 211 nn. 90–91
Esther, 3, 25, 27, 28, 76–95, 101, 102, 110, 139, 164, 165, 167, 170. *See also* Ahasuerus; Courts; Divorce; Family; Gentiles; Haman; Intermarriage; Vashti; Virginity; Zeresh
Euripides, *Hippolytus*, 17, 18, 24, 178 n. 43, 179 nn. 51–55
Eve, 5, 22, 23, 48, 133. *See also* Adam and Eve
Excommunication: canon law, 153, 159; Jewish law, 142, 152

General Index

Ezekiel, 58
Ezra, 3, 25–28, 58, 59, 62–67, 69, 73, 74, 75, 77, 88, 92, 139, 159, 165. *See also* Divorce; Gentiles; Intermarriage; Jerusalem; Nehemiah

Family: biblical and Jewish, 27, 58, 68, 70, 76, 77, 84, 85; membership in and identity, 33, 56, 58, 64, 68, 70, 73, 74, 76, 77, 84, 86, 87, 92; role in arranging marriages, 16, 34, 40, 42, 43, 51, 54, 73, 85, 87; social and political importance of, 94, 95, 102, 133, 134, 137. *See also* Aseneth; Dinah; Dowry; Esther; Gifts; Intermarriage; Jewesses; Jews; Marriage; Property

Gentiles, 3, 25, 30, 78, 135, 170; marriage with Israelites or Jews, 27–29, 72, 76, 77, 81, 84, 91, 92, 140, 143–49, 167; social relations with Israelites or Jews, 1, 69, 73, 80, 85, 88, 92, 98, 134, 137, 142, 147, 159, 167. *See also* Adultery; Aseneth; Bastards; Dinah; Esther; Ezra; Intermarriage; Jewesses; Jews; Marriage
Gerar, Abraham and Sarah in, 85
Geshem (enemy of Nehemiah), 67
Gifts, 45, 46. *See also* Dowry; Family; Marriage
Guest-friendship, 35–37, 40, 47, 48. *See also* Dinah; Hamor; Hesiod; Hospitality; Jacob

Haman, 77, 82–86, 88–92, 165, 170. *See also* Ahasuerus; Esther; Zeresh
Hamor (father of Shechem, host of Jacob), 35–37, 40, 42–44, 63, 71. *See also* Guest-friendship
Helbo (rabbi), 147
Helen (Greek beauty), 18, 39, 40
Heretics: canon law, 153, 154; Jewish law, 152, 159
Herodotus of Halicarnassus, *History*, 47
Hesiod, 35, 44. *See also* Guest-friendship
Hillel (rabbi), 25
Hippolytus, 17–19. *See also* Adultery; Euripedes; Phaedra
Homer: *Illiad*, 11, 16; *Odyssey*, 11, 14, 177 n. 31
Hospitality, 5, 7, 34, 35, 38, 40–42, 44–47, 96, 97, 165. *See also* Dinah; Guest-friendship; Jacob

Iliad. *See* Homer
Impediments, marital: canon law, 48; cultic disparity as a, 93, 94, 101, 135; Jewish law, 134, 140; Roman law, 29, 149, 155, 156. *See also* Intermarriage; Marriage
Impurity, women, 74, 95, 106, 109, 116, 140. *See also* Jewesses; Sex; Women
Intermarriage, 42, 54, 55, 87, 91, 92, 98, 158; biblical law and narratives, 28, 42, 50, 51, 54, 55, 60–69, 72–74, 80, 135, 144, 145; Jewish law, 72, 137, 138, 141, 143–49, 158; Roman law, 135, 148, 155, 156. *See also* Brides; Dinah; Divorce; Esther; Ezra; Family; Gentiles; Impediments, marital; Jewesses; Jews; Marriage; Nehemiah; Procreation; Women
Isaac (son of Abraham and Sarah), 25, 43, 45, 48, 57, 85, 161

Jacob, 40, 52, 57, 58, 71, 73, 93, 141; father of Dinah, 33, 35, 36, 38, 51, 61, 71, 168; guest of Hamor, 11, 35, 36, 42–44; husband of Rachel and Leah, 4–7, 10, 14, 46, 163. *See also* Dinah; Guest-friendship; Hospitality; Leah; Rachel
Jael (biblical heroine), 164
Jeremiah (prophet), 6, 164
Jerome (Christian theologian, c. 347–419 C.E.), 119, 120, 127, 128
Jerusalem, 9, 15, 23, 26, 59, 62, 64, 74, 76, 80, 122, 123, 150. *See also* Ezra
Jewesses: daughters, 27, 73, 84, 133, 167; identity of, 1, 2, 4, 15, 23–25, 28–30, 73, 108, 110, 112, 131, 133, 137, 138, 159, 165–68, 171; intermarriage, 27, 63, 73, 74, 80, 92, 100, 135–37, 144–49, 151, 155–57; wives, 24, 27, 28, 30, 77, 84, 154, 155, 159, 166, 167. *See also* Adultery; Brides; Childbirth; Family; Gentiles; Impurity; Intermarriage; Jews; Marriage; Widows; Women
Jews: fathers, 88, 15, 158; husbands, 27, 28, 154; identity of (male/female), 1, 2, 13, 10, 25, 49, 55, 72, 73, 75, 86, 92, 101, 117, 158, 165; intermarriage, 27, 63, 73, 74, 80, 92, 100, 135–37, 144–46; Roman law, 125, 151,

Jews: Roman law (*continued*)
153–55. *See also* Adultery; Family; Gentiles; Intermarriage; Jewesses; Marriage

Jezebel (wife of Ahab, rival of Elijah), 91, 96, 165

Joseph, 16, 50, 173; biblical, 161–63; intermarriage, 96, 97; in Joseph and Aseneth, 28, 76, 77, 81, 92–102, 146, 167, 168. *See also* Aseneth; Egypt; Property; Shimon

Joshua (rabbi), 9, 116

Judah: biblical, 50; land of, 7; Midrash Decalogue, 15, 17–22; rabbinic authority, 112, 122. *See also* Adultery; Meir; Midrash Decalogue; Miqṣat Ma'aśé ha-Torah; Tamar

Justinian (emperor, 527–65 C.E.), 117, 118, 124, 127, 128, 130, 158. *See also* Novellae, Justinian, *under* Roman Legal Sources *in* Index of Citations

Kalba Savua (father of Rachel and father-in-law of Akiva), 9, 10. *See also* Akiva; Rachel

Lamentations Rabbah, 5–8, 10, 14. *See also* Leah; Rachel

Leah (wife of Jacob, sister of Rachel), 7, 8, 45, 57, 71, 161, 163. *See also* Jacob; Lamentations Rabbah; Rachel

Learning: female, 23, 24, 132; male, 170

Levi: biblical, 38, 51, 54, 73; Jubilees, 71. *See also* Cozbi; Dinah; Shimon

Livy, *History of Rome (Ad urbe condita)*, 38, 52, 53, 60, 61, 67

Love: marital and conjugal, 4, 7, 10, 13, 34, 47, 53, 57, 66, 89, 93, 94, 101, 111, 112, 115, 128, 129, 146, 169; maternal, 8, 17, 66, 71. *See also* Children; Marriage; Procreation; Sex

Lucretia, 17, 26, 33, 49, 52–56, 108, 109. *See also* Adultery; Brutus; Rape; Sextus Tarquinius

Machiavelli, Niccolo: *Discourses*, 33; *Mandragola*, 108, 109

Marriage: biblical, 37, 48, 50, 57, 62–64, 100–102, 136; consent to, 37, 39, 40, 46, 47, 101, 136; Jewish law, 60, 65; Roman law, 39, 60, 61, 136. *See also* Adultery; Brides; Divorce; Dowry; Elephantine Papyri; Family; Gentiles; Gifts; Impediments, marital; Intermarriage; Jewesses; Jews; Love; Procreation; Property; Remarriage; Sex; Virginity; Widows; Women

Meir: Midrash Decalogue, 15–17, 19–20, 109, 171; rabbi and husband of Beruriah, 22–24. *See also* Adultery; Judah; Midrash Decalogue; Miqṣat Ma'aśé ha-Torah

Menelaus, 40

Mibtahiah, 100. *See also* Elephantine Papyri

Midrash Decalogue, 105, 177 n. 38, 179 n. 59. *See also* Judah; Meir

Midwives, 5, 162, 166

Miqṣat Ma'aśé ha-Torah (MMT), 74. *See also* Pseudepigrapha, Qumran, Elephantine Papyri, and New Testament *under* Index of Citations

Moab, 7. *See also* Cozbi

Molech, 72

Morality, sexual: biblical and Jewish, 24, 63, 64, 69, 70, 72, 73, 110, 120, 129, 132, 135, 155, 157; Christian literature, 25, 128, 135, 157, 170; Roman law, 52, 120, 122, 129, 130, 135, 170, 171. *See also* Adultery; Sex; Virginity

Moses, 6, 49, 50, 54, 72, 136

Naomi, 7

Nehemiah, 3, 25, 27, 28, 50, 57–59, 66, 68, 73, 77, 80, 88, 139, 158. *See also* Ezra; Intermarriage; Sanballat; Tobias

Noah, 133

Novellae, Justinian. *See* Roman Legal Sources *under* Index of Citations

Odyssey. *See* Homer

Ovid, *Art of Love (Ars Amatoria)*, 68

Paradise, 22

Paris (prince of Troy), 40

Penance, 122, 153

Penelope, 4, 11–14, 18. *See also* Akiva; Rachel

Pentephres (father of Aseneth in Joseph and Aseneth), 96, 97, 99

Phaedra, 8, 17–24, 81, 166. *See also* Hippolytus; Rape

Philo, 26
Phineas (priest, grandson of Aaron), 49, 52, 54–56, 73, 129, 163, 165. *See also* Cozbi
Pindar, *Nemean Odes V*, 16
Pliny, *Panegyricus*, 200 n. 48
Plutarch: *Advice on Marriage (Coniugalia praecepta)*, 107; *Romulus*, 67
Potiphar (father of Aseneth in Genesis), 16, 18, 81
Procreation, 4, 14, 60, 61, 74, 107, 129, 158, 164, 168. *See also* Adultery; Childbirth; Children; Intermarriage; Love; Marriage; Sex
Property, 43, 96, 99, 100, 124, 128, 153, 157. *See also* Aseneth; Divorce; Dowry; Elephantine Papyri; Family; Joseph; Marriage
Prostitution, 51, 72, 121, 124, 129, 157. *See also* Adultery; Sex
Pseudepigrapha. *See* Pseudepigrapha, Qumran, Elephantine Papyri, and New Testament *under* Index of Citations

Qumran. *See* Pseudepigrapha, Qumran, Elephantine Papyri, and New Testament *under* Index of Citations

Rachel: wife of Akiva, 9–14, 18, 99, 168–70; wife of Jacob, sister of Leah, 4–8, 45, 46, 57, 162–67. *See also* Akiva; Jacob; Kalba Savua; Lamentations Rabbah; Leah; Penelope
Rape, 17, 19, 23, 27, 47, 48, 50, 60, 61, 71, 73, 106, 129; biblical law, 26, 34–40, 48, 52–56, 66, 71, 73, 89, 165–67; Jewish law, 23, 106; Roman law, 49, 52–56, 129. *See also* Abduction marriage; Cozbi; Dinah; Lucretia; Phaedra; Sabine women; Seduction; Testimony; Women
Rashi, 23
Rebecca: Genesis, 8, 45–47; Jubilees, 57, 70, 71, 99, 161
Remarriage, 127, 152. *See also* Courts; Marriage; Widows; Women
Romulus (founder of Rome), 38, 44, 60, 61, 67

Sabine women, rape of, 26, 38, 47, 60, 61, 66–68. *See also* Rape

Sanballat, 67. *See also* Nehemiah
Sarah (wife of Abraham, mother of Isaac): Genesis, 57, 161; in Joseph and Aseneth, 99
Seduction, 23, 24, 33, 36, 53, 167. *See also* Adultery; Rape
Sex, 14, 17–20, 23–27, 63, 91, 92, 94, 95, 98, 145, 156, 158, 173; extramarital, 30, 57, 81, 106, 107, 129, 159; marital, 25, 114, 115, 122, 126, 135, 153; premarital, 38, 47, 72. *See also* Adultery; Impurity; Love; Marriage; Morality, sexual; Procreation; Prostitution; Women
Sextus Tarquinius, 53. *See also* Lucretia
Shamai (rabbi), 25
Shimon (son of Jacob, brother of Dinah): biblical, 38, 49–54; in Joseph and Aseneth, 94–95. *See also* Cozbi; Dinah; Joseph; Levi
Solomon (king of Israel), 50, 88, 90, 91, 96

Tamar: daughter of David, 33, 41, 42, 48; daughter-in-law of Judah, 51, 165. *See also* Amnon; Judah
Tertullian (bishop of Carthage, second to third centuries C.E.), 151
Testimony: Jewish law, 112, 114, 115, 122; Roman law, 122. *See also* Adultery; Rape
Theseus, 17, 24
Thucydides, *History of the Peloponnesian War*, 47
Tobias, 67. *See also* Nehemiah
Troy, 12, 40

Vashti (wife of Ahasuerus), 28, 77–84, 87, 90, 91. *See also* Esther
Virginity, 19, 23, 26, 30, 37, 39, 72, 73, 85, 89, 94, 95, 98, 106, 107, 134, 151, 163, 164, 166, 167. *See also* Celibacy; Chastity; Dinah; Esther; Marriage; Morality, sexual

Widows, 7, 9, 33, 138, 151; legal status of, 100, 128; remarriage, 94; social status of, 11, 13, 14, 26, 162, 167. *See also* Death; Jewesses; Marriage; Remarriage; Women
Women: communal identity, 1, 3, 7, 12, 14, 52, 110; legal status, 11, 13, 22, 27, 52, 117, 124, 125, 132, 137, 143, 148, 149;

Women (*continued*)
  reproduction, 5, 133, 158, 159; sexuality, 12, 131, 158; weaving, 155. *See also* Abduction marriage; Brides; Childbirth; Death; Intermarriage; Jewesses; Marriage; Rape; Remarriage; Sex; Widows

Yehud (Persian province in time of Ezra and Nehemiah), 26, 27, 57–63, 66–69, 75, 80, 88, 92, 165–67

Zelophehad, daughters of, 51, 55
Zeresh (wife of Haman), 77, 81, 82–84, 91, 92. *See also* Esther; Haman
Zeus, 20, 22
Zimri, 49–56, 129. *See also* Cozbi

Index of Citations

Hebrew Bible

Genesis
2:20, 132
2:23, 133
2:24, 134
4:1–2, 133
4:17, 133
4:18, 133
4:23–24, 132
5:1–32, 133
6:1, 133
10:1–32, 133
11:1–32, 133
11:29–30, 133
24:1–67, 183 n. 38
24:3–4, 70, 189 n. 48
24:4, 45
24:5, 46, 47
24:15, 181 n. 8
25:8–9, 70
27:3, 45
28:2, 189 n. 48
29:1, 46
29:1–35, 46, 47, 183 n. 38
29:11, 46
30:1, 5, 162
30:5–15, 72
30:6, 72
30:14–16, 6
30:21, 162
30:22–24, 162
31:1–54, 5
31:32, 5
33:18, 36, 183 n. 99
33:18–19, 35
33:19, 35
33:20, 35
34:1–31, 1, 26, 33–48, 50–52, 54, 56, 58, 59, 63, 66, 71, 73, 87, 91, 159, 163, 167, 168, 180 n. 2, 182 n. 26
35:1–29, 163
35:9, 183 n. 99
35:10–12, 183 n. 99
35:16–17, 5
35:19–20, 5
35:28, 43
38:28, 51
39:1–23, 81, 197 n. 3
39:12–18, 16
39:17, 81
39:19, 81
41:45, 92
48:1–22, 161
48:7, 162
48:22, 162, 182 n. 26
49:5–7, 162
49:30–31, 161

Exodus
1:15, 166
2:16–21, 183 n. 38
6:15, 50
12:1–51, 69
12:38, 186 n. 7
20:14, 2, 15
20:15, 105
20:17, 105, 201 n. 59
34:11, 209 n. 66
34:15–16, 50, 63, 65, 73, 85, 134, 192 n. 13
34:16, 81, 192 n. 18

Leviticus
18:18, 8
18:21, 207 n. 43
20:10, 198 n. 32
21:9, 70, 72
22:28, 6
24:9, 72
24:10–11, 166

Numbers

5:10–31, 18, 29, 105
5:11–31, 106, 111, 199 n. 37
5:14, 1, 26, 35, 114
5:31, 106
25:1–5, 49
25:1–6, 51
25:1–19, 49–52, 54–56, 73, 91, 159, 209 n. 66
25:6–18, 49
25:18, 56
36:1–13, 51

Deuteronomy

7:2–4, 209 n. 66
7:3, 143
7:3–4, 50, 63, 65, 73, 77, 85, 134, 144, 145
7:4, 81, 143, 192
21:10, 207 n. 42
21:10–14, 181 n. 12
21:13, 143, 144
22:22, 198 n. 32
22:23–24, 209 n. 69
23:4, 192 n. 13, 209 n. 66
23:4–9, 65
24:1, 65
24:1–2, 79
24:1–4, 187 n. 29

Joshua

23:11, 85, 209 n. 66

Judges

5:7b, 163
19:1–30, 41, 165, 181 n. 8

1 Samuel

4:19–22, 212 n. 4
4:20, 212 n. 4

2 Samuel

13:1–22, 33, 165
13:13, 33, 41
13:15, 41
13:20, 51

1 Kings

11:1–2, 192 n. 13
11:1–7, 88
11:1–13, 50, 85, 88, 90, 91
11:4–5, 90

Isaiah

14:1, 208 n. 57

Jeremiah

31:15, 7
31:15–17, 6

Ezekiel

23:37, 126

Hosea

4:14, 209 n. 69

Psalms

8:5–6, 170

Proverbs

9:17, 126, 203 n. 85
12:4, 10
12:10, 10
28:13, 16

Ruth

1:16–17, 7
4:11, 29

Esther

1:1–8, 78
1:5, 191 nn. 6, 7
1:9, 78
1:12, 81
1:20, 82
1:22, 80
2:1, 88
2:5, 80
2:7, 85, 193 n. 24
2:20, 193 n. 24
2:22, 86
3:1, 82
3:4, 85
3:8, 86, 92
4:7–17, 87
4:8, 87
4:11a, 89
4:13–14, 87
4:13–17, 88
4:14, 87

4:16b, 87
5:1, 90
5:10, 82
5:14, 83
6:8, 192 n. 23
6:13, 83, 186 n. 9
7:5, 90
7:6, 83
7:8, 83
8:1, 88
8:17, 191 n. 6
9:10, 82
9:12, 82
9:13, 82
9:25, 82
9:27, 191 n. 6

Ezra
4:1–2, 67
4:1–5, 64
6:19–22, 64
9:1, 186 n. 5
9:1–2, 60
9:1–15 and 10:1–44, 26, 61, 66, 92, 186 n. 5, 209 n. 66
9:2, 186 n. 7
10, 187 n. 26
10:3, 65
10:11, 66
10:15, 66
10:44, 68, 188 n. 36

Nehemiah
10:1, 193 n. 24
10:13, 209 n. 66
13:15–18, 80
13:23–24, 80
13:23–27, 191 n. 3
13:23–29, 80
13:24, 80
13:26, 88

Pseudepigrapha, Qumran, Elephantine Papyri, and New Testament

Jubilees
1:27, 69
2:25–27, 69
6:17–36, 69
15:33, 73
16:20–31:69
20:4, 70
20:8, 73
22:16–18, 73
22:18, 73
24:18–19, 69
25:1, 70
25:3, 189 n. 48
30, 70, 209 n. 66
30:2–4, 71
30:7, 72
30:11, 73
30:15, 73
40, 69
49:5, 73
50:8, 12–13, 69

Elephantine Papyri (Porten)
19, 97, 99, 100, 195 n. 53
B25, 100, 196 n. 61
B26, 101, 196 n. 62
C27, 99, 196 n. 59
C28, 99, 196 n. 60
C33, 101, 196 n. 65
D2, 101, 196 n. 64

Miqṣat Ma'asé ha-Torah (MMT)
74, 190 n. 53

1 Corinthians
7:12–15, 150

2 Corinthians
6:15, 152

Rabbinic Sources

Mishnah

Mishnah, Avot
1.1, 25
1.5, 201 n. 54

Mishnah, Gittin
8.5, 200 n. 42
9.10, 203 n. 87

Mishnah, Ketubbot
   1.6, 106
   2.9, 207 n. 38
   3.4–5, 197 n. 12
   7.4–5, 201 n. 53

Mishnah, Kiddushin
   3.5, 146, 208 n. 61
   3.12, 138, 139, 140, 141, 142, 143, 146, 148

Mishnah, Sotah
   1.1, 113
   1.2, 123
   3.5, 201 n. 54
   4.1, 134
   4.5, 114, 203 n. 85
   5.1, 125
   6.1, 124
   9.9, 111, 199 n. 39
   9.12, 200 n. 42

Mishnah, Yebamot
   2.4, 141
   2.5, 148
   6.6, 129

Tosefta

Tosefta, Hullin
   2.20–21, 206 n. 28

Tosefta, Kiddushin
   4.16, 207 n. 33, 208 n. 47

Tosefta, Yebamot
   8.7, 213 n. 16
   12.8, 203 n. 78

Palestinian Talmud

Palestinian Talmud, Avodah Zarah
   2.2, 203 n. 84

Palestinian Talmud, Ketubbot
   5.6, 197 n. 15

Palestinian Talmud, Shabbat
   14.4, 203 n. 84

Palestinian Talmud, Sotah
   1.1 (7b–d), 115
   1.2 (7e), 203 n. 77
   1.7 (17a), 124
   3.4 (19a), 176 n. 26
   5.1, 203 n. 82

Palestinian Talmud, Yebamot
   2.6, 207 n. 44

Babylonian Talmud

Babylonian Talmud, Avodah Zarah
   18a, 179 n. 61
   36b, 207 n. 37

Babylonian Talmud, Baba Metzia
   58b, 201 n. 54

Babylonian Talmud, Ketubbot
   51b, 201 n. 58
   62b–63a, 9, 177 n. 37, 212 n. 16

Babylonian Talmud, Kiddushin
   21b, 207 n. 42
   63a, 146
   66–68, 143
   68b, 144, 207 nn. 34, 44
   70b, 208 n. 57
   81a, 179 n. 57

Babylonian Talmud, Nedarim
   50a, 9, 10
   91b, 126

Babylonian Talmud, Sanhedrin
   57b, 149
   75a, 203 n. 84
   100a, 168

Babylonian Talmud, Shabbat
   118, 170

Babylonian Talmud, Sotah
   2c, 112, 114
   4a, 182 n. 17
   4a–b, 116
   5b, 116, 123
   7a, 122

17a, 197 n. 14
19a, 125
25a, 114, 123
25b, 114
25c, 114
47c, 199 n. 39

Babylonian Talmud, Yebamot
   17a, 207 n. 44
   23a, 207 nn. 34, 44

Roman Legal Sources

Codex Justinianus
   1.9.6, 156, 158
   5.5.2, 156
   9.7.2, 202 n. 68
   9.9.2 f. (Antonine), 211 n. 104
   9.9.5, 202 n. 64
   9.9.6, 202 n. 64
   9.9.17, 202 n. 64
   9.9.18, 201 n. 60
   9.9.19 f. (Diocletian), 211 n. 104
   9.9.20, 201 n. 59
   9.9.21, 202 n. 64
   9.9.22, 124
   9.9.29, 201 n. 62
   9.9.29.2, 202 n. 70
   9.9.29.4, 203 n. 90
   9.9.32, 203 n. 76

Codex Theodosianus
   3.7.2, 156, 206 n. 18, 211 n. 96
   3.14.1, 206 n. 18, 211 n. 98
   3.16.1, 202 n. 71, 204 n. 91
   9.3.1, 127
   9.7.1, 131
   9.7.2, 119, 121, 122, 202 nn. 67, 70
   9.7.7, 203 n. 76
   9.24.1, 182 n. 24
   9.38.1, 211 n. 105
   9.40.1, 211 n. 105
   11.36.1, 211 n. 105
   11.36.4, 128
   16.8.6, 211 n. 97

Digest
   4.4.37.1, 198 n. 24
   48.5.2.8, 201 n. 55
   48.5.40, 201 n. 59
   48.12.7–13, 201 n. 55
   48.15.2, 201 n. 55

Novellae, Justinian
   134.10, 128, 203 n. 79

Acknowledgments

To the invisible presence of Nicole Loraux I owe much of the inspiration for the introduction and the conclusion of this book. For the encouragement and support of Peter Brown and David Noel Freedman I owe less tangible but very real and lasting gratitude.

This project began its life at the Institute for Advanced Study at Princeton and came to an end at the Institute for Advanced Studies at the Hebrew University of Jerusalem. Fewer places offer a more exciting or challenging environment.

At Princeton, Peter Brown's Forum on Late Antiquity provided much food for thought. Michael Thomas Davis of the Princeton Theological Seminary and the Dead Sea Scrolls Project listened patiently to my ideas and provided indispensable guidance. Lellia Cracco Ruggini lent her gracious and wise ear.

In Jerusalem I learned a great deal from colleagues and participants in the workshop on Mechanisms of Canon Making in Antiquity. I remain grateful to the inspiring presence of Rita Finkelberg, Moshe Greenberg, Moshe Halbertal, Robert Lamberton, Christoph Markshies, Andrew Plaks, David Stern, and Guy Stroumsa. It was also a pleasure to converse with and listen to Hubert Cancik, Cristiano Grottanelli, Hayden Pellicia, and Shaul Shaked. I owe a special debt to Guy Stroumsa and to Rita for their trust in me and to David Stern for his kind words and encouragement. I also greatly benefited from conversations with Yossi Yahalom and Menachem Kister at the Hebrew University. My stay in Jerusalem was made particularly pleasant through the friendship of Ada and Amitai Spitzer, Sharon Stern, and Sonia Grober. Special thanks are also due to Ken Holum, director of the Caesarea Maritima dig, who took me and my students under his wing during two exciting seasons.

The pursuit of my research has been greatly facilitated by the Graduate Research Fund at the University of Kansas. The completion of the book has been greatly aided by the Vice Chancellor Book Subvention Award granted by the Hall Center for the Humanities at the University of Kansas. At the University of Kansas, Pam LeRow, of the Word Processing Center, has traveled with me through years of drafts and revisions with exemplary patience, and Lynn Porter and Paula Courtney, also of the Word Processing Center, supplied much-needed moral support. My colleagues, Jim Brundage, Skip Kay, and Rich Ring have lent their wisdom and experience. No words can adequately describe my lasting debt for the friendship that Roma Boniecka Biggins, Anna Cienciala, Elaine Darst, Gunda Georg, and Frau Georg have been always ready to extend.

Parts of this book have appeared in various forms and in various places. I am very grateful for permission to reproduce articles that appeared in the *Revue des études juives*, *Journal of Jewish Studies*, *Vetus Testamentum*, and *Zeitschrift der Savigny-Stiftung für Rechtsgeschichte (Romanistische Abteilung)*. I am also very grateful to Philip Davies and to H.-C. Schmitt for their kind understanding.

Daniel Boyarin read the manuscript and provided characteristically shrewd and penetrating comments. Steve Fine helped with useful references.

This book is dedicated to the memory of Hannes Olivier of Stellenbosch,
> a gentleman and a scholar,
>> and to the memory of her,
>>> the one who knows.

Finally, *tibadelna lechaim arukim*,
> Dvorah Sivan and Aliza Rodnitzki-Eilan.

www.ingramcontent.com/pod-product-compliance
Lightning Source LLC
Chambersburg PA
CBHW020646230426
43665CB00008B/331